The Story of Latin and the Romance Languages

MARIO PEI

The Story of Latin

and

the Romance Languages

With Appendixes partially written, compiled, and arranged
by Paul A. Gaeng, Chairman of Department of Romance Languages
and Literatures, University of Cincinnati

HARPER & ROW, PUBLISHERS

NEW YORK, HAGERSTOWN,

SAN FRANCISCO,

LONDON

FIRST EDITION

Designed by Sidney Feinberg

Library of Congress Cataloging in Publication Data

Pei, Mario Andrew, 1901–
   The story of Latin and the Romance languages.
   Bibliography: p.
   Includes index.
   1. Romance languages—History. 2. Latin
language—History. I. Title.
PC45.P4   440'.09   75–6352
ISBN 0–06–013312–0

76 77 78 79 10 9 8 7 6 5 4 3 2 1

Contents

APPENDIXES

Maps

Author's Foreword

Latin and its Romance descendants are here placed in the framework of three great forces that act upon language and tend to shape it—history, geography (including demography), and psychology. This book is primarily an attempt to balance these three factors and present them in proper perspective.

Historians of language have occasionally tended to underestimate the last two; structural linguists the first two. It is only the recently created "third force" in linguistics (geolinguistics) that has properly considered the role of geography and demography in the evolution of language, past, present, and future.

The part played by dramatic historical events and manifestations of raw power in determining the evolution of language and the relative importance of languages cannot be minimized, as is the tendency with some researchers. What would be the linguistic and cultural picture of the world today if "history had gone the other way"? If Greece had succumbed to the might of Persia at Marathon and Salamis, would our international words today be Iranian rather than Greek? If Carthage had overcome Rome, or if the Arabs had defeated the Franks at the battle of Tours, would we of the West be living today in a Semitic rather than an Indo-European world? If Harold's Saxons at Hastings had thrown William's Normans back into the sea, would this book not be written and read in a tongue far closer to German than present-day English actually is?

It is fashionable today to decry the importance of geography in determining the course of both history and language. After all, can't we fly around the world in eighty hours or less? The role of natural divides in determining language and cultural boundaries is no longer apparent to the modern eye. You ride or fly through, across, or over such former barriers as the Rhine, the Danube, the Mediterranean, the North Sea, the Atlantic, the Pyrenees, the Alps. But it was not always so, and linguistic and ethnic areas were for the most part determined and established when it was not so.

Some languages, like Celtic and Greek, have shrunk in size and extent. Others have disappeared, like Etruscan and Iberian. Still others have grown to tremendous proportions, like English, Russian, and Chinese. What has really shrunk, disappeared, or expanded is not so much the languages themselves as their bodies of speakers. These have disappeared or grown in numbers not as individuals or groups, but only as speakers of given languages. The descendants of the speakers of the original languages are there; but they are speaking something else.

What are the factors of prestige and desirability that lead to linguistic expansion, decrease, or disappearance? Are they predominantly material or spiritual? The fate of languages is, after all, only a facet of history, the result of historical changes that are often of a violent nature, but almost as often the outcome of spiritual movements that may be described as examples of mass psychology—Christianity, Islam, Buddhism, to name a few. Latin and its descendants have flown far on the wings of the first, Arabic has soared aloft on the second, Sanskrit and its offshoots on the third. English and Russian today are regarded, rightly or wrongly, as the bearers and mouthpieces of capitalistic and Communistic ideologies, by which they are in turn affected in their modern developments.

The influence of the written word upon speech, of literature upon language, is often a manifestation of mass psychology, and it is easily forgotten that this influence can be innovative and revolutionary almost as often as it is restrictive and conservative.

This book attempts to cast a complete battery of spotlights upon the evolution of the Latin–Romance language stream, rather than to focus on a single angle which, however precise, is necessarily incomplete and to some extent misleading.

M.P.

Acknowledgments

It gives me pleasure to acknowledge my indebtedness to the authors of the works listed in the Bibliography and cited in the text.

I am more particularly indebted to my dear friend and former student Professor Paul A. Gaeng, of the University of Cincinnati. He not only examined with the utmost care all of my material, supplying valuable suggestions and emendations. He also arranged the Appendixes and Bibliography from material worked out by me, and did originally Appendixes C, E, and I, dealing with the phonological and morphological development of Latin into the Romance languages.

I also offer special thanks to my friends of long standing, Professor Robert Fowkes of New York University and Professor John Hughes of St. Peter's College, both specialists in the Celtic languages, who carefully went over the Celtic material in Part II, Chapter 17, offering valuable suggestions and emendations.

M.P.

Introduction
The Miracle of the Romance Languages

The Romance languages are so called because they stem from the language of the Romans, which was Latin. The origin of the term is the Latin expression *romanice loqui,* "to speak in Roman fashion." Medieval Spaniards called their language *el romance castellano.* Speakers of Old French developed at an early period the verb *enromancer,* "to put into Romance." But early Italian speakers disdained the term, and preferred to style their language *il volgare,* "the vulgar tongue," implying that it was merely a vulgar or popular version of their ancestral Latin.

There had been foreshadowings of the term "Romance" even before the Romance languages themselves appeared in recorded form. Charlemagne's Edict of Tours, in A.D. 813, first made a clear-cut distinction between the *lingua latina,* the traditional Latin tongue, still official, at least in written documents, and the *lingua romana rustica,* the "rustic Roman tongue," current in speech among the masses. Since Charlemagne's empire included Germanic as well as Romance speakers, the counterpart of *lingua romana rustica* for the former was, fittingly, *lingua thiotisca,* the German tongue (Italians still call it *lingua tedesca*). But Italian records, even one century later, oppose *latinitas* (the Latin language) to *nostra vulgaris lingua,* "our vulgar tongue," though one of them states that the two languages are close (as, in a sense, they still are today). Even Dante, in 1305, called Italian *il volgare.*

The use of the term Romance to indicate the new popular tongue therefore seems to reflect primarily a French usage, born of an earlier consciousness of the dichotomy between the traditional Latin and the nascent speech of the masses. Later this usage spread to Spain, but only in part to Italy. French also are the subsequent developments of the word. In the Middle Ages Latin, now a purely cultural tongue, still used by clergy and scholars, was alone deemed worthy of theological, philosophical, legal, and diplomatic writings; the new, popular language was restricted, in written form, to what were then considered the "lowlier" fields of writing: poetry and prose fiction. Hence *roman*, something written in Romance, became the common term for a story or a novel; and since most novels dealt with earthly love, a love affair eventually turned into a "romance." But "Romance" also continues to describe the languages that sprang from the tongue of the Romans, and this is common usage in French, Spanish, even English and German. Italian still looks somewhat askance upon it; while it is perfectly possible to speak of *le lingue romanze*, Italian philologists prefer to call them *lingue neo-latine*, "neo-Latin tongues."

It is not an exaggeration to speak of the "miracle" of the Romance languages. There is indeed something in their genesis and unfolding that smacks of the miraculous. To begin with, they stem from a definitely known, fully described common ancestor, not from a hypothetical, unrecorded tongue supposed to have been spoken by the ancestors of the speakers of later recorded tongues, as is the case with Primitive Germanic, Primitive Slavic, and other members of the Indo-European language family.[1]

The Romance languages stem, directly, ascertainably, and beyond the shadow of a doubt, from Latin, one of the great languages of antiquity, whose records have come down to us in indisputable form. Latin changed in the course of its evolution, from its first recorded appearance around 500 B.C. to the time when it became altogether clear that it was no longer a popular, but only a cultural tongue at the beginning of the ninth century A.D. Its descendants, incidentally, seem to have taken individual language items from each stage in the evolution of Latin.

But this in itself is miraculous only by comparison with other groups. After all, a remotely similar case can be made for another branch of Indo-European, the Indo-Iranian, which, starting out with Sanskrit and Old Persian, evolved, slowly at first, into the Prakrits of medieval India and the Avestan of Persia, and then, by reason of successive waves of Arab and Mongol invaders, turned into the modern languages of Iran,

---

1. For a definition of Indo-European and a listing of the branches of the Indo-European language family, see Appendix A.

India, Pakistan, Bangladesh, and Sri Lanka, structurally quite different from the parent tongues, yet recognizably descended from them. Even more miraculous is the continued evolution of Greek, from its Minoan, Mycenean, and Homeric periods, through the Classical era of Athens and Sparta, to the Koine, the common tongue of the Byzantine Empire, and later into the language still spoken today in modern Greece. Here there was no jump, no break in continuity, no rise of new languages out of the old—only a steady flow of the stream of language from one century to the next.

The miraculous aspect of the Romance languages has two facets, one historical and minor, the other cultural and major. Historically, the Latin-speaking world was submerged, in its totality, by invaders of different speech. Normally, though not invariably, the invading conqueror imposes his language on the conquered population. This happened in the outlying provinces of the Roman Empire: North Africa, where Latin gave way to Arabic; Britain, where it yielded to Anglo-Saxon; most of the Danubian area, where it was replaced by Slavic and Magyar. But in the regions that formed the heartland of Latinity, Italy, France, the Iberian peninsula, it was the invaders, Goths, Longobards, Franks, Burgundians, Vandals, who, while setting up their own realms and a good many of their Germanic institutions, yielded to the subject populations in two all-important respects—religion and language: the two items on which consciousness and national culture are primarily based. The combination of these two elements is too significant to be considered coincidental. The Franks in Gaul, the Longobards in Italy, the Visigoths in Spain, built up their own strong monarchies, which endured for centuries. But all three accepted the Christian religion and the Latin language, though with modifications. The interlocking effect of religion and language, coupled with the mighty force of an ancient and venerated imperial tradition, will appear later. Christianity and Latinity not only survived, they flourished and spread, under the heel of the invaders, who paid them far more than lip service.

Again, this phenomenon has limited parallels elsewhere. The Anglo-Saxons, coming to England as pagan worshippers and Germanic speakers, gave up their traditional religion, though not their language. Later, when the French-speaking Normans overcame the stubborn resistance of Harold's followers, there was no longer a question of religion. Both were Christians. But it might have been expected that William's Normans would succeed in imposing their French speech on the Saxons they had reduced to churldom. However, English, the language of the conquered, survived, and eventually came out on top.

The true miracle is the cultural one. Latin, at its peak, was not merely a language of ordinary communication, serving more than half of Europe, all of North Africa, and large tracts of western Asia. It was also a cultural tongue of the highest order, second only, if at all, to Greek. Refined by its century-old contacts with Etruscan first, with Greek later, it had blossomed into a superb vehicle for literature, poetry, philosophy, religion, the art of government. Its cultural impact, which waxed as the physical Empire waned, was felt throughout all subsequent history, in the Dark Ages, the medieval period, the Renaissance, the centuries of the Enlightenment, down to the present and into the future. As it declined in popular use and was replaced by its direct descendants, these, in turn, repeating their progenitor's experience, blossomed from rough-hewn tongues of practical utility into new linguistic systems expressive of a new culture, a new bright civilization, until they stand forth today as among the greatest of living languages. The cultural development of the Romance languages was not an overnight process; neither had been that of Latin, their ancestor. It took centuries, many centuries, to shape them, mold them, build them up to the point where they could replace their illustrious forebear.

Latin had been in use for centuries before it could serve as a fit vehicle for such poets as Virgil and Horace, Juvenal and Ovid. The Romance languages, too, took centuries to produce the author of the *Chanson de Roland,* Turoldus, troubadour poets like Arnaut Daniel, Jofré Rudel, and masters of prose and poetry like Dante, Ariosto, François Villon, Lope de Vega, Calderón, Camões, and additional centuries to bring forth Carducci, D'Annunzio, Musset, Baudelaire, Verlaine, and the Rumanian Eminescu. Prose writers like Petronius and Apuleius foreshadowed the prose of Cervantes and Blasco Ibáñez, Boccaccio and Manzoni, Victor Hugo and Balzac, Eça de Queiroz and Veríssimo. The philosophy of Cicero and St. Augustine was, at a distance of centuries, duplicated by that of Descartes and Voltaire, Ortega y Gasset, Vico and Croce. Paralleling the historical works of Sallust, Livy, and Tacitus are those of Alfonso el Sabio, Froissart, Renan, Pirenne, Iorga, Menéndez Pidal.

Roman law, by which the Mediterranean world was once ruled, still prevails today. But the French Declaration of the Rights of Man, the Napoleonic Code, the writings of Machiavelli, Montesquieu, Rousseau, and Mazzini are worthy additions to the Roman legal, political, and institutional heritage. The Romans had produced little in the way of scientific writing to parallel that of the Greeks; the Romance countries produced, even before the advent of modern scientific thought, da Vinci and Galileo, and later Pasteur, Mme. Curie, Marconi, and Fermi. The artistic achievements of the Romans, most of them unfortunately anonymous and definitely under Greek influence, were easily equalled and surpassed by those of Michelangelo and Raphael, El Greco and Velázquez, Rodin and Picasso. The same is true of music, which the Romans cultivated in desultory fashion, but to which the Romance countries have contributed such names as Verdi and Puccini, Gounod, Bizet, and Debussy, de Falla and Granados, Villa-Lobos and Enesco.

The true miracle of the Romance languages is that of a brilliant father giving life to many equally brilliant sons, and this is truly without parallel in a language world where the parent language is often obscure, however distinguished its descendants; or where a noble ancestor, coming to the end of his life span, leaves behind offspring less renowned than himself.

Along with this highly unusual cultural phenomenon goes the collective prestige, influence, and power of the Romance nations, which, without establishing a world hegemony of the Roman type, nevertheless have expanded far beyond their original homelands and given rise to new, influential, powerful nations on other continents. But for this there are parallels in the astounding expansion of English and the less spectacular but highly impressive expansion of Russian. Thanks to Spanish and Portuguese explorers and settlers, the languages that stem from Latin today hold sway over practically all the American continent south of the Rio Grande; while French, though no longer the language of a vast colonial empire, is still official and semiofficial in more countries than any other tongue. Close to 500 million of the earth's nearly four billion inhabitants, or roughly one person out of eight, speak Romance languages. This puts them in the demographic forefront, on a par with the major tongues of China and India and with the languages of the Germanic, Slavic, and Indo-Iranian groups.

Such is the background of the languages we are about to present and discuss in their origins, their development, their ramifications and expansion, their predominant features. No language group is worthier of such discussion.

Part I

The Historical Background

1. *The Roman Character*

The amazing spreading of the Latin language from a limited area around the mouth of the Tiber to the entire Mediterranean world of antiquity coincides with Rome's territorial expansion. There is no understanding the one without a knowledge of the other.

In part, but only in part, these twin phenomena are linked with the force of Roman arms, the exercise of raw power, the forcible elimination of rivals that were too dangerous, the absorption and assimilation of vast ethnic groups that lent themselves to the process. This was inevitable in the world of the centuries that immediately preceded the Christian era. It must be viewed from the standpoint of that historical period, not of ours.

But along with armed might there was another element almost as important—the science of government, skill in diplomacy, the art of knowing how to turn bitter foes into potential allies, then into subsidiaries and satellites of the Roman state, finally into full-fledged Roman citizens, proud and happy with their ultimate status. Administrative ability, organizational skill, wise and basically fair laws, a system under which both groups and individuals could thrive and flourish, carrying on their activities in peace and comparative safety, all went into the melting pot. It is, in a sense, inconsequential that the system faltered and showed flaws at various times, even when it was most successful. That happens to all systems, at all times. It is equally inconsequential that the system ultimately broke down, as all human things must. What matters is that it successfully survived across a span of many centuries, gave rise to the nearest approach to world government and world peace

3

the world has ever known, and even after its downfall continued to inspire and guide Western man, as it still does today. Along with this there went a sense of discipline and self-control, a moral and ethical code that at the outset were of the first order, however much they degenerated in later times, with full recognition of the individual's rights as well as his duties and responsibilities to himself, his family, and the state; a skill in the limited technology of the period that, in its own way, surpasses ours, with road building, city planning, and the construction of dwellings, temples, public buildings, aqueducts second to none; a system of universal, though not compulsory, public education which had almost borne full fruit when the Empire collapsed; a military organization unparalleled in ancient times; methods of transportation by land and sea such as the world had never seen before, with consequent enhancement and expansion of commerce and industry.

There was a reverse to the medal, to be sure. The Roman system of military service was, at least in theory, universal for all able-bodied male citizens, and the period of enlistment was twenty years, longer than any modern draft. The religion of the Romans involved not only an Olympus of many gods and goddesses, all endowed with human failings along with supernatural powers, but also widespread superstitious beliefs and practices that cannot be described save as crass. The system of taxation was both relentless and oppressive, and as time went on it degenerated into one of the major causes of the Empire's decline. There was cruelty in the Roman way of dealing with enemies, particularly stubborn ones; widespread deportation and scattering of entire ethnic groups that proved difficult to assimilate and Romanize (the Jews, one of the major recipients of this practice, knew it as the Diaspora); methods of inflicting suffering and death that were ingenious and varied, as attested by the early history of Christianity (but many of them, like crucifixion, learned from the Carthaginians, were borrowed from Rome's enemies). Most depressing of all was a system of slavery whereby human beings of all races and colors were turned into chattels, and could be treated according to the owner's whim. This, at a later date, proved another cause of the great downfall.

It must be noted, however, that unlike the Roman virtues, which history has proved peculiar to the Romans, or at least possessed by them in far greater measure than by other peoples of antiquity, the Roman defects were the common property of all the nations of ancient times, with the partial, but only partial, exception of the Jews. Crete and

Egypt, Babylonia and Assyria, Persia and Greece, Phoenicia and Carthage, all shared with Rome, in equal or greater measure, the practices outlined above; witness the human sacrifices to the bull and to Moloch, the building of the Pyramids, the Babylonian captivity, the Carthaginian treatment of both prisoners and envoys. Such practices were current in the Middle Ages, as proved by the Jacquerie, the Inquisition, the religious wars, the burning of witches. They have not altogether vanished from the modern world, enlightenment and Christianity notwithstanding. Many of them find duplicates in Hitlerian and Stalinian outrages, the mass deportations that attended the end of World War II, the bombing of helpless civilian populations, the use of the atomic bomb, the slavery that endured till our own Civil War. It is perhaps unfair to picture Roman society as it is often pictured on the American screen, at its worst rather than at its best.

Add to this the evils that society as a whole has never been able to eliminate: nepotism and corruption, sprawling and inept bureaucracies, urbanism and welfare states, the relaxation of moral standards of conduct engendered by wealth and prosperity, the softness that arises in consequence of materialism and the worship of the "good" life. All of these increased as the Roman state grew and prospered, in precisely the same fashion that they have increased in our modern society. Under these circumstances, even virtues have a way of turning into vices. The rigid social discipline of Rome crystallized and fossilized, with social orders that became more and more meaningless save for the special privileges they entailed. The utter absence of racial and ethnic discrimination practiced by the Romans, who did not hesitate to extend citizenship to outsiders not raised in the Roman tradition, led to a decline of both patriotism and the sense of duty. The Roman introduction of a system of private ownership of property, replacing the primitive communism of many of the peoples they conquered and assimilated, while at first highly beneficial in arousing a sense of pride and individuality, eventually sprouted the well-known evils of capitalism and the concentration of wealth in the hands of a few. Even the Roman system of colonization not by segregation, but by intermingling and intermarriage of the conquerors and conquered may have given rise to divided loyalties, though of this there is little actual proof. Christianity, a great moral force that could have saved the Empire, was not allowed full play; first by the stubborn and long-drawn resistance of paganism; secondly by misguided interpretations that equated it with peace at any price and nonresistance to aggression; thirdly by the fact that while it was generally adopted by the barbarians who swarmed into the Empire, it was by them distorted to suit their own mundane purposes and violent habits, so that it gave rise to conditions and practices just as bad as those it had routed.

Above all, however, is the relentless march of history, which often repeats itself in part, so that at times it seems to move in a circle, but which is at all times subject to the iron law of change. It is the decree of nature that like all living organisms, nations, empires, institutions, must grow up to a certain point, then begin an inevitable decline, to the point of disappearance. They may continue to influence future developments, even when they no longer exist. But nothing in the material universe is eternal. The great empire of the Romans was no exception to the natural law of inevitable change. Nor was their language.

2. How Rome Gained an Empire

The mythical date of Rome's founding by Romulus and Remus, around the middle of the eighth century B.C., was followed by at least two centuries of semilegendary accounts, dealing largely with the seven Tarquinian kings of Rome. That the Tarquinian dynasty was of Etruscan origin seems certain; whether it indicates that Rome was a vassal state to the Etruscans during that period is more doubtful. The Romans themselves were definitely Indo-Europeans, of the Italic branch of the big family. The Italic branch, which occupied all of central Italy with the exception of Etruria on the western coast, and most of southern Italy, with a possible offshoot in Sicily, was linguistically subdivided into two subbranches: Latin-Faliscan and Oscan-Umbrian. The contribution to the Latin subbranch of Aeneas' refugees from Troy, as described in Virgil's *Aeneid*, may or may not have some foundation in fact.

Historical records in which one can place a degree of confidence go back to shortly before 500 B.C. They deal with the final expulsion of the Tarquinians and the setting up of the Roman Republic, with two elected magistrates, called consuls, a popular assembly, and a patrician senate, composed of the "best" (wealthiest and most influential) elements of the population.

The earliest history of Rome is largely one of defensive wars, fought by a city whose perimeter did not exceed twelve miles, against immediate neighbors, most of Latinian stock, whose ready absorption marks the beginning of Roman assimilative genius. This genius ultimately prevailed even in the case of the Sabines and Samnites, who belonged to the other branch of Italic, Oscan-Umbrian. It did not, at this early stage, prevail with the Etruscans, who maintained their independence until a much later date, or with the Gauls of northern Italy, who, sweeping down from the valley of the Po in the middle of the fourth century B.C., almost put an end to the city of Rome.

Through wars, alliances, intermarriage, and colonization, however, the Romans by 300 B.C. had gained effective control of the Italian peninsula, including even Etruria, but not Cisalpine Gaul,[1] which managed to retain a measure of independence until the end of the second Punic War, around 200 B.C. The Romans generally respected the individuality of the Greek cities of southern Italy, in which they recognized a degree of civilization superior to their own, and turned them into allies rather than conquests.

The beginning of the third century B.C. marked the end of the first period of Roman expansion, on continental Italian soil. Even though she faced one important overseas foe, King Pyrrhus of Epirus, the main engagements were fought in Italy. They were in the nature of a dress rehearsal for the life-and-death struggle for major expansion that was about to begin, and that was to be the first and most important step on the road to world hegemony for Rome.

Carthage (Kart Hadesht, or New City), on the African coast of the Mediterranean, located approximately where Tunis now stands, had been founded by colonists from Tyre, in Phoenicia, about the same time as Rome. The Phoenicians, of Semitic stock and closely related to the Hebrews, were among the foremost navigators and explorers of antiquity, and planted colonies and trading posts not only all over the Mediterranean, but even in Britain and along the Black Sea coast. The Carthaginians, like their Phoenician forebears, thrived and flourished through navigation and commerce. Like the Phoenicians, they ran into that other great race of navigators and traders, the Greeks. Clashes began around 550 B.C., just as the Romans were about to get rid of their kings and inaugurate the Republic. The Greeks had made numerous settlements in Sicily. The Carthaginians proceeded to take them over and subjugate them. Rome and Carthage, interestingly, had signed a treaty in 509 B.C., immediately after the expulsion of the Tarquinians, by the terms of which Italy was assigned to the Romans and Africa to the Carthaginians, but Sicily was left as a dangerous neutral zone. With their

---

1. Gaul on the Italian side of the Alps, embracing present-day Piedmont, Lombardy, Liguria, and Emilia.

sea power, which Rome still lacked, the Carthaginians were able to take over Sardinia and the Balearic Islands. But the Sicilian Greeks were hard to keep subdued, and fighting was constant.

Growing in power and wealth, Carthage claimed the monopoly of Mediterranean waters, and seized foreign ships between Sardinia and the Pillars of Hercules (later known as the Strait of Gibraltar). The Romans, engaged in their own struggles for Italian supremacy, at first did not dispute Carthaginian sea claims. But the clash was inevitable. It came when the Greek city of Messana (today Messina), relying on a treaty with Rome, asked for protection against Carthaginian aggression in 264 B.C. The Romans responded, and the first Punic War was on. It was a long and bitter war, lasting twenty-three years, and fraught with land and sea battles. The Romans won two naval engagements, then tried to invade Africa, but unsuccessfully. More fighting, on land and sea, took place in Sicily. Finally the war ended with an overwhelming naval victory at the Aegates Islands. The Carthaginians sued for an inconclusive peace, which they obtained, and tried to go home to lick their wounds. But there they were faced with a revolt of their own mercenaries, which they finally succeeded in putting down.

Unlike the Roman legions, which were a citizens' army, the Carthaginian land forces consisted mainly of hirelings drawn from a variety of countries, from the blacks south of the Sahara to the yellow-haired Gauls and swarthy Iberians. The largest element consisted of Libyans and Numidians, the original inhabitants of North Africa before the Phoenicians came, people of Hamitic stock, like the ancient Egyptians. (Their present-day descendants are the North African Berbers.) Officered by highly intelligent members of the Carthaginian aristocracy, and bolstered by the use of elephants that foreshadowed modern tanks, these motley forces were now reorganized by Hannibal in a deliberate plan to wreak vengeance on Rome for the defeat suffered in the first war. In the interim, the Carthaginians had occupied most of Spain, strengthening their hold on the western Mediterranean, now that the central part of the great inland sea was precluded to them. In 218 B.C. Hannibal launched an attack on Saguntum, an Iberian city of Spain that had sought a treaty of alliance with the Romans. Roman aid arrived too late to save Saguntum. While Roman forces were still laboriously working their way across the Alps and the Pyrenees to bring relief to a town already lost, Hannibal boldly struck across those same Pyrenees and Alps, picking up more Spanish and Gaulish mercenaries on the way. In a series of lightning-like strokes (not for nothing was his family name Barek or Barca, "light-ning"), he successively routed three large Roman armies sent out to meet him on Italian soil, then, veering to the east of Rome, proceeded into southern Italy to ambush and destroy the largest Roman force of all at Cannae (216 B.C.). The road to Rome lay open, but for some mysteri-ous reason Hannibal failed to take advantage of his opportunity. Rein-forcements from Carthage either were not sent or failed to meet him. His own brother's head, thrown into his camp by a Roman cavalryman, was his only notice that forces belatedly sent to help him had been destroyed. Hannibal withdrew from Italy, with the Romans in relentless pursuit. The battle of Zama, in North Africa (202 B.C.), put an end to Carthaginian power and to Hannibal himself. By the terms of the peace treaty that followed, Carthage lost its fleet and all save its African possessions, and was reduced to the role of a semivassal.

But the memory of Hannibal and how close he had come to destroy-ing Rome rankled in Roman hearts. Fifty years after Zama the Romans, on a trumped-up pretext, provoked a third and final Punic War, which ended with the utter destruction of Rome's rival.

Now the Romans, who in the course of a century had added Sicily, Sardinia, Corsica, southern Spain, Macedonia, and Egypt to their hold-ings, were at the height of their military power and in full naval control of the Mediterranean. Cisalpine Gaul (*Gallia togata,* "toga-wearing Gaul," from the fact that Roman citizenship was extended to its inhab-itants) had been subdued as early as 220 B.C. Both southern Spain and southern Transalpine Gaul (*Gallia comata,* "long-haired Gaul") were now added to the roster of Roman conquests, though northern Gaul was not to become Roman until the time of Julius Caesar, and northern Spain until the time of Augustus. Greece had been thoroughly subdued by 100 B.C., but the Romans, realizing they had much to learn from the Greeks, respected both their individuality and their language. Large in-roads were made into Asia Minor.

There was one frightening interlude, betokening the shape of things to come, around 100 B.C., when invading hordes of Germanic and Celtic wanderers, the Cimbri and Teutones, after ravaging Romanized southern Gaul and Spain, poured across the Alps to threaten the Italian homeland. But the consul Marius, with his invincible legions, met them, routed them, and cut them to pieces at Aquae Sextiae. By 100 B.C. Rome stood forth as the sole world power. There were rumblings of unrest from various quarters. In North Africa, Jugurtha, king of Numidia, raised the standard of revolt. Marius took care of him. Rome's Italic allies, Samnites and Sabellians, showed their teeth in the Social Wars. They, too, were defeated, with wholesale deportations of the more stubborn to Sardinia and Spain, and their replacement with more docile Umbrians from the north.

But this period also marks the beginning of downfall for Rome's democratic institutions, the rise of warring generals and dictators, proscriptions and wholesale massacres of political opponents, carried on first by the rival consuls, Marius and Sulla, followed later by Pompey, Crassus, and Caesar, still later by Anthony and Octavian, and the replacement of the Roman Republic by a "divine" emperor. During the first century B.C., however, Rome further extended her conquests and domains, with Caesar conquering northern Gaul, setting up an effective barrier to Germanic aggressions at the line of the Rhine, making a first incursion into Britain, to be followed by true conquest one century later, under the emperor Claudius and the leadership of Agricola. The inauguration of Octavian (Augustus) as the first Roman emperor coincided with the Christian era, completely unnoticed at its outset, and, far more important from the Roman viewpoint, the establishment of the *Pax Romana*—a Roman world of peace and prosperity, save at the remote fringes, along the Rhine and Danube and at the eastern end of Asia Minor, where Roman conquests bordered on the rejuvenated Persian Empire of the Parthians.

One more conquest of note was that of Dacia, the modern Rumania, which occurred under Trajan, around A.D. 100. This had far-reaching linguistic consequences that will appear later. In the early second century A.D., Hadrian made some minor additions to Rome's holdings at the eastern end of the Empire with the acquisition of Assyria and Mesopotamia (but these were difficult to hold against the hard-hitting Parthians).

One significant development of the period was the setting up of *limites*, or fortified borders, to protect Rome's territories from foreign incursions. One of these was Hadrian's Wall in Britain, where the Romans, having taken the part of the island that was worth taking, decided against subduing the wild Picts and Scots in the unproductive Scottish highlands, and limited themselves to protecting their Romanized British subjects. Another was the Rhine-Danube Wall, linking the two great natural lines of defense provided by the broad and deep-flowing rivers. Previously, the Romans had tried to extend their conquests beyond these

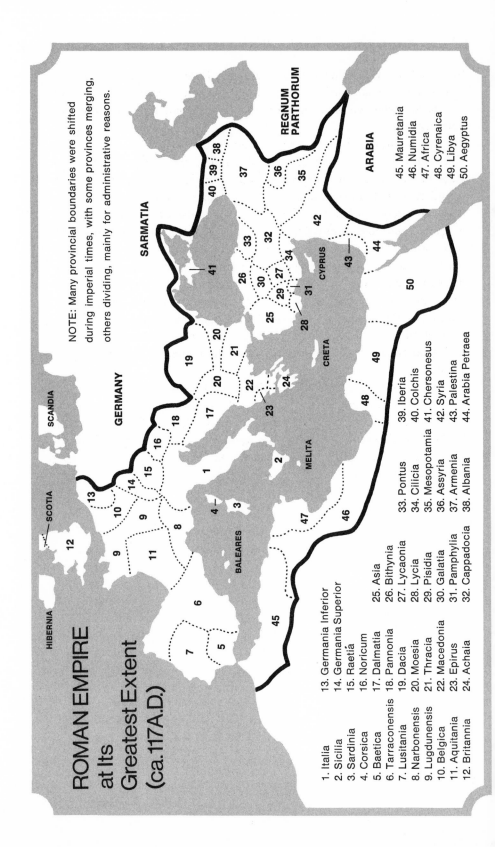

ROMAN EMPIRE
at Its
Greatest Extent
(ca. 117A.D.)

NOTE: Many provincial boundaries were shifted during imperial times, with some provinces merging, others dividing, mainly for administrative reasons.

1. Italia
2. Sicilia
3. Sardinia
4. Corsica
5. Baetica
6. Tarraconensis
7. Lusitania
8. Narbonensis
9. Lugdunensis
10. Belgica
11. Aquitania
12. Britannia
13. Germania Inferior
14. Germania Superior
15. Raetia
16. Noricum
17. Dalmatia
18. Pannonia
19. Dacia
20. Moesia
21. Thracia
22. Macedonia
23. Epirus
24. Achaia
25. Asia
26. Bithynia
27. Lycaonia
28. Lycia
29. Pisidia
30. Galatia
31. Pamphylia
32. Cappadocia
33. Pontus
34. Cilicia
35. Mesopotamia
36. Assyria
37. Armenia
38. Albania
39. Iberia
40. Colchis
41. Chersonesus
42. Syria
43. Palestina
44. Arabia Petraea
45. Mauretania
46. Numidia
47. Africa
48. Cyrenaica
49. Libya
50. Aegyptus

HIBERNIA
SCOTIA
SCANDIA
GERMANY
SARMATIA
REGNUM PARTHORUM
ARABIA
BALEARES
MELITA
CRETA
CYPRUS

lines, but Varus' excursion into Teutoburg Forest had proved counterproductive. Dacia, north of the Danube, heavily colonized by Roman
legionaries who intermarried with the local populations, was the only
outlying area.

This situation, which prevailed through the first two centuries of the
Christian era and into the early third century, was indicative of a new
state of affairs. Rome's expansion was over. Henceforth, the Romans
would stand behind their ancient Maginot Line and fight only defensive
wars, to protect what they had and keep outsiders from coming in.
Maginot Lines and purely defensive wars, as history reveals, are seldom
successful. In the case of the Romans, however, the *limites* provided at
least two centuries of *Pax Romana*, a period of relative peace, prosperity, expanding trade, travel, and education, public works that endure to
the present day, a standardization of language, customs, architecture,
housing, and technology that rivals that of modern America. This happy
state of affairs, if we so wish to term it, lasted through the reign of bad
and good rulers, to the time of the Antonine emperors and Marcus Au-
relius.

But the seemingly eternal Empire carried within itself the seeds of
its own doom. Coming events cast their shadow before, and the memory
of the bitter civil wars that attended the end of Roman democratic institutions, coupled with the even more ancient evils of slavery and urbanism, were a warning to the proud Roman citizen of A.D. 200 that nothing
is everlasting.

3. The Empire's Fall

The first century B.C. was characterized by bitter, destructive civil wars, and by the downfall of Rome's democratic institutions. The first two centuries of the Christian era were the golden age of the *Pax Romana*, under emperors who were often autocrats and tyrants. Across all three centuries the bell of doom was heard, tolling in the distance.

Even before Rome's final triumph over Carthage, a Greek historian who had come to Rome in 168 B.C. had observed and recorded the initial phases in the downfall of the democratic process, which he dispassionately (or perhaps cautiously) placed in the framework of world history. Kings who abuse their power are expelled, says Polybius; then an aristocracy or senate takes over the effective rule of the state. But the younger generations, raised in an atmosphere of liberty and permissiveness, do not appreciate the blessings of equality and freedom of speech. They are inclined to violence, and arouse the populace to disorderly action. Chaos prevails, until a new despot takes control. This fate, Polybius says openly, is reserved for the Roman state, which will inevitably follow Athens, Sparta, Carthage, in the historical cycle. The luxury of Greece is bad for the Romans, who are beginning to adopt it. Of the two forces by which a state perishes, external and internal, the latter is the more dangerous.

Sallust, a historian who lived between 86 and 34 B.C., describes the Roman society of his day as having developed strong class differences, with a growing body of large and small businessmen (but small landowners are still in the majority), an army that tends to become more and more a professional class, too many unemployed freemen because

14

of the competition of slave labor; he advocates a reduction in the concentration of wealth, scattering the urban unemployed, who are too prone
to crime and violence, into new colonies, and limitations on the use of
slave labor, particularly on farms and large estates.

In the same period, poets and orators like Horace and Seneca are
frankly pessimistic about Rome's future. Seneca in particular (60 B.C. to
A.D. 37) deplores the disappearance if democratic institutions: "You
can't resurrect liberty when the moral premises that made it possible are
gone." Livy, who lived between 59 B.C. and A.D. 17, expresses nostalgia
for the old days, and contempt for the servile, materialistic society that
has replaced them, as well as for the inferiority complex the Romans
show in connection with Greek culture. This, he says, first started after
the Macedonian wars, when the Romans began to hold banquets that
often turned into orgies. Love for "art," he complains, is often a mask for
greed.

More to the point is Lucan, a Spanish-born provincial (this may account in part for his sentiments) who lived in the middle of the first
century A.D. "This Roman peace of ours," he says at one point, "comes
with a master." Elsewhere he intones: "Long live the Galatians, the Syrians, the Gauls, the Iberians, because after the civil wars they will be
the Roman people! All the provinces weep. The more they know the
Romans, the more they hate them."

Tacitus, who lived between A.D. 55 and 117, takes a dim view of the
Pax Romana. After criticizing Augustus for abolishing the old institutions
in the name of "peace," he says that what prevails now is *non mos,
non jus*, "neither morality nor laws." The laws are discredited by violence, intrigue, love of wealth. The future is uncertain for all. He
deplores the new universalism: How can a culture and a moral code
created by the few for a few be extended to the many? How can the past
be inserted into the present without betraying it and doing it violence?
The society he sees before his eyes is vast, multiform, restless, beset by
economic troubles and by social and ethnic minority demands. He ad-
mires the virtues of the Germanic barbarians who are massing beyond
the Rhine-Danube barrier; among them there is no usury, no immoral-
ity, no taking on of vices in order to get ahead, no bribery or corruption.
They may, in fact, be compared to the Romans of an earlier day. As
mercenaries, they are already numerous in the Roman army, which
eventually will have no more Roman soldiers. The barbarians, who now
can lay claim to defending Rome against Rome's own degeneracy, will

inherit the Empire. Where there is no moral superiority, there is no right to rule.

Such are the prophecies, uttered while Rome was still mistress of the earth. One weakness of Roman society, slavery, is mentioned only glancingly by the prophets and critics, possibly because it was universal in the world of antiquity. They deplore the use of slave labor only because it deprives freemen of their right to earn a living. What the Roman historians failed to do was to look at slavery from the standpoint of the slaves. Yet the Romans should have known that viewpoint, expressed in no uncertain fashion in the great slave revolt of Spartacus, that three-year war (73–71 B.C.) which laid waste large tracts of Italy, and which Cicero called *foedissimum bellum,* "the most horrible of wars." It finally ended in a Roman victory, but its memory lingered on, to haunt the masters.

Yet at the outset of the third century A.D. all seemed well with Rome's world. The *limites* held firm; so did the legions, though now they were constituted mainly of barbarian mercenaries and provincial levies. One new element had entered the picture—the rising tide of Christianity. But its triumph was still a century or more in the future. At this point it was engaged in a vast underground struggle with other forces—the old pagan faith, which had added the emperors to the roster of its gods; the imported philosophies of the Stoics and Epicureans, favored by the old intellectual aristocracy; another eastern religion, Mithraism, an offshoot of the ancient faith of Persia, with its perennial conflict between the forces of good and those of evil, a dynamic faith of action, well suited to the professional military class. But it was Christianity, with its firm belief in the equality of all human beings in the sight of the one God, its unshakable faith in the survival of the individual in the hereafter, that appealed to those who had lost all hope in the things of this world—the slaves, the poor, the dispossessed and oppressed. As it slowly seeped up from the lowest to the higher classes of Roman society, it weakened what remained of the authority of the old power structure. It was the Establishment itself, with its ultimate reliance upon physical might and the force of arms, that was being slowly undermined.

The convergence of all these forces, internal and external, came to a head around the middle of the third century A.D. First the Alamanni and Franks broke through the Roman Maginot Line into what is today Belgium; they were temporarily contained. Then the Goths moved into

Dacia, the one outlying province beyond the Danube. The Roman settlers and their families were removed to the safer side of the river, the
province of Moesia, which was renamed Dacia to soften the blow to the
folks at home. The old Dacia was in part recovered later, but meanwhile
the Goths, who were wanderers, had moved on across the Balkans and
into Asia Minor, where they threatened some of the Greek cities.

Bad as were Rome's third-century troubles, they were as nothing compared to the happenings of the next hundred years. The only relief (a
doubtful one, from the standpoint of the Empire) was the triumph of
Constantine, his conversion to Christianity, and the final extension of
tolerance, and later full recognition, to that religion, still heavily beset
by its rivals. With this, however, came another symbol of downfall: the
transfer of the seat of government from Rome to Constantinople, shortly
to be followed by the establishment of twin emperors, one in each city.
There may have been in this some thought of returning to the old democratic institution of two consuls, but it is more likely that the now numerous and influential Christians saw Rome as a center of pagan worship
and pagan iniquities, and preferred to start again from scratch in a place
untouched by these evils.

The second half of the fourth century saw a large-scale Gothic invasion across the Danube, into the province of Moesia. True, it was
carried out with the consent of the Empire, and the Goths, now Christianized, but in the Arian form,[1] settled down more or less peaceably, at
least for a time. One of their bishops, Wulfilas, trained in Constantinople, even produced the first full-scale translation of the Bible into a
Germanic tongue, Gothic. There was also the splitting of the Gothic
hordes into two separate nations. Those who had crossed the Danube
into Moesia, later named Visigoths, or West Goths, eventually moved
on, first to Italy under Alaric, then to southern Gaul, ultimately into
Spain, where they founded a flourishing monarchy that endured till the
coming of the Moors in 711. The others, Ostrogoths, or East Goths, remained for a time on the north side of the Danube, under the overlordship of the Huns. Ultimately they, too, moved, first into the Balkans,
then into Italy, and established a short-lived empire of their own under
Theodoric.

Meanwhile, Franks and Burgundians were filtering across the Rhine

---

1. The Arian heresy held that Christ was not God, but the first of created beings,
thus casting doubt upon the doctrine of the Trinity.

into the old Roman province of Gaul. Shortly after 400 A.D., the Romans withdrew their last garrisons, desperately needed at home, from their outlying province of Britain, and left the Romanized Celts to struggle as best they could with the unsubdued Picts and Scots from the north and with the Angles, Jutes, and Saxons that raided the eastern coasts.

In 410, Rome had undergone the first of many final indignities—sack at the hands of Alaric, leader of the West Goths, who had tired of unkept promises to take care of his people. These same West Goths, having previously defeated the forces of the Eastern emperor at Adrianople, had been admitted by Theodosius as *foederati,* full-fledged allies. As a matter of fact, after their outburst of temper, they again took up their duties, and together with the Franks and the Romans put a stop to the invasion of the Huns at Châlons in 451.

The Eastern Empire was holding out successfully, and would continue to do so for another thousand years. But the Western Empire was finished. Vandals, Suevians, Alans, had poured into Spain and North Africa; Franks and Burgundians into Gaul. In Italy it was the turn of the Heruli, then of the Ostrogoths, though Germanic predominance in Italy was constantly disputed by the forces of the nearby Eastern emperors, particularly Justinian. Theodoric, leader of the Ostrogoths, set up a temporary kingdom in Italy that was almost successful. Then came the Longobards, of Suevian stock, fiercest and most uncouth of all the Germanic invaders. Unlike most of the other barbarians, who were partly Romanized and quite willing to merge with the local populations, they kept themselves apart from the Romans, setting up their own laws and institutions. But numerous as they were, they were not numerous enough to submerge the entire peninsula. Their kingdom extended over northern Italy (but not to the seacoast cities of Venice and Genoa) and as far south as Tuscany, with offshoots in the duchies of Spoleto and Benevento. The only major concessions they made to the local populations were to give up their Arian form of Christianity in favor of Catholicism, and to adopt, but slowly and only in part, the Latin language, at least for the purpose of codifying their laws. They stayed away from the coastlines, where they could be opposed by the sea power of the Eastern Empire, and were eventually subdued by Pepin and Charlemagne, whom the popes had called upon for help against Longobardic encroachments on the Papal States.

Now there arose a new menace, which concerned equally the Eastern Empire, what was left of the Western, and the unstable monarchies set up in various localities by the Germanic invaders (the Vandal kingdom of North Africa, centered around Roman Carthage, was a case in point). The rise of Islam, founded by Mohammed in southern Arabia around 622 A.D., had at first seemed remote. But in the first half of the seventh century the fanatical Moslems had accomplished what Rome had been unable to do—the overthrow of the Parthian empire. Persia and Egypt, then all of North Africa, were conquered by the warriors who planted the Crescent where the Cross had been. Libya, Numidia, Mauretania, fell swiftly to the Arab sword and the spell of a new, dynamic religion. Intermingled with the recent Berber converts to Islam, the Arabs in 711 crossed the Strait of Gibraltar, overthrew the long-standing kingdom of the Visigoths, and took possession of the entire Iberian peninsula save for the northern strip between the Cantabrian mountains and the Bay of Biscay. They poured across the Pyrenees into France, but were met and routed by Charles Martel and his Franks at Tours in 732. Henceforth Roman Spain, which had lived for two centuries under enlightened Visigothic rule, was carved into two unequal parts, Christian principalities in the north and Moorish caliphates in the south and center, where an Arab minority ruled over older Christian populations made up of Visigoths and Romanized Iberians.

Strongest and most stable of the new Germanic kingdoms that had arisen on Roman soil was the Frankish empire founded by Clovis before the year 500. Clovis not only expelled the Visigoths from most of southern France; he also was converted, with all his followers, to the standard brand of Christianity, which meant closer links with the Roman Papacy than prevailed, at least at the outset, in the case of either Goths or Longobards. The Merovingian dynasty he founded endured till 751, when Pepin, mayor of the palace, took over and established the Carolingian line. Charlemagne, the great emperor of the Middle Ages, forged an empire that extended over most of present-day France, Germany, Holland, Belgium, and northern Italy. It did not endure, but split into what were essentially modern France and modern Germany, thus setting up France as the first major Romance country to achieve national unity. By way of contrast, the Iberian peninsula, split into Moslem and Christian areas, did not become fully unified till the fifteenth century. Italy, with a Frankish kingdom in the north that later fell to the lot of the German emperors, evolving many free cities and small states; the domains of the pope in the center; and a kingdom in the south and in Sicily that was fought over by Byzantines, Saracens, Normans, Swabians,

French, Aragonese, found it still harder to achieve a measure of national unity, which did not come about until 1870.

The Roman Empire of the East, Greek in language and institutions, continued in existence until 1453, when it fell to the Turks, fully one thousand years after the Empire of the West had succumbed. But the nations that arose out of the great catastrophe in the West, strengthened by the infusion of new blood, were eventually to give an excellent account of themselves. In spite of their vicissitudes, they remained steeped in the Roman tradition. The stamp of Rome was indelibly upon them. The spirit of Rome inspired them, and urged them on to greatness.

4. The Rise of the Romance Nations

At what point in history did the inhabitants of the former Empire of the West, now intermingled with newcomers from the Germanic world, begin to cease thinking of themselves as Romans and start considering themselves Frenchmen, Spaniards, Italians? This point seems intimately linked with their consciousness of the tongues they spoke as still being the Latin of the Empire, however degenerated in their mouths, or as something apart, be it *lingua romana rustica, romance,* or *volgare.*

Some historians make the imaginary date of the breakup of Roman consciousness and the Latin language coincide with the fall of the Roman Empire of the West, in the fifth century. Others aver that while the disruption began at that point, or even earlier, the process was a slow one, continuing at least until the Moorish invasion of Spain in the early eighth century, when communications between most of the Iberian peninsula and the realm of the Franks were broken.

Three factors must be considered in assessing ethnic and linguistic change: geography, history, and human psychology.

Geographical barriers, which today are unimportant in the face of modern means of transportation—railroads, automobile roads, tunnels through mountain ranges, airplanes—had far greater importance in the days of a more limited technology. Rivers such as the Rhine and the Danube, mountain chains like the Alps, the Apennines, the Pyrenees, the Cantabrians, formed effective borders. Nature, rather than man, had circumscribed what later was to be France by means of the Atlantic, the Mediterranean, the Pyrenees, the Alps, the Rhine. The same Pyrenees, with seas on all other sides, cut off the Iberian peninsula from the rest of

Europe. Italy's borders were naturally set by the various arms of the Mediterranean and the Alps. The Romans had to a considerable degree overcome these obstacles of nature by their genius of organization and their road-building skill. When these skills failed, nature was sooner or later bound to come back into her own.

The strong, fully standardized civilization of Rome, with her highly centralized government, her military, fiscal, and educational systems, and the relative ease of travel and trade among the various regions of the Empire, could not and did not fail overnight. Repairs could be made then, as they are now, even after destructive wars and invasions.

Of even greater importance was the psychological factor of the Roman and imperial tradition, bolstered at the very time it began to fail by a great, new, spiritually unifying force, Christianity. The populations of the fallen Empire could not and did not overnight give up the habit of thinking of themselves as Romans and citizens of a world state. Even before the fourth-century triumph of Christianity, there was a sense of unity, one might almost say uniformity, that extended not only to the old populations of Italy and the provinces but even to the newcomers. The Roman Empire was a way of life, fully accepted by the barbarians who lived on its borders and clamored for admittance to its benefits, real and fancied. The Germanic tribes that settled permanently in the Western Empire had been seeping in for centuries, learning from the Romans the arts of both war and peace. This is particularly true of the Visigoths who ultimately settled in the Iberian peninsula, the Ostrogoths who were the first permanent invaders of Italy, the Franks, Alamanni, and Burgundians who came to a permanent halt in France, even the Vandals, who swept through all the major future Romance countries to found a kingdom in Africa. The later records of the Western Empire are replete with names of Germanic generals, like Stilicho the Vandal, who defended Rome and her Empire as if it had been their own. The large number of Germanic mercenaries who fought in the Roman armies were often as thoroughly assimilated as the Syrians and Dacians and Iberians and Gauls and Italians by whose side they fought. The Germanic invaders, with the probable exception of the Longobards (and they, too, succumbed in the long run to the Roman spell), did not hate the Empire. They wanted to be a part of it, mold it to their own purposes, possess it, even defend it. They were not too unlike certain groups of modern immigrants to the United States, unruly and troublesome at first, later, in the course of two or three generations, fully assimilated and turned into patriotic Americans, but who nevertheless, by reason of their ethnic background, tend to change the habits, viewpoints, and mores of an older America.

In the course of the fifth century a new expression arose (some say it was coined, or at least first circulated, by Paulus Orosius, a Lusitanian by birth, who lived and wrote at the time when the Visigoths were about to found their kingdom of Spain), *Romania,* which betokened the part of the former Empire that still preserved the Roman tradition and in which Latin, however bastardized, continued to be the popular language. The popularity of the expression is indicated by the fact that it was later applied to the short-lived Latin kingdom founded in the East by the Crusaders, was bestowed in the form *Romagna* upon an Italian region, and was taken over by the descendants of the former Dacians as the name of their entire country, *România.*

One additional factor needs considering as having a linguistic bearing. It is the extent to which some measure of a new, separate national consciousness ultimately managed to arise in each of the three main divisions of Romania—the French, the Spanish-Portuguese, and the Italian—separating them from one another and from their common Roman wellspring. This, too, hinges on the same three factors—geography, history, psychology.

France was the first of the three areas to achieve both a national consciousness and a new language clearly identifiable as separate from Latin. Julius Caesar had divided the area he was instrumental in bringing into the Roman commonwealth into Belgium, Aquitania, and Gaul proper. But he had overlooked the fact that even in his day the southeastern portion of Transalpine Gaul had already been brought under Roman control and subjected to Romanizing influences. This cleavage was later recognized in the division of Gaul into Narbonensis, the southeastern and southern region, closest to Italy, and Lugdunensis, the northern area, for whose annexation Caesar was more directly responsible. In addition, there were Aquitania, an extensive southwestern region bordering on the Pyrenees, and Belgica, the extreme north, covering the lands west of the Rhine near its mouth, and embracing not only what today are Belgium and most of Holland but also large areas of northern France and parts of Germany west of the river divide. It is possible that the cleavage between Gallia Narbonensis and Gallia Lugdunensis may have had something to do with the later cleavage between the Provençal and the northern French areas, with Aquitaine going, for the most part, to join the Provençal section and Belgica forming the meeting place between Romance and Germanic speakers.

Clovis, leader of the Franks who came into Gaul from the north and northeast, founded his Merovingian line around A.D. 500. He and his successors eventually overcame the Visigoths and Burgundians who had pierced the Empire's border further south, but the process was slow, and Frankish authority over the former Gallia Narbonensis was a bit shadowy for a time.

Two of Clovis' achievements were to establish a fairly centralized monarchy, which formed the basis for the later union of France's regions into a homogenized nation, and to accept, at the very outset, the Catholic form of Christianity linked to the Roman popes. This was to give the Church a position of prominence and importance on French soil that was duplicated only later and less thoroughly in Spanish-Portuguese and Italian territory. The centralized monarchy, while it worked well for later French unity, could not be said to favor the universal imperial idea. But the strong position of a church that claimed universality more than offset this. The Frankish kingdom, a local institution, nevertheless considered itself from its inception as forming part of a universal Christian Church steeped in the later Roman tradition, whose universal language was the Latin inherited from pagan and Christian Rome.

After many vicissitudes and internal conflicts, the Merovingian dynasty gave way to the Carolingian, founded by Pepin of Heristal, last of the mayors of the palace who had made themselves the real rulers. Charles Martel, said to have been an illegitimate son of Pepin, reinforced the French monarchy by uniting the Franks, with the valid help of the Church, to face the Moorish menace that swept in from Spain. Pepin himself forged new bonds with the Church by defending it from the aggressions of the Longobards. But it remained for Pepin's descendant Charlemagne to expand the Frankish realms into an empire reminiscent of the glories of ancient Rome, with control of northern France (Neustria), western Germany (Austrasia), southwestern France (Aquitaine), and northern Italy, wrested from the Longobards. It is also to Charlemagne's credit that despite his own illiteracy, he tried to bring back something resembling old Roman culture, importing Alcuin of York and Peter of Pisa to instruct his scribes and clerics in "good" Latin, and creating monastery schools that fostered Latin literacy. But it was also Charlemagne who gave first official recognition to the new popular tongue of his western domains, the *lingua romana rustica*.

Charlemagne's empire fell apart in the hands of his successors, and there was not only a final cleavage between the Franks of France and those of Germany but also the creation of a large buffer state between the two, called first *Lotharingia,* or Lorraine, later expanded into Burgundy, which for a period of centuries vied with the authority of the kings of France. There were Viking incursions along the coasts and up the great tranquil rivers of western France, culminating in the siege of Paris and the establishment of the Northmen in the region that bears their name, Normandy. From Normandy, a century or so later, the Northmen turned Normans moved on to the conquest of England, while retaining their French possessions. Long before this, there had been a parallel settlement of the ancient province of Armorica by British and Welsh refugees from the inroads of the Anglo-Saxons, with the consequent change of name of the region to Brittany. There was the growth in power and influence of the feudal nobles, forever clashing with the central authority and among themselves. But all the way through French history there was a broken line of rulers who managed to expand the royal power, authority, and domains, taking the leadership in the Crusades, like Louis IX; resisting the claims of the English, based on their original holdings in Normandy and Aquitaine, like Philip Augustus; or finally breaking the power of the feudal lords and the dukes of Burgundy, like Louis XI; as well as by inspiring semireligious crusades against the southern heretics, and thereby ending at one stroke the power of the counts of Toulouse, the Albigensian heresy, and the rich Provençal culture that had flourished, separately from that of northern France, in the eleventh and twelfth centuries. (Old Provençal culture disappeared in the thirteenth century, leaving only a series of local dialects where there had been the most promising literature of medieval Europe, sending its offshoots to distant Portugal and Sicily, and giving inspiration to Dante and his precursors.)

By 1500, when the period of overseas expansion begins, France was rid of the English claims that had beset her during the Hundred Years' War. Despite the earlier disasters of Crécy, Poitiers, and Agincourt, she had been carried on to victory, largely by the sacrifice of Joan of Arc. Now she was fully united, and ready to embark on her own career of empire-building. On European soil, this mission was carried on by Charles VII and Francis I, with doubtful results, but with much glory and prestige, as well as with the assimilation by the French of Italian culture and refinement.

The story of French overseas expansion will appear in a later chapter.

For what concerns the French homeland, it may be noted that the centralizing tendencies of earlier rulers were continued in the seventeenth century by the wise appeasement of Henry IV, the cunning of the two great cardinals and statesmen, Richelieu and Mazarin, the despotism of Louis XIV, who finally expelled the Huguenots, and in the eighteenth and nineteenth centuries by the ultranationalistic aspects of the French Revolution and the imperialism of the two Napoleons.

The main historical factor in the case of France is a centripetal tendency that begins with Clovis and ends with De Gaulle. The fact that some of its aspects in the eighteenth, nineteenth, and twentieth centuries are highly democratic is beside the point. France is today, despite her political parties and struggles, one of the best-knit nations in the world, with a spirit of national and cultural consciousness second to none, a basically strong administration and economy, and a unity and cohesion that never seem to fail, whatever the course of events—a worthy descendant of republican Rome. All this could not fail to influence the course of the language, which is among the most standardized and regularized in existence; its use in standard form among all classes of French speakers is far more general than is the case with other, less fortunate tongues whose speakers were not subjected to the same centralizing forces.

From the standpoint of the sixth and seventh centuries, the Iberian peninsula presented by far the most promising picture among the three main areas of the former Empire of the West. After the Suevians, Vandals, and Alans had swept across Iberia, most of them going on to North Africa in the fifth century, the peninsula fell to the Visigoths, the most civilized and Romanized among the Germanic invaders. They established, early in the sixth century, a monarchy that was elective, not hereditary, and that proved fairly stable, giving the region a century and a half of relative peace in a world beset by wars and bloodshed. They did not disturb the traditional layout of the Roman provinces, with Baetica in the south, Tarraconensis in the north and center, and Lusitania in the west. The Visigoths were already Christianized when they arrived, but belonged to the Arian sect, which was at odds with the Popes in Rome. They shifted over to Catholicism around A.D. 589 under King Reccared, but friendly relations with the Roman Church were established a full century later than they had been established by the Frankish monarchs, which meant that the participation of the Church in state affairs was not as complete as it was in France. Cultural activities of sorts were carried on during the Visigothic period, as evidenced by the work of Isidore of Seville and the comparatively correct Latin appearing in the documents that have come down to us.

But the Visigothic monarchy was beset by internal weaknesses, which led to its downfall in 711, when the North African Moors, at the invitation of some dissatisfied Visigothic noblemen, crossed the Strait of Gibraltar and inflicted a series of disastrous defeats on the royal armies. In less than five years the Moors conquered all of the peninsula south of the Cantabrian mountains. The Visigoths, however, held the line and desperately defended the last northern strip of territory left to them, successfully turning back the final thrust of the Moors at Covadonga, in 726.

From that point on, the peninsula turned into two hostile or semi-hostile regions, a series of Christian principalities in the north and Moslem emirates and caliphates in the south and center, where Christian populations lived on under Moorish overlordship, with a constantly shifting no man's land between the two areas. The extreme northern provinces, Galicia, Asturias, Navarra, the Basque region, constituted a shadowy, disunited realm out of which ultimately emerged the new kingdoms of León and Castile, which kept the Roman and Visigothic tradition, and eventually began to press down upon the weakened Moors in the slow process of the *Reconquista,* begun in earnest about 1050 and fully completed in 1492. One of its first fruits was the retaking of the ancient capital of Toledo, in 1085. Castile, León, and Galicia were united under Ferdinand I in the year 1035. At a much later date (ca. 1150) there was a similar union of the eastern group of northern provinces, Aragón, Navarra, and Catalonia. Córdoba was retaken by the Christians in 1236, Seville in 1248. The union of Ferdinand and Isabella marked the merger of the two kingdoms of Castilla-León and Aragón, marking the emergence of the modern state of Spain, the fall of Granada, last of the Moorish strongholds, the beginning of persecutions against both Moors and Jews who refused to be converted to Christianity, and Columbus' discovery of America, which changed the face of the world.

In the meantime, however, there had been the rise of the separate state of Portugal, founded largely by settlers from Galicia and León in the western lands liberated by the *Reconquista,* and recognized as a separate nation in 1279, though it was twice in its later history reunited with Spain.

The story of navigation, discovery, and the occupation of vast overseas territories belongs to a later chapter. Both Spain and Portugal profited enormously from these activities, and under Charles V and Philip II there was a vast expansion of Spain's domains, not only in the New World but also in Europe, with the conquest of the Low Countries and large areas of Italy. But economic exhaustion, population depletion due to emigration, and the defeat of Philip's Armada by the English fleet and the sea storms of 1588 led to a period of decadence that lasted through the seventeenth century and culminated in the loss of Spain's European possessions, and even of the fortress of Gibraltar. Napoleon's invasion of Spain, his attempt to set Joseph Bonaparte on the Spanish throne, and the Peninsular War, in which Wellington, with the collaboration of both Spaniards and Portuguese, finally expelled the French, contributed to plunge Spain into deeper depression, and these events were followed by the revolt of Spain's American possessions in the early nineteenth century. The final stage in Spain's decline was the Spanish-American War of 1898, in consequence of which Spain lost Cuba, Puerto Rico, and the Philippines. The modest resurgence of Spain after the great Civil War of the 1930's is a tribute to the power of endurance and will to survival of the Spanish people.

But while Spain was reduced in power and influence, her offshoots, on American soil, have grown in numbers, productivity, and importance. There is today a Hispanic world that embraces not only Spain and the few overseas possessions she has left but the new, vibrant countries of South and Central America, the Antilles, and Mexico, which retain the Spanish tradition and language and hark back in part to the same Iberian, Roman, and Visigothic ancestry as does Spain herself.

Portugal has been more fortunate than Spain in retaining until recently part of the vast colonial empire it once had. Portugal's major territorial loss has been that of Brazil, a country that embraces nearly half of South America. But Brazil, too, continues the Portuguese tradition and language.

The geographical force that has had the greatest influence in the development of the Iberian peninsula is its relative isolation from the rest of Europe, with only the passes of the Pyrenees to supply communication in the days before the appearance of modern transportation. Historically, the Iberian peninsula's development was subjected to the disruptive force of the great Moorish invasion, which partially paralyzed its normal evolution. But the tremendous contributions brought to the Spanish-Portuguese civilization by the Moors and the Jews cannot be minimized. To them are due the growth of such pursuits as astronomy, mathematics, chemistry, philosophy, architecture, partly assimilated by the Arabs from earlier contacts with the Greeks. These were eventually passed on to the rest of

Europe. The Moorish occupation retarded the ultimate unification of Spain, which had begun under the Visigoths, and this is reflected in the number and varieties of Spanish dialects, enhanced by overseas migrations and surviving to the present day, and in the widespread lack of acceptance of the Castilian standard. Psychologically, the evolution of the peninsular nations is affected by their long semi-isolation from common European influences and by the long and bitter struggles of the *Reconquista,* leading to stubborn pride, haughtiness, occasionally intolerance.

Yet throughout their long history both peninsular countries retained their basic Roman heritage, in more conservative and undiluted form, perhaps, than other Romance countries. The Moorish overlay is just that— an overlay. Spain and Portugal, with all their distant offshoots, are worthy descendants of Rome.

Italy, homeland of the Romans, and the base from which they began their career of world unification, found herself at the close of the period of Germanic invasions in a worse state of disruption than either of the other two major Romance areas.

In the north, Charlemagne had set up on the ruins of the Longobardic realm a Frankish kingdom that extended from the Alps to Terracina in the vicinity of Rome, and that endured for more than a century. The central part of the peninsula was governed, not too effectively, by the Popes. The south, with Sicily, was vaguely subject to the Eastern Roman Empire, which was Greek. But soon the Saracens from North Africa began to harass the Italian coasts; they invaded and occupied Sicily. At the same time, the Northmen, coming into the Mediterranean, made destructive raids on the extended coastlines, while the Frankish north was temporarily thrown into confusion by a Magyar invasion.

In self defense, the cities, not sufficiently protected by distant central authorities such as the Frankish Empire and that of the Byzantines, undertook to set up their own fortifications and select their own military leaders. Here was the beginning of the Italian city-state, later typified by Milan, Venice, Genoa, Pisa, Florence, Amalfi: an ideal environment for individuality and creativity, but hardly conducive to any form of national unity. When the Frankish rule in the north was replaced by that of the Holy Roman Empire, which was in effect German, the situation did not change for the better. The German emperors were remote, and at first cared little about their Italian possessions. The northern cities became more and more independent, vying and fighting with one another. In the south, some Norman adventurers who had gone on a pilgrimage to Rome and had tarried to aid the southern cities against Saracen raids and Byzantine encroachments decided to liberate Sicily from Saracen rule, and succeeded in setting up a Norman kingdom of Sicily in the latter half of the eleventh century. At about the same time, the German emperors started to worry about their Italian possessions, and began a series of attempts to enforce their authority which went on until 1176. They also clashed with the Popes. One episode involved Henry IV and Pope Gregory VII, and ended with the humiliation of the former at Canossa in 1077, because the Popes had learned to make effective use of the spiritual weapon of excommunication directed at an entire nation in reprisal for the misbehavior of its ruler. But while the Popes were temporarily victorious, the issue rankled, and there ensued a long and bitter struggle between Popes and emperors which was highly disruptive to the Italians, who took sides in the conflict. Guelphs (supporters of the Popes) and Ghibellines (followers of the emperors) were terms that lasted for centuries and gave rise to many struggles and reprisals, not only among different cities but within the same city. On a military plane, the greatest of medieval German emperors, Frederick Barbarossa, who made the last serious attempt to subject northern Italy, was soundly routed by the league of Lombard cities at Legnano in 1176.

Now began a period of pre-Renaissance prosperity and achievement for the free Italian cities, but on a separate, disunited plane, with the rise of *condottieri* (leaders) and *compagnie di ventura* (bands of mercenaries that served the interests of different cities). Seafaring city-states like Venice and Genoa covered themselves with glory, but also fought destructive wars with each other. In the papal domains, various noble families came into prominence, and either dominated the Popes or selected them outright from their own number. The only bright spot was Sicily, where the Normans had been succeeded by the Hohenstaufens, whose greatest king, Frederick II, made his court a center of learning, enlightenment, arts, and letters.

Beginning about 1300, the fiercely free and independent northern and Tuscan cities, which had preserved a measure of democratic liberty, began increasingly to fall into the hands of despots, who fostered the arts and sciences, but repressed opposition. Increasingly, they called in foreign powers to their aid, or made use of foreign mercenaries—French, German, Spanish, Swiss. The Italians, who could not unite, were now faced with unification at the hands of foreigners. Charles VIII of France invaded

Italy. The Aragonese took possession of Naples. The battle of Pavia between Francis I of France and Charles V of Spain and Germany took place on Italian soil, with the Italians as onlookers. In 1527 there was a sack of Rome, despite the presence of the Pope. Florence fell. From 1530 on began a period of foreign ascendancy, Austrian in the north, Spanish in the south. All the French could do after their defeat at Pavia was to take Corsica from a weakened Republic of Genoa.

The French Revolution and Napoleon put a temporary halt to this state of affairs, but Napoleon's liberators turned out to be merely a new army of occupation, with a new French kingdom of Italy in the offing. At the end of the Napoleonic wars, peace was restored to a fragmented Italy, dominated in the north by Austria, which held Lombardy and Venice and protected a couple of Austrian-inspired grand duchies in Florence and elsewhere; in the center by the Popes; and in the south and Sicily by a branch of the Bourbon dynasty.

But the auspices were finally ripe for unification, under the aegis of the counts of Savoy, who held Piedmont and Sardinia. The *Risorgimento,* which lasted from the fall of Napoleon to 1870, proceeded by gradual stages, first with the annexation of Lombardy after a victorious war against Austria in which the kingdom of Piedmont and Sardinia was assisted by Napoleon III; then with the annexation of Venice and Venetia, in consequence of the Austro-Prussian war of 1866; then with Garibaldi's amazing conquest of the southern Kingdom of the Two Sicilies, which he wrested from the Bourbons and offered up to the cause of unification under the House of Savoy; lastly with the occupation of the Papal States and of Rome itself in 1870. It was now possible to speak of a united Italy.

But unification had been long delayed. Vast rifts had developed in the course of centuries among the various regions of Italy, differences that were cultural, economic, linguistic, psychological. Of the three major Romance areas, the one that was Rome's heartland is even today the least homogeneous. That is being remedied by modern technologies and techniques, but the effects of disunion endure. Not the least of these is the fact that Italy, despite the ability and genius of her navigators and discoverers, failed utterly to participate in the settling of the New World, first discovered and explored by Italians.

On the other hand, millions of Italians migrated across the Atlantic in the nineteenth and early twentieth centuries to settle in both North and South America. But as latecomers, they were absorbed by the countries that received them.

Geographically, Italy's position lent itself to all sorts of raids and invasions, both by land and sea. Historically, its cleavage into north, center, and south, created by the fall of the Roman Empire, endured across the centuries. This led psychologically to an inability to unite, but also to a quickening of local and individual genius.

One thing that did not fail was the Roman and Latin tradition, which was fiercely preserved through all vicissitudes. In some ways, the modern Italians are the farthest removed from the ancient Romans, with their stern social discipline; in others, notably language and cultural outlook, they are the closest.

Smallest of the Romance areas, and geographically detached from the others, is Rumania, which occupies approximately the same area as Trajan's province of Dacia. But the movements of the Romanized Dacians and the Roman settlers are shrouded in mystery by reason of the third-century invasion of the Goths.

After more than a thousand years, Rumania emerged. But the historical development of the country in its formative period is so strangely intertwined with the linguistic development of the Rumanian language, and presents such puzzling features, that it is best left for later discussion in a separate chapter.

5. The Overseas Expansion
of the Romance Nations

In antiquity, the prize for navigation and exploration went to the Phoenicians, the Greeks, the Carthaginians. They, so far as we know, were the first to venture out of the relatively safe Mediterranean into the great ocean that lay beyond the Pillars of Hercules, as far as the northern coast of Spain, the British Isles, the West African coast. The Romans, while they made themselves masters of the Mediterranean and sailed to Britain, were not by nature inclined to navigation, and took it as an indispensable part of their empire-building mission and of the trade they developed. Their favorite campaigns were by land.

Before the fifteenth century of our era, the great ocean-going navigators were the Scandinavian Vikings. They not only raided all the coasts of Europe and sailed up the rivers to attack peaceful towns and monasteries; they also discovered Iceland, Greenland, and, if we accept the story of Leif Ericsson's Vinland, the North American continent. But the last discovery did not bear fruit; nor did other, generally unsubstantiated voyages by Irish, Welsh, and Breton fishermen, who may have approached Newfoundland and other nearby regions.

During the Middle Ages and the early Renaissance, the Mediterranean was dominated largely by the great seafaring Italian republics, Venice, Genoa, to a lesser degree Pisa and Amalfi. Productive navigation and exploration beyond the Strait of Gibraltar really began in the early fifteenth century with the Portuguese.

The Portuguese had a special incentive and special conditions that impelled them out into the Atlantic—an extended coastline, nearly all of which faces the ocean, and no land access to the rest of Europe save through Spain, a country with which the Portuguese were often at odds.

Almost a century before Columbus, Prince Henry the Navigator had shown the way up and down the West African coast. By the middle of the century the Portuguese had occupied the Azores, Madeira, even portions of Guinea on the African mainland, and initiated what was to be a later bane to modern civilization, the practice of trading in black slaves from the West African regions. In 1486 Bartolomeu Diaz rounded the Cape of Good Hope and sailed up the east coast of Africa. By 1490 the Portuguese had established friendly relations with the one Christian country of Africa, Abyssinia, the mythical land of Prester John. Going on to India under the leadership of Vasco da Gama (1498), they later established trading posts along the Indian coasts, in Cochin, Calicut, Goa, and Diu, then went on to the Moluccas and China, where they occupied Macao. The basis of a Portuguese empire that in small part survives to this day was thus laid. Magellan (Magalhães) crowned Portugal's glory (though he sailed for Spain), with the rounding of Cape Horn and the first circumnavigation of the globe between 1519 and 1522.

The Portuguese did not take part in the initial discovery and exploration of the American continent, not even that part of it which was later to be theirs. Brazil was first discovered and partly explored by a Spaniard (Pinzón, 1499). But the Portuguese under Cabral arrived there the following year and took possession. They engaged in successful warfare against the other colonizing nations, Spain, Britain, France, Holland. The last three nations were finally circumscribed to what later became British, French, and Dutch Guiana. Portugal established a more or less uncontested dominion over the vast east central region of South America. It was to Brazil that they brought large numbers of African slaves, and slavery persisted in Brazil almost as long as it did in the United States. But long before it was abolished in 1860, the Portuguese settlers in Brazil had decided to follow the ancient Roman policy of intermarriage and integration, both with the blacks and with the natives. A rough estimate of the racial composition of the population of Brazil today is that it is 45 percent pure white (this includes the numerous latecomers from Italy, Germany, Spain, and other European countries), 14 percent pure black, 8 percent pure Indian, and 33 percent of mixed blood. The Portuguese government moved to Brazil during the Napoleonic wars, but in 1822 the country declared itself a separate empire, though ruled by an emperor who was a member of the Portuguese ruling dynasty. The empire gave way to a republic in 1889.

The overseas expansion of Portugal has meant, roughly, a 1,000 percent increase in the number of people who speak the Portuguese language and subscribe to Portuguese culture. This includes not only Brazil, with its vast area and population, but formerly Portuguese African areas (Mozambique, Angola, Guinea), the Portuguese part of the island of Timor, Macao, and even such Indian cities as Goa, Damau, and Diu, where the local Indian population was happy and proud of its full-fledged Portuguese citizenship before India's military take-over.

To Spain belongs the glory not merely of having given Columbus the opportunity to discover the new world but also of having settled and colonized that world to an extent second, if at all, only to that of the English. The story of Columbus' voyages in search of a new route to the Indies is well known. So is the story of Cortés' conquest of Mexico in 1520, of Pizarro's conquest of Peru in 1533, and of the many voyages of exploration and discovery carried out by such men as Balboa, Coronado, Cabeza de Vaca, de Soto, Pedro de Mendoza, Ponce de León. By the time of the American Revolution the Spanish overseas empire included not only all of South America (with the exception of Brazil and the Guianas), Central America, Mexico, most of the larger Antilles, wide areas of what is today U.S. territory (California, Arizona, New Mexico, Texas, Florida) but also the Philippines and many islands of the Caroline and Mariana groups, as well as the Canary Islands and small regions on the West African coast. Politically, most of these lands were later lost to Spain in the early part of the nineteenth century, when Bolívar and San Martín carried on wars of independence that resulted in the emergence of the present-day Spanish-speaking countries of South America, while Iturbide fulfilled the same mission for Mexico. But long before these countries became independent, they had been Hispanicized, at least as to language, customs, and cultural outlook. Racially, all sorts of differences appear among them: while Argentina, Chile, and Uruguay are at least 75 percent pure white, Peru, Bolivia, and Paraguay are 75 percent Indian or of mixed blood; Mexico is 20 percent white, 37 percent Indian, 43 percent mixed. Argentina, Chile, and Uruguay, like Brazil, have received large groups of Italians, Germans, and other European immigrants. It is estimated that at least 10 percent of Argentina's population is of Italian extraction.

The result is that despite Spanish territorial losses, the number of people who speak Spanish and subscribe to Hispanic culture has increased at least 600 percent in relation to that of the homeland in the course of the last five centuries. Spanish-Americans are highly independent, and have rejected the possibility of uniting into one vast federal union similar to that of the United States. But they are also intensely proud of their Spanish heritage, and while they do not combine politically, they intermingle freely as *Hispanos:* people of Spanish culture, even if not 100 percent of Spanish blood.

French overseas expansion, while as extensive as that of the English, Spanish, or Portuguese, was less fortunate in enduring results. In their earlier colonizing career, the French clashed with the English both in India and on the North American continent, and lost out in both encounters. The clash in India began in the late seventeenth century, and was over by 1757, at which time all the French had left were one or two coastal towns (Pondichéry was voluntarily relinquished to India in very recent times).

In North America the story was different. Here the French gained an excellent foothold in what is now eastern Canada with the explorations of Cartier and Champlain, and began to establish an empire that was proudly named "New France." The explorations of Joliet, Marquette, and La Salle from the Great Lakes down the valley of the Mississippi led to the establishment of vast additional French holdings, vaguely labeled "Louisiana," which embraced far more than the present-day state that bears that name. But the most promising settlement of all, along the valley of the St. Lawrence, was brought under British rule by Wolfe's victory over Montcalm at Québec in 1759. What endured was a large French-speaking and French-thinking population that today numbers over six million, mostly in the Province of Québec, and that has sent offshoots into the New England states, northern New York, and, by reason of British mass deportations of recalcitrant French speakers to the bayous of Louisiana (where Acadiens turned into Cajuns), even to the U.S. South. All that politically remained to France were the islands of St. Pierre and Miquelon. It was left for Napoleon to lose Haiti to the rebellious black slaves, and to sell the vast tract of Louisiana to the United States. In South America, France was restricted to French Guiana; in the Antilles, to the islands of Guadeloupe and Martinique.

Undeterred by earlier failures, France went on to build herself a second colonial empire in Africa and the Far East in the course of the nineteenth century, beginning with the occupation of Algeria, followed at a distance by that of Tunisia, and the seizure of Indochina, which occurred during the last two decades of the last century, while at the same time vastly expanding her seventeenth-century holdings in western and central Africa. But this was a different type of colonization, occurring in lands already thickly populated by their original inhabitants, with relatively few settlers from France. The French linguistic and cultural veneer that was overlaid on the native population was not the sort of thing that could take too deep a root in the relatively brief time left before the end of the era of colonialism. Accordingly, while many of the new independent nations that have arisen in Indochina and what was formerly French-speaking Africa (and this includes Zaire, the former Belgian Congo) maintain close cultural and economic relations with France and Belgium, and most of them still use French as one of their official languages, the French flag flies over only a small fraction of the territories that France once held.

There is, however, another aspect that concerns French culture and the French language. By reason of historical predominance in European affairs over many centuries, the language and culture of France are so widely studied and pursued in other countries all over the world that their pervasiveness has been exceeded, and that quite recently, only by that of English.

Italian overseas expansion has been solely of the migratory type, despite the prominent role played by Italian navigators and explorers in the discovery of the New World.

Columbus, a Genoese, was the first to come to America in such fashion that his discovery had lasting consequences; but Columbus, having vainly tried to convince his native Genoa and Portugal that his ideas were valid, had to sail under the Spanish flag, and to Spain went the power and the glory and the profit of his discovery. Another Genoese, John Cabot, was the first to reach the North American continent with lasting results; but Cabot sailed for England. His son Sebastian, sailing for Spain, explored part of the coast of Brazil and the La Plata River. Verrazzano, who first discovered the Hudson River and the present location of New York, sailed under the French flag. Amerigo Vespucci, who gave his name to the New World, seemingly by reason of a misconception to the effect that he had been its discoverer, reportedly made four voyages to the American conti-

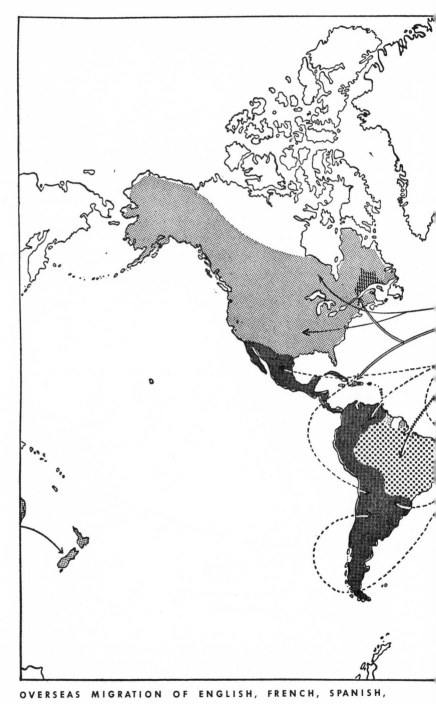

OVERSEAS MIGRATION OF ENGLISH, FRENCH, SPANISH,
AND PORTUGUESE

ENGLISH
SPANISH
PORTUGUESE
FRENCH

nent, but his account, contained in letters whose originals were lost, and which may have been mistranslated, lends itself to considerable doubt.

Italian overseas migration to both North and South America has been heavy, particularly in the latter half of the nineteenth century and the early decades of the twentieth. It did not, however, lead to any occupation of territory in the name of an Italy that was just beginning to exist as a united nation. The descendants of millions of Italian emigrants to the United States, Canada, Argentina, Brazil, and other American countries continue to some extent the Italian tradition, but regard themselves as nationals of the countries where they were born, and speak their national languages far more fluently than they do Italian.

Rumania, smallest of the Romance nations, has had no overseas expansion and comparatively little overseas migration. The ties that the descendants of its emigrants (of whom there are a considerable number in the United States) feel toward their country of origin are, like those of the Italians, purely cultural.

Part II

The Linguistic Evolution

1. The Tongues of Ancient Italy: Archaic and Pre-Classical Latin

At the dawn of history the languages of the Italian peninsula and the island of Sicily appear to have belonged to the Indo-European family[1] with one notable exception, Etruscan, and some doubt attaching to a few other groups. On the basis of very scanty indications, Corsica and Sardinia are assigned by some scholars to the Iberian linguistic system, which, like Etruscan, may have belonged to a prehistoric "Mediterranean" family of languages antedating the coming of Indo-European speakers.

In the extreme north, along the crest of the Alps, a few "Rhaetic" inscriptions point to the existence of a race whose linguistic affiliations, like those of the Veneti of the northeast, the Messapians of the heel of the Italian boot, and the speakers of the tongue represented by the "Sabellian" or "East Italic" inscriptions of the central Adriatic coast, have been described as lying with an equally mysterious "Illyrian" spoken on the other side of the Adriatic. Inscriptions and glosses[2] for all these languages, as well as for the "Liguric" of the region around Genoa, permit us only to surmise that they were probably of Indo-European stock.

The tongue of the inhabitants of Cisalpine Gaul was undoubtedly Celtic, probably closely allied with the Gaulish spoken beyond the Alps, but here, too, the material is scanty and uncertain.

The Sicani and Siculi of Sicily and the toe of the Italian boot also seem to have spoken Indo-European tongues, and in the case of the Siculi a definite Italic connection seems likely.

---

1. For a chart of the branches of Indo-European, see Appendix A.
2. A gloss is an interlinear or marginal notation in an ancient or medieval manuscript giving a translation or explanation of a word or passage.

Etruscan, which still constitutes a linguistic enigma, seems to have been a non–Indo-European tongue, probably transplanted to Italy by overseas migrations from Asia Minor before 1000 B.C.[3]

The Greek colonies of southern Italy and Sicily supply a Hellenic element in the picture. Punic, an offshoot of Phoenician (a Semitic language), was brought by the Carthaginians to western Sicily in historic times.

The backbone of linguistic ancient Italy was formed by the languages of the Italic branch of Indo-European, subdivided into Latin-Faliscan and Oscan-Umbrian.

Latin, the language of Rome, had for its closest neighbor Faliscan, and Latinian dialects seem to have been spoken by other groups in the vicinity of Rome. Oscan, the predominant tongue of southern Italy, was spoken by many groups, chief among them the Sabines and Samnites. Umbrian was the predominant tongue of central Italy east of the Apennines.[4]

The linguistic picture of ancient Italy prior to Roman expansion is therefore one in which Indo-European languages of three different branches, Italic, Greek, and Celtic, predominate. Numerically, Italic speakers probably constituted an absolute majority of the peoples of pre-Roman Italy; but the Cisalpine Gauls, who occupied all of the Italian northwest, drove a spearhead to the upper Adriatic, and on one occasion threatened Rome itself, must have been quite numerous; the Etruscans, who had come to the west central coast of Italy before 1000 B.C. and had developed a great civilization from which the Romans took inspiration, must also have been numerous, extending their tentacles north into the valley of the Po, south as far as Capua, and into the city of Rome itself; the Greeks, though scattered along the southern coastlines and in eastern Sicily, had founded many flourishing towns.

The speakers of assuredly Italic languages, stretching from the upper Adriatic coast southward to the mouth of the Tiber, occupied the eastern half of central Italy and all of the south save for the Greek colonies and what may have been left of the Messapians in the heel of the boot.

There is plenty of evidence that the Latin-speaking Romans, as they began absorbing and Romanizing their neighbors and turning them into Latin speakers, borrowed rather extensively from their languages. These early borrowings, however, were homely words, indicative of an earthy,

---

3. For a brief discussion and samples of the Etruscan language, see Appendix B.
4. For a brief discussion and samples of Oscan, Umbrian, and Faliscan, see Appendix B.

primitive civilization. Latin forms like *asinus,* "donkey," and *caseus,* "cheese," seem to be Oscan or Umbrian rather than Latin in origin, for Latin would have turned *s* between vowels into *r* (*ausis,* the word for "ear," for instance, turned into *auris*). The appearance in many Italian words of a characteristic Oscan *f* where Latin has *b* between vowels (It. *scarafaggio* from Latin *scarabeus,* "beetle"; *bifolco* from *bubulcus,* "ploughman"; *bufalo* from *bubalus,* "wild ox") indicates that Oscan forms with *f* must have existed in the Vulgar Latin speech, even if unrecorded.

The earliest Latin inscription on record is the Praenestine Fibula, a belt buckle found at Praeneste, a few miles from Rome, and said to go back to the seventh century B.C. Its message goes: *Manios med fhefhaked Numasioi.* In Classical Latin this would run: *Manius me fecit Nummerio* ("Manius made me for Nummerius"), a true ancient trademark combined with the name of the consumer, almost a modern commercial.[5]

Next in order of archaism is the Viminal Vessel, dated in the fifth century B.C., a part of which runs as follows: *Duenos med feced en manom einom Duenoi ne med malo statod.* This in Classical Latin would be: *Bonus me fecit in* (*contra*) *Manum enim* (*sed*) *Bono ne* (*per*) *me malum stato* (*sit*)[5] ("Bonus made me against Manus, but let no harm come to Bonus through me"). Was this cup designed to contain a poisoned drink? If so, would the perpetrator have left such a definite clue to his identity?

Between the Archaic and the Pre-Classical are two inscriptions from the third century B.C., one from Spoleto, the other from the tomb of Lucius Scipio, brother of Scipio Africanus, on the Appian Way. The first runs: *Sei quis scies violasit Jovei bovid piaclum datod.* In Classical Latin this would be: *Si quis sciens violaverit Jovi bove piaculum dato* ("If someone shall knowingly violate this, let him offer expiation to Jupiter with an ox"). The second goes: *Honc oino ploirume cosentiont r*(*omai*) *duonoro optumo fuise viro* (or *virorum?*) *Luciom Scipione.* Here the Classical Latin would have: *Hunc unum plurime* (or *plurimi*) *consentiunt Romae bonorum optimum fuisse virum* (or *virorum*) *Lucium Scipionem* ("Most people in Rome agree" [or "they generally agree in Rome"] "that Lucius Scipio was the best of good men" [or "that Lucius Scipio was the best man among the good"].[5]

The picture that emerges from this older Latin material is that of a language still uncontaminated by higher cultural influences, and still fairly close to its Indo-European ancestry; therefore it is closer to other

5. For an analysis of the linguistic features of this and other Archaic and Pre-Classical inscriptions, see Appendix B.

early-recorded Indo-European languages, such as Greek, than it would be at a later date. The case endings often duplicate those retained by Greek; the verbs show a reduplication in the perfect tense that is practically universal in Greek, but only occasional in Classical Latin; there are numerous diphthongs that survived in Greek, but turned into simple long vowels in later Latin (*ei* to *ī; oi* and *ou* to *ū*).

Yet there are also features that anticipate later Romance development (the fall, or disappearance, of final *-m*, and of *n* before *s;* the confusion of similar vowels in the unstressed position, which resulted in the interchange of *e* and *i*, of *o* and *u*), attesting to certain long-range tendencies that were apparently suppressed in the Classical period, but may have run as an undercurrent in the more popular language until they again emerged, before or after the Empire's fall. It is upon archaic features of this type that many experts base their belief in a popular or "vulgar" Latin that ran parallel with the more refined variety appearing in official documents and literary works.

The changes appearing in the Latin language from the inception of its records to the time of the Punic Wars are self-evident. They are confirmed by a chance statement made by Polybius (the Greek-born historian and observer mentioned earlier) that the differences between the Latin of his time and that used in treaties by the ancestors of the Romans of his day were such that even the most learned had difficulty in understanding those treaties. Even in the heart of the Classical period, Cicero and other writers mention the archaic and rustic features displayed in the language of earlier orators.

The quality of *rusticitas*, "rusticism," may carry greater implications than it would today, and point to the long survival of Italic dialects (Oscan, Umbrian, Faliscan) akin to Latin, yet differing from it. This quality is still mentioned in the first century of the Christian era.

As for non-Italic influences in the early Latin language, Livy, who lived during the final decades of the first century B.C. and the initial ones of the first century A.D., referring in his writings to events that had taken place in the fourth century B.C., has this to say: *Tum romanos pueros sicut nunc graecis ita etruscis litteris erudiri solitos* ("At that time Roman boys were taught Etruscan, as they are now taught Greek"). Some of those Etruscan words rubbed off on the Roman learners. Among Latin words said to be of Etruscan origin are *satelles*, "satellite," *caerimonia*, "ceremony," *fenestra*, "window," *autumnus*, "autumn," possibly even *vinum*, "wine," and the name of Rome itself, *Ruma*.

Popular slang is also current in some of the literary works that have come down to us, notably the comedies of Plautus (early second century B.C.), which indicate a rich, ebullient popular tongue, not too unlike the slangy American of today.

The general image that appears from an examination of the material at our disposal points to a Latin language close to its Indo-European ancestry at its source, but developing and unfolding as it progresses, and subject to all the influences that still affect language today—gradual evolution of sounds and grammatical forms; borrowing of words, possibly even of syntax, from neighbors, first near, later remote; willingness to absorb the cultural experiences of others; social stratification, with a popular variety streaked with slang and vulgarisms, but also an upper-crust language that gradually crystallizes and slowly develops into a rich, abundant, tightly knit tongue capable of expressing all the shades and nuances of meaning that will appear in the literature of its Golden and Silver ages, from the first century B.C. to the fourth century A.D.

2. The Classical Period

By the year 100 B.C. Roman society had crystallized into what might be called its imperial mold, even though the Republic was to go on for nearly a century. It was a society openly based on class distinctions, with an old patrician aristocracy now turned into a senatorial class; an upper middle class that continued the ancient equestrian order, but which now consisted largely of businessmen, merchants and traders, manufacturers and builders, owners of large and medium estates, all or most of whom had achieved a measure of prosperity; a still numerous, but gradually dwindling class of small landowners, who found the going increasingly more difficult by reason of burdensome taxation and the competition of large agricultural enterprises run with slave labor; a growing mass of city dwellers, some gainfully employed in various trades and occupations, but many unemployed, and living mainly on government bounty; and a numerous class of slaves, both urban and rural, who enjoyed no human or civil rights beyond what their masters chose to give them, but who could on occasion be freed or purchase their own freedom, in which case they went to join the two lower classes.

The language, too, was essentially crystallized, at least in its official aspects. Beginning with Varro (first century B.C.), in imitation of what had been going on in Greek for some centuries, there had come into being a group of grammarians of the prescriptive type, who laid out the rules for the use of "good" Latin, partly on the basis of usage, more largely in accordance with traditional and archaic standards, ultimately in accord with their own learned whim. Official documents, works of literature and philosophy, military records, inscriptions on commemorative monuments (but not on tombstones), even the *Acta Romani Populi Diurna*, the official news bulletin posted up each morning in the Forum for the guidance and information of the people, all were couched in this "official" Latin, which apparently everybody understood, even if his or her own personal speech did not quite meet its standards.

It is this official Latin that has come down to us in our high school and college courses. Did it reflect the spoken language? Approximately to the same extent that the language of *The New York Times* or Internal Revenue forms reflects the spoken language of the New York subways and slums; but also of the New York Stock Exchange, the government bureaus, the suburbs, the wide open spaces of our West.

Was this language in widespread spoken use not merely in Rome, but throughout the provinces? That depends on the duration of the Roman occupation of any given area. For what concerns the areas of major interest to us (Italy, France, Spain and Portugal) the Roman occupation lasted from the third, second, and first centuries B.C. to the fifth century A.D., from a minimum of four hundred to a maximum of seven hundred years. The linguistic changeover from Oscan, Etruscan, Iberian, and Gaulish to Latin did not take place overnight, as the evidence indicates. But even the four-century minimum is a long time, and lends itself to leisurely change.

What variety of Latin was carried to the provinces, the official language, or the more racy, spicy, slangy tongue of the legions? Seemingly, both.

What of that more racy, popular, slangy tongue? What was it like? To what extent did it coincide with and differ from the Classical variety we learn in school today? Here the evidence is not as abundant as we should like it to be, but it is ample. From the graffiti of Pompeii, from popular tombstone inscriptions, from the occasional direct quotations of such lower-class characters as appear in the works of Plautus, Apuleius, and others, we can reconstruct it to a considerable degree. It differs from the literary and official language in its use of slangy words and constructions, in its vogue of short, choppy sentences of the simple variety rather than the majestic flow of the involved syntax of the poets and orators, but it is basically the same language, though socially stratified, just as the language of Emily Dickinson and Winston Churchill is basically the same language as that of the Lower East Side and Whitechapel. Its essential sound, word, form, and sentence structure is the same. There is no record of linguistic incomprehension between master and slave, between senator and welfare client, where both are speaking what goes for Latin. Our only records of linguistic incomprehension appear where an outlying province has still not been thoroughly Romanized and Latinized. But even here, the proof of the pudding is in the eating. We know that in some areas the process of Latinization was not sufficiently deep to do away with the native speech, as was the case in Britain; in other areas, Latin was ploughed under by another occupation, as in North Africa or in the lands east of the Adriatic. But in what today are Italy, France, Spain, and Portugal, there is no question that Latin came out on top. It must have been firmly grounded in the language habits of the people to have triumphed over both the original languages and the ones brought in by the later invaders.

The Roman writers are not particularly distinguished as linguistic observers, generally taking language for granted. Yet they give us, *en passant,* some precious information concerning the state of the disappearing native languages in the expanding Roman realm. Festus, a third-century A.D. grammarian, tells us that Volscian, a tongue of the Oscan branch of Italic, was still in use in the second century B.C. Cicero, in the first century B.C., speaks of the quality of *rusticitas,* which may easily imply non-Latin Italic influences, such as Oscan; but he uses the past tense in connection with it: *rustici dicebant,* "the rustics used to say"; *rustico sermone significabat,* "in rustic language used to mean." The impression he leaves with us is that *rusticitas,* in his time, was a thing of the past. Two writers from the first century A.D., Quintilian and Verrius Flaccus, remark on the *patavinitas,* "Patavian quality," of Livy and the *praenestinitas,* "Praenestine quality," of Vectius as things of the past. But are they referring to their writing (if so, no perceptible trace of any local usage appears in what has come down to us), or to their speech or intonation?

Quintilian (first century A.D.) specifically informs us that in his day all Italy spoke the same Latin, but *Italiotes* (non-Roman Italians) could be recognized by their accents, as individual metals can be identified from their ring. The implication seems to be that by Quintilian's time the Latinization of the Italian peninsula was complete, save for local intonations, which appear in practically all languages at all periods.

What of the outlying provinces, particularly Spain and Gaul? Here Cicero, in the first century B.C., speaks of *verba non trita Romae,* "words not current in Rome," that are used in those two provinces, and also of the need for interpreters for visitors to Rome from Spain and Africa. He further states that in Spain a Córdoba-born poet had offered up to Pompey some verses he had composed in the great general's honor, but that these verses were *pinguibus sonantibus*, "heavy-sounding." We are left in doubt whether he is referring to the quality of the versification or the native accent of the Spanish poet as he declaims his verses in Latin.

Spanish-born orators and writers, like Seneca and Lucan, have been explored, to the extent that we have their writings or records of their activities, to determine whether the quality of their Latin differs from that of native-born Romans. All that has resulted is their predilection for the demonstrative adjective-pronoun *iste*, "this," to the practical exclusion of others. Spanish preserves this demonstrative in the form *este*, but so do Old French (*ist*) and colloquial Italian (*sto*).

Tacitus, at the end of the first century A.D., tells the story of a Spanish peasant who had killed the praetor Lucius Piso, and when questioned refused to identify his accomplices: *voce magna, sermone patrio, frustra se interrogari clamabat* ("in a loud voice, and in his native language, he shouted that he was being questioned in vain").

There is a slightly suspect report that when the emperors Hadrian (first century A.D.) and Septimius Severus (second century A.D.) made their maiden addresses to the Senate, the senators tittered at the Spanish accent of the first and the African accent of the second; but there is some doubt that Hadrian was actually Spanish-born; in any case, the incidents would be no more significant than if Easterners today were to titter at Senator Sam Ervin's Southern accent.

The Ulpian Code, in the early third century A.D., gives definite indication that some of the background languages were still in use in the outlying provinces: *fidei commissa quocumque sermone relinqui possunt, non solum latino vel graeco, sed etiam punico vel gallicano, vel alterius cujuscumque gentis* ("wills may be left in any language, not only Latin or Greek, but also Punic or Gaulish, or in the tongue of any other nation").

The fourth century A.D. gives us some precious indications from the writings of St. Jerome, compiler of the Vulgate, to the effect that Gaulish was still used in the city of Treviri (now Trier, in western Germany, but at that time in eastern Gaul): *Galatas, excepto sermone graeco, quo omnis Oriens loquitur, propriam linguam eandem paene habere quam Treviros* ("the Galatians [of Asia Minor] in addition to Greek, which is spoken throughout the entire East, have their own tongue, which is almost the same as that of the inhabitants of Treviri"). The added bonus in this statement is the passage to the effect that Greek was the tongue of common intercourse of the eastern part of the Empire. Jerome also informs us: *cum et ipsa latinitas et regionibus quotidie mutetur et tempore* ("since the Latin language itself changes day by day, both by region and in the course of time"). This could be turned into a generalization concerning all language which would do honor to a modern linguist.

Jerome's contemporary Augustine, bishop of Hippo in North Africa, offers an interesting incidental statement: *proverbium notum est punicum, quod quidem latine vobis dicam, quia punice non omnes nostis* ("there is a well-known Punic saying, which I shall repeat to you in Latin, since not all of you know Punic"). The indication here is that Punic, the background language of North Africa, is rapidly giving way to Latin in the mouths of the younger generations.

Considering the chronology of these testimonials, it would seem that the non-Latin languages of Italy had practically disappeared from spoken use by the beginning of the Christian era, leaving only local intonations behind them; while in the outlying provinces, a dwindling use of the original languages continued down to the end of the fourth century A.D., not fully disappearing until after the fall of the Empire. The report that in some remote forest areas of Gaul there was still a remnant of Druidic worship and of the old Gaulish language in the time of Charlemagne probably has some truth in it; while in Spain the present survival of Basque proves that where the Romans did not extend their full authority, a background language can continue in use to this day. Nevertheless, the triumph of Latin in the four Romance countries of the West appears to have been all but absolute.

The factors favoring linguistic uniformity have already been mentioned: roads and other systems of communication and transportation; uniform, all-pervasive (and grinding) taxation; colonization (Roman, not British, style, by settling down and intermarrying with the native population); deportations and scattering of populations among other populations, with Latin as the sole common means of intercourse; military service, with recruits from various areas thrown together with no common language but Latin, which was also the language of command; communal property replaced by Roman private ownership; the prestige and pride of Roman citizenship; the mighty force of Christianity, with Latin as its sole official language in the West. One more factor needs bringing out, in view of the widespread belief in the ignorance and illiteracy of Roman times: the Roman school system, not compulsory, but free and open to all. Here again the words of Roman writers and historians are of interest, even though they are incidental.

Plutarch, the Greek biographer (50–120 A.D.) informs us that in the first century B.C. the Roman general Sertorius founded at Osca (now Huesca, in Spain) a school for the Iberian population, and adds that the local people were both proud and happy to attend. The language of instruction was, of course, Latin.

Livy tells us that at Carteia (modern Cádiz, also in Spain) a school had been founded for the Ibero-Roman population, with some four thousand lower-class pupils in attendance. Pliny mentions schools, run with public funds, at Cremona and Como, in northern Italy (the first was attended by Virgil). Tacitus, writing about the Roman general Agricola (first century A.D.), states that while in winter quarters in what is today Brittany, he passed his time teaching Latin to the Armorican tribesmen, later founding at Bibracte (or Augustudunum, today Autun) a great university open to all Gauls, which is mentioned in the third century A.D. by Eumenius, and which endured till the invasions. Suetonius, at the beginning of the second century A.D., speaks of grammatical studies that are carried on in all the provinces, especially in Gaul.

In the fourth century A.D. Symmachus, prefect of Rome, writes in a letter to a friend that he is sending his son to study at the university of Lugdunum in Gaul (now Lyon), because there he will learn to speak a better brand of Latin than is spoken in Rome. The fifth-century Theodosian Code provides for government-paid *grammatici* (teachers of grammar) to be located in all towns and villages throughout the Empire.

After the Empire's fall, but two centuries before Charlemagne, Theodoric the Ostrogoth, conqueror of Italy, ordered his learned prime minister Cassiodorus to reform the decaying Roman school system and bring back some measure of classical learning; while Chilperic, one of the Merovingian Frankish kings, who died in 584, undertook the task of reforming the Latin alphabet by the addition of some letter symbols to represent new sounds that had crept into the language; unfortunately, the precise nature of his proposed additions is lost to us.

The tradition of Latin grammarians, begun at the outset of the first century B.C. by Varro and his *De Lingua Latina,* continued throughout subsequent centuries, with, among many others, Verrius Flaccus in the first century A.D., Probus in the third or fourth, and went on long after the Empire's fall, with Macrobius in the fifth century A.D., Priscian in the sixth, Isidore of Seville in the seventh.

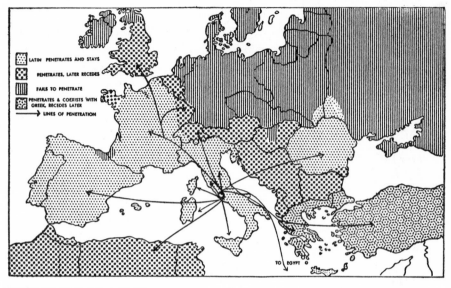

LATIN PENETRATES AND STAYS
PENETRATES, LATER RECEDES
FAILS TO PENETRATE
PENETRATES & COEXISTS WITH GREEK, RECEDES LATER
→ LINES OF PENETRATION

TO EGYPT

EXPANSION OF LATIN

The type of Latin advocated by the grammarians is essentially the language that has come down to us as Classical Latin, a language which no doubt represents both an ideal and a reality. It is the language used in military accounts, like Caesar's *Gallic War;* in addresses directed not only at the Senate but also at the people assembled in the Forum, like Cicero's Catilinian Orations, the language of which differs only slightly from that used by Cicero in his letters addressed to friends; in literary prose of the type of Petronius' *Satyricon* and Apuleius' *Golden Ass;* even in Jerome's Vulgate and Augustine's *City of God.* There is little ground for the contention that these works represent a language which was written but not spoken. Considering the frankly propagandistic aim of some of these works, particularly Cicero's Forum orations and the Biblical version, the language in which they were couched must have been at least generally understood, in the same fashion that uneducated Americans at the time of Franklin D. Roosevelt were able to understand the language of his fireside chats, even if they could not duplicate it in their own speech.

When it comes to the language of poetry, the story is different. Latin prosody has its own highly complicated rules, coupled with the use of archaisms and special terms, and a freedom of word order that often calls for piecing the meaning together as though one were unscrambling a puzzle. But people, even of the educated classes, normally do not speak in verse.

What was the nature of this Classical Latin language, which certainly prevailed in the Empire's officialdom and among the more educated classes, and was at least understood by the lower orders of society, from roughly 100 B.C. to A.D. 400, and probably beyond?

3. The Classical Latin Language

The portion of the Classical Latin language that can be expected to appear in written records is fully at our disposal, in any good modern Latin grammar. Any such grammar will give us the grammatical forms and syntactical structure of the language, while any comprehensive Classical Latin dictionary will tell us what words from that language appear in the mass of documentary evidence still available to us. This mass is considerable, despite the fact that perhaps only ten percent of all Classical Latin writings have escaped the influx of the barbarians and later acts of barbarism to come down to our times. It is quite likely that not too many words in literary usage during the days of the Republic and the Empire have escaped our researchers.

This, of course, applies to the written, standard, official language. There are two things that our grammars, dictionaries, and linguistic studies cannot reveal, save exceptionally: the more popular, slangy tongue of the lower classes; and the precise sound structure and pronunciation of even the official language at any given period within the five hundred years that constitute the Classical era. These are the two elements of language most subject to change, far more than the grammatical and syntactical structure or the literary lexicon. Also, in the absence of living speakers and modern recording devices, they are the most difficult to pinpoint. Accordingly, they will be placed last in our description, and portions of them will be reserved for the later discussion of Vulgar Latin.

In its grammatical structure, Classical Latin was a typical Indo-European language of the older type. (In the matter of historical records, only two Indo-European languages antedate Latin, both of other branches: Greek and Sanskrit.) This ancient structure has largely disappeared from the modern Indo-European world, where only Slavic and Baltic tongues preserve it, with perhaps the addition of one Germanic tongue that has been described as a linguistic living fossil, Icelandic. Some (but by no means all) of its features survive in other modern tongues of the family, including even English, a language that tends more and more to depart from the original pattern. If one wishes to study the ancient structure of Indo-European in modern times, the recommended widespread modern language is Russian, which duplicates most of the typical features of such ancient Indo-European languages as Sanskrit, Greek, Latin, Gothic, Old Norse, Anglo-Saxon, Old Irish, Old Church Slavonic. From a study of modern Russian we can learn two things: (1) how an ancient Indo-European language operated, and (2) how such a language was not at all beyond the reach of even an illiterate speaker, despite features that impress most modern learners with a Western background as "difficult" and "complicated," only because they are unfamiliar and contrary to the language habits and patterns in which the learners have been raised. It can never be sufficiently stressed that languages are never difficult or complex to their own speakers, who grow up hearing and using them, accommodating their thought patterns to them, and assimilating them by a process of endless, mechanical imitation and repetition to the point where they become a part of the individual's nature; whereas a new language that is being learned at the adult stage is subjectively "easy" or "difficult" to the learner in proportion to how much or how little it coincides with that learner's previously established language habits and patterns.

Ancient languages of the Indo-European family (and this includes Latin) had several distinct characteristics: clearly defined notions of (1) *number* (singular for one, dual [usually for objects that come in pairs], and plural for more than two, or progressively, as the dual becomes archaic, more than one); (2) *gender* (masculine, feminine, and neuter, reflecting to a considerable degree the distinction between animate and inanimate, and, for animate objects, male and female, but with certain qualifications, due seemingly to the personification of inanimate objects, whereby such objects may appear grammatically as masculine or feminine as well as neuter); (3) *case* (indicating whether the noun or pronoun, with its modifying adjectives, participles, articles, etc., is subject, object, possessor, or in some other relation in the construction in which it is used); (4) *person* (speaker, person addressed, person or thing spoken of); (5) *tense* (time of action); (6) *mode,* or *aspect* (action viewed as actually occurring, or potentially occurring, or as commanded to occur, or in the abstract; action viewed as occurring at one definite point in time, or as being repeated, continued, or habitual); (7) *voice* (active if the subject is acting, passive if the subject receives the action, middle, or reflexive, if the subject acts upon himself or in his own interests).

In addition, the primitive Indo-European language provides for well-defined word pigeonholes, or parts of speech, which are clearly identifiable by both their form and their behavior, rather than by their meaning: nouns, adjectives, pronouns, articles (but this category is often omitted, as happens in Latin and Russian), verbs, adverbs, prepositions, conjunctions, interjections. The last three categories are generally invariable and uninflected; all the others undergo changes, usually by means of endings, sometimes by modifications of the root itself. The system of morphological endings and internal changes is basic in Indo-European structure, though it appears in various forms and to varying degrees in other language families as well. It lends itself to freedom of word order, and tends to minimize the role of syntax: in English, "Peter sees Paul" is the only word order possible to convey a certain meaning; in Latin, there are six possible arrangements: *Petrus videt Paulum; Paulum videt Petrus; Petrus Paulum videt; Paulum Petrus videt; videt Petrus Paulum; videt Paulum Petrus.* All six convey the identical meaning, though some are more frequently used than others. What makes this interchange possible is the *-us* ending of *Petrus,* clearly indicating that it is the subject, no matter where it is placed, and the *-um* of *Paulum,* which shows that it is the object, regardless of its position in the sentence.

In Latin, nouns are clearly identified as such by the fact that the ending indicates number (singular or plural), gender (masculine, feminine, or neuter), and case (nominative for subject, genitive for possessor, dative for indirect object, accusative for direct object, vocative for direct address, ablative for a variety of uses such as those English expresses with prepositions like *in, on, with, by,* etc.).

The adjective is subject to the same system, but while the noun is restricted to one gender, the adjective may appear in any one of the three; further, it may indicate degree (positive, comparative, superlative, as in English *free, freer, freest*).

The pronoun, depending upon its nature and use (personal like *you*, demonstrative like *this*, possessive like *your* or *yours*, etc.), may behave like a noun or like an adjective.

The verb, indicating action or state of being, shows by its ending (sometimes by internal change) the person and number, occasionally even the gender, of the doer of the action, and also the tense, mode, and voice of the action.

The adverb is invariable save that, like the adjective, it may show degree (*well, better, best; poorly, more poorly, most poorly*).

Complications arise, from the standpoint of the adult learner, from the fact that nouns and adjectives fall into several distinct regular declensional systems, each with its own set of endings, while verbs fall into four distinct conjugational systems, each again with its own set of endings.[1] Many irregular forms also exist, for most of which there is a historical explanation. All these complexities naturally seem bewildering to the learner, but the native speaker has many years of constant repetition and imitation in context to assimilate these seemingly complicated forms, and uses them naturally by the time he grows up, whether or not he is conscious of the grammatical rules involved.

In the matter of vocabulary, the Latin language, which had begun its career of refinement under Greek influence in the second century B.C., continued to refine itself and expand in the Classical period by the coining of new words, the recombination of others, and the expansion of meanings of old words to cover new needs, but above all, by an endless process of borrowing from its mentor, Greek. This process had begun to a limited degree when the Romans had established their first contacts with the Greek colonies of southern Italy and Sicily. It expanded after the Macedonian War and the conquest of Greece, continued and grew in the Classical period, receiving a mighty impulse under Greek New Testament influences when the Empire turned Christian, and was broken only by the invasions that separated the East from the West. It was to be resumed later, during the Renaissance, and particularly after the fall of Constantinople to the Turks in 1453; but by that time Greek loan words found their way not only into the conventionalized Latin of the Renaissance, but, more importantly, into the new languages, Romance and otherwise, that were finally blossoming forth into full

---

1. For a limited sample of regular Latin declensions and conjugations, see Appendix C.

languagehood. When we examine a full-scale lexicon of Classical Latin, we are left with the impression that almost half of the Classical vocabulary was borrowed from Greek, appropriated, Latinized, and naturalized. Here are words like *hora*, "hour," *theatrum*, "theater," *machina* or *macina*, "machine," *cathedra*, "chair," (which goes on to become French *chaise*, English *chair* and *cathedral*, even Spanish *cadera* ("hip" in popular speech), *camera*, "vault," (which has become not only the modern *camera* but also, previously, French *chambre* and English *chamber*), *piper*, "pepper," *butyrum*, "butter," *spatha*, "spade," (also French *épée*), *schola*, "school," *petra*, "stone," *platea*, "street," (eventually *place*, *plaza*, *piazza*), *gubernare*, "to govern," *triumphus*, "triumph," (also *trump*), *angelus*, "angel," *presbyter*, "priest," (French *prêtre*, Italian *prete*, Spanish *preste*, English *Presbyterian* and *Prester* [*John*]), *crypta*, "crypt," (also *grotto*), *apotheca*, "storeroom," (surviving in French *boutique*, Italian *bottega*, Spanish *bodega* and *botica*), *phalanx*, "battle array," (French *planche* and English *phalanx*, *planchette*, and *plank*).

The actual period of Latin borrowings from Greek can often be roughly estimated from the form the Greek word took in Latin. *Porphyra* turning into Latin *purpura* (French *pourpre*, English *purple*), *byrsa* turning into *bursa* (French *bourse*, Italian *borsa*, Spanish *bolsa*, English *purse*), indicate borrowing at a period when Greek still pronounced the letter upsilon (Υ) as *u* rather than as *ü*, as it did later, when Latin borrowings show *i* or *y* (by the tenth century, in Greek, the sound became *i*).

More words came into Latin during the Classical period from the language of the Gauls than from that of the Iberians, whose words are generally restricted to the languages of the Iberian peninsula, entering other Romance languages, if at all, at a later period (like *bizarro*, "bizarre"). Some of the Gaulish words were probably borrowed by Latin in its Archaic and Pre-Classical periods, considering the early contacts between Romans and Cisalpine Gauls. Among Latin words attributed to Gaulish (Celtic) origin are *caballus*, "nag," (this is somewhat doubtful, however), *camisia*, "shirt," *camminus*, "road," "path," *caminus*, "fireplace," "chimney," *basiare*, "to kiss," *carrus*, "cart," "chariot," *bracae*, "pants," *lancea*, "lance," *ambactus* "slave," "ambassador."

There is also the suspicion, but it is difficult to confirm, that the Romans borrowed some of the numerous Germanic words that eventually appeared in the Romance languages during the Classical period, from border contacts, or through Germanic mercenaries in the Roman armies.

Sapo, "soap," definitely was such a word. How many of the hundreds of Germanic loanwords that appear in our lexicons of Post-Classical and Vulgar Latin may have come in while Latin was still in its Classical period we can only surmise. Such words would naturally have been shunned as vulgarisms by the literary language prior to 400 A.D.

The Romans, detesting the Carthaginians, borrowed very few words from the Punic of the latter. *Magalia,* "cluster of huts," appears in Virgil; *mappa,* "tablecloth," (eventually giving English both *map* and the "nap" of *napkin*), *saccus,* "sack," *byrsa,* "purse," (the name of the citadel of Carthage, which coincided in form with Greek *byrsa*), are more likely to have come in through Greek. Some Hebrew and Aramaic words came in from the East with Christianity (*abba, mammona, seraphim*), but quite late in the Classical period, and through the intermediation of Greek.

We come now to that most elusive portion of language—sounds and accentuation—where all we have at our disposal is written records and descriptions left by prescriptive grammarians, who naturally tend to present an ideal rather than a reality.

The Classical Latin consonant scheme was rather poor in sounds. It had the plosives *t, d, p, b, k* (represented by *c*), *g;* the fricative *f,* but not *v;* neither of the two *th* sounds; neither of the velar fricatives that appear today in Spanish, the *j* of *jarro* and the *g* of *pagar.* There was an *s,* but no *z* sound. There were an *l* and an *r,* the latter probably a lingual trill, similar to that of Spanish or Italian today. There was an *h,* which tended to disappear in pronunciation. The nasals *n* and *m* were there, but *n* tended to disappear before *s,* and *m* to be dropped in the final position. The glide sounds of *w* and *y* existed, the former represented in writing by the same V symbol that served for long or short *u,* the latter by the same *I* symbol that served for long or short *i* (the symbols *u* and *j,* which appear in modern Latin books, are much later creations).

Conspicuously missing from the Latin consonant scheme, in addition to those mentioned above, were all the palatal sounds represented in English by the *ch* of *church,* the *j* of *joy,* the *sh* of *shore,* the *zh* sound of *pleasure,* the *ny* of *canyon,* the *ly* sound of *million;* also the affricates *ts* of *its, dz* of *adze.* Yet all of these arose in Romance, and their career may have begun in the Post-Classical period, if not earlier, at least in popular speech.

The evidence is overwhelming that in the Classical period *c* and *g* were invariably velar, regardless of the nature of the following vowel (*Cicero* pronounced KEE-ke-ro, not CHEE-che-ro; *Caesar* pronounced KY-sar, not CHE-zar), and that *villa* was pronounced WEEL-la, not VEEL-la. The pronunciations in use in the Catholic Church are authentic enough, but did not come into vogue, save possibly in a few lower-class circles, before A.D. 400. This is proved not merely by the statements of grammarians, which might be suspect, but by Greek transcriptions of Latin words, and by the many loanwords borrowed from Latin by Germanic and Celtic languages before the invasions (German *Kirsch,* and *Kaiser* from *cerasia* and *Caesar,* for instance, as against the later *Zins* from *census;* or Welsh *gwin* from *vinum*).

The Classical Latin vowel scheme included five vowels, *a, e, i, o, u,* which could be either long or short, independently of whether they were stressed or unstressed. All of these vowels were pure, that is to say, uncontaminated by the glides that are so numerous in English so-called long vowels, where "long *a*" is the sound of *e* in *met* followed by a *y*-glide, "long *u*" the sound of *u* in *rule* preceded by a *y*-glide, etc. The best modern counterpart of the Classical Latin vowel system appears in modern German, where the five vowels, both long and short, have approximately both the quantity and the quality they had in Latin. There were also diphthongs (in the Classical period, *ae, oe, au, eu*), with the sounds, respectively, of *ai* in *aisle, oi* in *oil, ou* in *house,* and the *e* of *met* followed by a *w*-glide. These, being compounded of two sounds, naturally counted as long.

The main point to remember is that long vowels, short vowels, and diphthongs could all appear in a stressed or in an unstressed syllable. To duplicate this feature in modern times, we have to go to a language like Czech, where in a word like *dobrý,* "good," the stress falls on the first vowel, which is short, but the final, unstressed *ý* is prolonged in pronunciation (DŎ-bree); Czech uses the acute accent mark to indicate length of vowel, not place of stress. In a sense, this is in conflict with natural tendencies, which are to lengthen the vowel we stress and shorten the ones that are unstressed.

To complicate matters (and this was no figment of the grammarians, for the system we are about to describe appears in all words, popular as well as learned), the place of the accent, or stress, was determined in Classical times by the length, not necessarily of the vowel, but of the entire syllable. The syllable was considered long if it contained: (1) a long vowel, (2) a diphthong, (3) a short vowel followed by a consonant in the same syllable. This placed a great deal of emphasis on syllabification, the breaking up of words into syllables. Syllabification was not merely a written-language device to determine how to split words at the end of lines, but something that deeply affected the pronunciation of the spoken tongue.

The Latin system of syllabification, still faithfully followed today by the Romance languages, dictated that a single consonant between two vowels should go with the following, not with the preceding vowel. This made, and still makes, a great deal of difference between the pronunciation of a Romance language like Spanish or Italian and that of a Germanic language like English. If we compare English *gen-er-al* with Latin *ge-ne-ra-lis,* or Italian *ge-ne-ra-le,* or French *gé-né-ral,* we find that the English syllables, often ending in consonants, are choppier than the Latin-Romance, with only the stressed vowel clearly pronounced, the other vowels coming out with the indefinite sound called "schwa" by the linguists. The Latin-Romance vowels, on the contrary, are clear and definite, whether stressed or unstressed.

What happened if a double consonant occurred, or if two different consonants appeared together inside the word, as in *annus,* "year," or *septem,* "seven"? They were normally split, one going with the preceding, the other with the following vowel (*AN-nus, SEP-tem*). There was one notable exception: a plosive or fricative (*c, g, t, d, p, b, f*) followed by a liquid (*l, r*); such a combination was counted as a single consonant, and went with the following vowel (*PA-trem,* not *PAT-*rem, "father" in the accusative case). This syllabic division, with its notable exception, persists to the present day in the languages descended from Latin. This means in turn that in *PĂ-trem,* which had a short *a* not followed by a consonant in the same syllable, the syllable was considered short, but in *PĂR-tem,* "part" in the accusative case, where the *r* split from the *t* and went with the preceding vowel, the syllable was considered long, in spite of its short vowel.

These complicated rules are of primary interest to students of Latin poetry, since it is syllable-quantity, not vowel-quantity pure and simple, that determines whether a foot in a line of Latin verse is a dactyl, an iamb, a trochee, or a spondee. But it profoundly affects the spoken language, since it determines where the accent falls in any given word of more than two syllables. Not only does the popular accentuation follow the Classical rule, but the place of the accent remains unchanged, save exceptionally, when Latin, Classical or Vulgar, transforms itself into the Romance languages.

The rule for where to accent a Latin word of more than one syllable is that in a two-syllable word the stress falls on the penult (next to the last), which is also the first syllable in the word; only in a few very exceptional cases do we have evidence of a two-syllable word being stressed on the final. If the word has three or more syllables, the stress falls on the penult if the penult *syllable* (not necessarily its *vowel*) is long (*ma-RĪ-tus,* "husband," but also *fe-NĔS-tra,* "window"). If the penult syllable is short (that is to say, has a short vowel not followed by a consonant in the same syllable), the stress falls on the antepenult, or third from the end (*O-cu-lus,* "eye," *CA-li-dus,* "warm").

All this, however, is purely mechanical. The real problem of the Classical Latin accent lies in its essential nature. It shares with its older sisters, Greek and Sanskrit, the feature of being based on musical pitch rather than the stress of the voice that is natural with us of the modern Western world. The name itself of the phenomenon is a clue to what the "accent" should ideally be; *accentum* is a compound form of *ad-cantum,* "a singing to" a given syllable. In this respect, Sanskrit, Greek, and Roman grammarians are unanimous. The accentuation of their respective languages is, ideally, a lilt, a raising of the pitch of the voice, not an extra burst of vocal energy. Some of them even give us a precise definition: the stressed syllable should be raised three and a half notes above the other syllables of the word. This means that a word like *amō* should

be pronounced *á͗mō,* not *á-mō.* In modern times, traces (but only traces) of this system of accentuation appear in the well-known lilt of some Scandinavian languages, notably Swedish and Norwegian, and, occasionally, in Serbo-Croatian and Lithuanian. Languages outside of the Indo-European family (Chinese, for instance, with its system of tones) make plenty of use of musical pitch; but in these languages it is generally used to differentiate meanings, while in the earliest Indo-European languages on record there is no convincing indication that it was so used.

In Greek and Latin the objective reality of this type of accentuation is indicated by the fact that the versification of these languages derives its rhythm from the alternation of syllabic quantities (long and short syllables), not at all from the place where the accent falls.

Was this seemingly unnatural system of accentuation prevalent among all classes of society? Was it rather primarily a rhetorical device, reserved for the use of poets and orators as they declaimed their verses and speeches? Here the evidence is conflicting. Stress accentuation of the modern type inevitably entails greater prominence for the stressed syllable and vowel, which are favored with the bulk of the speaker's vocal energy, and a corresponding weakening of unstressed syllables and vowels, which have to be contented with what vocal energy is left. Among the consequences are the weakening, shortening, blurring, and occasional fall of unstressed vowels, particularly those closest to the favored stressed vowels, immediately before and after the stressed syllable, but also in the final syllable. This phenomenon, known as syncopation when the weakened medial vowel falls, occurred rather frequently in Archaic and Pre-Classical Latin, before cultural and literary influences took the upper hand (in Pre-Classical Latin, *maxumus* and *maximus, optimus* and *optumus,* interchange, and we have seen final *-o* and *-u,* final *-e* and *-i,* being confused (see p. 45); even fully Classical Latin permits the interchange of *calidus* and *caldus,* the latter with full syncopation of the unstressed posttonic vowel). Prehistoric Latin is supposed to have had accentuation of the stress variety on the initial syllable, which accounts for the vowel change from *annus* to *biennis,* from *facio* to *conficio,* representing a weakening of a vowel that loses its accented status.

Is it possible that the pitch accent represents an aristocratic standard, while the stress accent coincides with popular tendencies? That in the earlier period of royal and republican Rome "popular" forces in language were in control, with their "natural" stress accent, but that as society became crystallized and the upper classes took the leadership, they imposed their favorite pitch upon at least the official and literary language? That the stress accent ran as an undercurrent throughout the Classical period, again taking the upper hand as the Empire and the prestige and authority of the ruling aristocracy weakened?

The triumph of the stress accent, with its concomitant phenomena of the weakening and fall of unstressed vowels, occasionally of entire unstressed syllables, seems to be at the root of the major sound transformations that distinguish both Vulgar Latin and the initial stages of transition from Latin to Romance. These sound transformations, in turn, had far-reaching effects on the morphological and syntactical structure of the language, though they were not alone in producing the sum total of change. Other factors were the growing isolation of Latin-speaking communities as systems of transportation fell into decay, the growing ignorance of linguistic standards as the educational system of the Romans dwindled and all but disappeared, the distortions inherent in the assimilation of Latin by people originally speaking other tongues. Working against these disruptive factors were the survival of Roman and imperial consciousness and the continued use of Latin by Western Christianity. Where these were stronger and more vital, resistance to change was greater, which accounts in part for the diverse development, here more radical, there more conservative, displayed by the various Romance dialectal varieties, even within what later became a single nation (consider, for example, the radical sound transformations displayed by some northern and southern Italian dialects as against the conservatism of the "national" language, based on the central dialects, those closest to the influence of the Church in Rome).

It was the popular Vulgar Latin that emerged as the winner in the historical process of change. But the role and importance of the official Classical Latin, and its participation in the creation of new national standards, cannot be minimized. All through the period of transformation, between A.D. 400 and 800, and on into the early Romance period, we are faced with a vast number of what are described as "learned" or "semilearned" forms, words and constructions that refuse to obey the laws of popular sound-change, and that go back to the original Latin. Many of these survive today, and they were joined throughout the Renaissance and up to our own days by hosts of additional learned words and constructions deliberately inserted into the languages by literate people who still had the Latin tradition. Were the early ones due to religious influence? Legal use? Scholarly or literary influences? Plain old conservatism? A mixture of all of these?

Whatever the explanation, it is an oversimplification to describe the emergence of the Romance languages as the triumph, pure and simple, of the Vulgar Latin of the lower classes. The role of Classical Latin in the formation and development of the new languages cannot be overlooked.

4. The Triumph of Vulgar Latin

What is meant by Vulgar Latin? Here we run into a terminological nest of hornets, with broad historical and chronological complications. Partial synonyms for Vulgar Latin are Popular Latin, Folk Latin, Low Latin, even Medieval Latin (the equivalence of the last depends on where you begin and end the Middle Ages).

In Classical Latin itself, we find such expressions as *sermo rusticus* (merely "country language," or Latin streaked with Oscan and other influences?); *sermo urbanus* ("city language" in general, or city language of the upper classes?); *sermo plebeius* ("plebeian language"; this seems to come closest to lower-class language); *sermo cotidianus* ("everyday language"; but whose? That of Cicero and people of his class when they conversed rather than when they wrote or orated, or that of a cross section of the population?). There seem to be parallels for these terms in the seventeenth-century French of Fénelon and Féraud (*genre élevé, genre simple, genre vulgaire, genre familier, style oratoire*), but do they really correspond in meaning?

One rather extreme school of thought holds that throughout the entire history of Latin, from its very inception, there was a dichotomy between lower- and upper-class language, so that Vulgar Latin would have run an uninterrupted parallel course with official Latin through Archaic, Pre-Classical, Classical, Post-Classical times, and on into the shadowy centuries that followed the fall of the Empire. Against this hypothesis is the expression *prisca latinitas*, "old, primitive, original Latin language," by which some Roman writers seem to imply that there was an early period when Latin was essentially one speech, with little or no class

67

cleavage. This does not seem too unreasonable at a time when Roman society was basically agricultural and military, small in numbers, with its territorial extent limited to Rome and its immediate environs.

But for the most part, Roman writers are delightfully (or tantalizingly, or even irritatingly) vague about what went on in their real spoken language, as opposed to the ideal language presented by their grammarians. From other writers, we would gather that the real class cleavage began only with the immediate Pre-Classical period, the Punic Wars perhaps, with a Vulgar variety running side by side with official Classical Latin till the Empire's fall, and taking the upper hand in the vicinity of 400 A.D. Another school of thought prefers to reserve the term "Vulgar Latin" for the language that emerged after the invasions, and speaks of the centuries between 400 and 800 A.D. as the "Vulgar Latin period," further claiming that this Vulgar Latin was geographically very little differentiated, being essentially the same in Gaul, Spain, and Italy.

Most of the direct statements on the issue of class differences in language come rather late, though indications of such differences appear early. Cicero, who in the first century B.C. puts *rusticitas* into the past, favors us with a new term for what went on in his present: *barbarismus*, which he defines as *cum verbum aliquod vitiose effertur*, "when some word is badly uttered," (he also offers *solecismus*, "the lack of proper agreement," but he seems to have borrowed that from Greek). One century later, Quintilian says: *aliud esse latine loqui, aliud grammatice* ("it's one thing to speak Latin, something else to speak grammatically"); on the one hand, he admits that some people speak without regard for the rules of grammar; but on the other, he credits such speakers with speaking "Latin." Festus, in the third century A.D., gives a sample of Vulgar usage, *ut auriculas oriculas*, with the word for "ear" not only put into the Vulgar diminutive form, but mispronounced in such a way as to point to later Romance development. Probus, in the same century, offers a much more detailed commentary, but this presents chronological problems which lead us to place it at the end of our listing.

Augustine, toward the end of the fourth century, comes out quite definitely with his popular preferences, at least for purposes of addressing lay audiences: *sic enim potius loquamur; melius est nos reprehendant grammatici quam non intelligant populi* ("let us therefore prefer to speak this way; better for the grammarians to criticize us than for the people not to understand"), a rather strong statement, implying lack of comprehension if the elegant Latin of his writings is used in his sermons to the masses. One rare written sample of his spoken-language preference is the use of *ossum* for *os*, "bone," so that it may not be confused with *os*, "mouth"; the possibility of this confusion in turn indicates that the popular language no longer made a distinction between the short *ŏ* of *ŏs, ŏssis* and the long *ō* of *ōs, ōris*. Consentius, a fifth-century Gallo-Roman grammarian, states that the Gallo-Romans pronounce long *i* like long *e*, or shorten the double *l*, using *vēlla* or *vīla* for *vīlla* (the first trait is not reflected in French, or any other Romance language; the second appears in French). He also offers *tottum* for *totum*, "all," "every," which does foreshadow a specifically French development, but appears also in Italian, and *triginta*, "thirty," stressed on the first instead of the second syllable, which is later reflected in all Romance languages.

Another piece of documentary evidence of a grammatical nature comes from the seventh- or eighth-century Glosses of Reichenau, which lists words that have apparently become obsolete in the popular tongue and explains them by paraphrase. A few samples are: *transmigrat—de loco in loco vadit* ("migrates"—"goes from place to place"); *sexagenarius —qui LX annos habet* ("sexagenarian"—"one who has sixty years," as any Romance language would phrase it); *oppidis—castellis vel civitatibus* ("in fortified towns"—"in castles or cities"; *oppidum* disappears from Romance, but both *castellum* and *civitas* survive).

Most valuable to us of all Roman grammarians is Probus, who probably lived in the third century A.D., and who may have lived in Rome or in Africa. Having composed one of the customary essays on grammar, Probus also thought of adding an appendix, in which he listed over two hundred words and expressions which he thought were mishandled in popular usage, giving first the "correct" form, then the "incorrect" (occasionally he mixes them up). It is, of course, the incorrect forms that primarily interest us. There is, however, one serious drawback which the *Appendix Probi* shares with many other pieces of documentary evidence at later periods; the manuscript that has come down to us is not his own, but an eighth-century copy. Since copyists of manuscripts are notorious for amending and adding to the originals from which they copied, we cannot be altogether sure whether the errors mentioned by Probus pertain to his own period, or to any of the five subsequent centuries. Here is a brief sampling of the forms he cites:[1]

columna ("column") *non colomna*	*coquens* ("cooking") *non cocens*
calida ("warm") *non calda*	*sibilus* ("whistle") *non sifilus*
olim ("formerly") *non oli*	*mensa* ("table") *non mesa*

---

1. For a linguistic analysis of these samples, see Appendix D.

pauper mulier ("poor woman")	*vinea* ("vineyard") *non vinia*
non paupera mulier	*auris* ("ear") *non oricla*
vetulus ("old") *non veclus*	*februarius* ("February") *non febrarius*
tabula ("table") *non tabla*	*aqua* ("water") *non acqua*

There is no question that the "wrong" forms show progression of the spoken tongue toward Romance, with some favoring one later Romance language, others another.

So much for direct statements of writers and grammarians commenting specifically on the state of their language. Their testimony, however, is flanked by a truly impressive mass of material, in the form of both inscriptions and documents, that has come down to us. Each of these has its own drawbacks. The inscriptions on tombstones, which have been transcribed into several large volumes subdivided by regions of the Roman Empire, while they lend themselves fairly well to localizing phenomena of change and vulgarism in space, do not invariably give a clear picture as to time. Not always are they dated with absolute precision, by some such statement as "died in the fourth year of the reign of Emperor Hadrian." They can easily be subdivided into pagan and Christian by their wording and symbols (*d.m.s.* for *dis manibus sacrum*, "consecrated to the gods of the underworld," is a clear indication of paganism, while references to one God, or to the Trinity, characterize many of the Christian inscriptions). But since paganism and Christianity coexisted for many centuries, this only serves to assure us that a Christian inscription cannot antedate the spreading of Christianity in the West, while a pagan inscription is not likely to appear beyond A.D. 500. A few excerpted samples of both types, between A.D. 400 and 700, are given below, with Classical Latin versions and English translations.[2]

Pagan Inscriptions:
. . . ispose rarissime fecit (Africa)
sponsae rarissimae fecit
("made to his beloved wife")

Lepusclu Leo qui vixit anum et mesis undeci et dies dece e nove perit septimu calendas agustas. (Tusculum, 404 A.D.)
Lepusculus Leo (or Lepusculo Leoni) qui vixit annum et menses undecim et dies decem et novem (or undeviginti) periit septimo (die) kalendas augustas. ("[to] Lepusculus Leo who lived one year and eleven months and nineteen days, died on the seventh day before the Kalends of August.")

---

2. For a linguistic analysis and additional samples, see Appendix D.

Christian Inscriptions:
Deus magnu oclu abet. (Rome)
Deus magnum oculum habet.
("God has a large eye.")
Si aliquis sepulchru istum biolare bolueri abea anathema da patre et filiu et scm
spm. (Rome)
Si aliquis sepulchrum istum violare voluerit, habeat anathema a patre et filio et
sancto spiritu. ("If anyone should wish to violate this sepulcher, let him have
a curse from the Father and the Son and the Holy Ghost.")

. . . menbra ad duus fratres (Gaul)
membra duorum fratrum
("the remains of two brothers")

The graffiti of Pompeii are localized both in space and time (first
century A.D.), definitely antedating all Christian and many pagan inscriptions. They offer such forms as *ama, valia, peria* (for *amat, valeat,
pereat;* "he loves," "let him be well," "let him die"); *verecunnus* (for
verecundus, "ashamed," "bashful"); *scriserunt* (for *scripserunt,* "they
wrote"); *settembris* (for *septembris,* "of September"). An inscription that
appears in a Pompeiian house says: *abiat Venere Bompeiiana iratam qui
hoc laeserit/habeat Venerem Pompeiianam iratam qui hoc laeserit* ("let
him who damages this have the anger of the Venus of Pompeii").[3]

From the inscriptional material certain conclusions may be drawn:
(1) up to the beginning of the eighth century the language, though
incorrect, is still Latin; (2) it is fairly uniform throughout the Western
part of the former Empire, and shows widespread features that later
become universal in the Western Romance languages; (3) occasionally
an inscription shows a feature that later becomes characteristic of the
specific Romance language arising in the region where the inscription is
found; but there are also occurrences of phenomena later developing in
regions other than that where the inscription appears.

The documentary evidence from A.D. 400 to 700 is nothing if not
abundant. Unfortunately, practically all of it is subject to the same
drawback that was noted for the *Appendix Probi:* the original writing
took place in a given century, but the earliest extant manscript is a copy
from a later century, leaving us in doubt whether the language that
appears is identical with that used by the author, or reflects emendations
and additions made by the copyist. To get original manuscripts, where

---

3. For a linguistic analysis, see Appendix D.

we can be sure that the language is that of the writer, we generally have to wait until the eighth century.

Nevertheless, the features displayed by Vulgar Latin writings are of considerable interest, especially when the writer confesses that he is not a scholar, is ignorant of grammar, and writes as he speaks, as is the case with Gregory of Tours, who lived in sixth-century Gaul (the manuscripts are of the early eighth century). A comparison of his language with that of two contemporaries, Pope Gregory the Great of Italy and Isidore of Seville of Spain, is revealing.

In the writings of Gregory of Tours, we find such expressions as *spectante matri meae*, "while my mother was looking on"; the correct ablative absolute construction would call for *spectanti matre mea;* ignorance of the proper use of cases might supply a plausible explanation, coupled with the tendency, shown elsewhere, to interchange final *-e* and *-i*, final *-o* and *-u; omnes populus*, "the entire people," is another sample of this confusion; it should be *omnis populus*, or, better, *totus populus. Victuriam* for *victoriam* shows the confusion of stressed long *o* and short *u*, which eventually led to the merging of the two sounds. Gregory also uses *omnia* in the sense of "all things," a usage later reflected in early Italian *ogna*, but not in French. *Mulierem clamare fecit*, "he had the woman called," is definitely a Romance construction (*il fit appeler la femme, fece chiamare la donna*), though with Latin words. *Vestra utilitas* (literally "your usefulness," used in the sense of a polite singular "you") is indicative of the Romance tendency that later blooms into Spanish *Vuestra Merced, Usted*, and Italian *Vostra Signoria, Vossia*, but is shunned in French, which prefers a plain *vous*.

By way of comparison, here is a passage from Isidore of Seville, who died in 637 (the manuscript is of the eleventh century): *Tunc enim miseri homines, et quod pejus est, etiam fideles, sumentes species monstruosas, in ferarum habitu transformantur; alii, feminei gestu demutati, virilem vultum effeminant* ("Then some wretched men, and, what is worse, even the faithful, putting on monstrous disguises, are transformed into the semblance of wild animals; others, changed for the worse by feminine gestures, effeminate their manly faces"). Isidore is deploring the celebration of the New Year with wild parties in which men disguise themselves as animals or women, much as might happen today. There is nothing un-Classical about this language.

A letter from Pope Gregory (590–604; but the manuscript is of the eleventh century) to the Bishop of Marseilles runs in part: *Latorem vero praesentium dilectissimum filium nostrum Cyriacum, monasterii patrem, vobis in omnibus commendamus, ut nulla hunc in Massiliensi civitate mora detineat* ("We entrust to you in all things the bearer of these presents, our beloved son Cyriacus, father of a monastery, so that no delay may detain him in the city of Marseilles"). Again, the language is altogether Classical.

Since most original writing at this period was done by people who were trained in the Classical Latin that was still official throughout the Roman world of the West, it is not surprising that most of the writings of the fifth, sixth, and seventh centuries that have come down to us show relatively little Vulgar influence. This appears to a greater degree in legal formulas which were drawn up for the benefit of lawyers and scribes, who probably would have had a difficult time trying to express in writing the points they discussed with their clients. Here some traces of the Vulgar language appear, as evidenced by this excerpt from the *Formulae Andecavenses* ("legal formulas of Angers"), composed in the sixth century, with the extant manuscript from the eighth: *Si fuerit qui contra hanc cessione ista quem ego in te bona voluntate conscribere rogavi . . .* ("If there should be anyone who [wants to object] to this cession which I in good faith have ordered to be written to you . . ."). Here *cessione* should be *cessionem*, and should not be followed by *ista*, which is redundant in view of the preceding *hanc*, making it sound somewhat like "this here cession"; *quem* should be the feminine *quam*, to agree in gender with its antecedent *cessione; in te*, which from the Classical standpoint sounds like "against you," would better be expressed by *tibi; conscribere rogavi* should be *conscribi jussi*, and displays the confusion of active and passive infinitives which later shows up in Romance (*j'ai fait écrire une lettre*, "I have caused a letter to be written").

One interesting document, in the nature of a travelogue of the period, is the *Peregrinatio Sylviae ad Loca Sancta* ("Sylvia's Pilgrimage to the Holy Places"). It was composed by a fairly literate nun, probably from Spain, who wrote in the early fifth century (but the manuscript is from the eleventh). Composed in a discursive, almost breezy style, her story sounds like that of a present-day tourist with special religious interests, viewing holy spots and relics, interviewing abbots of monasteries and other holy men, seldom if ever running into any unpleasantness, and never once mentioning language difficulties or the use of interpreters. Among individual features of her writing which could be styled non-Classical rather than downright Vulgar are: *ymnos* for *hymnos*, "hymns," and *habundare* for *abundare*, "to abound," indicating uncertainty in the use of an initial *h-* that was no longer pronounced, or, if it was, could be misplaced, as it is by modern London Cockneys; *septimana* for the more elegant Greek *hebdomadas*, "week"; *sedete vobis*, "sit down," (*sedeo* is not used reflexively in Latin, but is so used in the Romance languages; in addition, the reflexive pronoun should be the accusative *vos*, rather than the dative or ablative *vobis*). Sylvia is also much given to the excessive use of demonstratives (*ille, iste, ipse*) with nouns, foreshadowing the later emergence of the Romance definite article, and of *ibi*, "there," used like French or Old Spanish *y* and Italian *vi*. She uses *toti* for *omnes*, "all," (French *tous*, Spanish *todos*, Italian *tutti*), as well as such phrases as *in giro mensa*, "around the table," (reminiscent of Italian *in giro alla tavola*); *sexta hora se fecerit*, "it had become the sixth hour," (French *il s'était fait six heures*); *de ante cruce*, "before the cross," (a combination of prepositions frequent in later Romance formations; *de ab ante* to French *devant*, Italian *davanti*).

The evidence at our disposal seems to indicate that throughout the fifth, sixth, and seventh centuries there was still substantial unity both in the written language and in the spoken tongue of the regions that later became France, Spain, Portugal, and Italy, with proper allowance made for local words, idioms, and intonations. Nevertheless, there is also evidence of a trend toward change, with phenomena that point in a general Romance direction rather than toward any specific Romance language. In fact, certain traits that appear in the inscriptions and documents of one country later show up in another.

The phenomena that appear universally are: syncopation of unstressed vowels; confusion of final vowels; merger of certain stressed vowels; occasional sonorization (voicing) of intervocalic consonants; palatalization where velar consonants (*c, g*) are followed by the front vowels *e* or *i* (but this we can only surmise from later developments, because the spelling seldom changes), or where a Latin *e* or *i* in hiatus (before another vowel) turns into a *y*-glide that affects the preceding consonant. These all seem linked to the disappearance of the Classical pitch accent and the reinforcement of the popular stress accent, which thus emerges as the primary source of linguistic sound change. Other phenomena (loss of final *-m*, occasionally of final *-s*; loss of initial *h-*; fall of *n* before *s*) are a continuation of what went on much earlier, not only in Classical, but even in Pre-Classical times. Cases of confusion in the use of the Latin case system may be an outgrowth of the weakening of final vowels by reason of growing stress elsewhere in the word, coupled with uncertainty of standards and ignorance of grammatical rules.

It is interesting to speculate on what may have been the cause for the triumph of the popular stress accent. The disruption that attended the invasions and threw the Roman social structure into confusion cannot, of course, be minimized. Along with that, however, was the enthusiasm, bordering on euphoria, that attended the process of Christianization, a movement that welled up from the lower classes until it reached the emperors themselves. It was as though the lower orders of society, freed from the older restraints imposed upon them from above, were striving to give vocal expression to their new-found joy both in the assurance of equality in the eyes of the one true God, and in the certainty of a continued existence after death, in which every individual, however exalted or humble his station in this life, would be judged on his own spiritual merits. This boundless faith, which we of a colder, more materialistically scientific age find it difficult to understand, was the mainstay of the so-called Dark Ages, which with all their horrors and excesses nevertheless flowered forth into the age of the mighty cathedrals, with their gargoyles and saints, their mosaics and stained-glass windows, their new civilization centered about the churches and the church squares, which furnished the background for the resurgence of music, poetry, and theatrical performances.

For what concerns the language, there is little doubt that it was supported and kept from degenerating at too fast a pace by the Latin that continued in use throughout the Roman West. Many scholars support the theory that side by side with the earlier Vulgar Latin of common popular intercourse there ran a Christian Latin, which was the common tongue of Christianization and conversion, and which was characterized by its own vocabulary and usage—a language whereby Christians understood one another without revealing their identity in the days of pagan persecutions, a sort of Aesopian language wherein meanings were changed so that only the initiate would grasp the true message, in much the same fashion that Communists and fellow travelers in recent times knew what they meant when they used expressions like "democracy," "progressive," or "peace-loving."

But just as the Aesopian language of Communism finally broke forth into the open, so that it no longer deceived anyone, so the Christian language ultimately became official, and many words lost their ancient sense and assumed the new meanings they still hold in the Romance and other languages. Among them: *sacramentum,* originally "soldier's oath," later "sacrament"; *tirocinium,* once "military indoctrination," then "religious training"; *paganus,* once "civilian," "village dweller," later "pagan"; *adversarius,* once "opponent," then "enemy of mankind," "the devil"; *pax,* from "end of war" to "cessation of persecutions" to "family of Christians," ultimately "kiss of peace and brotherhood." Even Greek loanwords joined this parade: *martyr,* from "witness" to "one who dies for the faith"; *angelus,* once "messenger," later "God's messenger," "angel"; *catholicus,* from "universal" to "Catholic."

The Roman world, fortified by its new faith, had weathered and survived the fifth-century invasions, absorbing and assimilating the invaders, and attaining a new unity and a new stability under the shadow of the Cross. It was relatively easy for this new Roman world to forget that there were outside forces that did not accept the Word of Jesus, just as it had been easy for their ancestors four centuries earlier to forget that there were people living beyond the remote *limites* of the Empire who did not accept the authority of Rome.

The language, both spoken and written, reflected this new sense of security in spiritual unity, this brotherhood in the Christian faith. What did it matter if some, particularly among the powerful, transgressed the commands of Christ? They were still within the circle. Sinners could repent, and be forgiven, prodigal sons be brought back into the fold of Christianity.

Had this new stability endured, the chances are that the Latin language, in its new classical-vulgar-religious guise, would have developed in the same fashion as the Greek of the Eastern Empire, continuing to transform itself, but in slow, orderly fashion, evolving and perfecting a koine that already existed, with an eventual split into a *katharevousa* and a *demotike,* the former, close to the ancient language save for its sound structure, used for exalted purposes, the latter for everyday, informal intercourse, particularly among the lower classes; but even the *demotike* is easily identifiable as a direct descendant of the ancient tongue.

Instead of this, there was a new break, a new geographical and historical cleavage that not only destroyed the basic unity of the language, giving rise to separate languages based on separate national consciousnesses and entities, but also acted as a precipitant for the hitherto slow process of general change and transformation, reshaping the structure of the language into new, separate systems which, while still similar, were yet different.

This catalytic process occurred at the outset of the eighth century with the Moorish invasion of Spain, and the consequent interruption of communications between the Spanish-Portuguese area on the one hand, the French-Italian on the other. Its full effects did not manifest themselves all at once, coming into the full light of day in the ninth and tenth centuries. But its initial manifestations appeared in the eighth century itself, with a deterioration in the language of the documents that is far greater than all that had appeared in the three previous centuries. And these documents of the eighth century, unlike the earlier ones, are largely original, not later copies, which means that here we have fewer chronological doubts.

The end of the eighth century is the *terminus ad quem* for Vulgar Latin, at least in a large portion of the Romance area. Beyond this point, the new Romance languages begin to make their appearance, cautiously and hesitatingly at first, then more boldly, even while the bulk of writing is still done in what is meant to be Latin. But from this point on, we know that this Latin, however corrupt, is no longer the language of the people, even though it continues to infiltrate, and to be infiltrated by, the spoken tongues of the masses.

5. The Great Break

Between 400 and 700 A.D. Latin had undergone a process of transformation, less visible than it would have been audible to a trained modern linguistic observer, if one had been around to listen. Yet the changes are fairly evident, even to the eye of a careful philological examiner.

To begin with, there was the obliteration of both Classical pitch accent and Classical vowel quantity, the distinction between long and short vowels that made it possible for an educated Classical speaker to distinguish between the long *ā* of *pāter* and the short *ă* of *măter*, or between *lātus*, "broad," "wide," and *lătus*, "side." The new "rule," if such it can be called, is that stressed vowels are long, unstressed vowels short: *pătrem, mătrem*, become *pātrem, mātrem;* the *a* of *lătus*, "side," becomes as long as that of *lātus*, "wide," with the result that the two words are confused, and the one for "wide" drops out, to be replaced by *largus* or *amplius*. But this change cannot appear in writing unless we use short and long marks over *a*, which the Romans and their descendants did not do.

The quality of long *ā* and short *ă* was identical, and remained unchanged. In the case of the other pairs of long and short stressed vowels, lengthening the shorts did not affect the quality they had taken on in the course of their evolution. While in Archaic, possibly even in Pre-Classical Latin, each pair of long and short *e*, long and short *i*, long and short *o*, long and short *u*, had had, to the best of our knowledge, the same quality, this state of affairs had subtly changed somewhere along the line (the scattered evidence appears in Roman grammarians such as Lucilius, Terentianus, Victorinus, Consentius, all the way from the late second century B.C. to the fifth century A.D.). Save for the two *a*'s, which retained the same quality, originally long vowels assumed a closed quality, short vowels an open quality, as in modern German. But as the short vowels lengthened under the heavier stress, the closed quality of long *ē* led to its confusion with short *ĭ* (notice that if one prolongs the sound of English short *i* in *it*, one achieves a sound very similar to that of German *e* in *Zehn*, or of Italian closed *e* in *freddo*, or of French *é* in *été*). In like manner, originally short *ŭ*, prolonged, merged with long *ō* (again, if you prolong the sound of *u* in English *full*, you achieve a sound closer to that of German *o* in *loben*, or Italian closed *o* in *mondo*, or French *ô* in *nôtre*, than to the sound of English *u* in *rule*). This meant that when stressed, Classical long and short *a* merged, with no difference in sound. Short *ĕ* retained its open quality, like the *e* of English *met*, but prolonged. Long *ē* and short *ĭ* merged, with the sound that appears in French *été*, prolonged. Long *ī* retained its original quantity and quality, similar to that of *i* in English *machine*. Short *ŏ* retained its open quality, similar to that of British-pronounced *pot*, but lengthened. Long *ō* merged with short *ŭ*, with the sound of French *nôtre*. Long *ū* retained its original quantity and quality, sounding like the *u* in English *rule*.[1]

This in turn meant that in the place of the ten Classical stressed vowels, five long and five short, Vulgar Latin developed a system of seven accented vowels, all long. But the Latin system of writing provided only five symbols. There was no trouble about using *A* to represent the now universally long stressed *a; I* for the long *ī* sound; *V* for the long *ū* sound. *E* could continue to be used for the old short *ĕ*, and *O* for the old short *ŏ*. But how to represent the sound of *e* (as in French *été* or German *Zehn*), which resulted from the merger of Classical long *ō* and short *ĭ*; or the closed sound of French *nôtre*, which came from the merger of Classical long *ō* and short *ŭ?* To scribes and stonecutters not well trained in Classical spelling, this could only lead to confusion, using the symbols *E* and *I*, more or less indiscriminately, for the new long closed *ē* sound, and the symbols *O* and *V* for the new long closed *ō* sound. Accordingly, we find Classical *fidem* appearing as *fedem, dēbet* as *dibet, amōrem* as *amurem, tŭrma* as *torma*. Seldom, if ever, do we find "mistakes" that do not reflect the pronunciation, such as **pidem* for *pĕdem, *veta* for *vīta, *bunum* for *bŏnum, *lona* for *lūna*.

Unstressed vowels, on the other hand, tended to shorten (if they were originally long) and become blurred, so that originally long and short *e*'s

---

1. For a table showing these sound changes, see Appendix E.

and *i*'s on the one hand, *o*'s and *u*'s on the other, were confused in writing. Accordingly, we find *curona* for *cōrona*, *dibere* for *dēbere*, *pescare* for *piscare*. In the final syllable, we find *amare* for *amarī*, *spirito* for *spiritū*, and, with loss of final -*m*, *muro* for *murum*. But in the syllables closest to the dominant stressed syllable, the blurring could go to the point of complete fall, or syncopation: *calda* for *calida*, *domnus* for *dominus*, *frigdum* for *frigidum*.

These are the main indications we have of the initial process of change that leads gradually from a Latin to a Romance vowel structure. Other phenomena, such as the voicing of plosive consonants between vowels (*pagare* for *pacare*, *amadus* for *amatus*) and palatalization (*vinea* appearing as *vinia*) are occasional at first, become more widespread later. They, too, seem due to excessive stress.[2]

It is probable that these and many other phenomena we have mentioned earlier were far more current in speech than they were in writing. After all, there was still a written-language tradition, which scribes and stonecutters had to learn, however imperfectly, in order to be able to write at all. English speakers, who use spellings that often go back to Middle English pronunciation, hardly need to be reminded that "nite," "offen," "I should of done it," "watcha gonna do," come closer to popular American pronunciation than the "correct" "night," "often," "I should have done it," "what are you going to do." But they show up only in the writing of the semiliterate.

The eighth century began much as the seventh had ended, with a stability of sorts: a fairly enlightened, fairly unified Visigothic monarchy in the Iberian peninsula; a well-established Frankish Merovingian kingdom that extended over northern France and western Germany; an Italy whose northern area was under the heel of the Longobards, who were forever encroaching on the papal domains of the center and had even extended their power to parts of the south, but who stayed away from the coastlines, where they could not cope with the sea power of the Byzantine Empire of the East (the Byzantines held Ravenna, most of the southern seacoasts, and the island of Sicily, and the Longobards had never succeeded in subduing the nascent sea republics of Venice and Genoa).

---

2. See Appendix E for intervocalic plosives and palatalization.

The year 711 saw a disaster for the Western Roman world that was almost the equal of the fifth-century Germanic invasions. Mohammed's Arabs from southern Arabia, filled with the fiery zeal of a new-found, dynamic faith, had swept the rest of the Arabian peninsula, the Sassanid empire of Persia, Mesopotamia, Armenia, Damascus and Jerusalem, parts of Asia Minor, then, turning westward, Egypt, Carthage, North Africa, converting the inhabitants as they went. Joined by the North African Berbers, and favored by treachery among the Visigothic nobility, they now crossed the Strait of Gibraltar into Spain, inflicted disastrous defeats on the Visigothic armies, and in the course of a few years made themselves masters of most of what is today Spain and Portugal, leaving only confused, isolated Christian principalities in the north, and breaking communications between France and most of the peninsula. Some historians claim that they even penetrated and dominated the north for a brief period, but that Christian groups held out in individual fortresses, *castella*, whence the name of *Castilla*. However this may be, they effectively broke the unity of the Roman West. Then, in 720, they attempted to go further, into France, with the avowed purpose of pressing on to Rome, submerging the entire Christian world, and turning it Moslem. Parts of the old Roman province of Narbonensis fell to them. They thrust northward toward Poitiers and Tours, the "holy city" of the Franks. Here they were met and routed by Charles Martel, son of Pepin of Heristal, founder of the Carolingian dynasty that replaced the Merovingians. This victory saved Western Christianity, but Charles' efforts to recover Narbonensis were only in part successful, and the no man's land that separated France not only from Spain's Moors but from Spain itself remained for a long time on the French side of the Pyrenees.

Charles had studied Moorish tactics well, and knew that the invaders relied on their swift, light-armored horsemen to conduct blitzkrieg-style activities against their more heavily armored Christian foes, long on infantry and short on cavalry. To counteract these tactics, he organized a cavalry of his own, financed in large part by the Church of France, which perceived the mortal danger not only to the country but to itself. Under the earlier Merovingians, the Church had acquired, through gifts and bequests, enormous properties, and it is estimated that one-third of all lands and edifices in the Frankish realm had become Church property. The Church in France was far more than a spiritual entity. It was a temporal power, working, for the most part, hand-in-glove with the royal authorities, and forming with them a highly efficient Establishment. Considering itself the depositary of its own enormous wealth, it took on all the functions of a welfare state, caring for the poor, erecting and administering hospitals and shelters, and fostering such education as still existed. This state of affairs had gone on during the Merovingian centuries. Between 500 and 700 A.D., there had been held in France twenty-five Church Councils dealing with the condition and relief of the poor, as against only five in Spain, and none in Italy. The explanation may lie in a greater fervor of religious zeal on French soil than in the other countries, a more literal and sincere interpretation of the precepts of Christ. It is also possible that this spirit of religious enthusiasm led to a greater departure of the popular language in France from the old Latin standards than occurred in the other countries.

If the documentary and inscriptional evidence is of any value, it would seem to indicate greater conservatism in the matter of language on Spanish soil than in either France or Italy. But the Moorish invasion of 711 put a definite end to the earlier Spanish state of affairs. Eighth-century material, both documentary and inscriptional, from the free Christian north is both scanty and uncertainly dated. In part, this is due to the extensive Moorish occupation, which covered most of what is today Spanish and Portuguese territory. The original Ibero-Roman-Visigothic inhabitants continued to live and speak their Latin-based language (now named Mozarabic, literally, "among the Arabs") under the new masters, but their writing disappeared even more utterly than did that of the Anglo-Saxons during the two centuries that followed the Norman conquest of England. It came back to life in the tenth and eleventh centuries, but in either Arabic or Hebrew characters, which shed a good deal of light on the pronunciation. But by the time the first Mozarabic writings appeared, the language had undergone probably drastic transformations in the course of the previous two centuries, and must be characterized as a variety of Romance, to be discussed later. Consequently, the development of Spanish Vulgar Latin into Spanish Romance can only be described as a big leap in times of storm and stress, with a broad gap in our written-language evidence.

Semisubmerged by the Moslem wave, northern Spain has no reliable documents to show until the end of the ninth century. Here are two samples.[3]

---

3. See Appendix F, for additional samples and discussion.

Accepi ad te pretium pro ipsam meam portionem (A.D. 887) ("I received from you a price for my inheritance"). The only Vulgar features here are the confusion of *ad* for *a; pro* in the sense of "in exchange for," like later Spanish *por;* the use of *ipsam,* functioning possibly as a definite article.

. . . *monte que dicunt Adspera* (887) ("the mountain which they call Aspera"). *Que* for *quem* indicates at least the fall of final *-m,* at most the emergence of the new Spanish relative pronoun; *dicunt* for *dicitur* is one of the standard Romance replacements of the Latin passive voice.

The first unmistakable sample of Spanish appears in the vicinity of A.D. 950, more than a century after the appearance of the Oaths of Strasbourg of 842, the earliest French document. It will be discussed later.

In Italy, there is considerable documentary evidence from the eighth century, consisting in part of the Code of Laws of the Longobards, which displays more and more of the customary Vulgar Latin features, with the insertion of many Germanic words. Other Italian documents of the period, mainly from central Italian areas, display an abundance of Vulgar features. In view of the fact that the central dialects of Italy are highly conservative of Latin sound structure, some of the written features could be ascribed indifferently to Vulgar Latin or early Italian. But the basic sentence structure, however Vulgar, is still Latin, and this state of affairs continues into the ninth and early tenth centuries. Here is a sample.[4]

From an *Examen Testium* ("Examination of Witnesses"), Siena, 715: . . . *et fecit ibi presbitero uno infantulo habente annos non plus duodecim qui nec Vespero sapit nec Madodinos facere, nec Missa cantare* ("and there he made a priest out of a little boy not more than twelve years old, who neither knows how to conduct Vespers or Matins, nor how to sing the Mass"). At issue is the authority of two bishops, each claiming jurisdiction over certain parishes; the witness is testifying that one of them exercised his functions in a highly irregular and inefficient fashion. Of interest here is the use of *-o* endings where Classical Latin would require *-um* (*presbitero, uno, infantulo, Vespero*), combined with fall of *-m* in *habente, Missa,* foreshadowing Italian conditions (but these phenomena appear in French documents of the period as well); the use of an indefinite article and a diminutive form in *uno infantulo;* the shift from

---

4. For additional samples and discussion, see Appendix F.

unvoiced to voiced plosive in *Madodinos* (but Italian later appears with the original unvoiced *t* in *mattino, mattutino,* and this phenomenon is more characteristic of Spanish or French than of Italian); the use of *sapit* for classical *scit* (but the use of *sapio* in the sense of "to know" as well as "to taste" appears occasionally in Classical Latin). On the other hand, *annos* is definitely a Latin accusative plural (Italian would have *anni*).

The first unmistakably Italian document appears in 960, more than a century after the appearance of the first French document. It will be discussed later.

Spain's disastrous Moorish invasion and subsequent occupation may have been the prime reason for the final breakup and the emergence of the Romance languages, but it was conditions peculiar to France that led to French emerging first, more than a century before the others, at least in recorded form that has come down to us. For this many reasons have been advanced: a greater preponderance of the Germanic element in the population of northern France than elsewhere; a greater breakdown in Latin standards by reason of a less educated scribal class; a greater intensity of the stress accent, possibly engendered by religious fervor. Two ascertainable facts are that for eighth-century France we have at our disposal a collection of authentic, original documents, precisely dated, which offer clues as to certain historical happenings not otherwise recorded; and that certain pronouncements made by Charlemagne in the late eighth and early ninth centuries had consequences that might almost be described as predictable.

The documents, covering the years 703 to 717 and 750 to 799, were composed in the royal chanceries of Childebèrt III, Chilperic II, Pepin the Short, both as mayor of the palace and as king, Carloman, and Charlemagne. Scattered among them are a few documents done for private clients by private scribes, but equally original and authentically dated.

For what concerns the royal documents, the earlier ones, done under the Merovingians, display all the features that we associate with late Vulgar Latin, as described earlier. But the ones composed in the second half of the century, while still far from Classical, are largely correct, particularly in their spelling and the use of case endings. Some are exact copies of the earlier ones, but with corrections. A comparison is instructive:

No. 46 of Tardif's collection, dated 716: Oportit climenciae princepale, inter citeras peticionis, illut que pro salute adescribetur, et pro divino nominis postolatur, plagabile auditum suscipere . . .

No. 61, dated 768: Oportet climentiae principali, inter citeras petitiones, illud quod pro salute adscribitur et pro divine nominis postulatur, placabile auditum suscipere . . .

("It behooves the chief clemency [the royal authority] among other petitions to take up, having heard it, and when it is subject to legal procedure, that which pertains to salvation and is being presented on behalf of God's name . . .").

The only spelling irregularities appearing in the second passage are *climentiae* and *citeras,* where *i* replaces unstressed *e.* Further on in the document, the earlier has *facetis vobis amicis de mamona iniquetatis,* the later *facite vobis amicos de mammona iniquitatis* ("make for yourselves friends of the mammon of iniquity"). Here the earlier *facetis* reflects the peculiarly French plural imperative, which borrows its ending from the indicative. Uncorrected is *pro divine nominis,* which should be *pro divino nomine.*

These corrections, which are widespread in the later copies of earlier documents, arouse the suspicion that Pepin had issued orders to his scribes to consult their Latin sources and amend at least the grosser errors into which the earlier scribes had fallen, thus initiating the corrective process later pursued by Charlemagne, which was to prove counterproductive.

That Pepin's written-language reform did not extend beyond his chancery is shown, however, by contemporary private documents, which display the growing degeneration of the language that one might expect in the course of half a century. No. 67, a private deed of sale dated 769, shows this: *Constat nus at alliqua fimena nomine Nautlindo vindemus tibi pecia de maso probrio jures meo.* . . . An attempt to put this into something resembling Classical Latin might run: *Constat nos alicui feminae nomine Nautlinde vendere (tibi) (pecia de maso) proprii juris mei* ("It is stated that we are selling to a certain woman named Nautlinde [to you] a piece of farmland of my own property"). Outside of the inconsistency of "we" versus "my own property," we find the new Romance indirect object construction with *ad* replacing the Latin dative; confusion of stressed and unstressed vowels, including the finals, is in evidence throughout; consonants are similarly mishandled, with *probrio* replacing *proprio; pecia de maso* introduces not merely a Romance construction, but words not used in Latin but used in French and Provençal (*pièce de mas*). The language, even though notarial, is evidently degenerating at a fast pace when unsupported by such grammatical instruction as may have been available in the royal chancery.

In the year 787, Charlemagne, seemingly perturbed by the ravages he sensed and heard in his Latin-speaking domains, wrote in a letter to Bishop Baugulfus that good Latin usage should be urged on Christians, "so that those who strive to please God by a decorous life may not neglect to please Him also by decorous speech. . . . We exhort you to study letters . . . precisely with the aim that you may be able to penetrate more easily and more accurately into the mysteries of the Holy Scriptures." This was apparently meant to inspire the bishops and priests to reform their own usage in their sermons and homilies.

Did Charlemagne hope that better language uttered by the officiants in church would in part rub off on their audiences? It is possible. We must at any rate assume that the churchmen followed the emperor's admonition, and strove for better usage, in the same fashion as the royal scribes. But we must also assume that here they ran into a major problem, that of understanding. The language, for whatever reasons, had degenerated at a faster pace in northern France than elsewhere, and an attempt to couch church sermons and the reading and interpretation of the Gospels in Latin, even the somewhat sub–Classical Latin of the Vulgate, threw into confusion church audiences that had hitherto been able to understand priests speaking substantially their own tongue and making the necessary adjustments when they read from the Vulgate.

It took some decades to convince Charlemagne that his exhortation to the clergy to use a decorous speech was doing more harm than good. The popular language was too far gone along the road to change to be pulled back into anything resembling a Latin orbit. And since church attendance and church services were of paramount importance to the masses in those days, when they filled all spiritual and intellectual needs, Charlemagne eventually had to call off his reform, reverse himself, and acknowledge the existence of a new, different language in his western domains.

At the Council of Tours in 813 it was his decision that *et ut easdem homilias quisque aperte transferre studeat in rusticam romanam linguam aut thiotiscam, quo facilius cuncti possint intellegere quae dicuntur* ("and that each one openly exert himself to translate those same homilies into the rustic Roman tongue or the German, so that all men may more easily understand what is being said"").

The message is clear. French Romance had been born, and this was its baptismal certificate. But three more decades had to go by before we could be favored with a sample of the new "rustic Roman tongue."

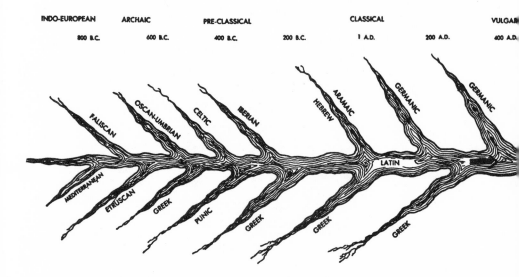

THE LATIN-ROMANCE LANGUAGE STREAM

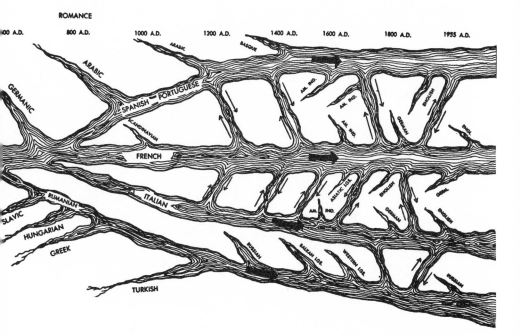

6. The Dawn of the Romance Languages

At Charlemagne's death, in 814, his vast empire, covering most of what is today West Germany, France, northern Italy, Belgium, and Holland, was inherited by his son Louis the Pious, a weak ruler. Louis died in 840, and his domains fell to the lot of his three sons, Charles, Louis, and Lothair. Charles, surnamed "the Bald," received the overlordship of the western regions of Neustria, corresponding roughly to modern France, and inhabited by people who spoke for the most part the language inherited from the Gallo-Romans, with its new Frankish admixture. Louis, surnamed "the German," received the regions east of the Rhine, which were German-speaking. Lothair took for his portion a broad band of territory, from the North Sea to the Alps and the Mediterranean, plus the extensive areas of northern Italy that Charlemagne had wrested from the Longobards. But this division did not become definite until the three brothers had had a falling out, due to the fact that Lothair wanted to establish his right to the imperial title and his overlordship over the others. A brief and indecisive war ensued, in the course of which Charles and Louis agreed to form a treaty of alliance, binding themselves to mutual assistance and to signing no separate peace with Lothair. They felt, democratically enough, that this arrangement should be not merely publicized among, but ratified by, their respective followers. Meeting on the plain of Strasbourg on February 14, 842, each ruler took the oath of mutual aid and no separate peace in the language of the other's army. The two armies were called upon to ratify by voice, each in its own language, the oaths taken by their rulers. The entire procedure was described at length in an account composed in fair Latin by Nithardus, who was another (illegitimate) grandson of Charlemagne. This account appears in its entirety in Nithardus' *Historiae,* which gives the full description of the controversy among the three brothers and its outcome, and has fortunately come down to us in a copy composed in the same ninth century that saw the events described. He gives us the full text of all four sections of the oath, the one spoken in French by Louis the German, that spoken in German by Charles the Bald, that spoken in French by Charles' followers, that spoken in German by Louis' army.

The German texts of the Strasbourg Oath are of great interest to Germanic philologists, but are not quite the earliest records of Old High German at our disposal. The French texts, on the other hand, are of paramount interest to students of Romance because they are unquestionably the earliest unmistakable record of a Romance tongue thus far discovered.

The full text of the French-language oath taken by Louis the German, preceded by Nithardus' comment in highly acceptable "reform" Latin, runs as follows:

Lodhuvicus, quoniam maior natu erat, prior haec deinde se servaturum testatus est.
("Louis, since he was the elder, then swore first that he would keep these [pledges]".)
Pro Deo amur et pro cristian poblo et nostro commun salvament, d'ist di in avant, in quant Deus savir et podir me dunat, si salvarai eo cist meon fradre Karlo, et in aiudha et in cadhuna cosa, si cum om per dreit son fradra salvar dift, in o quid il mi altresi fazet; et ab Ludher nul plaid nunquam prindrai qui, meon vol, cist meon fradre Karle in damno sit.
("For the love of God and for the safety of the Christian people and our own common safety, insofar as God grants me the knowledge and the power [to know and to be able], so will I assist this my brother Charles, both in help and in all things, as one by justice should assist his brother, provided he does the same with me; and with Lothair I shall never make any pact which, of my will, may be to the detriment of this my brother Charles.")

The language is unmistakably French, not Latin, Classical or Vulgar.[1]

Reconstructing the passage first in literal Vulgar Latin, then in literal French, this is what we get:

Vulgar Latin: Pro Dei amore et pro christiano populo et nostro communi salvamento, de isto die in ab ante, in quantum Deus sapere et potere mihi donat, sic salvare habeo ego ecce istum meum fratrem Karolum, et in adjuta et in cata una causa, sic quomodo homo per directum suum fratrem salvare debet, in

---

1. For a linguistic analysis, see Appendix G.

hoc quid ille mihi alterum sic faciat; et ab (cum) Lothario nullum placitum numquam prehendere habeo qui, meo volo (mea voluntate) ecce isti meo fratri Karolo in damno sit.

French: Pour (l')amour de Dieu et pour (le) peuple chrétien et notre commun sauvement, de ce jour en avant, en quant Dieu savoir et pouvoir me donne, si sauverai je ce mon frère Charles, et en aide et en chaque chose, si comme on par droit son frère sauver doit, en quant il me fasse autresi (de même); et avec Lothaire je ne prendrai jamais nul plaid (arrangement) qui (selon) ma volonté, soit en dommage à ce mon frère Charles.

Another Old French manuscript definitely assigned to the ninth century (about 880) is the *Sequence of St. Eulalia,* which also happens to be the first work of literature composed in a Romance tongue. The same manuscript also bears a Latin version which deals with the saint, but is not at all a translation of the French. Lives of saints and accounts of their martyrdom, both in prose and in verse, had been quite common in late Vulgar Latin literature, and this work seems to be an early attempt to put a favorite genre into the new and uncertain linguistic medium. The first ten of its twenty-nine lines run as follows:

Buona pulcella fut Eulalia, / Bel avret corps, bellezour anima.
Voldrent la veintre li Deo inimi, / Voldrent la faire diavle servir.
Elle nont eskoltet les mals conselliers, / Qu'elle Deo raneiet chi maent sus en ciel.
Ne por or ned argent ne paramenz, / Por manatce regiel ne preiement;
Niule cose non la pouret omque pleier / La polle sempre non amast lo Deo menestier /

("Eulalie was a good girl, / She had a beautiful body, a more beautiful soul.
The enemies of God wanted to overcome her, / Wanted to make her serve the devil.
She does not listen to the evil counselors / That she should renounce God Who dwells up in heaven.
Neither for gold nor silver nor attire, / For royal threat or entreaty;
Nothing could ever bend her / So that she would not continue to love God's service.")

The poem goes on to state that she was led into the presence of the pagan emperor Maximian, who urged her, but to no avail, to renounce Christ. She gathered her strength, and preferred to endure torture rather than lose her virginity. And so she died in an aura of saintliness. She was thrown into the fire so that she might quickly burn; but she was sinless, therefore the flames did not harm her (literally: therefore she did not cook). The pagan king would not yield to the evidence of his own eyes.

He ordered her head to be struck off with a sword. The girl offered no objection; she wanted to leave this world, and besought Christ to receive her. In the form of a dove she flew to heaven. We all pray that she may deign to intercede on our behalf, so that Christ may have mercy upon us after death, and let us go to Him through His mercy.[2]

From the tenth century is the Valenciennes or Jonah fragment, which seems to be the text of a sermon composed partly in Latin, partly in French, by a preacher commenting on the final chapter of the Jonah prophecy. The text is badly damaged in spots. Here is an excerpt, with the French words in italics:[3]

Dunc, co dicit, Ionas profeta habebat *mult laboret e mult penet a cel* populum; *e* faciebat *grant iholt,* et *eret mult las* et preparavit Dominus *un edre sore sen cheve, quet umbre li fesist e repauser s'i podist . . . e cum cilg eedre fu seche, si vint grancesmes iholt* super caput Ione . . .
("Then it says this, Jonah the prophet had greatly labored and greatly suffered with those people, and it was very warm, and he was very tired, and God prepared an ivy over his head, that it might make shade for him and he could rest there . . . and when that ivy was dry, there came a very great heat over Jonah's head . . .")

Two manuscripts appearing on the same eleventh-century parchment, are attributed to the late tenth or early eleventh century. One, the *Passion du Christ* ("Passion of Christ") was evidently copied from a Provençal manuscript by a French-speaking scribe, who blended French and Provençal forms. The other, the *Life of St. Léger,* is in Old French. Both are quite lengthy (240 lines for the first, 516 for the second).

The eleventh century gives us the *Life of St. Alexis* (625 lines) for French, with four separate and differing manuscripts, and the 267-line *Boethius* for Provençal. Later in the century, French will produce the masterpiece of Old French literature, the *Chanson de Roland* ("The Song of Roland"), with over four thousand lines, which means that Old French is entering upon its "classical" stage.

French had appeared not merely as a language, but as a literary medium before the end of the ninth century; Provençal as a translation medium before the end of the tenth, as a literary language in its own right by the middle of the eleventh.

Italian makes its first definite appearance as a language in 960, con-

2. For a linguistic analysis, see Appendix G.
3. For a linguistic analysis, see Appendix G.

tinuing into the eleventh century, but only for notarial, devotional, and inscriptional purposes, and blossoming forth as a literary tongue only in the twelfth.

Consciousness of the separation between Italian and Latin had appeared, however, at the beginning of the tenth century. An account of the crowning of King Berengarius, in 915, states that the senate sang *patrio ore*, "with their ancestral mouths," but the people shouted *nativa voce*, "in their native tongue." In 916, Gonzo, writing to the monks of Reichenau, says: *Licet aliquando retarder usu nostrae vulgaris linguae, quae latinitati vicina est* ("It is allowable that I may at times be slowed up by the use of our vulgar tongue, which is close to Latin"). An epitaph of Pope Gregory V says of him: *Usus francisca, vulgari et voce latina, instituit populos eloquio triplici* ("Using the French, the vulgar, and the Latin tongue, he inspired the people with his triple eloquence"). But this comes in 999, and the vulgar tongue had already appeared in writing thirty-nine years earlier.

The four Montecassino formulas for the use of witnesses, composed between 960 and 963 in Capua, Sessa, and Teano, all in the vicinity of the famous Benedictine abbey, appear in the body of Latin documents describing lawsuits concerning certain lands. They seem to have been prepared for the use of peasants who did not understand Latin. The first one runs: *Sao ko kelle terre, per kelle fini que ki contene, trenta anni le possette parte Sancti Benedicti* ("I know that those lands within those boundaries which here contains [are herein described] for thirty years the party of St. Benedict owned them").[4]

The Italian eleventh century offers a postscript in verse, added to a legal document, which indicates that the writer suspected the donor of having been drunk when he made out the donation: *Ista cartula est de caput coctu; ille adjuvet de illu rebottu qui mal consiliu li mise in corpu.* ("This document is from a cooked head [fool]; may he enjoy the orgy that put bad counsel into his body"). The language falls into a classification that might be construed as bad Vulgar Latin or equally bad early Italian. But the Italian definite article (*illu*) appears, as also the indirect object pronoun (*li*).

The Church of St. Clemente in Rome has a fresco depicting one of the saint's miracles, with words issuing from the mouths of the characters in the fashion of modern comic strips. One character says: *Fili*

---

4. For a linguistic analysis, see Appendix G.

de le pute, traite ("Sons of bitches, pull!"). Another says: *Albertel, trai* ("Albert, pull!"). Albert himself says: *Falite dereto colo palo, Carvoncelle* ("Get behind it with the pole, Carvoncello!"). St. Clement, using rather poor Latin, says: *Duritiam cordis vestris . . . saxa traere meruistis* ("Because of the hardness of your hearts, you deserved to pull stones!"). The big stone was apparently moved by the saint's words where it had previously failed to respond to material efforts.

There is also an eleventh-century confession formula from Umbria, of which these are excerpts:

Me accuso de lu genitore meu et de la genitrice mia, et de li proximi mei, ke ce non abbi quella dilectione ke me senior Dominideu commandao . . . de la decema et de la primitia et de offertione, ke nno la dei siccomo far dibbi. . . . Et qual bene tu hai factu ui farai en quannanti, ui altri farai pro te, si sia computatu em pretiu de questa penitentia. Se ttou judiciu ene ke tu ad altra penitentia no poze accorrere, . . . si sie tu reppresentatu ante cospectu Dei, ke lu diabolu no te nde poza accusare.
("I accuse myself of my father and my mother, and of my relatives, that I did not have for them that love that my lord God commanded . . . of the tithe and the first fruits and the offering, that I did not give it as I should have done. . . . And whatever good you have done or will do henceforth, or another will do for you, may it be counted as the price of this penance . . . so that you may be represented before the presence of God, so that the devil may not accuse you of it.")[5]

It is only in the twelfth century that literary passages begin to appear, in various localities, bearing dialectal traits that are to be expected before the emergence of a national literary tongue. Chief among them are the *Ritmo Cassinese*, the *Ritmo Marchigiano di Sant'Alessio*, and the *Ritmo Giullaresco Toscano*. Their subject matter will be discussed later.

The thirteenth century sees the appearance of a language that may be truly described as nationwide, in Sicily, Bologna, Florence, and Umbria.

On Spanish soil, the first unmistakably Spanish document is a series of glosses, some of which are translations of individual words in the text, while a few are fairly lengthy. They appear in a devotional book composed in rather poor Latin at the monastery of San Millán, in Old Castile (but close to the border of Rioja, which verges on Aragonese territory), about the middle of the tenth century. The glosses were evi-

---

5. For a linguistic analysis, see Appendix G.

dently meant to explain to readers the meaning of Latin forms and passages that might no longer be understood. Among individual words we find:

Repente ("suddenly")—*lueco* (this becomes *luego,* which has rather the meaning of "then," "later").

suscitabi ("I aroused," "I raised")—*lebantai, levantavi;* later it becomes *levanté.*

submersi ("I submerged")—*trastorne.*

conmotiones ("movements")—*moveturas.*

et tertium veniens ("and the third one coming")—*elo terzero diabolo venot* ("the third devil came"); later *el tercer diablo vino.*

indica ("shows")—*amuestra.*

inveniebit ("will find")—*aflarat;* later *hallará.*

non nobis sufficit ("does not suffice us")—*non convienet a nobis* ("does not suit us").

siquis ("if anyone")—*qualbis uemne* ("whatever man"); later *cualquier hombre.*

quid agas ("what you may do")—*ke faras* ("what you will do"); later *qué harás.*

ayt enim apostolus ("for the apostle says")—*zerte dicet don Paulo apostolo* ("certainly says Saint Paul the apostle").[6]

A *Nodicia de Kesos* ("Account of Cheeses") on the reverse of a parchment in Latin appears later in the tenth century, while for the late eleventh or very early twelfth there is a Mozarabic poem in Hebrew characters by Iehuda ben-Levi, of which one stanza runs:

Vayse meu corachon de mib;	"My heart goes away from me;
Ya, Rab, si se me tornarad?	Oh, Lord, will he come back to me?
Tan mal meu doler li-l-habib!	So great is my grief for my beloved!
Enfermo yed; cuando sanarad?	He is ill; when will he get well?"

Here *rab,* "master," "lord," is Hebrew; *li-l-habib,* "because of the loved one," is Arabic. *Tornarad, sanarad, yed,* show late retention of a weakened final *-t. Mib* is from *mibi,* formed on the analogy of *tibi, sibi,* like Old Italian *mebe, meve.*

Like Italian, Spanish becomes thoroughly literary in the twelfth century, with a play about the Magian Kings, and the *Cantar de myo Cid,* the masterpiece of Old Spanish literature.

---

6. For additional passages and a linguistic analysis, see Appendix G.

7. Medieval Romance Languages and the Rise of Romance Literatures

For historical periods when there were no audial recordings (these began only at the beginning of the twentieth century) or descriptive grammars of the modern type (satisfactory ones, from the scientific standpoint, don't begin to appear until the outset of the nineteenth century), one has to rely upon four different devices to ascertain the state of the spoken language. First, there are spoken-language reconstructions based on processes of induction and deduction; these can be highly ingenious, but also highly misleading. Next come the stray remarks that appear in writers of the period under consideration; we have seen this method at work in our chapters on Classical and Vulgar Latin: good as far as it goes, but it doesn't go far enough. Third are practical grammars designed to impart one language to speakers of another in terms of the second language: a doubtful testimony until we get to the Renaissance and even beyond, by reason of the lack of linguistic training and the sketchy methodologies and comparisons of the authors. Lastly, there is the internal evidence supplied by the language itself through its literary output; this is by far the most satisfactory and abundant source of information, but it, too, is subject to certain drawbacks.

The language of literature generally represents a sublimation of the spoken tongue, which puts on, so to speak, its Sunday clothes for the occasion. The writer is normally conscious of the need to put his best foot forward when he writes, and will seldom write exactly as he speaks. His language is apt to be stilted, overprecise, overinvolved, to show traces of archaism and cultural influences. If he is writing poetry (and poetry constitutes well over half of the literary output of the early

Romance centuries), his language will be forced into an unnatural mold set by the requirements of rhythm, the number of syllables to a line, the rhyme or assonance. There may be conscious or unconscious imitation of earlier models, earlier works, earlier forms. There is almost certain to be a dialectal influence, supplied by the writer's own dialect background or by that of his model, occasionally by a mixture of both (the tenth-century Clermont poem known as the *Passion du Christ* is a perfect example of this blending; here the scribe, evidently a northern Frenchman, copied from a Provençal model, which was in turn based on the Biblical account, in the Latin of the Vulgate, of the Passion of our Lord Jesus Christ; the result is a hodgepodge of northern French, Provençal, and, to a lesser degree, Latin forms).

Yet the value of documentary, literary evidence must not be underestimated. The medieval writer, generally speaking, expects his poem to be read out loud, to an audience of people less literate than himself who must nevertheless be reached by the message he conveys. He can be over their heads only to a very limited degree, or he will lose them. The nature of early medieval literature, particularly in verse, is highly propagandistic, almost to the same extent as the commercial "messages" we are faced with on radio and television. It is highly unfair to discount the evidence of the written language as a reflection of what was being spoken, just as it would be unfair today; in fact, even more so, considering that the general cultural level in the Middle Ages was far more uniform than it is today. Lords and barons and their ladies were, for the most part, just as illiterate as their servants and retainers. Just as all listened together to the sermons and Gospel readings in the churches, so all congregated in the main hall of the castle to listen to a northern French *jongleur* who recited or sang a *chanson de geste,* or even to a Provençal troubadour singing his love lays.

Medieval Romance poetry has its roots deep in the literature of an earlier period, the centuries that intervened between the fall of the Roman Empire and the rise of the new western European empire of Charlemagne. These were centuries of profound religious feeling, characterized by works that dealt largely with the lives of Christian saints and martyrs. Hence it is not surprising that when the new vernaculars first appeared in literary form, they should bear the stamp of the older Christian tradition and relate the tales, mostly of suffering and violent death, of the same saints and martyrs.

In northern France, at the close of the ninth century, we get the brief, episodic *Sequence of St. Eulalia*, who was martyred for her faith by the Roman emperor Maximian. This is followed at a distance by the *Life of St. Léger*, a politically inclined saint who was prime minister of some of the Merovingian kings of early France and also underwent martyrdom, and the *Passion du Christ*, taken straight from the Biblical account. Then there is the ancient Syrian legend of St. Alexis, who was not martyred, but lived and died in the service of God.

In Spain, the most ancient literary document, from the early part of the twelfth century, is the account of the visit to the court of King Herod of the Magian kings. In southern France, literature opens with the eleventh-century story and maxims of Boethius, the Christian author of *The Consolation of Philosophy*, who lived about 500 A.D., followed by the life story of St. Foi d'Agen, who was martyred about the year 300. In Italy, it is another version of the legend of Alexis, along with a mysterious poem from Cassino which some have interpreted as a piece of heretical Albigensian propaganda, cleverly disguised as a seemingly harmless account of the meeting of two wise men seeking the truth.

But new forms, new ideas, were in the making. By the eleventh century, the era of Christian mysticism was over. Northern France and Spain were aroused by a warrior spirit fostered by the Moorish invasions and the Crusades, and in these countries there was a flowering of songs of war and liberation, in the earliest of which the old religious spirit still ran strong, but which soon turned into military epics pure and simple. In the south of France, inspired perhaps by songs of veneration for Our Lady, perhaps by Moorish songs of earthly love, it was the lyric strain that prevailed, the song of worship for one's lady, carried by the troubadours through the Mediterranean lands and spreading to Italy and Portugal. The early literature of the Romance countries, stemming from a seemingly universal religious base, thus branches out into two different and opposite directions. On the one hand, we have the French *chansons de geste* and the Spanish *cantares*, tales of doughty deeds of arms; on the other, the love lays of Provence, Sicily, and Portugal, glorifying sometimes tender, chivalric love, sometimes the raw passions of the flesh. Here and there, as in the *Canticles of Saint Francis of Assisi*, the old religious spirit raises its head, almost submerged by the twin terrestrial waves that describe the deeds of man in a material existence compounded of lust of battle and lust of sex.

First and greatest among the war epics of northern France is the *Chanson de Roland,* composed toward the end of the eleventh century by Turoldus, a Norman abbot, whose purpose it probably was to arouse enthusiasm for the freeing of the Holy Land from the Saracens, a process then barely beginning. The abbot wanted to depict the infidel Moslems as the enemies of Christendom, make them living, breathing characters who would inspire a hatred born of fear in the masses destined to march to the liberation of Christ's Sepulcher. The Holy Land was far away, and its Saracen occupants remote and unknown. But there were other Moslems closer at hand, the Moors of Spain, who three centuries before had overrun the Iberian peninsula and stormed at the very heart of France. They had been routed in the bloody battle of Tours in 732 by Charles Martel, leader of the Franks who had been the ancestors of the eleventh-century Frenchmen. Half a century later, Charlemagne, mightiest of medieval emperors, had led an expedition into Spain with the half-avowed purpose of hurling the Moors back across the Strait of Gibraltar into Africa. His campaign was indecisive, but around it legends sprang up—one, in particular, about the last stand made by Charlemagne's nephew Roland in the Pyrenean passes, protecting the army's retreat. The treachery of Roland's own stepfather, Ganelon, had been the cause of Roland's death, for which the emperor had exacted a terrible vengeance.

Actually, the historical details were different. Charlemagne's rearguard had been attacked not by the Moslems, but by the Christian Basques, who from the cliff tops had rolled down huge stones on the heavily armored Franks in the pass below. The rearguard had been utterly destroyed. Egginhard, friend and chronicler of Charlemagne, mentions among the fallen one Count Roland, prefect of the Breton March, an important leader, but apparently not related to the emperor. Charlemagne, on hearing of the massacre, turned back with his army, but on arriving at the scene he found that the Basques, having plundered the baggage train, had fled into their mountain fastnesses. Nothing was left for him to do but bury the fallen and return to France.

For three centuries, popular but unwritten songs and dirges about the slaughter of Roncevaux continued to be recited and embellished, until Turoldus, a full three hundred years later, wove them into a single epic, much as Homer is said to have pieced together the *Iliad* out of earlier brief epic fragments dealing with the fall of Troy. The Anglo-Norman poet Wace, who accompanied William the Conqueror at the Battle of

Hastings, tells us that the *Chanson de Roland* was sung by William's men as they joined battle with Harold's Saxons in 1066. If this is true, it must have been an earlier, briefer version, for the full version of the *Chanson de Roland* that has come down to us is over four thousand lines long and is dated in approximately 1075. At any rate, Turoldus' version of the Roland story is vastly different from Egginhard's earlier and more sober account. It is picturesque, heroic, historically inaccurate, but highly stirring and imaginative.[1]

This highly dramatic tale fired the imagination of the medieval world, which was ripe for this type of writing after the Great Penance of the early Middle Ages. The *Chanson de Roland* became the prototype of the historical novel as we know it today. It spread like wildfire from France to Spain, Italy, Germany, England, Scandinavia, in almost literal translations or in widely diverging versions. The story was told and retold. For three centuries France was flooded with epic poems stemming directly or indirectly from the *Chanson de Roland*. The *chansons de geste*, or tales of doughty deeds, became the universal fare of king, knight, cleric, retainer, artisan, merchant, and serf. In some of these imitations the original heroes became the villains and vice versa. Each of Roland's twelve peers was written about in his own epic.

In the twelfth and thirteenth centuries especially, the story of Roland pervaded the scene of world literature, sweeping far beyond national borders to all the countries of Western Europe. There were Provençal, Dutch, German, Norse, Spanish, even Welsh versions. The first Italian version gave rise to one of the earliest cases on record of a deliberately constructed international language, the Franco-Italian, or Franco-Venetian, whose purpose it was to permit a French jongleur to recount his story to an Italian audience in a tongue close enough to his own to allow the full retention of the original rhythm and assonance, yet near enough to that of his audience to permit them to grasp his utterances. The Italian fourteenth, fifteenth, and early sixteenth centuries were dominated by the Roland legend, with such writers as Barberino, Pulci, Boiardo, Berni, Ariosto, and Tasso vying with one another to produce new, highly distorted, highly imaginative versions of the original.

Spain was influenced in its epic output, from the *Cantar de myo Cid* through *Fernán González* and the ballads of Bernaldo del Carpio, down to Cervantes and his *Don Quixote*. In England, we have not only Wace

---

1. For a brief summary of the plot and samples of the language, see Appendix H.

but also the fifteenth-century *Rowlandes Song,* Caxton's *Life of Charles the Great,* and even a remote influence that appears in some of Shakespeare's plays. The memory of Roland lingers on today in the puppet shows of Italy and the painted wine carts of Sicily, where the exploits of Roland, Oliver, and Charlemagne, of Ganelon and his evil men of Mayence, of the Paladins of France, are still acted and depicted.

Turning to the epic output of Spain, we find that the Spaniards, after an early translation of the French version, of which only about a hundred lines have come down to us, decided to bring forth their own national epics. The first and best of these is the *Cantar de myo Cid,* a semihistorical account of the exploits of Rodrigo Díaz of Bivar, the medieval *caudillo* who, having been banished from his own lands because of the machinations of his enemies, nevertheless retook Valencia from the Moors. The four-thousand-line poem goes on to relate how he regained the king's favor, and how his two daughters were married to the *infantes* of Carrión, who treated their brides in shameful fashion. But the Cid proved through his champion that the unworthy husbands, in name only, were in the wrong, and the girls were rewed to better men.[2]

The *Cid* and other native Spanish epics were undoubtedly more historically accurate than the *Chanson de Roland.* But they lacked the powerful dramatic appeal of the French epic, and the Spaniards turned again to the original source of inspiration, giving it a new, nationalistic twist. They devised a character, Bernaldo del Carpio, who in numerous ballads is described as rebelling against his uncle Alfonso of the Asturias, who had invited Charlemagne into Spain to fight the Moors. But Alfonso had also granted the French emperor overlordship over the Spanish realm without consulting his barons. Bernaldo was incensed at this. But he was even more incensed at the death of his father, who had been imprisoned by Alfonso at the time of Bernaldo's birth because he had secretly wed the king's sister. So Bernaldo joined with his rebel bands the Moslem forces of Marsile in order to drive the Franks from Spain. In a new version of the battle of Roncevaux, Bernaldo slays Roland with his own hand, and forces Charlemagne to withdraw into France.

The Basques, who historically were the true victors at the pass, also decided to get into the literary picture. There is a brief Basque epic, the *Altabiskarco Cantua* ("Song of Altabiskar") that tells the story from the

---

2. For brief passages from the *Cid,* see Appendix H.

Basque viewpoint, and in highly accurate fashion. But there is some suspicion in scholarly circles that it may have been manufactured as late as the nineteenth century, since there is no earlier record of it.[3]

The other main branch of early Romance poetry lies in the lyric field, and here it is southern France that sets the pace. Earliest of the Provençal troubadours was Guillem IX, count of Poitiers and duke of Aquitaine, who lived at the end of the eleventh century and, in the words of one of his biographers, "roamed the land to deceive the ladies." The Provençal love lyric dominated the twelfth century, but came to a rather abrupt close at the beginning of the thirteenth, when the crusade against the Albigensian heresy turned southern France into a wasteland.

Unlike the northern French *jongleurs,* who were professional singers of the *chansons de geste,* the Provençal troubadours were mostly men of noble or seminoble origin who delighted in singing the praises of fair ladies, many of them married to other men. The nature of the love affairs they describe is such that frequently the identity of the lady to whom the poem is directed has to be concealed. This in turn leads to a style that is often obscure and strange, but which met with great favor in Italy, in Portugal, and even in northern France, where it had to face the competition of the native epic.

Not all Provençal poetry consists of songs of love. There are also political diatribes, and some of the earliest military epics appear in Provençal form. We have at least one glorification of war from the pen of Bertrand de Born, a Provençal poet who is said to have lived for a time at the court of King John of England. There were even among the Provençal writers men who hated women instead of enthroning and worshipping them. Marcabru, inventor of the *trobar clus* ("closed singing," or "hidden style"), says, among other things: "I never loved and never was loved." Worse yet, he adds: "Famine, pestilence, and war do less evil upon earth than the love of a woman."

But few of his contemporaries agreed with him. In most of their writings, whether they be *pastorelas* (shepherdess songs), *albas* (dawn songs), *sirventés* (songs of flattery), or *tenzós* (songs in which two characters, usually a man and a woman, sing alternate stanzas), we find outright worship for the object of the troubadour's love, or a brutal, frankly

---

3. The opening stanza, with a translation, is given in Appendix H. The reader is reminded that Basque is not at all a Romance language, and not even Indo-European.

expressed desire to possess it. Both are on occasion shrouded by the mysterious *trobar clus*, in which the poet veils the lady of his heart and the circumstances leading to their love affair in words that are puzzling and bewildering.

Arnaut Daniel, a man whose fame spread far beyond his own borders, to the point where his work was extravagantly praised by Dante, gives us a sample of this strange style, of which a portion is quoted in Appendix H. If the English translation is bewildering, the Provençal original is no less so. What sort of adventure is the poet describing? The repeated appearance of the word "uncle" in his poem has led some to think that his love affair was with the young wife of his own kinsman, real or imaginary. He also speaks of a mysterious chamber, which no man dares enter, but where he has enjoyed and will enjoy love's pleasures, and of the claw and beak of a *losengier* ("flatterer," or "slanderer"), possibly a courtier who knows of the affair and is going to reveal it to the outraged husband. Interestingly, even the music to which this poem is set has come down to us.

One of the most typical of Provençal poets was Rambaut de Vaqueiras, a man who traveled widely and knew most of the tongues of southern Europe. He did not hesitate to put his polyglot accomplishments to good use in his poems, which describe personal experiences. In one of them, he uses no fewer than five languages, his native Provençal, Italian, French, Gascon, and a mixture of Spanish and Portuguese. He claims that his unhappy love affair has thrown his tongues into confusion, so that he uses a different language in each stanza; when he comes to the *envoi* (short concluding stanza), he speaks two lines in each of the five tongues. This linguistic *tour de force* from the Middle Ages has led to the inclusion of his poem in practically all anthologies that deal with medieval languages.[4]

In another of his poems, Rambaut uses the form variously known as *tenzó* (literally "tension"), *contrasto* (the Italian term), and *jeu parti* (literally "split game," because the utterances are split between the two participants; but since the outcome of the game lies in the balance till the very end, the term *jeu parti* has given rise to English *jeopardy*, a situation of potential danger). In the variety of *tenzó* favored by Rambaut, a man urges a woman to yield herself to him, while she resists his advances. Only the closing lines will tell whether he achieves his purpose

---

4. See Appendix H.

or not. Here Rambaut uses a bilingual form. He speaks in Provençal, while the lady who is the goal of his desires replies in the Genoese dialect of Italian.[5]

The Provençal style spread to Italy, giving rise to the *dolce stil nuovo,* "sweet new style," of Cavalcanti and other precursors of Dante and Petrarch. But it found its most numerous imitators at the Sicilian court of Frederick II of Hohenstaufen, the German emperor who far preferred his southern realms to his native Germany, and who surrounded himself with poets from all parts of Italy and from foreign shores. One of the earliest writers of the Sicilian school was Cielo d'Alcamo, whose *contrasto* is an echo of that of Rambaut de Vaqueiras. Here a young stranger pleads for the love of a Sicilian girl, who at first rejects him. Unlike the participants in Rambaut's *tenzó,* both speak good medieval Italian, with perhaps a touch of Sicilian dialect.[6]

Pre-Dante literature in Italy is also well represented by the religious, ascetic, strangely beautiful poetry of Saint Francis of Assisi and his Umbrian school. In his *Cantico delle Creature,* the saint gives thanks and blessings to the Lord for all His bounty—the sun, the moon, the stars, the earth and fire and water, the changing seasons, and, last of all, Death, which ushers in a more enduring life. He uses no definable poetic form, and his poetry might be described as free verse, in the ultramodern style. Yet the poetic qualities are there.[7]

Spreading to Galicia and Portugal, the Provençal love lyric encountered there a seemingly earlier, native, popular strain, the song of love and longing and the sea, in which a maiden expresses her concern for her lover, who has sailed far away. This *Cantiga de Amigo,* which gathers in itself the well-known Portuguese spirit of *saudades,* or nostalgic longing, blends well with the new tone that comes from southern France. It is exemplified by some of the *cantigas* of Martin Codax, a thirteenth-century Galician poet.[8]

More tinged with the influence that stems from Provence is a song of love, attributed to King Sancho.[9]

With the dawn of the Renaissance, new influences come into Por-

---

5. For an excerpt, see Appendix H.
6. For an excerpt, see Appendix H.
7. For an excerpt, see Appendix H.
8. For an excerpt, see Appendix H.
9. See Appendix H.

tuguese poetry, notably the classical epic that is so well reflected in the *Lusíadas* of Camões. But Camões also wrote briefer works that reflect the earlier strain, like a lyric in which he bewails the untimely death of the woman he loved.[10]

In one sense, it may be said that early Romance poetry is only a transitional form bridging the gap between the classical literature of Greece and Rome and the new modern literary forms produced under the influence of the Renaissance which appear from the fourteenth century on. But it may also be argued that the literature of the Middle Ages represents a more indigenous, spontaneous growth on Romance soil, something that is free from the artificiality of the intellect and stems more directly from the heart, something that is closer to the soul of the people. At any rate, we discover in it abundant proof that human nature does not change throughout the centuries, that the themes that pervade the literature of today were present then. War and violence, loyalty to an ideal or a person, refined and spiritual love between the sexes, love of a more earthy, material nature, the search for God, manifestations of sorrow and bereavement, all deeply human qualities, equally characteristic of all ages, are well represented.

Above all, there is little question that the emotional nature of this type of poetry, directed to people of all social classes and educational levels, is couched in a true reflection of the popular spoken tongue, perhaps the best reflection that is available to us in the absence of modern audial records.

---

10. For an excerpt, see Appendix H.

8. *Old French and Old Provençal*

Referring to a language, the adjective "old" can be used chronologically, to indicate a period of time; when "old" is used in this sense, it means that the language, while it progresses, does not alter its basic structure. The "old" forms of Italian, Spanish, Portuguese, are still accessible to the modern reader with, perhaps, the aid of a glossary to explain words, uses of words, and a few grammatical forms that have become archaic.

In the case of languages like French and Provençal (and, to an even greater degree, English) the term "old" has a deeper meaning. It is the basic structure of the language, its combination of morphology and syntax, that has changed. This means that the "old" language is accessible only in spots to the modern reader without a special and separate course of study. It is, to all intents and purposes, a different tongue from the one he knows, though related to it.

If we take our own tongue, "Old English" is synonymous with Anglo-Saxon. The breaking point between Old English and modern English comes some centuries after the Norman Conquest and before the time of Chaucer, when the English language emerged from the relative obscurity that had enveloped it while Saxons and Normans lived on separate planes, with the latter using a type of Norman French that differed more and more from the French of France, while the former, left to their own linguistic devices, continued to use their Germanic tongue, but with growing admixtures from the language of the conquerors. When, in the fourteenth century, the English court, nobility, and clergy went over to the language of the once conquered and despised Saxons, that language had undergone vast transformations. By the time Chaucer used it in his writings, there is no question about its identity with the English we know, as proved by its basic comprehensibility to a modern reader. We can, if we wish, set up a transitional period, Middle English, covering the centuries from the twelfth through the fifteenth; but the relative paucity of written works composed in English prior to the fourteenth century, and the fact that those that appear still lean rather heavily in the direction of Old English rather than modern English makes the classification one of convenience rather than of structure and vocabulary.

In the case of French, one finds a somewhat similar situation. Between the appearance of the earliest French documents in the ninth century and the full flowering of French as a literary tongue there is a span of more than two centuries which has already been described. The appearance of the *Chanson de Roland* in the latter half of the eleventh century marks the full final development of a language that has broken all links with its ancestral Latin and will thenceforth be used as a full-fledged literary and cultural medium. But that language is still quite remote from the French we learn in high school. In fact, it is doubtful whether an English speaker equipped with high school and college French, or even a native Frenchman who has not followed special studies, can make more than a stab at the meaning of many of the *Chanson's* four thousand or so lines. Translations of Anglo-Saxon works into modern English abound, but from Chaucer on it is only exceptionally and for special purposes that one gets translations of so-called Middle English into modern English. In French, translations of the *Chanson de Roland* and subsequent *chansons de geste* into modern French are quite current, and it is only after the time of François Villon (middle of the fifteenth century) that the French high school student or general reader is faced with original texts (explanatory notes are beside the point).

By way of contrast, the Italian reader is normally given his Cielo d'Alcamo, Francis of Assisi, even Dante, in the original. The Spanish reader is similarly treated to his *Cantar de myo Cid* and *Siete Infantes de Lara*. The point is that while the language of Dante or the *Cid* represents an older, archaic state of what is basically one language, the Old English of *Beowulf* and the *Ormulum*, the Old French of the *Roland*, are, structurally, different languages from the modern English and French tongues, and have to be approached as semiforeign languages even by native speakers. At the same time, it must be admitted that the spread between the Old French of the *Roland* and the modern French of Lamartine is not quite as great as the distance that separates the Old English of *Beowulf* from the modern American of Poe.

This separate status, in which Old French is accompanied by its Gallic kinsman Old Provençal, sets the languages of the French area apart from the other Romance languages of the West. Its basis is the transitional double case for masculine nouns, adjectives, and articles, a holdover from the elaborate Latin six-case system; this double case fails to appear in the other Romance languages of which we have an unbroken record. The fact that Old French and Old Provençal can distinguish by means of an ending (or the lack of an ending) between subject and object case is altogether peculiar to those languages among the Romance tongues of the West. (Rumanian, too, has a double-case system to this day, but by a different formation and with a different function.)

Phonetically, the Old French language, which ultimately prevailed in its Francien form, based on the dialect of Paris and surrounding regions, is a tongue characterized by a strong stress accent which is perceptibly absent from the modern language, and gives Old French a rhythmical flavor similar to that of modern English. If we are correct in our analysis, it was this stress accent, continuing and even increasing over the centuries, that was primarily responsible for the severance of Old French from the Latin sound structure and for its striking phonetic divergence from other, more conservative languages such as Spanish and Italian. The manifestations and consequences of this heavy stress accent are obvious: more abundant diphthongization and other changes in stressed vowels, greater weakening and fall of unstressed vowels, particularly in the final syllable, weakening of consonants between vowels, evidenced by voicing (sonorization) of unvoiced consonants and fall of voiced consonants; all this to the point where Latin *dormitorium* becomes *dortoir,* and Latin *monasterium* turns into *mostier.* Palatalization of velars goes farther than in other Romance languages, with *caballum* turning into *cheval, causa* into *chose, gallina* into *jeline.* Nasalization is a fairly regular phenomenon, though normally not indicated by the spelling (*montem* to *mont*).

But it is in the field of morphology and syntax that the Gallo-Romance tongues display their individuality to the best advantage. Where Latin could arrange a subject-verb-object sentence in any of six ways, Old French still preserves that possibility. ("The dog sees the deer"):

Latin	Old French
canis videt cervum	li chiens veit le cerf
canis cervum videt	li chiens le cerf veit
videt canis cervum	veit li chiens le cerf
videt cervum canis	veit le cerf li chiens
cervum videt canis	le cerf veit li chiens
cervum canis videt	le cerf li chiens veit

Italian, to express the desired meaning, has to rely on word order, like English (*il cane vede il cervo*). Spanish, by the somewhat ambiguous device of using the preposition *a* (which normally marks an indirect object) before a personal direct object ("deer," as an animate being, is personalized) can duplicate the French tour de force (*el perro ve al ciervo, el perro al ciervo ve*, etc.; *a* + *el* contract into *al*). But if the object is thoroughly inanimate, Spanish becomes as helpless as Italian (*el hombre ve el muro*, "The man sees the wall").

What can have been the cause of this partial conservation of Latin morphological structure, which is at loggerheads with the far greater evolutionary tendencies of Gallo-Romance in the matter of sound changes? One would be tempted to attribute it to the phonological phenomenon of the French conservation of Latin final *-s*, which Italian drops (*murus* becomes *murs* in Old French, and both *murō* and *murum* become *mur*, while in Italian all three forms turn into *muro*). But Spanish, like French, conserves Latin final *-s*, so that on a purely phonological basis it too could have developed a double case; yet Spanish chose not to do so.

One interesting, though largely unproved theory, is that the greater religious fervor that prevailed in France led to a good deal of direct rendering of the Latin Vulgate, particularly the Gospels, into the popular language in the churches for the edification of the masses, and that the preachers found it far easier to modify the Latin into the vulgar tongue if they retained some of the older case distinctions, more specifically the opposition between nominative singular (with final *-s*) and accusative or oblique singular (without *-s*), and also between nominative plural (without *-s*) and accusative or oblique plural (with *-s*), which would have permitted them to translate freely without having to rearrange the word order of the sentence. But of this we have no direct evidence, though some circumstantial evidence appears in documents like the *Fragment de Valenciennes* of the ninth century, where some of the fragmentary utterances appear twice, first in Latin, then in the vulgar tongue, with some elaboration and paraphrasing.

The two-case system for masculine nouns, fully operative from the inception of French documents, continues in use through the ninth, tenth, eleventh, and twelfth centuries, with only occasional lapses, which are nevertheless indicative of a trend toward a final and complete merging of the cases. In the thirteenth century signs of breakdown become more frequent. By the end of the fourteenth, the breakdown is complete. Generally speaking, it is the nominative forms, both singular and plural, of masculine nouns that disappear, and the oblique case remains as the single case of modern French, which thus rejoins the languages of the Italian and Iberian peninsulas.[1]

Again, the causes of the fourteenth-century change are obscure. The disappearance from pronunciation of final -s, which had been strongly pronounced in the earlier centuries, is advanced as the most likely single cause, along with a tendency to standardize the word order of the simple subject-verb-object sentence. By the fifteenth century the language is definitely in its modern state, at least for what concerns morphology. Whether there could have been any conscious or unconscious desire to imitate the sentence structure of Spanish and Italian is doubtful. The fact remains, however, that today a word-for-word translation from one Western Romance language into another is both feasible and customary.

The Old French period is marked in vocabulary by a certain progressive diminution of the Germanic element brought in by the Franks, coupled with noticeable accretions of Latin words and word-formations, and a certain amount of borrowing from sister Romance languages, especially Provençal; this along with Arabic and other Oriental words brought back by the Crusaders.

The Crusades, originating on French soil and frequently led by French kings and leaders, were also responsible for the spreading of the French language abroad, to the point where French began to assume the aspect of an international tongue. But for this there were other causes: the earlier start of French as a literary tongue than any of the other Romance languages, and its vast literary output, particularly in the field

---

1. There are quite a few cases, however, where both nominative and oblique survive, and come down into modern French with a semantic differentiation, turning them into two different nouns. Latin *homo, companio,* nominatives, give rise to *on, copain,* while the oblique forms *homine(m), companione(m)* become *homme, compagnon.*

of military epics, Arthurian romances, and, to a lesser degree, semididactic works of the type of the *Roman de la Rose,* popular *fabliaux,* mystery plays, even historical chronicles. It must also be remembered that France enjoyed during this period a larger measure of national unity than any other European nation, with the possible exception of England, and that it was demographically superior to the other countries of Western Europe, having a more numerous population than England, Italy, Spain, or Germany.

Summarizing, Old French was a language of strong stress, with more Latin stressed vowels transformed into diphthongs than any other Romance tongue; more unstressed and final vowels falling out; more intervocalic consonants progressing from unvoiced to voiced and from plosive to fricative, or to complete disappearance; more palatalization of velars, and more nasalization of *n*'s and *m*'s in syllable-final position. In short, there was a greater change from the original Latin than in the kindred languages; this was coupled with conservatism in the matter of the morphological structure and function of nouns and adjectives, leading to a greater freedom of word order than appears in modern French.

Old Provençal shares with Old French the distinctive feature of a two-case system which sets nominative apart from accusative, or oblique, in masculine nouns; Old Provençal goes perhaps a trifle further than its sister Gallic tongue in frequently extending the two-case system even to feminine nouns, something that French does far more sporadically. The machinery is the same in both cases: a distinct -*s* ending in the nominative singular and oblique plural, the lack of an ending in oblique singular and nominative plural.[2]

But aside from this all-important morphological characteristic, there is less similarity of phonological development between Old French and Old Provençal than there is between Provençal and Spanish, or Provençal and Italian.

What might be described, with qualifications, as "standard" Old Provençal does not diphthongize, save under exceptional circumstances, the

---

2. For Latin nouns that do not have -*s* in the nominative singular, the distinctive feature of the Latin original is normally retained: Latin *imperator, imperatore*(*m*) become Old French *emperedre, emperedour;* Latin *tropator, tropatore*(*m*) become Old Provençal *trovaire, trobador;* however, despite the fact that the distinction is already clear, both languages often add an -*s* to their nominative singular forms on the analogy of the majority of masculine singular nouns that have come by their -*s* legitimately; *emperedre, trovaire* are often flanked by *emperedres, trovaires.*

stressed vowels of Latin. There is syncopation of unstressed vowels to approximately the same degree as in French, but Latin final -*a* remains -*a* in Provençal, as in Italian or Spanish, instead of weakening into a schwa (or "mute" *e*) as in French. On the other hand, stressed Latin *u* is rounded into *ü*, as in French (some Provençal scholars disagree, but the evidence seems to be on the side of *ü*). Stressed *a* remains unchanged in Provençal, as in Spanish and Italian, instead of changing to *e* when free (i.e., at the end of a syllable), as in French. Voicing of intervocalic consonants occurs in Provençal, but to a lesser degree than in French. Provençal conserves the Latin diphthong *au*, which French turns into *o*; it does not palatalize *c* before *a*, as French does. But nasalization often goes farther than in French, with the nasal consonant disappearing completely (Latin *bene* to French *bien*, Provençal *be*). This mixture of phonological features, while it definitely sets off Provençal from French, also differentiates it from Italian, Spanish, even Catalan, to which it is closest.

A third classification is favored by some linguists for a collection of related dialects of eastern and southeastern France, western Switzerland, and extreme northwestern Italy. The dialects of this region, to which the collective name of Franco-Provençal has been given, while conforming to the general medieval two-case system of the entire Gallic area, agree in their sound structure sometimes with French, sometimes with Provençal, sometimes partly with the one, partly with the other (Latin -*are* verbs regularly appear as -*er* in French, -*ar* in Provençal; the Franco-Provençal dialects regularly show -*ar;* but if Latin -*are* is preceded by a velar consonant, they show -*ier*, like French).

What may have been the cause of the cleavage of the entire area of what was once Gaul into two separate linguistic systems (three, if we accept Franco-Provençal)? Caesar's threefold division of Gaul into a Belgian, an Aquitanian, and a Celtic area is not of much help. His Belgian area later becomes part of northern French (the Walloon dialect of Belgium, while distinctive, shows an overwhelming majority of northern French features); his Aquitanian area covers the modern Gascon area, but extends much farther into present Provençal territory. If we try to place the cleavage during the long period of Roman rule, it could be pointed out that the Provençal area coincides, very roughly, with Rome's Gallia Narbonensis, the northern French area with Gallia Lugdunensis. Others point to the fact that the Provençal area coincides roughly with the kingdom set up by the Visigoths in southern Gaul before they moved on to Spain, while northern French coincides with the region settled by the Franks; they even make the Franco-Provençal area coincide with the settlement of the Burgundians. Lastly, there is the undisputed historical fact that the Frankish monarchy, when first set up, extended its effective authority only to northern France, though it claimed to rule the entire country, and that the south of France was subjected to outside influences, not only from the Visigoths and Burgundians but also from the Spanish Moors and even the Byzantines and Genoese.

However this may be, the Old Provençal language was both a linguistic and a cultural reality from the early eleventh century through most of the thirteenth (that it existed even earlier is proved by the obvious Provençal admixture in the tenth-century *Passion du Christ*). But Old Provençal was more than a language and a literature. It was a way of life, far more luxurious, ostentatious, and gay than that of its grim northern neighbor. Both literature and way of life came to an end with the Albigensian Crusade, conducted by Philip Augustus of France and led by Simon de Montfort, on the somewhat specious pretext that the inhabitants of Provence were heretics and devil worshippers. The language remained, but as a series of oral dialects that tended more and more to degenerate into local patois. Attempts to revive Provençal as a literary tongue in the fourteenth century and later were unsuccessful, as was Frédéric Mistral's nineteenth-century Felibrigian revival, on the basis of a compromise of modern spoken dialects.

But the literary influence of Provençal, while short-lived, was far-reaching and enduring. The lyric forms of the troubadours penetrated Italy, Spain, Portugal, Germany, England, even northern France. They live on to this day.

9. Old Spanish, Portuguese, Catalan

Many linguists believe that the nascent Romance of the Iberian peninsula during the Visigothic period (ca. 500–711 A.D.) was marked both by substantial unity and by greater conservatism of the ancestral Latin than appeared elsewhere in the former Roman world. This seems to be borne out by the apparent lack of any consciousness of a break in Latin continuity indicated by the writers of the period (notably Isidore of Seville, who gave evidence of linguistic interest in his work on etymologies). There is also the fact that the language of the inscriptional material and the Vulgar Latin documents of the area, as well as its earliest Romance documents, indicate less in the way of regional diversities than appears at a later date. Also, what we are able to reconstruct of early Mozarabic from the *aljamiado* forms in Arabic and Hebrew script is of a strongly conservative nature.

Nevertheless, from the very inception of Romance documents, there is one morphological feature in which the languages and dialects of the Iberian peninsula reveal themselves as more innovational than those on the French side of the great divide: they all, without exception, indicate reduction of the all-important Latin case system to a single case, with rejection of the possibility of an opposition between nominative and oblique which the retention in pronunciation of final -*s* would have made possible.[1] In the singular, the single case of the Iberian languages may be

---

1. Had Spanish-Portuguese taken the same course as French-Provençal, the form most likely to have been taken by an imaginary Spanish two-case system for second declension masculine nouns would have been the following:

    Nominative singular—*ille mūrus* to (*el*) *muros*
    Oblique singular—*illum mūrum* (or *illō mūrō*) to (*lo*)*muro*
    Nominative plural—*illī mūrī* to (*li* or *le*) *mure*
    Oblique plural—*illōs mūrōs* to (*los*) *muros*

either the result of a merger of Latin accusative and ablative (with help from the dative), or the extension of the accusative to the exclusion of all other Latin cases; in the plural, the second hypothesis seems undeniable.

For the rest, the Iberian languages display, in varying degrees, conservative and innovational features. The latter are most pronounced in Castilian, the dialect that is at the root of modern Spanish, but with qualifications. The innovations appear definitely to a lesser degree than happens on the French side of the Pyrenean divide.

Dialectal divergences of a relatively minor nature begin to appear with the earliest documents. They seem based on the political subdivisions that arose after the Moorish conquest rather than on the earlier Roman subdivision of the peninsula into the three great areas of Tarraconensis, Baetica, and Lusitania. Also, they merge gradually into one another, without any sudden, definite geographical break such as can be observed in France or Italy. Lastly, the boundaries are fluctuating, advancing or receding in accordance with historical vicissitudes.

The entire peninsula south of the Cantabrian mountains having fallen into the hands of the Moors in the second decade of the eighth century, both literary production and the official use of Visigothic Romance in that area came to an abrupt halt. It is to be assumed that the Romance form known as Mozarabic continued to be spoken by the Christian populations, which, though subject to Arabic speakers, were still in the majority. The reflections of spoken Mozarabic appear only occasionally in Arabic and Hebrew script. To the extent that it can be reconstructed from these sporadic records, Mozarabic seems to have been fairly unified and strongly conservative.

In the free Christian north, five dialect bands begin to appear in the late tenth and eleventh centuries: Galician in the west; then, proceeding eastward, Leonese, with an Asturian subspecies; Castilian; Navarro-Aragonese; Catalan. Strongest of the Christian principalities was that of León, which exerted a measure of control over Galicia. The original Castilian area was small, being confined to the coastal region around Santander, and sandwiched in between Navarro-Aragonese and Basque-speaking regions to the east and the kingdom of León to the west. Navarro-Aragonese was confined to Aragón and Navarra, and soon fell under the influence of Catalonia, concerning whose language both historians and linguists entertain some doubts. The Catalan region was very much under French and Provençal influence, forming the Spanish March which bordered on the region of Septimania, a borderland at the eastern extremity of the Pyrenees where relatively easy passage between France and Spain is possible, and incursions on both sides were frequent.

The peninsular dialects (or languages), as they begin to unfold, all show common features, some to a greater, others to a lesser degree. Morphologically, all agree on a single case form for masculine as well as feminine nouns.

In phonology, stressed vowels retain the Vulgar Latin pattern, with opposition between open and closed *e*, open and closed *o*. Castilian is the first to indicate diphthongization of open *e* to *ie*, of open *o* to forms that fluctuate between *uo, ue,* and *ua*. Unlike what happens in French, this diphthongization occurs both in the free and the checked position, but does not occur when the vowel is followed by a palatal or by a palatalization. The phenomenon spreads quickly to Aragonese on the east (in fact, some claim it may have originated in western Aragonese), somewhat more slowly to Leonese on the west, and with the added feature that it is not impeded by a following palatalization. It does not extend to the two extremes, Galician on the west and Catalan on the east. Stressed *a* regularly stays unchanged, and there is no rounding of *o* or *u* into *ö* or *ü*. Syncopation of unstressed vowels is not quite so drastic as in the French-Provençal area, and some proparoxytonic words endure, in popular as well as learned forms. Final vowels generally remain. There is some weakening of final *-as* into *-es*, notably in Catalan and Asturian. Final long *-ī* weakens into *-e;* final *-o* and *-u* generally remain, but fall in Catalan; final *-e* tends to fall, particularly when it is not needed as a support vowel for a preceding consonant cluster; this phenomenon is fairly universal at the eastern or Catalan end, but is progressively more resisted as we move westward.

Intervocalic unvoiced consonants tend to voice, turn from plosives to fricatives, and fall, but to varying degrees and at different points of time in the different areas. The tendency toward palatalization of certain consonant groups (*pl-, fl-, cl-, -ct-, -mn-, -ll-,* etc.) is general, but occurring in varying degrees and at different points in time, and the ultimate outcomes are often quite different. Nasalization appears in Catalan to the same drastic degree as in Provençal, to the point of complete disappearance of the nasal consonant. It also appears in Galician-Portuguese, but rather late, and it is of a different type from that of French, Provençal, and Catalan.

At the outset of the era that followed the Moorish invasion, Galicia was closely united with the Leonese-Asturian realm. But from the eleventh century on, the Galician push to the south led to the reconquest of Coimbra in 1064, of Lisbon in 1147. The liberated regions constituted themselves into a separate kingdom of Portugal in 1143, and as the Portuguese drive southward continued, Portugal acquired roughly its present boundaries in 1250, enabling the Portuguese to boast that their Reconquest was completed over two centuries before that of Spain. In the process, however, they became separated from their original homeland, and Galicia, while linguistically linked to Portugal, politically remained with Spain. The Galician language (or dialect, as we choose to view it) has far more points of contact with Portuguese than with Castilian (no diphthongization of short *e* and *o;* metaphonic influence of final on accented vowels; *ai, au* becoming *ei, ou,* but not progressing to *e, o; pl-, fl-,* and *cl-* groups shifting to the palatal sound of English *sh* (spelt *ch* in Portuguese), not to *ll-;* nasalization; use of *tenere* as an auxiliary in preference to *habere;* even the fall of *-n-* and *-l-* between vowels (but this, if we believe the testimony of Mozarabic documents, not until the late tenth century).

The kingdom of León, which preferred to use Galician as its literary language, displays hesitation in most of these matters, diphthongizing short *e* and *o* only sporadically at first, then to a greater degree as the Castilian influence grows stronger, and producing the diphthongs even before a palatal; and halting the evolution of *-li-* and *-cl-* at the *-ll-* stage instead of going on to the *j* of *ojo,* originally pronounced like the *s* of *measure;* of *-ct-* at the *-it-* stage instead of progressing to *-ch-,* pronounced as in *chef;* of *ai, au,* at the *ei, ou* stage instead of reducing them to *e, o.* Squeezed between an expanding Castilian on the east and an expanding Portuguese on the west, Leonese falters, fluctuates, and ultimately relinquishes its claim to separate languagehood.

Castilian, most innovative of the Iberian varieties, shares with Navarro-Aragonese the tendency to diphthongize Latin short *e* and *o,* to reduce *ai* and *au* to *e* and *o,* to carry palatalization of various groups to further lengths than the other dialects (but this in part occurs after the end of the medieval period).

Most characteristic of Castilian sound changes is the transformation of initial Latin *f-* into an *h-* that ultimately becomes silent; but this phenomenon, too, seems relatively recent (fourteenth century at the earliest, at least for what concerns documentary evidence). Some linguists believe that the change is due to Basque influence (Basque has no *f-* sound); others that it goes back to the Iberian substratum, and that even the Ibero-Romans pronounced Latin *f* as a bilabial rather than a labiodental spirant, with this bilabial subsequently becoming an aspirated *h*- sound (that a bilabial *f* interchanges readily with an aspirated *h* before certain vowels is indicated by modern Japanese, and even by some southern Italian dialects). The later disappearance of aspirate *h* in pronunciation has many parallels, including the *h*-mute and even the *h*-aspirate of French.

Historically, Castile, an outgrowth of León, became semi-independent, then was reunited to León, but this time it was in the lead. The medieval kingdom of Castile and León continued for some time to use Galician as a literary and poetic tongue, but its official tongue was Castilian rather than Leonese. It was this tongue that predominated in the later stages of the *Reconquista*, that mingled in the south with the language of the Mozarabic population, giving rise to Andalusian, and that ultimately became modern Spanish, for which "Castilian" is often used as a synonym, though more and more guardedly as it spreads to the New World.

Navarro-Aragonese, closely linked to Castilian at its western end, merging with Catalan at the eastern, is more conservative than Castilian in its medieval period. It tends to preserve intervocalic unvoiced consonants,[2] and initial groups like *cl-, pl-, fl-*. On the other hand, it diphthongizes Latin short *e* and *o* into *ie* or *ia, ue, uo,* or *ua*, respectively, even if a palatal follows. But it does not generally go along with Castilian in palatalizing *muito* to *mucho*, or *fillo* to *fijo* (modern *hijo*).

The union of Aragón and Navarra was completed in 1076. The fusion of the Navarro-Aragonese kingdom with Catalonia in 1137 led to the formation of an eastern Spanish realm that rivaled the western one constituted by León, Castile, Galicia, and the Asturias. Aragonese and Catalan were both used in the early days of the eastern fusion, but Cata-

---

2. This feature is noticeable in the earliest Spanish document, the Glosses of San Millán, which comes from La Rioja, a region that practically straddles the Castilian-Aragonese linguistic border; see Appendix G.

lan, the more literary and commercial language of the two, tended to become more and more the official tongue. This situation was reversed in 1469, when Isabel of Castile and Ferdinand of Aragón were married. While this union did not lead to any immediate linguistic changes, it strengthened the position of Castilian, which had already established itself as the speech of the leading group in the reconquest of Spain from the Moors. Catalan continued in official use in the former kingdom of Aragón, while Aragonese, already fairly close to Castilian, began to sink to the rank of a dialect.

Most distinctive of the peninsular languages is Catalan, which many believe had its roots on the French-Provençal side of the Pyrenean divide. It is quite true that by and large Catalan resembles Provençal more than it does Castilian, both linguistically and for what concerns literary development. In the most important morphological respect, however, Catalan agrees with the Hispanic complex, displaying a single case from the very inception of its documents. A secondary point is that Catalan does not round *u* to *ü*, as do the French and Provençal dialects (for certain reservations concerning the rounding of *u* in Provençal, at least in the medieval period, see p. 113). Also, there is a slight tendency to retain proparoxytones, and *au* becomes *o*, as in Castilian, instead of remaining *au*, as in Provençal.

For the rest, Catalan largely agrees with Provençal. There is no diphthongization of stressed Latin short *e* and *o* save where a palatal follows. Final *-a* is retained, as in both Provençal and Castilian, but in the plural the *-ās* ending weakens to *-es;* this also happens in Asturian, probably by sheer coincidence. Final *-u, -o, -e,* even *-i,* are dropped, as in Provençal and French. The voicing process for intervocalic unvoiced plosives follows the Provençal pattern, but the latter is not startlingly different from the Castilian. Nasalization is on the Provençal model, with frequent complete disappearance of the nasal consonant. A further reminder of the French-Provençal system is the occasional appearance of Latin *illōrum* as the third plural possessive (but this also appears in early Aragonese, which has *lures* corresponding to Catalan *llurs*). Some Catalan palatalizations partake of both Provençal and Castilian, with split orthographies (Latin *-nn-* to Spanish *-ñ-,* Catalan *-ny-,* Provençal *-nh-;* Latin *-ll-* to Spanish and Catalan *-ll-* as against Provençal *-lh-*).

In several respects, Catalan displays its own individuality, as in the vocalization of various consonants that become final (Latin *pacem, cru-*

cem, pedem, tenetis to Catalan *pau, creu, peu, teniu,* versus Provençal *patz, crutz, pe, tenetz*).

While French linguists normally view Catalan as an offshoot of Provençal, and Spanish linguists claim it is a peninsular dialect, the Catalans themselves proudly insist that it is a separate Romance language. In this view they are probably justified.

During medieval times, Catalan was extended to the Balearic Islands and the entire Valencian region, which today speak their own subvarieties of Catalan, even to the region of Alghero in western Sardinia. Catalan is also spoken on the French side of the Pyrenees, near the coast, in the region of Roussillon, with a sharp break at the line of the Corbières. This sharp break is not paralleled on the Aragonese side, where Catalan and Aragonese merge gradually into each other.

In the matter of vocabulary, the peninsular languages display their individuality not so much in the common Latin base (though it has been claimed that certain words come from a more archaic stage of Latin than the words adopted in French and Italian) as in the words inherited by Hispanic Latin from the mysterious and largely unknown Iberian substratum, or acquired at various times from close contact with the Basques, whose language may or may not go back to Iberian, or even be linked with the Caucasian languages. Most of this element remains confined to the peninsular languages, though a few picturesque words, like *bizarro,* have been carried to the other Romance languages and even to non-Romance tongues.

Far more important is the vast vocabulary accretion that Spanish and Portuguese received from the Arabic of the Moors, a great deal of which moved on to other western languages. Arabic words that are internationally spread from the Iberian peninsula often carry the Arabic article *al-* (*alchemy, alcohol, alkali, algebra,* etc.), and this distinguishes them from the words that entered the European languages by way of the Arabs who conquered Sicily and held it for well over a century. (The Spanish *alcázar* is an Arabized Latin *castrum;* the same word appears in Sicily as *Cassaro,* the shore drive of Palermo). It is of interest that many words brought into the peninsula by the Moors had previously been borrowed by the Arab conquerors from the Greek and Latin of pre-Moslem North Africa (the Greek *oryza,* for instance, gives rise to the Spanish *arroz*). Lastly, Spanish and Portuguese, when they finally emerge, do not always coincide in making use of Arabic loanwords. At the Spanish-Portuguese

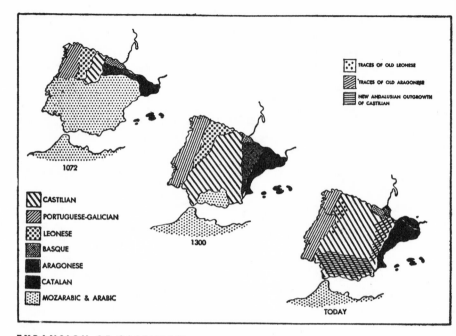

TRACES OF OLD LEONESE

TRACES OF OLD ARAGONESE

NEW ANDALUSIAN OUTGROWTH OF CASTILIAN

1072

CASTILIAN

PORTUGUESE-GALICIAN

LEONESE

BASQUE

ARAGONESE

CATALAN

MOZARABIC & ARABIC

1300

TODAY

EXPANSION OF CASTILIAN

As Castilian speakers take the lead in the reconquest of Spain from the Moors, their speech acquires greater prestige than that of adjoining groups (Leonese, Aragonese) and tends to squeeze them against Portuguese and Catalan. The latter, farther removed from Castilian, show greater resistance.

border one notices the customs-houses, *aduana* on the Spanish side, *alfândega* on the Portuguese; both are Arabic, but from different Arabic words. Portuguese uses the Arabic-derived *alfaiate* for "tailor"; Spanish the Latin-derived *sastre*.

The Germanic element in both Spanish and Portuguese is not quite as abundant as it is in French or Italian, and seems to have in large part antedated the Germanic invasions of the peninsula, indicating that the invaders, particularly the Visigoths, had already gone over to Vulgar Latin when they arrived.

This mixture of tongues, including not only Indo-European Latin, Greek, Germanic, and Celtic, but also Semitic Arabic and Hebrew and non-Indo-European Iberian and Basque, imparts to Spanish and Portuguese a distinctive international flavor which could lead early Spanish philologists, like Juan de Valdés, to claim that Spanish was indeed a

composite rather than a basically Romance language. But French philologists managed to fall into the same error concerning French, and at
a later date and with less justification than Valdés.

At the beginning of the period that follows the Moorish invasion of
711, the indications, scanty as they are, point to a substantial unity for
the primitive Romance of the Iberian peninsula, with the gradual emergence of the five great dialect bands: Galician, with its later offshoot
Portuguese; Asturo-Leonese; Castilian; Navarro-Aragonese; Catalan. Subsequent historical factors lead to the emergence of three of these (Portuguese, Castilian, Catalan) as full-fledged languages, and the relegation
of Asturo-Leonese and Navarro-Aragonese to relative obscurity by the
year 1500. As one would expect from general linguistic history, each of
the three survivors developed its own dialectal varieties. All three were
firmly established, with Spanish (in its official Castilian variety) and
Portuguese on their way to gigantic overseas expansions that would
eventually set them among the world's leading languages.

Catalan, not so fortunate by reason of its political link to Castilian,
was destined for a stormy career that would involve no further expansion, but rather a restriction of its area, speaking population, and influence, and relegation to the post of a secondary language overshadowed
by the dominant Castilian that was once its partner and equal, a melan-
choly example of what blind historical forces can do to a flourishing,
promising language. But this does not deter its unbowed speakers from
continuing to cultivate and cherish it, both in spoken and in literary form,
to the present day.

10. *Old Italian (with Sardinian, Rheto-Rumansh, Dalmatian)*

Italy, home and heartland of the Latin language and the Roman Empire, was the first of the future Romance lands to achieve Latin linguistic unity, if we are to believe the testimony of Quintilian (see p. 50). But during the period that intervened between the earlier Germanic invasions (middle of the fifth century) and the appearance of the first Romance written records (ninth century for France, tenth for Spain and Italy), Italy had become, politically speaking, the most fragmented of the Roman lands. The Merovingian and Carolingian dynasties in France had led to a substantial process of unification, equalled and probably surpassed in the Iberian peninsula during the two centuries of Visigothic rule. Even after the Moorish invasion, the linguistic unity of northern Spain had scarcely been broken, while in the south the Mozarabic of the Christian population had become largely frozen.

In Italy, successive waves of Visigoths, Heruli, and Ostrogoths had swept the country, encountering two lines of resistance—the papal domains and the Byzantine south. Theodoric the Ostrogoth had almost succeeded in establishing a Germanic kingdom of Italy, but after his death in 526 the Byzantine armies of Belisarius and Narses had swept it away in 552, only to see Italy reinvaded from the north in 568 by the Longobards, who for over a century enjoyed possession of northern Italy with the sole exception of a few coastal cities, encountering once more the resistance of the papal domains and the Byzantine south. In 754 and again in 774, Pepin and Charlemagne had come to the rescue of the Papacy, taking over the Longobardic north in the process. But early in the ninth century the new Saracen menace from North Africa had engulfed Sicily and wrested large portions of the south from its Byzantine occupants. In consequence of these happenings, Italy had been broken into three large cultural units marked by fluctuating boundaries: a north, reaching down into Tuscany, which had been heavily exposed to a three-fold Germanic influence—Ostrogothic, Longobardic, and Frankish; a central area, including the city of Rome and extending to the middle Adriatic, in which the Latin tradition, both imperial and ecclesiastic, managed to live on; and a south, subjected to the Greek-speaking Byzantines and the Arabic-speaking Saracens.

Now, as the end of the first Christian millennium approached, and the first documents of the popular tongue began to make their timid appearance, new historical forces were on their way to confirm and add to the process of fragmentation: the overlordship of the German emperors over the north, proclaimed by Otto I in 962, but attended by a shadowy sovereignty that left the inhabitants of the cities largely free to develop their own interests and institutions; and the Norman reconquest of most of the south and of Sicily (the latter completed by 1060). But the power of the German emperors was broken by Barbarossa's defeat at Legnano at the hands of the embattled Lombard League in 1176, which led to the emergence of the northern city-states as small but fully independent political units; while in the south and Sicily the Norman rule gave way to the Swabian, which was in turn overthrown by the French followers of Charles of Anjou, who remained for a time in southern Italy, but were quickly expelled from Sicily by a popular revolt (the Sicilian Vespers), and replaced by the Aragonese.

That this lack of political unity led to linguistic confusion and the burgeoning of local dialects is beyond dispute. On the other hand, in spite of all historical vicissitudes, the Italian soil, homeland of the Latin language and seat of the Christian Church that had made that language its own, preserved a measure of the Latin cultural tradition that the other Romance lands could not duplicate. This is perhaps why the consciousness of the break between the popular tongue and the cultural and ecclesiastical Latin came later to Italy than to the other countries. There had been a "vulgar" variety of Latin even back in the days of the Empire. In the absence of a new standard, the local spoken dialects could still be regarded as continuators of that "vulgar" tongue, even while an earnest effort was made to use the "real" Latin both in writing and in ecclesiastical and learned speech.

But this self-deception, fostered even by Dante around the year 1300, could not be continued indefinitely, particularly in the face of an ever-growing body of vernacular writings, even of a literature of sorts.

The earlier documents we have described all bear a clearly identifiable dialectal imprint, and this continued to the end of the twelfth century and beyond. Then, around the middle of the thirteenth century, spurred by an ever-increasing literary production, there came the beginning of a purely literary language, destined to serve the entire country. But it was by its very nature an aristocratic tongue, for the use of the nobility, the clergy, the universities (the latter two only whenever they might condescend to come down from the still thoroughly current scholarly Latin); then spreading gradually to the wealthier and more leisured classes, the merchants, artisans, and tradesmen of the cities. The tillers of the soil, who still constituted the overwhelming majority of the population, were thoroughly illiterate, and had no occasion to travel, blissfully continued to speak their local dialects, already widely divergent and tending to diverge more and more.

Here begins the great Italian dichotomy between language and dialect, later synthesized in the *Questione della Lingua,* a problem that beset the best minds of the Italian Renaissance and that is still basically unsolved today.

The linguistic reality has to do with the popular, spoken, living dialects, which are barely beginning to give way in modern times to the great forces of modern standardization—literacy and education, widespread travel, and, above all, the mass media of oral-aural communication, spoken films, radio, and television. The theory around which the great *Questione* revolves is the nature and origin of the literary language, which, in the exaggerated words of an expert observer not too long departed, "everyone reads and writes but no one speaks."

It was historical reality that led to the growth on Italian soil of dialectal varieties far more divergent and mutually incomprehensible than in any other Romance land. But whence came that beautiful literary tongue that finally emerged in the poetry of Dante and Petrarch and the prose of Boccaccio? Was it merely a sublimation and refinement of the Florentine dialect common to all three? Was it, as Dante seems to imply in his *De Vulgari Eloquentia* of 1305, a compromise language put together for the sake of literary and cultural opportunism out of mixed contributions from north, south, and center, a sort of primitive Esperanto for the use of the various and variegated Italian regions? Was it something that had been slowly and painfully evolving through the centuries, mainly for commercial reasons, among the seafarers who plied Italy's extensive coastlines, and who had to communicate with the inhabitants in every port they touched, be it southern Palermo and Amalfi, central Pisa and Leghorn, northern Genoa and Venice? Was it something that developed at Italy's early and flourishing universities, Bologna and Salerno, Milan and Florence and Rome, where students from every part of Italy, who could communicate among themselves and with their professors in Latin, neoclassical or macaronic, had also to communicate with the local townsfolk, who knew no Latin?

All these hypotheses are possible, if not equally plausible, and all probably hold some measure of truth. As for the fact that the Italian language, when it finally emerges, has more points of contact with the central dialects than with the northern and southern extremes, that is to be expected, from the very bridge position of those central dialects, coupled with their relatively conservative features. That a language conceived primarily for literary purposes should from its outset be heavily infiltrated with ancestral Latin, that too is to be expected. Where else but to the firmly established, polished tongue of their Roman forebears would the Italians turn when at a loss for a word, an expression, a grammatical construction?

The first full blooming of an Italian literary school took place in Sicily, at the court of Frederick II of Hohenstaufen, a lover of culture who gathered to his side not only educated people from all parts of Italy, but from foreign lands as well, notably Provence. Most of the writers of the Sicilian school use a language which, though interlarded with Provençal literary terms, cannot be described save as Italian. One of them, Stefano Protonotaro, uses a polished Sicilian dialect which stands out starkly against the contributions of the others. Cielo d'Alcamo, said to have been the first of the school, uses an Italian that is rather liberally sprinkled with Sicilian terms and forms. For the others, it is claimed that their original contributions were in Sicilian (though they were by no means all Sicilians), like Protonotaro's, but that the original manuscripts have disappeared, and what we have are copies found in Tuscan libraries and evidently adapted by Tuscan scribes to the tongue of their own region. This is quite plausible, considering the practices of medieval scribes and copyists. The fact, however, remains that it was Sicily, not Tuscany, that first witnessed the birth of a full-blown native Italian literature, however much influenced by Provençal.

Almost contemporaneous with the Sicilian school is that of Bologna, headed by Guido Guinicelli. He and his followers are described as Bolognesi of culture and refinement, and the *Dolce Stil Nuovo* which they created is a fair model of literary Italian. Here the question of Tuscan influence and Tuscan copyists of original manuscripts again comes up. The local dialect of Bologna, a Gallo-Italian variety, goes with Piedmontese, Lombard, and Ligurian, and in many respects outstrips them all in diverging from the Italian literary standard. Could Guinicelli have created his *Dolce Stil Nuovo* in an original Bolognese, which would be more difficult than Sicilian to transpose into Florentine? Or did he pick up in Florence the refined language in which his writings appear? If so, why? Florence enjoyed in Guinicelli's days a measure of commercial and financial predominance, but not too much of a literary one, since Dante, Boccaccio, and Petrarch had not yet appeared. Could his have been a deliberately esthetic choice, based on the fact that Florentine makes a more favorable impression on the ear than does Bolognese? Or did Dante's *Volgare Illustre* already exist in embryonic form, and were Guinicelli and his followers among the first to avail themselves of its possibilities? These questions still await an answer.

Nor is the answer made easier by the fact that Umbrian writers, like Francis of Assisi and Jacopone of Todi, and even Tuscans, like Guittone d'Arezzo, display abundant localisms in their writings. But since their spoken forms are central Italian, they come close enough to Florentine standards not to arouse too much notice or controversy.

However all this may be, whether Dante was right or wrong in describing his ideal *Volgare Illustre* as basically a compromise language, embodying the best of north, south, and center, leavened with strong doses of Latin, the nature of the literary language that unmistakably existed from Dante's time on stands revealed as without doubt the most conservative of the official Romance tongues, both in its phonetic structure and its vocabulary; yet with qualifications, for where this language decides to follow the general Romance phonetic trends it more than holds its own in the matter of drastic innovations. Compare, for example, Latin *tenere habeo* with French *tiendrai*, Spanish *tendré*, Italian *terrò*; or Latin *rapidum* with Spanish *raudo*, Italian *ratto*, side by side with "learned" *rapido*; or Latin *fabula* with Italian *fiaba* and *fola*, side by side with semilearned *favola*. Italian displays more doublets and triplets (words that evolve in learned, semipopular, and full popular fashion) than any of its sister languages; and we are only begging the question, and justifying Dante's composite-language view, when we attribute the ultrapopular developments to dialectal influences or borrowings.

In the matter of phonology, one prominent linguist has gone so far as to assert that the sound structure of Italian had already been reached by the year 400 A.D. This is an exaggeration, but it is a fact that by and large the phonetic scheme of Italian stays closer to that of our reconstructed Vulgar Latin than does that of any other Romance tongue with the exception of Sardinian.

The Vulgar Latin seven-vowel scheme still appears in the stressed vowel pattern of Italian, with the conservation of *a*, long *i*, and long *u;* the merger of long *e* and short *i* into closed *e*, in opposition to the open *e* that comes from Latin short *e;* the parallel merger of long *o* and short *u* into closed *o*, in opposition to the open *o* that comes from Latin short *o*. The only concession to further Romance trends is the diphthongization, by no means universal, of open *e* into *ie*, open *o* into *uo*. There is no metaphonic effect[1] upon stressed vowels from final vowels, such as appears generally in Portuguese, Rumanian, and most Italian dialects of the north and south, and occasionally in French and Spanish. Final vowels survive better than they do elsewhere in the Romance world, with only the occasional, often optional fall of *-e* and *-o*. Syncopation of unstressed vowels is widely resisted, but with numerous and sometimes startling exceptions; yet the very numerous Italian proparoxytones can by no means all be described as of learned origin (Latin *numerum* to learned *numero*, popular *novero*).

Consonants resist voicing in Italian to a greater degree than in other Romance languages, with the possible exception of Rumanian. Yet the normal Romance trend of unvoiced plosive to voiced plosive to voiced fricative to complete fall is often in evidence. Italian not only resists simplification of double consonants, but often doubles single consonants; regionally, this is a process most frequent in the southern and central dialects, almost completely absent in northern varieties. There is plenty of palatalization in Italian, but no nasalization, save dialectally. Where Italian outstrips its sister tongues is in the general dropping of Latin final consonants, particularly morphologically significant *-s* and *-t*, as well as *-m*.

In morphology, Italian joins the Iberian rather than the Gallic system

---

1. For an explanation of this term, see Appendix E and the Glossary.

in reducing the Latin case system to a single case from the outset of its documents. But while the singular of nouns and adjectives parallels Iberian development, the plural shows forms in -*i* and -*e* that seem derived from Latin plural nominatives. For this there is apparent justification in the fact that with the fall of final -*s* the distinction between singular and plural would have been lost had plural forms been derived from Latin accusative plurals. Numerous other theories concerning the Italian plurals have been advanced (see Appendix I).

The Italian verb system follows rather closely that postulated for Vulgar Latin, but Latin second and third conjugations merge save in the infinitive.

The Italian definite article is complicated by numerous euphonic forms that are to be used in conjunction with the sound that follows, and these in turn combine with various prepositions in similar schemes. But some of these developments come rather late, and may be due to dialectal conflicts. Personal pronouns retain to a slightly greater degree than in other Romance languages vestiges of the Latin case system (e.g., nominative *egli*, accusative *lo*, dative *gli*, ablative *lui*).

The Italian vocabulary, especially of the literary variety, is more firmly based on Latin than is the case in other Romance languages. Borrowing from the parent language is extremely easy for a tongue whose basic phonetic pattern remains close to the ancestral one. This also means that in the case of many words the distinction between popular and learned development is hard to make. What else could *capra* have become in central Italian but *capra*, with no palatalization of *c* before *a*, and conservation of stressed and final *a* and of the intervocalic -*pr*- group? *Raro* from *rarum* could very easily be popular, quite unlike French *rare* (whose popular development would have been *rer), were it not for the presence in the language of *rado*, which shows a popular change from *r* to *d* that parallels *chiedere* from *quaerere*. The literate speaker of Italian undertaking to read Classical Latin without having studied it has very little trouble understanding the individual words; his difficulty is in putting them together so they will make sense (Dante had remarked that his *Volgare Aulico* was Latin without the rules of grammar; this was somewhat of an exaggeration, and a modern linguist would say instead that the morphology and syntax had undergone a radical transformation in passing from Classical Latin to standard Italian, while the phonology and vocabulary had changed relatively little).

But this free-and-easy vocabulary interchange between Latin and Italian does not at all mean that Italian is lacking in loanwords from the most disparate sources, as well as in new formations based on Latin roots, prefixes, and suffixes. In addition to the very numerous words that Latin had borrowed from Etruscan, Oscan, Greek, Celtic, Germanic, and other sources, some of which are attested in Classical times, others hypothetical, there are the many words brought in by the Ostrogoths and Longobards, a few possibly even by the Franks. Many Arabic and Persian words came into the early literary language, some by way of Sicily, others from the Crusades, still others from Spain. Many were the French and Provençal words that entered Italian through early literary and cultural contacts, along with suffixes of French and Provençal origin that lent themselves to processes of word formation (among them *-aggio; -iere,* with its variants *-ieri* and *-iero; -anza*). Dante's lexicon and those of his contemporaries and immediate successors give abundant evidence of all these borrowings, plus many occurrences of words that come not only from the Tuscan dialects but from those of the north and south, giving further credence to Dante's conglomerate theory.

Italian, in its literary variety, appears firmly fixed by the beginning of the fourteenth century, and develops from that point on as a cultural tongue for all of Italy, with fairly prompt official recognition in all or most of the country's fragmented political units.

The dialects continue in local spoken use, and several of them have given rise to flourishing dialectal literatures, which are, however, inevitably influenced by the standard literary tongue. This is particularly true of Roman, Neapolitan, Sicilian, Milanese, and Venetian.

With the final unification of Italy in 1870 there was a definite, though at first not too successful, attempt to impose the literary language as a spoken standard, mainly through the instrumentality of the schools and the governmental bureaucracy. It is only in very recent times, with the reinforcement supplied by spoken films, radio, and television, that the process of spreading the national standard among the younger generations has gained a considerable measure of success, to the point where the dialects are beginning to be threatened, if not with extinction, at least with drastic restriction, even among the masses of the population.

The rich variety of Italian dialects will be discussed in a later chapter. There are also, however, spoken wholly or partly on politically

Italian soil, three varieties that by reason of their strongly individualistic features can hardly be classed as Italian dialects, and are best described as separate Romance "languages," even though they lack the national, official status usually associated with the word "language." This in spite of the fact that some linguists, including Dante, have at various times, often for political rather than linguistic reasons, described them as dialects of Italian.

On the island of Sardinia there appear two varieties, Logudorese in the center of the island, Campidanese in the south, which in the opinion of most experts fail to meet the tests that would affiliate them with the Italian system (chief of these tests is the fall of Latin final -s, and consequent derivation of plural forms from what seems to be the Latin nominative rather than the accusative). The northern Sardinian dialects, Gallurese and Sassarese, not only pass the tests, but are definitely linked with Corsican, which is a central Italian dialect.

Central Sardinian Logudorese is in the matter of sound structure by far the most conservative of all Romance varieties. For what concerns stressed vowels, it follows not the Vulgar Latin, but rather the Classical Latin scheme, with merger of long *i* and short *i*, of long *u* and short *u*, instead of the more usual long *e* short *i*, long *o* short *u*, combinations. There is no diphthongization whatsoever. It preserves the final vowels of Classical Latin, with *o* and *u* kept separate (but final short *i* goes with the *e*'s). It keeps intact Latin velars before front vowels, and preserves Latin final -s and -t, as well as *pl-*, *cl-*, *fl-*, groups. On the other hand, it labializes Latin *qu* and *gu* into *b* or *bb* (*equa*, "mare," to *ebba*), turns Latin -*ll*- into a high alveolar -*ḍḍ*- (*bello*, "beautiful," to *beḍḍu;* this happens also in Sicilian, Calabrian, and Corsican), turns -*gn*- into -*nn*- (*legnum*, "wood," to *linnu*). There is a minimum of progression from unvoiced to voiced plosives between vowels. Plural forms are definitely from the Latin accusative, as in the Iberian languages. The definite article is derived from Latin *ipse*, not from *ille* (this happens also in varieties of Catalan, in Provençal, and occasionally in Sicilian and some of the mainland Italian southern dialects). Campidanese, while it goes along with Logudorese in most of these features, shows traces of Sicilian or possibly mainland Italian influence.

Historically, the aboriginal inhabitants of Sardinia are said to have been of "Libyco-Iberian" or possibly Liguric origin, and have left no documentary or inscriptional traces. From about 500 B.C. to the time of the First Punic War Sardinia was under some measure of Carthaginian influence. The island was among the first Roman conquests outside of the Italian mainland, and Roman rule was established in 238 B.C. Little is heard of Sardinia in Roman times, save that it was one of Rome's grain and mineral producing regions, and was also used as a place of deportation for rebellious Italian populations, such as the Oscans who resisted Rome in the Social War, and later for recalcitrant Jews and Christians. The relative remoteness and inaccessibility of the island led to a state of isolation which is suspected of being the main cause of the archaism of the Sardinian language.

After the fall of the Empire, Sardinia was subjected to incursions by the Vandals, temporary occupation by the Byzantines in the sixth century, new incursions by the Saracens from the eighth to the eleventh century. Later it was a bone of contention between the seafaring republics of Genoa and Pisa. It finally fell to the lot of the Aragonese at the outset of the eighteenth century; this led to the formation of a Catalan-speaking settlement at Alghero, on the western coast. It was later awarded to the dukes of Savoy, who united it to their holdings in northwestern Italy and transformed it into the Kingdom of Sardinia, which was the springboard for the ultimate unification of Italy.

While there is next to no literary production in Sardinian, there are eleventh- and early twelfth-century charters composed in both Logudorese and Campidanese, of which excerpts appear in Appendix J.

The Rheto-Rumansh system, considered by some linguists a separate Romance division, by others an extension, with conservative features, of the Gallo-Italian and Venetian dialects of northern Italy, by still others a connecting link between the Italian and the French, the Provençal, and particularly the Franco-Provençal systems, appears in several geographically separated areas: the Engadine-Grisons section of Switzerland; several valleys of Tridentine Venetia (Mareo and Val di Fassa among them); and the Friulian plain of northeastern Venetia, up to and including the Carnic Alps. While the Swiss variety is freer from Italian influences and more characteristic than the others, the Friulian is numerically the most important. As against some 50,000 Rumansh speakers on Swiss soil, and a few thousands in the Italian Alpine valleys, there are about half a million speakers of Friulian varieties.

Among the general characteristics of the Rheto-Rumansh group are the diphthongization of Latin short *e* and short *o* in the checked as well as in the free position; the diphthongization of Vulgar Latin closed *e* into *ei;* occasional change of stressed *a* to *e,* particularly after a palatalized velar, as in Franco-Provençal; rounding of long *u* into *ü* (but this mainly in the Swiss varieties); fall of final vowels save *-a,* which often weakens into *-e* (in Friulian there is also a feminine plural in *-is,* of uncertain origin); the general palatalization of the *ca* and *ga* groups; conservation of *cl-, pl-, fl-;* voicing of intervocalic unvoiced consonants, and fall of intervocalic voiced consonants. Morphologically important is the conservation of final *-s,* accompanied by a single case based on the Vulgar Latin accusative, or oblique (but this may have happened in Romance times).

Historically, the Rheto-Rumansh system is supposed to have originated with the Roman legions sent in early imperial days to form part of the barrier against possible Germanic invasions (the name Friuli comes from *Forum Julii,* "the Julian Gateway"). Place-names and other linguistic evidence indicate that the Rheto-Rumansh area was at one time much more extensive than it is today, stretching on the east as far as Trieste, and receding slowly from the mountain-crests and even the German areas on the other side of the Alps under the pressure of Germanic speakers.

The earliest document is, possibly, the Glosses of Kassel of the eighth or ninth century; but the indications are uncertain, and there is a distinct possibility that this early Germanic-Romance glossary and phrase book may represent a French or Franco-Provençal variety of Romance. The first sure documentation is a twelfth-century translation of a Latin sermon, which gives evidence of strong links to the Gallic system, including possible traces of a two-case declension.

For the Friulian variety, there are documents that go back to the end of the thirteenth century, but even at that early date they show signs of heavy Venetian linguistic infiltration. The Swiss variety split with the Reformation into a Catholic Surselvan and a Protestant Engadine variety, which survive to the present day. Both the Swiss and the Friulian varieties have developed in the course of recent centuries a fairly extensive popular literature.

In 1938, the Swiss government, reacting to Mussolini's claim that Rheto-Rumansh is a dialect of Italian, declared it to be a fourth "national" (but not "official") language of Switzerland. Despite the bolstering effects of this proclamation, there are signs that Swiss Rumansh tends more and more to give ground to German, the predominant language of the Grisons Canton. In like manner, Friulian, once beset by Venetian, is yielding ground to standard Italian.

Samples of both Swiss and Italian varieties appear in Appendix J.

The Dalmatian system stands out by reason of the fact that it is today completely extinct, though it has left traces of its former existence. It is supposed to be the continuator of the Vulgar Latin of the Roman province of Illyricum, on the eastern shore of the Adriatic, separated from Moesia and the Balkans by the Dinaric Alps.

The Romance-speaking inhabitants of the region are mentioned in the tenth century by Byzantine chroniclers; but even then they were hard-pressed by the southern Slavs who had overspread most of the Balkan area. At a later date, in the fourteenth century, they are described by a French visitor to Ragusa as being hemmed in by the Slavs, who have occupied most of the countryside, on the east, and by the Venetians, who have seized most of the cities, on the west. Another visitor reports a few words of the local Dalmatian dialect: *pen,* "bread," *teta,* "father," *chesa,* "house," *fachir* "to make." There are some medieval Ragusan documents, transcribed in Bartoli's study on Dalmatian, but they are so infiltrated with Latin and Venetian that they tell us little about the state of the local language. Dalmatian became more and more restricted, till in the late nineteenth century it became circumscribed to the island of Veglia (Krk) at the head of the Adriatic. Bartoli managed to record in transcription the speech of the last surviving speaker, Antonio Udina, before the latter's death.

From his study, the following facts appear concerning the language in its late nineteenth-century form: Vegliote (the dialect of the island of Veglia) seems to form a link between the eastern Italian dialects, Venetian, Abruzzian, and Apulian, and Rumanian. It displays extreme diphthongization of stressed vowels; strong conservatism, with practically no voicing or fall, for intervocalic consonants, but, like Rumanian, simplification of double consonants; conservation of the velar consonant sounds before *e* and sometimes before *i,* coupled with palatalization of *k* before Latin long *u,* pointing to a possible rounding of the *u* into *ü,* and of *qui* and *gui* to the sounds of English *ch* and *j.* In morphology, there is no indication of a double case, while the fall of final *-s* brings about the seeming use of Latin nominative forms in the plural, as in Italian. In these respects, Dalmatian would qualify as an Italian dialect. In the absence of satisfactory historical records, little can be said concerning the evolution of Dalmatian, though attempts have been made to reconstruct its phonetic development on the assumption that it was influenced by Serbo-Croatian.

A sample of nineteenth-century Vegliote, as reported by Bartoli, appears in Appendix J.

11. The Mystery of Rumanian

There are two problems connected with Rumanian, both complicated by the utter absence of reliable documents, particularly of a linguistic nature, before the sixteenth century of our era. This is in strong contrast with what appears in the Romance languages of the West, where there is an unbroken continuity of documentary evidence, however one may choose to interpret it.

The two questions that continue to plague Romance linguists and historians have to do with: (1) the origin of the Rumanian language, its point of separation from ancestral Latin, and the possible migrations of its speakers during its formative period; (2) the affiliations and links of Rumanian with the Western Romance languages, particularly those of the Italian and Dalmatian systems.

The Rumanian language is subdivided into a number of dialectal varieties, of which the main one is the Daco-Rumanian of Rumania as it exists today. Daco-Rumanian spills over the political borders into the provinces once known as Bessarabia (now the Moldavian S.S.R. of the U.S.S.R.) and Bukovina (now mostly incorporated into the Ukrainian S.S.R.). There are also smaller groups of Daco-Rumanian speakers in present-day Yugoslavia and Hungary. Of the twenty-two million inhabitants of Rumania proper, it is estimated that at least 85 percent have Daco-Rumanian as their mother tongue, while the linguistic minorities on Rumanian soil include some two million Hungarian speakers and perhaps half a million German speakers, both concentrated in the big bend of the Carpathian mountains of Transylvania, along with Bulgarians, Turks, and Tatars in Dobrudja, Serbians in Banat, and Jewish speakers of Yiddish scattered throughout the country. Daco-Rumanian is subdivided into three main subdialects, Transylvanian, Wallachian, and Moldavian, the last of which predominates in Bessarabia and Bukovina as well as in Moldavia.

Macedo-Rumanian is the language of half a million or more speakers (who also style themselves Arumanians) in northern Greece, eastern Albania, and southern Yugoslavia. A variant of Macedo-Rumanian is Megleno-Rumanian, spoken by a small enclave on Greek soil, northwest of Salonika. There are a few thousands of Istro-Rumanian speakers in the Val d'Arsa of Yugoslavia, near the Italian border, completely isolated from the other groups, but claimed to have been once connected with the Morlachians, or Mavrovlachs (Black Rumanians) of Dalmatia, now completely extinct.

Historically, the original Dacians are said to have been of "Thraco-Illyrian" stock, further described as a probable blend of Celtic Indo-Europeans with an aboriginal Iberian or "Mediterranean" population. They were known as Getae to the Greeks, as Daci to the Romans, and seem to have been a people of fairly high civilization, with a ruling aristocracy that may have given rise to the later boyars. Their best-known king, and also the last, was Decebalus, who successfully defied the Romans for a time, but was eventually defeated by Trajan's legions in A.D. 106. Eutropius, a fourth-century historian, implies that many of the original Dacians were killed, with many more fleeing beyond the pale of Roman power, and that they were replaced by Roman settlers.[1]

Others suppose that there was large-scale mingling of Trajan's settlers with the original Dacians. A list of Trajan's auxiliaries indicates that they were largely drawn from Spain, Rhetia, and Syria, while a Gaulish legion is mentioned as having participated in the earlier fighting against the Dacians. This would give the "Romans" who settled the province a highly international flavor, even though we may suppose that they were Romanized and Latinized.

After a relatively brief span of one and a half centuries of Roman occupation, the emperor Aurelian, under the pressure of the Ostrogoths, decided to withdraw the Roman legions from Dacia. To what extent the legions were accompanied in their retreat by the settlers *ex toto orbe*

---

1. *Trajanus . . . ex toto orbe romano infinitas eo copias hominum transtulerat ad agros et urbes colendas.* ("Trajan . . . had transferred there infinite numbers of men from the entire Roman world to settle the fields and cities.")

romano is not altogether clear. How many of them stayed behind in the face of the advancing Ostrogoths and made their peace with the invaders? Eutropius informs us that Aurelian *abductos Romanos ex urbibus et agris Daciae in media Moesia collocavit* ("placed the Romans transplanted from the towns and fields of Dacia in the center of Moesia"), and the section of Moesia to which they were transplanted was renamed *Dacia Aureliani,* "Aurelian's Dacia," possibly to make the refugees feel less homesick for the lands they had left behind. The original Dacia, north of the Danube, was later reoccupied by the Romans. Did the transplanted settlers move back *en masse* to their original homes? Did they do so only in part, or not at all? Could the ones who stayed north of the Danube when the Ostrogoths came in, and those who moved back to old Dacia when the Ostrogoths left, have been the ancestors of the present Daco-Rumanian speakers, while those who remained in their new location in Moesia gave rise to the speakers of Macedo-Rumanian and Megleno-Rumanian?

However this may have gone, another mighty invasion of the Balkan region by a new race, the Slavs, in the sixth century, threw the entire region into turmoil, cut communications between the Balkans and the West (though not between the Balkans and Byzantium), and led to presumed new mergers and new wanderings for the Latin speakers of the Balkan area. A Byzantine seventh-century writer gives, in connection with a Thracian campaign of the Byzantines in 587, what may be the earliest sample of Rumanian: *Torna, fratre!* ("Turn back, brother!"). But even if authentic, this could be merely a sample of Balkan Vulgar Latin. The word *sculca,* "awake," "out of bed," also mentioned as dating from this period, is derived, or at least connected with, Rumanian *a se culca* (from Latin *se collocare*), "to lie down," "to go to bed," with a hypothetical privative *ex-* prefixed.

In the sixth century there begins to appear in Byzantine writings the term *Vlachoi,* "Vlachs," "Wallachians," who are engaged in resisting the Slavs. This term, which passes on into Slavic and even Hungarian (*oláh, olasz*), seems to be of Germanic origin, possibly introduced by the Ostrogoths, and is related to the *Wealh,* applied by the Germanic invaders of the West to Romance speakers, and even to English *Welsh,* which the Welsh, who call themselves Cymri, never use. Its original meaning is uncertain (perhaps "foreigners"), but it carried even then a derogatory connotation. Modern German still speaks of *die Welschen* in the sense of "foreigners," particularly Romance speakers; but the derogatory connotation has largely been lost, as indicated by German Swiss *die welsche Schweiz* for the French-speaking cantons.

Further reference to the Vlachs is made by Byzantine writers in the tenth century in connection with the Bulgarian empire that had been established in the Balkans, of which the Vlachs were a part. The Arumanians are specifically described as located in Epirus. At the beginning of the eleventh century, the Magyars, who had previously occupied what is today Hungary, seized Transylvania, which their writers call *Pascua Romanorum*, "the grazing lands of the Romans." This seems to imply that some form of Roman culture had survived in that area. It was the Magyars who in the thirteenth century established, under their suzerainty, the principalities of Wallachia and Moldavia, thereby strengthening the theory of the development of Daco-Rumanian in the original area of Trajan's Dacia. But almost at the same time we are informed of Rumanian bridgeheads and settlements north of the Danube established from the south under the leadership of Radu Negru, which gives credence to the Moeso-Illyrian theory of reimportation of the language and its speakers from the lands south of the Danube. Could Daco-Rumanian have resulted from a blend of the tongue spoken by descendants of the Daco-Romans who never moved away from Dacia, but withdrew to the Carpathian fastnesses of Transylvania and kept their culture and tradition alive, with the speech of the Macedo-Rumanians who moved up from the south? There are in the Transylvanian dialects survivals of Latin words which in standard Rumanian have been replaced by Slavic loan words (*nea*, "snow," from Latin *nivis*, which in standard Rumanian is replaced by *zăpadă*, for instance). On the other hand, standard Rumanian shows a postposed definite article (*lupul*, "the wolf," from *lupum illum* or *lupus ille*), which it holds in common with other Balkan languages of non-Romance stocks, such as Bulgarian and Albanian, and which appears nowhere else in the Romance world (it might be argued that *lupus ille* is quite possible in Latin, though *ille lupus* is somewhat more frequent, and that the postposed article may simply have been a Rumanian choice of word order, made possible in part by Rumania's complete lack of contact with the Romance languages of the West).

Satisfactory Rumanian texts begin to appear early in the sixteenth century,[2] but by that time the Balkan region had fallen under the dominion of the Turks, who established a shadowy protectorate over the Rumanian

---

2. Samples of early Rumanian texts appear in Appendix K.

principalities, later more fully exercised through their Greek-speaking Phanariote emissaries. Bible translations from Old Church Slavonic, Greek, and Hungarian began to appear, along with sermons, homilies, and lives of saints. The language was Rumanian, the script was the Cyrillic used by the Eastern church in its Slavonic version. A moderate Roman Catholic influence began to infiltrate from Hungary about the end of the seventeenth century, but it was mainly restricted to Transylvania, which was under Hungarian rule. It was perhaps due to this influence that the Rumanians began to become aware of a Latin tradition, which had been altogether lost in the Balkans. In the middle of the seventeenth century Basarab introduced the Rumanian language, still in Cyrillic script, into the churches and schools in the place of Slavonic. The eighteenth century saw the beginning of Russian influence in Rumanian affairs, and while the Russians protected their Rumanian fellow Christians from the Turks, they also laid claim to Bessarabia, where there was and is a mixed population of Rumanians and Ukrainians. Moldavia and Wallachia finally united into a single realm, and a kingdom of Rumania was established in 1881. But long before that time a movement had grown for the replacement of the Cyrillic script by the Roman alphabet. Starting in 1830 with Lazar and Eliade, the alphabetic reform came to full fruition about 1880. During the intervening fifty-year period, the Rumanians, now keenly aware of their Latin origin, went about relatinizing their language, with wholesale importation of words from Latin, French, and Italian to replace many of the older, firmly established loanwords from Slavic, Greek, Hungarian, and Turkish. This gives the literary language of such modern writers as Eminescu and Alecsandri a strongly Romance flavor that does not altogether coincide with the popular speech. Since World War II and the Communist takeover in Rumania linguistic studies have followed a more historically scientific and less emotional approach. This, however, does not in any way detract from the fundamental nature of the language, which in spite of its many foreign borrowings is in its phonetic and grammatical structure strongly Latin-Romance, and very clearly linked to the Romance languages of the West.

The second and lesser problem in connection with Rumanian is whether it shows a stronger link to the centro-southern Italian system and what we can reconstruct of Dalmatian from Vegliote than with the Romance languages further to the west. Here, too, the evidence is mixed and inconclusive.

In the matter of sounds, Rumanian merges Latin stressed long *e* and short *i*, but not long *o* and short *u* (the two *o*'s go together, and so do the two *u*'s). Only Latin short *e* shows unconditional diphthongization into *ie*. While there is no nasalization of the French-Provençal or Portuguese type, stressed vowels are changed by the presence of a following *n* or *m*, assuming a closer sound (*a* to *î* or *â*, with a sound similar to *y* in English *rhythm; e* to *i; o* to *u*). A strong umlaut influence is exerted by final vowels upon the stressed vowels, with consequent diphthongization (*solem*, "sun," to *soare*). There is a definite weakening of final vowels, including *-a*, but their fall is only partial and, as attested by the older documents in Cyrillic script, fairly late. There is weakening, but little syncopation, of pretonic or posttonic vowels, giving the language a proparoxytonic rhythm at least equal to that of Italian and more pronounced than that of Spanish or Portuguese. There is very little voicing of unvoiced intervocalic plosive consonants, or fall of intervocalic fricatives, save for the labials *b* and *v* (*caballum*, "horse," to *cal*); on the other hand, Latin double consonants are regularly simplified. Palatalization of velars before front vowels is reminiscent of that of Italian. There is fall of final *-m, -s, -t*, and rhotacism of intervocalic *l* (*solem*, "sun," to *soare*). One phenomenon peculiar to Rumanian (it has only a partial parallel in Sardinian) is the labialization in intervocalic position of *-qu-, -gu-*, to *-p-*, *-b-*, (*aqua*, "water," to *apă; lingua*, "tongue," to *limbă*), as well as of *-ks-, -kt-*, to *-ps-, -pt-* (*lactem*, "milk," to *lapte*).

Morphologically, Rumanian is in a class by itself, with a double case which, unlike that of French-Provençal, merges Latin nominative and accusative into one case, Latin genitive and dative into another (occasional archaic vocative forms seem borrowed from Slavic).[3]

Plural nominative-accusative forms seem, as in Italian, to be derived from Latin nominatives. This may or may not be occasioned by the fall of final *-s*. The Rumanian adjective follows the general Romance system, and agrees with its noun in all positions. The postposed definite article, concerning whose origin opinions differ, may appear with the noun or the adjective, but, save archaically, not with both. There is a faint resem-

---

3. Taking Latin *lupus*, "wolf," as the basis, Rumanian has *lupŭ*; but *lupus ille*, *lupum illum*, become *lupul*, which is used as subject or direct object; *lupō illui* becomes *lupului*, "of or to the wolf"; *lupī illī* becomes *lupii*, "the wolves," subject or direct object; *lupīs illōrum* becomes *lupilor*, "of or to the wolves." There is some controversy as to whether the Rumanian case endings are carried primarily, or even exclusively, by the suffixed article, or appear in the noun as well, as feminine nouns of the type of *capră* would seem to indicate (the genitive-dative is *capre* [from *caprae*] if the definite article is not used; *caprei* [from *caprae illei*] is used to mean "of or to the goat").

blance to Spanish in the use of *pe* with a definitely known direct object (*a dat pe singurul lui fiu,* "gave his only son"), to French in the occasional use of *al* to indicate possession (*al meu,* "mine"). The Rumanian verb generally follows the Romance pattern, but the future is formed with an auxiliary that represents Latin *velle,* "to want," (*voi cântà,* "I shall sing"; etymologically, "I want to sing"), instead of the customary Romance *habere,* "to have." The phrase and sentence structure of Rumanian sometimes shows wide divergence from that of the Western languages. Certain constructions ("I want that I come," where other Romance languages use "I want to come") seem to have been borrowed from Greek.

The Rumanian vocabulary has perhaps a larger percentage of non-Latin loan words than any other Romance language, as is no doubt to be expected when one considers historical conditions, and this applies even to the borrowing of formative suffixes. While a speaker of French, Spanish, Portuguese, or Italian could understand most of the Latin element in the Rumanian vocabulary, he would be helpless without special study in the face of anything longer than three or four consecutive words. Where the words are of Latin origin, the Italian speaker would have the best chance of recognizing them.

The elements that Rumanian has in common with the centro-southern Italian system and the Dalmatian as represented by Vegliote are primarily the fall of final -*s* and the consequent derivation of plural forms from what appears to be the Latin nominative plural. Whether this represents an actual link or merely a parallel chance development is yet to be ascertained. The treatment of intervocalic occlusives (lack of voicing), while at first glance it seems promising, is contradicted by the highly contrasting treatment of Latin double consonants (the strong gemination tendencies of centro-southern Italian versus the general simplification of Rumanian, which reminds one of French, Spanish, and Portuguese). In other respects, Rumanian displays, along with undoubted Latin origin, a sturdy individuality, unhampered by the constant interrelation that prevailed among the Western Romance languages during their most formative period. Under the circumstances, it seems more reasonable to view Rumanian as a fourth major Romance subdivision than to link it with centro-southern Italian and Dalmatian into an "eastern" Romance, to which is opposed a "western" Romance composed of Spanish-Portuguese, French-Provençal, and the dialects of northern Italy.

12. The Renaissance

It is easier to describe the Renaissance than to define it, or even to local-
ize it in time. To some experts, the Renaissance began in thirteenth-century
Italy, even before Dante, Petrarch, and Boccaccio, with the flowering of
Guinicelli's and Cavalcanti's *Dolce Stil Nuovo*. It then spread gradually
during the ensuing centuries to the other countries of Western Europe,
merging in the fifteenth century with the Humanism fostered by the fall
of Constantinople and the consequent rebirth of Greek studies in the
West, coupled with the invention of printing and the voyages of discovery. Other scholars perceive the Renaissance in terms of the decay of
feudal institutions and the rise of absolute monarchies, the new nationalistic currents engendered by the Hundred Years' War, particularly in
France, the coming to age of a true middle class, a liberation of the currents of thought that culminated in the Reformation, the beginning of
modern science heralded by Galileo and Copernicus. Still others view it as
primarily a cultural rebirth of many facets, stemming from the slow, un-
even progress achieved during the Middle Ages in the fields of literature,
art, and architecture, philosophy and theology, but now turning away
from other-world ideals to face the reality of the things of this existence
under the inspiration of resurrected and rediscovered classical models
that had been lost and forgotten.

Linguistically, the Renaissance marks the final and full emergence of
national standards, the relegation of local dialects to an inferior status as
vehicles of widening systems of communication and trade, the setting up
of new classical standards and ideals, not merely for the rediscovered and

144

reexplored ancient languages, but for the new vernaculars now come of age. This in turn meant, as had been the case in ancient Rome, that the new languages, while becoming more widespread, fell again under the spell of an intellectually aristocratic class, conservative in spirit and suspicious of lower-class or local innovations, whose unconscious aim it would be, once the standards were set, to preserve them unchanged as much as possible, thus slowing down the swift flow of phonological and morphological change that had characterized the Middle Ages, at the same time that it expanded vocabularies, literary production, and the use of stylistic devices. The natural consequence of all this would be, in the centuries that followed the Renaissance, that the written form of the language would again exercise dominion over the spoken tongue, as it had in the days of Classical Latin.

In Italy, where the cultural aspects of the Renaissance were first manifested, there was a swift and early crystallization of the language around a cluster of three outstanding names: Dante, Petrarch, and Boccaccio. Long before the end of the fourteenth century, the basic form of what was to become the Italian national standard was set. This language, the *Volgare Illustre* whose existence Dante had denied, but which he used in his *Divine Comedy* and other Italian writings, was basically upper-crust Florentine, with an admixture of other Italian dialects (but a predominance of the Tuscan ones is noticeable), plus abundant borrowings from the three other tongues Dante knew best: Latin, French, and Provençal. The Latin element was particularly strong in the Italian writings of all three fourteenth-century luminaries. This was natural, since they were all scholars deeply grounded in Latin, whose Latin writings were in the nature of a foretaste of the Humanism that would bloom a century after them. Greek actually began to be taught in Florence in 1360, nearly a century before the fall of Constantinople and the invasion of Italy by Greek scholars.

There was one element missing from the picture, that of universality throughout the country that the new language was supposed to serve. Thirteenth-century Florentine predominated only in Tuscany, and not everywhere in Tuscany. The rest of Italy accepted it as a literary medium, but not much else. The north, broken up into a mosaic of city-states that had turned or were turning into petty autocracies, continued to use its own dialects for all purposes save that of writing poetry or exalted prose.

Rome was culturally out of the running by reason of the chronic absence of the Popes. The south, now broken up into a kingdom of Naples and one of Sicily, was even less responsive than the north.

But fourteenth-century Italy was a land of many resources, much trade and travel and intellectual activity. There were merchants, minstrels, artists, soldiers of fortune, who moved easily from one part of the country to another. The ancient and established universities, such as Bologna and Salerno, were joined by new ones, in Florence, Perugia, Siena, with an attendant movement of students and scholars. The long coastlines of Italy and the ease of navigation helped the good cause. The new Italian language spread, though it was still largely the property of a restricted class of people.

Relatively little of this early phase of the Italian Renaissance spread to the other countries of Europe, though it did extend, sporadically, even to England, where Chaucer absorbed and utilized some of Boccaccio's writings. The Iberian peninsula, still in the throes of its *Reconquista,* was largely untouched. France, struggling through its Hundred Years' War, was too busy to pay too much cultural attention to its southern neighbor, though the Italian link with Provence, from which Italy had gained much of her inspiration, was still strong.

In France, the Renaissance did not really get under way until the fifteenth century, though the groundwork had been laid earlier. The Hundred Years' War, with its preliminary clashes and attendant side horrors, such as the Jacquerie, had served a few useful purposes. It had aroused a nationalistic feeling, born of unpleasant contacts with the English, that had not been there before.[1] Another result was the decay of the feudal aristocracy, which had proved itself unequal to the task of providing the sinews of war, both military and financial, and the consequent rise of the absolute power of the French kings, from Philip Augustus to Louis XI.

Linguistically, the confusion occasioned by the fundamental change-over from a two-case system reminiscent of Latin to the single case that the languages of the Iberian and Italian peninsulas had adopted from their very inception had come to a close, and the French language was beginning to assume its modern aspect, at least for what concerned mor-

---

1. One example is the *Vaux-de-Vire* of Olivier Basselin, in which he urges his fellow countrymen to oppose the invaders from across the Channel, whom he describes as *ces godons, panches à pois,* "these pea-bellied goddams," referring to the favorite cuss-word of England's sturdy yeomen.

phology and syntax. The unconscious desire for what might be called simplification of structure was manifested in other ways, such as the leveling out through the process of analogy of many of the startling irregularities in verbs, inherited, through the working of phonological "laws," from Latin.[2]

There was also the matter of word order, which now assumed a regular subject-verb-object pattern.[3]

But these historical and linguistic developments by themselves would not have added up to a French Renaissance had they not been furthered by a few whiffs from the culture, both classical and new, that blew up from the south, a new interest in the Latin that the scholars of France had used by rote during the Middle Ages, curiosity about the formation of a kindred Romance language suitable for any and all uses, literary, philosophical, commercial, even bureaucratic. The French fifteenth century was still marked by fluctuations and drastic changes in pronunciation, by the continued survival of the dialects in speech and occasionally in writing. But now there was the adoption and adaptation of Latin words into the language, a growing breach between the French of the masses and that of the ever-expanding class of scholars and writers. The full flowering of French in its Francien variety, with its use in official documents, the courts, and the royal administration, would not come to pass until the sixteenth century. But even in the late fifteenth there was a filtering into French of some of the ancient Greek culture that the refugees from the fall of Constantinople had brought to Italy; and the effects of Gutenberg's printing press were beginning to be felt, though the initial output of the presses was in Latin and Greek rather than in French.

---

2. As a single example, the Old French present of *aimer* was *aim, aimes, aimet, amons, amez, aiment,* with *ai* in the forms where the stress falls on the root, *a* where it falls on the ending; now, by a process of conscious or unconscious imitation, *amons, amez,* took on the *ai* of the root-stressed forms. In like manner, the present of *prover,* from Latin *prŏbare,* had been *pruef, prueves, pruevet, provons, provez, pruevent,* in accordance with the phonological law that Latin stressed short *o* turns into the diphthong *ue* (later *eu*), but unstressed short *o* remains *o* (later *ou*). Had this gone on into the present, we would have today *preuve, preuves, preuve, prouvons, prouvez, preuvent.* Here the root-stressed forms imitated the unstressed ones, and modern *prouver* has *ou* throughout.

3. The old two-case system had permitted such constructions as *le rei veit li cuens,* "the count sees the king," where the form *li cuens* identified itself as the subject by its form and ending (the oblique, or objective, form would have been *le comte*), and *le rei* identified itself as the object (the nominative, or subject, form would have been *li reis*). From the fifteenth century on, with only one form at the disposal of each noun, the only possible arrangement to indicate the desired meaning was *le comte voit le roi,* as is the case today.

The Iberian peninsula, geographically remote from the Mediterranean center and preoccupied with its own specific problems, was largely untouched by Renaissance influences in the fourteenth century. Its main concerns were the expulsion of the last Moors, the separate unification of the two kingdoms of Spain and Portugal, the setting up of peninsular standards, political, institutional, religious, and linguistic. The literary output of the various peninsular kingdoms, while fairly abundant, shows little trace of outside influence.

This state of affairs continued into the fifteenth century, whose preoccupation was with voyages of discovery and exploration into new worlds rather than with the study of antiquity. Even Nebrija's grammar of the Spanish language, at the very end of the century, displays little knowledge of antiquity and classical sources beyond what would have been available to a medieval scholar.

But when Spain began its phenomenal career of conquest on the European continent, at the outset of the sixteenth century, it was reached by both the Renaissance and Humanism, and assumed a belated but noble role in both.

The Italian fifteenth century shows a surprising swing away from the national vernacular (or *Volgare Illustre*), now fully established, and into humanistic antiquity. This was in part due to the influx of Greek refugees, in part to the discovery of numerous lost Latin works, which had to be codified, edited, and very often translated. Translation had now become an art and a vogue, since the printing press made publication possible and put books within the reach of a rapidly growing intellectual class. This situation presented advantages and disadvantages, depending on one's viewpoint. Robert A. Hall, Jr., for instance, points to the fact that printers were generally scholars and translators as well, and made wholesale appropriations of Latin and Greek words which they put into their Italian translations, and thus, ultimately, into the Italian language. More pessimistically, his Italian colleague, Angelo Monteverdi, focuses on the element of laziness on the part of the translators, who found it easier to appropriate such Latin words as *vir*, "man," and *dives*, "rich," turning them into *viro* and *dive*, than to seek current vernacular equivalents, and to put such Latin constructions as the ablative absolute and the accusative with the infinitive into Italian rather than recouch them in the forms they had assumed in the spoken language; in proof of his contention, he cites the identical process in operation for such other model languages as

French and Provençal, from which Italian borrowed *ostello, motto, gioia, giardino, allegranza, lusinga,* and extends it to other languages besides Italian. Portuguese, in its official documents, uses the traditional Spanish *el rei* instead of the native *o rei;* Provençal borrows *joi* from French; Rabelais forms *cécité,* "blindness," from Latin *caecus,* forgetting the existence of French *aveugle* (formed centuries earlier from *ab oculo*), from which **aveugleté* could have been formed (* indicates a hypothetical form which is not recorded).

Be this as it may, some of the results of the double process of printing ancient works in their original languages and also in vernacular translations seem fairly clear. The original Latin works led to Ciceronian standards for the scholarly Latin of the Renaissance which were perhaps too high, and led to the downfall of Latin as a means of intercommunication. Scholars began to abandon Latin and to try to use more and more the now polished vernaculars. In this they may also have been inspired by considerations of the wider popular market now available, so that while Latin was being exalted and purified it was also becoming more restricted and losing some of its international prerogatives.

Another side effect of printing was that it lent itself to the growing spirit of secularism, relaxing the stranglehold that had been exercised by churchmen over the written language during the Middle Ages. Still another was the increasing tendency toward linguistic uniformity for what concerned spellings, punctuation, the use of the standard dialect. It confirmed first the Florentine ascendancy for Italian, then the Francien for French, ultimately the Castilian for Spanish.

The sixteenth century, which saw the full triumph of the Renaissance in France, also witnessed the beginning of its decline in Italy, after the great sack of Rome of 1527, which marked the effective end of Italian liberty from foreign domination. The French and Spanish invasions, using Italy as their battleground, could do little to prevent the flowering of a second, purely literary Renaissance, featuring such giants as Ariosto and Tasso, or the continuation of classical studies and research. If anything, they fostered a stronger national consciousness, born of foreign oppression, along with a new outburst of religious feeling, occasioned by the Reformation, the Counter Reformation, and the Council of Trent. The decay came from within, and it took the form of excessive introspection and linguistic controversy on a topic which, while linguistically important, was doomed in advance to fruitlessness, the *Questione della*

Lingua. Was literary Italian, now consecrated by over two centuries of production, basically Tuscan, and more specifically Florentine, or was it the conglomeration of dialects at which Dante had hinted in his *De Vulgari Eloquentia?* Rivers of ink flowed on the subject, from the quills of such men as Bembo, Machiavelli, Speroni, Tolomei, Castiglione, Trissino. From the standpoint of linguistic history, the question was absorbing, and provided a field for the display of high and varied talents. From another angle, it was sterile, nonproductive, wasteful of energies that might have been concentrated on more creative topics. It confirmed Italian in its role as a primarily written-language medium, made speakers self-conscious in its use, and led to artificiality and the worship of petrified models. One of its by-products was the first of language academies, the Accademia della Crusca, whose prime mover was Cardinal Bembo, and whose avowed purpose it was to fix usage in accordance with the dictates of the best minds of the period. Meanwhile, the spoken, popular language, left to its own devices, tended to flow back into its old dialectal channels, while foreign influences, particularly Spanish, but French and German as well, made themselves increasingly felt.

But for this there were compensations. While Italian and the Italian dialects were absorbing a great deal from the speech of the foreign mercenaries who trampled Italian soil, they were also contributing mighty exports of words and forms and constructions to the tongues of the invaders. More than any other century before the twentieth, perhaps, it may be claimed that the sixteenth was the century of the greatest linguistic interchanges, especially among the three major Romance languages. Italy exported to France a host of words and forms which France re-exported to other European, non-Romance lands, particularly England, words like *soldato, campo, costume, banco, capriccio, carezza, calma, capitano,* suffixes like *-issimo* and *-esco.* To Spain went *novella, piloto, sentinella;* from Spain came *bizarro, sosiego, lindo,* along with myriads of words that Spanish and Portuguese explorers had brought back from America, Asia, and Africa, words like *piroga, patata, chicchera, indiano, tifone, zebra, banana.*

In France, where the vernacular in its Francien form had triumphed in 1539 to the extent of becoming the official tongue of the documents and courts, the spirit of nationalism combined with imitation of Italian models to give rise to works like du Bellay's *Défense et illustration de la langue française* of 1549, and Henri Etienne's protest of 1598 against the Italianization of the French language. But while these and other works did much to bolster the confidence of the French in the value of their own tongue, they did little to stem the flow of borrowings from Italian. The same may be said of Spain, where Valdés' *Diálogo de la lengua* (1535) attempted to enlighten Spanish speakers as to the origins and merits of their Castilian tongue, but could not check the flow of words and forms from Italian. The nationalistic movement extended even to Portugal, where in the earlier works of Gil Vincente the characters spoke Castilian, but in the later ones Portuguese.

The spreading of national languages was aided by the new religious movements of Reformation and Counter Reformation. Calvin's *Institution chrétienne,* a work of Protestant propaganda, originally appearing in Latin in 1536, was reissued in French in 1541.

This was a period when religious, political, and literary factors combined to set the definitive form of the Romance languages. There was still much confusion of spelling usage, but the printers, to whose interest it was to foster uniformity, began the difficult work of spelling standardization, not fully completed even today. There were also abortive attempts at creating phonetic spellings, and extending spelling regularization to the dialects that were still in written use.[4]

Latin became more and more restricted to a scholarly class, and even this scholarly Latin failed to escape the effects of spelling reform (it was at this period that *j* and *v* were differentiated from *i* and *u* in Latin works).

The burgeoning science of the period, striving for mass appeal, increasingly turned to the national languages as a linguistic medium. But at the same time there began to arise processes of codification and standardization, particularly on the part of grammarians, who found it simpler to try to force the new languages into a Latin grammatical mold than to construct new grammatical bases founded on spoken-language reality. Without yet following Italy's lead in the creation of a language academy, both France and Spain began to look longingly in the direction of a body that would set and fix all rules for the use of the languages and the admissibility of new words. In France, the writers of the Pléiade set the style, and even the satirical wit of Rabelais could not deter the language from entering a new state of quasi-classical crystallization.

By the end of the sixteenth century, the Renaissance process was

---

4. Bruno Migliorini reminds us that in the writings of the previous centuries, a dialectal form like Venetian *doge* could appear in the forms *doxe, dugie, dogio, docio.*

over. There was still plenty of confusion and fluctuation in spelling, and even in pronunciation and grammatical forms. There was a use of local dialects that would be viewed as intolerable today. But French, Spanish, Portuguese, Italian, had attained, in rough outline, what was to be their modern form. In their respective domains, each was official. Latin, still abundantly used, purified and Ciceronized, had sunk to the role of a purely cultural language, save in the Church and in a few universities. The age of the vernaculars was at hand. They had finally replaced the ancestral classical language, having themselves attained classical status.

Change in sounds and grammatical forms, which had gone on apace in the earlier centuries, was slowed up by the Renaissance, since such change reflects popular, "anonymous" rather than aristocratic, individualistic development, which is best mirrored in vocabulary and syntax.

Very little of a fundamental nature in the two "popular" divisions of linguistic development took place in Italy after the time of Dante. In the Iberian peninsula, certain phenomena generally associated with the dialect of Lisbon (*ou* to *oi*, as in *cousa, coisa;* nasalized *e* pronounced as *ai*, as in *bem;* the uvular pronunciation of *r*) seem to have developed between the thirteenth and the fifteenth centuries. In Castilian, the merging of *b* and *v* into two positional variants appears by the fifteenth century; initial *f* to *h* begins as far back as the fourteenth, but is apparently not completed till the end of the fifteenth. The progression of Latin velar *c* before front vowels, which had from the outset assumed the sound of *ts*, went on during the fifteenth and sixteenth centuries to Castilian unvoiced *th* and to the *s* of Portuguese and many regions of Spain. The change of *ç, z,* from *ts, dz,* to *s* or *th,* and of *x* (originally indicating a *sh*-sound) and *j* (originally the sound of *s* in *measure*) to the present *kh-* or *h*-sound is definitely a sixteenth-century phenomenon. No major morphological changes appear in Portuguese. In Spanish, we have the modern distinction between *tener* and *haber,* "to have," with the latter reduced to the status of an auxiliary (*tengo un libro,* "I have a book"; *lo he leído,* "I have read it"). The modern opposition between *ser* and *estar,* "to be" (*el hielo es frío,* "ice is [inherently] cold"; *el agua está fría,* "the water is [temporarily] cold") was not fully fixed until well into the seventeenth century.

On French soil, the reduction of the two-case system to the modern state of affairs, sporadically heralded in earlier centuries, is completed by the fifteenth, as is the regularization of word order into the subject-verb-object pattern of modern times. Phonetic change continues at a slower pace, particularly among the vowel sounds. Noteworthy is that of the diphthong *oi*, which had progressed from *oy* to *óe*, *oé*, and *wé*, and which now achieved its final stage, *wa;* this was a popular Parisian phenomenon which did not gain official currency until after the French Revolution had brought about the triumph of the masses and petty bourgeoisie, and of some (by no means all) of their speech forms. (It is rumored that the Marquis de Lafayette, in 1832, still said *mwe* and *rwe* for *moi* and *roi.*) In any event, it failed to spread to several of the French dialects, notably the Norman, which was exported to the French New World settlements in Canada and parts of New England.

13. The Rise and Fall of Romance Dialects

The question of what is a language and what is a dialect has long agitated the world of linguistics. Several answers have been suggested: (1) A language is what is official and nationwide; a dialect is what does not have government recognition. If this answer is accepted, the official Romance languages, five in number, are French, Spanish, Portuguese, Italian, Rumanian; everything else is dialects; this view leaves out of consideration such factors as history, geography, literary output, widespread use in one region of a national unit; it excludes Provençal, Catalan, Sardinian, Rheto-Rumansh, Dalmatian, from the roster of Romance languages. (2) A language is what has a literary tradition and output; a dialect is what lacks this feature. This makes languages not only of Provençal and Catalan, but also of Galician, Picard, Norman, Milanese, Neapolitan, Venetian, Sicilian, while it relegates to the status of dialects Sardinian, Dalmatian, to some extent even Rheto-Rumansh. (3) A language exists where the speakers of two or more varieties, using their own language forms, manage to achieve a satisfactory degree of mutual understanding; where this is not achieved, you have separate languages. This would mean that Italian and Spanish, in their official varieties, are one language, but that Sicilian and Venetian are separate languages.

Each answer is obviously unsatisfactory, though the first comes closer to general popular acceptance than either of the others.

Dante, when he recognized, classified, and partly described the Italian dialects of his day, used instinctively a scientific criterion that was not fully developed until modern times,[1] when linguistic atlases of vari-

---

1. He reduced the major varieties to fourteen, while at the same time bringing out the fact that each was subdivided, even within the same town, so that if one wanted to be precise he would have at least a thousand local dialects.

ous national areas revealed on the one hand the infinite multiplicity of separate linguistic forms that could be described as dialects of one language, on the other the fact that some order could be brought out of this confusion by bringing together under one general classification those local varieties which hold many features in common.

Dialects are the best illustration at our disposal of the natural, centrifugal force that is forever at work in language. Left to its own devices, the speech of any one group will tend to diversify and change, both in time and in space. From the standpoint of time, the spoken language is subject to innovations the nature and source of which can only occasionally be precisely determined (though the two factors of imitation due to the social prestige of an individual or group, and of imperfect hearing and imitation of their elders by new generations of speakers seem paramount). Spatially, the separation of a speaking group into two or more groups by reason of partial migration to new areas leads inevitably to innovations in both groups which are not common to both, and to consequent dialectal diversification.

An opposite, centripetal force becomes operative only when society turns localized and stable. Its manifestations are a strong central government, a set of religious, ethical, and political principles, an established tradition, even if this is purely oral. These cultural and psychological factors then tend to take the upper hand, and lead to a unification of a chosen speech form, or dialect, with the consequent subordination of other dialects, even to the point of disappearance. Of these two processes, which seem to alternate in the life of language, we have seen exemplification in the history of the expansion of Latin, which caused the disappearance of other speech forms, both related (Oscan, Umbrian, Faliscan) and unrelated (Etruscan, Iberian, Punic), and at the same time gradually crystallized into its Classical form. But even though we have scanty records of what actually happened, there is little doubt that the Vulgar Latin of the masses had some measure of dialectalization, even while the Roman Empire was at its height.

With the fall and fractioning of that Empire, the natural, centrifugal forces of language again took sway. Low cultural and literary levels, and the isolation of localities previously united by Roman roads, trade, schools, military service, uniform government administration, created new dialectal borders where none had existed before. These boundaries were often favored by geography, as where the Alps and Pyrenees formed natural barriers, even more often created by history, as when different invading groups assumed control of different territories.

As the forces of diversification deepened, the dialectal differences of a previously fairly unified Vulgar Latin grew more profound. The dialects of Vulgar Latin then crystallized into units that were still subject to centrifugal conditions, and they subdivided further into subdialects that grew in number and diversity.

At the outset of the era of Romance documents (ninth and tenth centuries), it is not difficult to distinguish between what comes from France, Spain, or Italy (though one is occasionally faced in the texts of one country with a form that later becomes characteristic of another, like the *buona* in the French *Sequence of St. Eulalia*). What is difficult to establish is a precise dialectal differentiation in the texts of any one country.[2] But the dialectal status of our texts becomes much clearer as we advance into the eleventh and twelfth centuries. It is possible that some of the dialectal features expected in the earliest texts do not appear because they had not yet arisen, though many other as yet undisclosed factors may have been at work.

By the year 1300 the dialect picture is quite clear, and it is one that with minor retouches still exists today. The difference between 1300 and today is that in 1300 the dialects were strong, living realities, where today, after centuries of new centralizing, centripetal forces, they may be described as relegated to the background, if not yet moribund.

By 1300, in the Iberian peninsula, Galician-Portuguese was well on its way. With the political severance of Galicia from Portugal, Portuguese had developed into a northern (Tras-os-Montes, Entre-Douro-e-Minho), a central (Beira-Lisbon), and a southern (Alemtejo-Algarve) variety. To these would be added in due course of time the forms that appear today in Madeira and in the Azores. Still later, with overseas migration, will come the varieties of Brazilian Portuguese (the Northeastern of Bahia, the Carioca of Rio de Janeiro, the Paulista of Rio Grande do Sul).

In what was later to be Spain, the dialectal roster, shorn of Galician

---

2. There is considerable controversy over the localization of the language of the Oaths of Strasbourg, the *Sequence of St. Eulalia*, even the *Life of St. Léger* and the *Story of St. Alexis*, in France. While we know where the Testimonial Formulas of Monte Cassino originated, a seemingly northern form like *sao* disturbs the experts. The Glosses of San Millán give indication of a possible dialect mixture.

and Catalan, which would give rise to separate languages, shows an Asturo-Leonese, a Castilian, and a Navarro-Aragonese division. The first and last would gradually become more restricted, while expanding Castilian would go on to merge with Mozarabic in the south to create Andalusian, in the west to give rise to Estremeño. Overseas, with the discovery of the New World, Castilian-Andalusian was destined to give rise to new dialectal varieties, which can be broadly subdivided into a Mexican-Central American, an Antillean (Cuba, Puerto Rico, Dominican Republic), a northern South American (Venezuela, Colombia, Ecuador), a central South American (Peru, Bolivia), a southern South American (Paraguay, Uruguay, Argentina, Chile). There is, in addition, the highly conservative Judaeo-Spanish of the Sephardic Jews, now spoken mainly in North Africa, the Balkans, Istanbul, and Israel.

Catalan, which at first seemed destined to merge with Aragonese, broke off abruptly by reason of political factors and carried on as a separate language, with an eastern and western subdivision on Spanish soil, a Roussillon variety on the French side of the border. It later expanded to create Valencian and Balearic varieties, and even a Sardinian outpost at Alghero.

The cleavage on Gallo-Romance soil between northern French and Provençal is evident and clear-cut from the very inception of documentary evidence, but it is only in the course of time that the subdivisions of each become definite. While the north, by the end of the twelfth century, appears subdivided into Francien, Picard, Champenois, Walloon, Lorrain, Bourguignon, Angevin, and Poitevin areas, the south shows cleavages into an area east of the Rhône, which may be called Provençal proper, and an area to the west in which developed Languedocien, Auvergnat, Limousin, and Gascon (the last showing stronger divergences than do the others, which has led some to think of possible Basque influences, others that Gascon may be the descendant of Julius Caesar's Aquitanian).

The Franco-Provençal subdivision, if we accept it, is more difficult to classify than either French or Provençal, by reason of interlacing isoglosses.[3] One possibility is Lyonnais, Franche-comtois, Savoyard, on French soil, Valdostan on the Italian side of the border, and the speech forms of the cantons of Valais and Vaud on Swiss territory.

---

3. An isogloss is a linguistic line of demarcation on a map, like the one separating Low German *dat* from High German *das*.

In modern times the Gallo-Romance varieties continue, but tend to be more and more relegated to the role of patois (local spoken but unwritten forms) rather than literary dialects. Mistral's attempt to revive Provençal as a literary medium led to a new classification into Provençal proper (sometimes rechristened "Mistralien"), as against a general Occitanian west of the Rhône.

The three main varieties of Rheto-Rumansh are the Swiss (Engadine) of the Grisons Canton, the Friulian of northeastern Venetia, and a series of separated speech forms in the mountain valleys along the course of the Adige, in the general region of Trent, and extending north as far as Bolzano.

For Italian, Dante's classification had established the separate existence of a Tuscan group, a Corsican, one for Umbria, the Marche, and northern Latium, including the city of Rome, an Abruzzo-Campanian, a Calabro-Lucanian, an Apulian, a Sicilian, accompanied by the lower half of Calabria, a Venetian-Istrian, an Emilian, a Lombard, a Piedmontese, and a Genoese. To these, Dante's classification adds Friulian and Sardinian, which modern linguists would regard as separate Romance varieties, spoken on Italian soil but not forming part of the Italian system. This classification holds up reasonably well today, with minor modifications. Some of the links that bind together Lombard, Piedmontese, Emilian, and Genoese do not apply to Venetian, though the five are sometimes lumped together in a "north Italian" classification. Tuscan, Corsican, and the speech forms of Umbria, the Marche, and northern Latium may be described as a central group that forms the backbone of the Italian literary language, while the dialects of the south and Sicily lend themselves to classification into an upper tier (Abruzzo-Campanian, Calabro-Lucanian) and a lower tier, consisting of the tip of the boot and the island of Sicily, with Apulian agreeing in part with one, in part with the other.

There is no way of classifying the dialects of Dalmatian that may once have existed, but for what may be called Daco-Illyrian (or Rumanian), the compact mass of former Dacia (present-day Rumania, plus Bessarabia on Soviet soil) may be subdivided into Moldavian, Wallachian, and Transylvanian units, while the Rumanian of Macedonia shows a split into Macedo-Rumanian proper (or Arumanian) and Megleno-Rumanian. Then there is a small, isolated Istro-Rumanian enclave near the Italian-Yugoslav border, which is characterized by strong influxes from the languages on both sides (Italian and Venetian on the one hand; Slovenian and Serbo-Croatian on the other).

Several points of historical, geographic, and cultural interest are stressed by Monteverdi and may be summarized here:

(1) The official language, once it is established, becomes the tool of bureaucrats, notaries, lawyers, the courts, the army, the schools. It would be strange indeed if it did not infiltrate the local dialects, in addition to thrusting them into the background.

(2) Historically, dialects have been known to disappear before the encroachments of the national languages (the local dialects of Lyon and Geneva are cited as cases in point); this encroachment is more likely to occur along important lines of communication, such as waterways. However, the national language thus accepted and spoken in such areas continues to be colored by the former dialects, even if the coloring takes the form only of an intonation. (This is reminiscent of Quintilian's statement about the Latin of his period, universally spoken on Italian soil, but with surviving background intonations.) Monteverdi even speaks of new, modern Vulgar French, Vulgar Spanish, Vulgar Italian, functioning as Vulgar Latin probably once did.

(3) The literary function is essential to the proper survival of a dialect. In Italy, where this function was operative longer than elsewhere (it even continues into the present period), such speech forms as glorified literary Neapolitan, Sicilian, Milanese, Venetian, Roman, have an excellent chance of survival. On the other hand, the literary function must be complete to the point of exclusivity for the dialect to qualify as a language. Catalan, which was a literary language before 1464, sank to the role of a semiliterary dialect when many of its writers went over to Spanish, and this dialect status endured till the middle of the nineteenth century, when Catalan once more became a full-fledged literary language.

(4) It is, generally speaking, one particular dialect that initially provides the literary backbone of a national or literary language: Francien, in its Parisian variety, for French; Tuscan, in predominantly Florentine form, for Italian; the Castilian of Toledo (rather than that of Burgos), once the *Reconquista* had freed that city, for Spanish; initially Galician, but later Lisbonese, for Portuguese; Limousin for medieval Provençal. This does not at all exclude the possibility of admixture from other dialects, or, for that matter, from foreign languages.

Additional cultural factors are presented by Rebecca Posner, who pictures the Picard-Norman dialect complex in France as being at the outset more productive of literature than the Francien area; but the latter not only had the capital and court but also such monasteries as

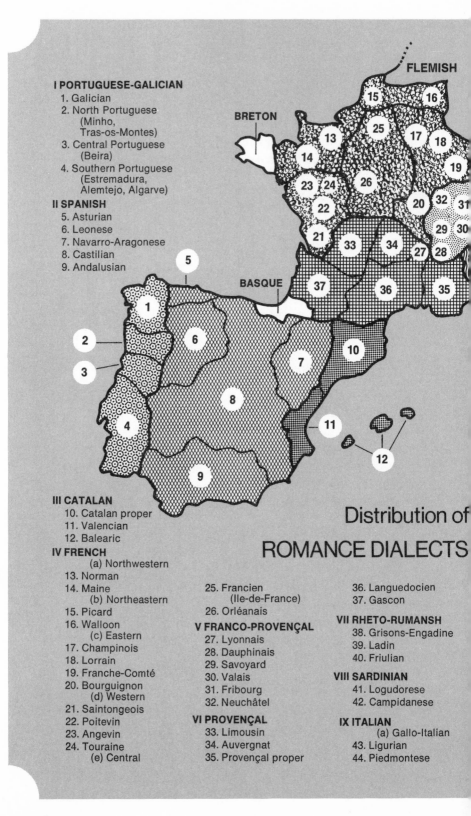

I PORTUGUESE-GALICIAN
1. Galician
2. North Portuguese (Minho, Tras-os-Montes)
3. Central Portuguese (Beira)
4. Southern Portuguese (Estremadura, Alemtejo, Algarve)

II SPANISH
5. Asturian
6. Leonese
7. Navarro-Aragonese
8. Castilian
9. Andalusian

FLEMISH

BRETON

BASQUE

III CATALAN
10. Catalan proper
11. Valencian
12. Balearic

IV FRENCH
   (a) Northwestern
13. Norman
14. Maine
   (b) Northeastern
15. Picard
16. Walloon
   (c) Eastern
17. Champinois
18. Lorrain
19. Franche-Comté
20. Bourguignon
   (d) Western
21. Saintongeois
22. Poitevin
23. Angevin
24. Touraine
   (e) Central

25. Francien (Ile-de-France)
26. Orléanais

V FRANCO-PROVENÇAL
27. Lyonnais
28. Dauphinais
29. Savoyard
30. Valais
31. Fribourg
32. Neuchâtel

VI PROVENÇAL
33. Limousin
34. Auvergnat
35. Provençal proper

36. Languedocien
37. Gascon

VII RHETO-RUMANSH
38. Grisons-Engadine
39. Ladin
40. Friulian

VIII SARDINIAN
41. Logudorese
42. Campidanese

IX ITALIAN
   (a) Gallo-Italian
43. Ligurian
44. Piedmontese

Distribution of

ROMANCE DIALECTS

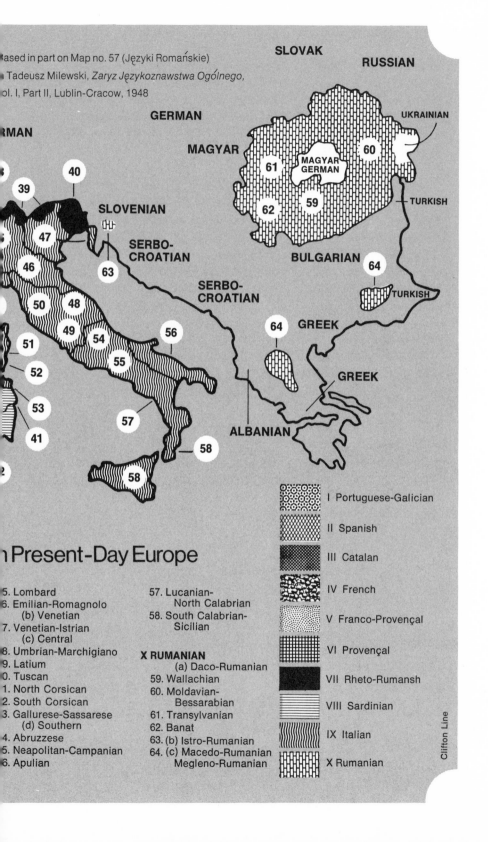

SLOVAK

RUSSIAN

Based in part on Map no. 57 (Języki Romańskie)
Tadeusz Milewski, *Zaryz Językoznawstwa Ogólnego*,
Vol. I, Part II, Lublin-Cracow, 1948

UKRAINIAN

GERMAN

RMAN

MAGYAR

61   MAGYAR
GERMAN   60

40

39

62   59

TURKISH

47   SLOVENIAN

46   SERBO-
CROATIAN

63

SERBO-
CROATIAN   BULGARIAN   64

50   48

49   54   56   64   GREEK   TURKISH

51   55

52   GREEK

53   57

41   ALBANIAN

58

58

Present-Day Europe

5. Lombard
6. Emilian-Romagnolo
   (b) Venetian
7. Venetian-Istrian
   (c) Central
8. Umbrian-Marchigiano
9. Latium
0. Tuscan
1. North Corsican
2. South Corsican
3. Gallurese-Sassarese
   (d) Southern
4. Abruzzese
5. Neapolitan-Campanian
6. Apulian

57. Lucanian-
    North Calabrian
58. South Calabrian-
    Sicilian

X RUMANIAN
   (a) Daco-Rumanian
59. Wallachian
60. Moldavian-
    Bessarabian
61. Transylvanian
62. Banat
63. (b) Istro-Rumanian
64. (c) Macedo-Rumanian
    Megleno-Rumanian

I Portuguese-Galician

II Spanish

III Catalan

IV French

V Franco-Provençal

VI Provençal

VII Rheto-Rumansh

VIII Sardinian

IX Italian

X Rumanian

Clifton Line

Saint-Denis, where much copying of manuscripts was done. As the monks copied, they deliberately or unconsciously adapted the original Picard to their own native Francien. The same factor was seemingly at work in Italy, where Tuscan scribes translated or adapted as they copied manuscripts from other regions. The originals were often lost, and only the adaptations survived.

Lastly, it may be stressed that a dialect, literary or purely oral, has exactly the same linguistic features as a national language: a sound structure, a morphological-syntactical setup, an independent lexicon. All of these features may coincide to a greater or lesser degree with those of the official language. It is altogether possible to construct a descriptive grammar of a dialect, in all respects similar to that of a standard language. The popular conception of a dialect as a distorted, inferior variant of the national language is, scientifically speaking, to be shunned, being as groundless as that of inherently superior and inferior races or social groups.

On the other hand, it is not to be denied that the national, official language carries in practice greater prestige and advantages, and can be put to more practical uses than a dialect, save in very specific situations.

So perhaps the best way to differentiate between a language and a dialect is to say that there is no intrinsic difference between them, but that a language is a dialect that has been lucky to the extent of gaining official recognition, while a dialect is a potential language that has failed to run into this good fortune.

14. *The Romance Languages Go Overseas*

Only three of the five official Romance languages need be seriously considered in this connection, as having given rise to transoceanic variants of themselves. When the exploration and colonization of the Americas began, in the final decade of the fifteenth century, Rumania was not yet a national unit, while Italy, which contributed so much to the discovery and exploration of the New World, not having managed to achieve unification, was not in a position to send out organized groups of colonists. The three expanding languages were Spanish, Portuguese, and French.

In all three cases, it is well to remind ourselves that by the outset of the sixteenth century the languages had achieved official status and a measure of standardization, but that the dialects were still powerfully alive and active. In addition, the bulk of the colonists came from the lower rather than the upper social echelons of the three countries. While members of the aristocracy often led exploring expeditions, and supplied the officialdom once settlements were made, and while all three countries, being intensely Catholic, sent out priests and missionaries along with their soldiers and settlers, the people who left their European homelands to seek either fortune or permanent homes in the New World were necessarily, in their majority, members of the working classes. The upper crust is normally too well off and satisfied with its status to want to leave it. This does not mean that there were not included among the explorers and settlers fairly numerous upper-class adventurers who wanted to make things better for themselves by bringing back to the homeland some of the fabled treasures that existed in fact (as in Mexico and Peru) or in fancy (El Dorado, the Seven Golden Cities of Cibola, Florida's Fountain of Youth).

In addition to these historical, sociological, and cultural factors that in part account for the developments the old languages underwent in their new homes, there are also two general linguistic principles that apply. One is the natural centrifugal tendency of all language to become differentiated into dialects when the speakers part company, especially when communications between the two separated groups are difficult, as was the case in the sixteenth century. One has only to think of the tongue of the Low German speakers who went off to Britain and became Anglo-Saxons, and how in the course of a few centuries it differentiated itself from the speech of those who had remained on the European mainland, so that by the time of King Alfred it is quite easy to distinguish between Old English and Old Low German or Frisian. But the French, Spanish, and Portuguese of America did not have to go through the distressing changes and additions forced upon Anglo-Saxon by Danish and Norman invasions, and are therefore still recognizably French, Spanish, and Portuguese, whereas the distinction between English and Frisian, Dutch, and Low German became profound after the Danelaw and the Norman Conquest.

Secondly, there is a tendency, which the linguists have explained only in part, for a language to become conservative when it migrates to new quarters, and to crystallize into the mold of the time of the migration, while the tongue of the homeland keeps on evolving at normal pace. This conservatism is especially noticeable in the areas of phonology and morphology-syntax, which are predominantly subject to popular influences; much less in the field of vocabulary, where the influx of new words from the languages with which the immigrants come in contact leads to innovations that frequently are carried back to the old country, but almost as often become part of a restricted local lexicon. On the other hand, the emigrant group is keenly conscious of its origin, especially at the outset, and anxious to keep up its home ties. It therefore imports to the best of its ability the cultural innovations that occur in the homeland. It is only at a later date that it becomes conscious of a separate culture of its own, and develops a spirit of linguistic nationalism directed against the mother country, as when some people speak of an "American" language distinct from English, or of a "Brazilian" distinct from Portuguese. Rebecca Posner felicitously calls this phenomenon a "love-hate" relation, not too different from that which characterizes the younger generations with respect to their parents and elders.

Generally speaking, the New World variant of a Romance language is characterized by a more relaxed articulation and less respect for traditional "correctness" in the use of the language. Both these phenomena may be attributed, at least in part, to the lower social origin of the settlers, though the factor of racial mixture, where applicable, may also play a part. Both these features are quite noticeable in Antillean Spanish (Cuba, Puerto Rico, Dominican Republic), where the black admixture is heavy, and in Brazilian Portuguese (Brazil was the first country to abolish black slavery, but its Portuguese homeland had also been the first to initiate it, in 1434, and the black admixture in Brazil is larger than in other Latin American countries).

Along with this, there are archaic features, often of dialectal origin, which appear in the American varieties of all three languages. Canadian French, in particular, reflects seventeenth- and eighteenth-century Norman rather than Francien. But it has been subjected to strong English influences in the course of its history, and some linguists attribute its lax articulation to English contacts.

The Portuguese of Brazil shows clearer unstressed vowels than that of Portugal and less diphthongization in words like *baixo, primeiro, tirou* (often pronounced *baxo, primero, tiró*), along with a tendency not to palatalize final *-s* (*muros,* pronounced *murush* in Portugal, *murus* in Brazil). This probably reflects the state of Portuguese at the time of the migrations, as does also the greater freedom of grammatical constructions (object pronoun before the verb as well as attached). The more frequent use of diminutives, particularly *-inho* (*cafèzinho,* "little cup of coffee"), on the other hand, seems to be merely an exaggeration of a propensity that appears in Portugal.

There is a Portuguese-Brazilian Academy, which meets about every ten years for the purpose of regularizing and standardizing the language that should be common to both countries. Since language academies notoriously have little effect on the spoken tongue, the efforts of the Academy are directed especially at achieving a common orthography, with identical spellings and use of diacritic signs, such as accent marks. Even this limited objective is not always attained, and it is often possible to distinguish a work written and published in Brazil from one done in Portugal by its orthography, much as is the case with American and British English (*labor/labour, center/centre, defense/defence*, etc.).

As is natural in the case of a language extending from the north temperate zone to the Antarctic, American Spanish shows greater variety than either American Portuguese or American French, and it has been subjected to far more detailed study.

There is general agreement that outside of vocabulary, which can differ markedly from country to country, in accordance with local conditions, the differences are fewer than one might expect. The question of the influence exerted by the background American Indian languages upon American Spanish phonology has been thoroughly gone into, but outside of matters of local intonation, such as the singsong of Andean Spanish, which seems to come from Quechua, and the constant confusion of *e* and *i*, of *o* and *u*, in the Ecuadorean Andes (Quechua has only the three cardinal vowels, *a*, *e*, and *o*), there is little to report.[1] (The high-tension Mexican *s* may be due to Nahuatl influence.)

Generally speaking, Spanish America prefers a pronunciation varying from *y* (*zh* or *j* in the far south: Argentina, Uruguay, Chile) to *ly* for Castilian *ll* (*calle*, "street," prounounced *caye* or *cazhe*), and one varying from *s* to *th* for *c* before front vowels and *z*.[2] Final -*s* ranges from the Castilian high apical to the gentle aspiration or downright evanescence of Antillean (*venceremoh* or *venceremo*, the latter actually appearing on a Cuban revolutionary banner, for *venceremos*). The strongly rasped velar Castilian *j* (*kh*) is generally reduced to *h*. Medial *d, g, r*, are often lost, especially in Antillean (*pa naa* for *para nada*). But these phenomena are all to be found in one or another of the local dialects of Spain, and seem to be due to the dialectal background of early Spanish settlers, many of them from Andalusia. In the imperfect subjunctive American Spanish shows a strong preference for the -*ra* form over the -*se* (*no creía que viniera* rather than *no creía que viniese*, "I didn't think he'd come"). There is a fairly widespread use of *vos* with a plural, or even a singular verb, with *te* as the accusative form, and *ustedes* as the plural (the inverse phenomenon of *tú, te, tuyo*, with a plural verb, also occurs). Argentinians tend to stress *vámonos, dígale*, on the last syllable.

---

1. This is the majority opinion; linguists like Rodolfo Lenz, however, go so far as to claim that the vulgar speech of Chile is Spanish with Araucanian sounds.

2. This occasionally leads to vocabulary changes to avoid confusion, as where *caza*, "hunting," is replaced in Cuba by *cacería* to distinguish it in speech from *casa*, "house."

Mosotros often replaces *nos, nosotros.* Archaisms of the type of *es nacido* (for *ha nacido* or *nació,* "he was born"), and *truje* (for *traje,* "I brought") are also current. Chileans often use *donde,* "where," for *en casa de,* "at the house of," as in *donde mi tío,* "at my uncle's house," but this phenomenon appears elsewhere in Spanish America, and even in Spain.

William Entwistle points to the fact that borrowings from Spanish by the American Indian languages cast considerable light upon the state of the Spanish language at the time of the conquests. Both the native languages of Mexico and those of South America indicate that at that period there was still a clear-cut distinction in pronunciation between *b* and *v,* which have since merged into two positional variants of the same sound; that the *s* of the Conquistadores was the apical sound of Castilian rather than the dorsal *s* of Andalusian; that *ç* and *z* (pronounced, respectively, *ts* and *dz*) had already merged. In like manner, *x* and *j* of medieval Spanish (*sh, zh*) had merged into *sh,* but this had not yet turned into the *kh*-sound of today, while initial *f* had become an *h* that was still aspirate, but with a tendency to vanish.

Entwistle also localizes the American Indian languages from which Spanish borrowed words that were later passed on to other European languages, including English. *Canoa, cacique, maíz, huracán, sabana, batata, barbacoa, tabaco,* come from the Antillean Indian tongues (Arawak, Carib). Of Mexican origin are *tomate, aguacate* (English *avocado*), *cacao, chocolate, coyote, tamale, mezcal, pulque.* From Quechua and Aymará are *chinchilla, pampa, vicuña, quina* (quinine), the *coca* of Coca Cola, *guano, roto* (still used in Chile in the sense of "peasant"). Tupi supplies *tapioca, ananás, curare,* while Araucanian Mapuche gives *gaucho* and *poncho.*

In modern times, the Spanish of America has undergone French and English influences to a greater degree than that of Spain, which has, however, accepted most of the Latin American acquisitions. Forms like *remarcable, pichón,* "pigeon," *bisutería,* "jewelry shop," from *bijouterie*), have gotten into Spain via Latin America, along with English borrowings like *tranvía, lifte, espiche,* "speech," *futbol.* American English has latterly contributed *bluff, líder, repórter, selfmademan.*

There are many vocabulary divergences in the countries of Latin America, not all due to borrowings from American Indian languages. The *peón* of Mexico is a *guajiro* in Cuba, a *roto* in Chile. *Gringo,* which to the Mexicans means an American, is applied in Argentina to all foreigners, especially Italians, while recent Spanish immigrants are called

Godos, "Goths," a reminder of the Visigothic strain. In the matter of modern technological terminology, there is often wide divergence among Spanish American countries. An automobile tire may be a *goma, llanta,* or *neumático;* gasoline may be *gasolina, bencina, esencia,* depending on the country you happen to be in. This often reflects the source (American, British, French, Italian) from which the innovation came (the English counterpart appears in British *petrol, lorry,* versus American *gas, truck*). There is also an entire range of words that usage has made improper or suggestive in one country, while they retain their pristine innocence in another. It will be well, for instance, to avoid *rapariga* for "girl" in Brazil (though it is quite all right in Portugal), and use *moça* instead; compare the British and American uses of *bum,* or even *wench.*

From a literary point of view, both American Spanish and American Portuguese have been extremely productive, rivaling in modern times the literary output of the mother countries. Since the literary output circulates freely from one side of the Atlantic to the other, the linguistic interchange has gone on apace, producing a richness that equals that of the British-American interchange. Spanish and Portuguese writers, self-exiled from the Franco and Salazar regimes, have done much writing and publishing in Latin America.

Canadian French has not participated in a similar manner in French literary activity by reason of its past cultural subordination to English, but there is reason to expect that as the political and economic status of its speakers improves to the point of equality, it, too, will take up the burden of contributing to the French literary stream. The same may be said of the French of Haiti.

Italian emigrants to both North and South America and their American-born descendants have contributed much to the languages of their host countries, both in the matter of words and expressions and in the field of literature. The latter activity, however, has generally used English, Spanish, and Portuguese as its medium, even when describing the experience of the emigrants-immigrants.[3] Yet there are occasional

---

3. In the United States, for instance, one may mention from the 1890's on such names as Costantino Panunzio, Giuseppe Cautela, Garibaldi Lapolla, Louis Forgione, Angelo Valente, Bernard De Voto, Frances Winwar (Vinciguerra), Paul Gallico, Hamilton Basso, Jerre Mangione, Pietro Di Donato, Charles Calitri, Luigi Creatore, Guy Talese, and the poet Ignace Ingianni, who for years directed a magazine (*Simbolica*) devoted exclusively to poetry. (See Rose Basile Green, *The Italian-American Novel,* Cranbury, N.J.: Fairleigh Dickinson University Press, 1974).

samples of works done by Italian-Americans, both in North and South America, originally composed in Italian, or even in French.[4]

---

4. Bernardino Ciambelli, whose abundant fictional output, in Italian, ran from 1893 to 1919; the poet Riccardo Cordiferro, whose writings appeared for many years in *La Follia di New York*, which he directed; Italian-American writings in French came from Luigi Ventura, in the 1840's, and Giacomo Beltrami, whose account of his explorations in the upper Mississippi valley (*La Découverte des sources du Mississippi*) was published in New Orleans in 1824, and forms the basis of Augusto Miceli's *The Man with the Red Umbrella*, Baton Rouge: Claitor, 1974.

15. *The Beginning of Modern Times*

Depending upon the individual viewpoint, some linguists describe the seventeenth and eighteenth centuries as a period of consolidation, regularization, purification, codification; others, more pessimistically, as an epoch of stagnation, when ceremony, pretentiousness, pomposity, and pedantry prevailed in both manners and language. There is, to be sure, a difference in the way different countries reacted to the end of the ebullient Renaissance and the establishment of national standards.

Spain, having achieved its supreme literary triumphs by the middle of the seventeenth century, gradually went over to a Gongorism that was high-flown, verbose, stylized, and had little connection with the spoken tongue of the masses, succumbing thereafter to the literary currents and fashions that came from France. Something similar happened in Portugal, after the sixteenth-century glory of Camões. Italy, which had in many ways set the pace throughout the early and later Renaissance, worn out by internal strife and foreign domination, sank into a baroque style that prevailed in literature as well as in art and architecture, and resulted in the highly artificial Arcadian school of Cavalier Marino. As Spain's military and political predominance in European affairs waned, that of France increased. Spain, Portugal, Italy, looked increasingly to France for inspiration. Italy had founded the first language academy in 1587, but it was Richelieu's French Academy of 1635, with its Forty Immortals, that was imitated by Spain at the outset, by Portugal at the close, of the eighteenth century. Grammars and grammarians flourished everywhere, but they based themselves on Latin and Greek grammatical models rather than on current speech. As the international prestige of the French language grew, that of the Italian decreased, save perhaps in the field of musical terminology, where Italy retained a strong lead that endures to the present day. Many musical terms, *opera* and *piano* among them, passed from Italy to France and other countries in the seventeenth century. French predominance continued through the eighteenth century and into the nineteenth.

The new absolutism of the French monarchy, coupled with the Counter Reformation, may have played an indirect role in the new spirit of precision and authority, the worship of reason and clarity and elegance in language, at least in written form, that characterized the French of the Golden Age. There was as a by-product an unfortunate straightjacket effect upon the language. The stringent prescriptions and prohibitions of Malherbe, who banned words and constructions, archaisms, dialectalisms, neologisms, colloquialisms, foreign borrowings, that he did not personally approve of; the more gentle, but equally binding suggestions of Vaugelas; the appearance of the Port Royal grammar, offering a Classical Latin mold for all languages; the chauvinistic pronouncements of Rivarol, insisting that French was the tongue best suited for universal use; even the antics of the *Précieuses;* all played a part in this movement, which was basically aimed at the triumph of reason, logic, precision, and featured a rationalism and cult of the abstract that were excellent for the stage and diplomacy, but made syntax inflexible and arbitrary, and deprived the language of a good deal of its former elasticity. Yet this language of the Age of Enlightenment, now definitely a literary instrument of the highest order and especially suited for the use of the court and government circles as well as of the world of stage and books, gave rise to a literary output of which France is intensely and justly proud, and whose luminaries include Corneille, Racine, Molière, Rousseau, Diderot, La Rochefoucauld, La Fontaine, Voltaire, and others far too numerous to mention.

Nor is it to be thought that during this period the French language stood still. To begin with, despite the strictures of Malherbe and his school, the appropriation of words and constructions from Classical Latin and Greek, and the coinage of new words based on classical roots, went on unceasingly. The growth of science called for neologisms, and these were supplied from an inexhaustible stock of Latin and Greek roots. Such words as *molecule, equilibrium, microscope, telescope, antenna, apogee,* many of which had first been coined in Italy, then passed on to France and other countries, entered the language at this period. Other words came into French from Spanish, and are particularly noticeable in the works of Corneille. English and German influences were beginning to make themselves felt, though they became much stronger in the eighteenth and particularly the nineteenth century. Lastly, the popular tongue was busy making its own innovations, both in pronunciation and vocabulary, though the first were generally suspended as vulgarisms until the French Revolution set them free and gave them currency in higher circles. The favoring of an *e*-sound that was closed where syllable-final, open where checked, concerning which there is still controversy today,[1] seems to have begun at this point, along with the uvular rather than the trilled pronunciation of *r*, and possibly even the use of the imperfect indicative rather than the imperfect subjunctive in the *if*-clause of a contrary-to-fact condition. More important yet, the shift of so-called *l mouillé* (as in *fille, Bastille*) from an *ly* to a *y* sound, and the shift of written *oi* from *wé* to *wá* are characteristic of the lower-class and petty bourgeois French of the Parisian masses prior to the Revolution, which established their hegemony over the former aristocratic forms. Words like *fourbe, gueux, dupe, gaffe, chic, épatant, narquois, gosse, polisson,* were pure cant in the seventeenth and early eighteenth centuries, where today they are accepted as at least nationwide slang.

One side effect of the domination exerted by classical scholars over the seventeenth-century language appears in the field of orthography, where etymological but unpronounced consonants were often inserted into words that had previously been more or less phonetically spelled.[2] It has also been noted that French and English retain etymological spellings that Spanish and Italian have given up in favor of phonetic ones (*hydrogène, hydrogen,* versus *idrógeno, idrogeno*).

Spelling simplification and regularization are featured in the same period by both Italian and Spanish. The former finally regularized the use of certain consonants and consonant groups, such as *ch* to indicate a velar pronunciation before front vowels, the precise use of *j, qu, gu.* Spanish finally gave up the use of *ç* in favor of *c* before front vowels, *z* before back vowels, and the use of *x* in favor of *j* to represent the new

---

1. How should one pronounce the first two words in *Les lais de Marie de France?* Should a pronunciation distinction be made between *j'aimerai,* "I shall love," and *j'aimerais,* "I should love"?

2. Words like *vingt,* "twenty," *doigt,* "finger," *compter,* "to count," stemming from Latin *viginti, digitum, computare,* are cases in point. English still retains the etymological spelling in *doubt,* which French, having gone through *doubter* (from *dubitare*), has finally relinquished.

velar fricative that had developed out of both. Phonetically, Spanish went over to a universally unvoiced pronunciation for *s*, and dropped the aspiration of *h* stemming from initial *f-*. It also made universal the rule for the use of *a* before a definite personal direct object, which had appeared sporadically since the days of the *Cid*, and which Portuguese had rejected.

Spanish foreign borrowings, which in the sixteenth century had been largely Italian, now became overwhelmingly French. Italian, which had favored Spanish borrowings at an earlier period, also turned more and more to French.

Italian, too, like French, though controlled by an intellectual aristocracy, began to admit to its more popular reaches, and even to the *Commedia dell'Arte*, underworld terms like *gonzo* "sucker," *birba* "sly one," *furfante* "scoundrel," *truccare* "disguise," *camuffare* "disguise."

The seventeenth-eighteenth century period may be described as one of predominantly French ascendancy on the European scene, with Italy, which had set the tone of the Renaissance in the fourteenth and fifteenth centuries, and Spain, which had dominated the sixteenth, progressing at a slower pace. The eighteenth century in particular saw French linguistic, literary, philosophical, and political influence extended to many non-Romance countries, chief among them the Prussia of Frederick the Great and the Russian Empire of Catherine the Great.

The French Revolution, which closed the eighteenth century, and the Napoleonic period, which opened the nineteenth, confirmed this trend. French, the language of a now formalized culture and already the tongue of diplomacy and international relations, was further spread by Napoleon's career of conquest. French ideas, to some extent revolutionary and lower-class, to an even greater degree representative of a dominant bourgeoisie, democratic in a limited sense, equalitarian in a political but not in an economic frame, liberty-loving within the limits of middle-class propriety, inclined to universal brotherhood, but under the aegis of France, were carried by French arms, with varying results, to the Iberian peninsula, to a still badly disunited Italy, to a Germany that was only a very loose conglomeration of independent states, to the Low Countries, even to the great absolutistic empires of the Hapsburgs and the czars. It made no difference that in all these countries there was military, political, and ideological opposition to the great French flood. The ideas took root, even if they were to sprout forth only half a century later, and in the meantime, despite Napoleon's fall, the sweep of the

French language and French culture across Europe, and even across the ocean, continued. As all people who laid claim to culture once knew Latin, now they all knew French. It is no accident that at the Congress of Vienna it was the language of France, the defeated nation, in which the proceedings were carried on. This French linguistic and cultural pre-dominance was to continue unabated throughout the nineteenth century, beginning to wane only after World War I, when Wilson's ignorance of French forced English into a position of parity at the Versailles peace conference.

One additional fruit of the French Revolution and the Napoleonic era was the initial impulse it gave to popular education generally and to literacy in particular. In 1800, the general literacy average of both the United States and the more advanced countries of Europe was in the neighborhood of 20 percent, about the same as what is estimated for the Roman Empire at the height of its power. But the shackles of illiteracy, along with those of slavery, were destined to be broken in the course of the nineteenth century.

16. *The Modern-Contemporary Period*

Historical, literary, and linguistic periods seldom coincide precisely with centuries; but centuries supply a convenient classification for such periods, even if they are chronologically somewhat out of line. The eighteenth century comes to a close in 1800. Should the French Revolution and the Napoleonic era that followed it be viewed as a prolongation of the eighteenth century, or as the starting point of the nineteenth? Or as an epoch of transition? As a unit of history, mores, and culture, the nineteenth century runs on into the early years of the twentieth, and its close is marked by the First World War of 1914–1918, at whose outset a British statesman, Viscount Grey, remarked that the lamps were going out all over Europe, and would not be lit again in "our" lifetime. He probably meant that Western civilization, as his generation had known it, was at an end, and he was right.

The Revolution and Napoleon had transformed the pattern of absolute monarchies and respect for authority in most fields, as it had prevailed in previous centuries, into a new era of political (though not yet economic) democracy. The Great War, destined to end all wars, not only missed its mark, but ushered in a new age of dictators, and government controls over individual activities and national economies exercised by a class, party, or political group, usually in the name of "democracy" and "the People." All this was coupled with a phenomenal, undreamt-of growth in populations, trade, industry, communications, science, technology, and invention, far outstripping that of all previous centuries, whose end is not yet in sight. But all this material progress was, and still is, largely unattended by moral and ethical maturity, and a consciousness

175

of duties to go along with rights, on the part of either individuals, governments, or national units. However one may wish to view these developments, it was altogether natural that this vast political, economic, and social ferment should be reflected in both literature and language.

The Napoleonic wars, arousing the middle classes to a leadership once held by royalty, aristocracy, and clergy, also awakened a spirit of fierce nationalism, a consciousness of race, language, and tradition, that gave rise to the vast romantic movement that dominated most of the nineteenth century. Here it was Germany, aroused from its dynastic loyalties and torpor by the din of French arms and the humiliation of Queen Louise of Prussia, inspired by Lützow's Night Riders and the exploits of Blücher to rout the invader from beyond the Rhine, that gave the signal. Herder, Goethe, Schiller, and the Grimm brothers in the fields of literature and mythology heralded a Romantic movement of which the cult of the Middle Ages was a distinctive feature. This cult spread to England, where it produced the historical novels of Walter Scott and the Gothic mysteries of Horace Walpole, as well as to France, Spain, and Italy. Neoclassicism and the worship of reason were all but forgotten as French writers turned to the previously scorned "Gothic" period for their inspiration. This novel interest, spreading to the linguistic field, gave rise to the beginning of scientific historical linguistics, with Schlegel, Rask, Bopp, Jakob Grimm, pointing the early way to the Indo-European field, and Friedrich Diez applying the comparative methodology specifically to the Romance languages a little later.

But literary romanticism had a second aspect, which was to lead to literary and linguistic realism: the study of the life, customs, and speech of the popular masses; hence the mixture of topics and treatments that appear in the works of Chateaubriand, Lamartine, Victor Hugo, Vigny, Musset, Gautier, Baudelaire, Mallarmé, Maupassant, Daudet, Balzac, Flaubert, Verlaine, Zola, Rimbaud.

The mighty French literary output dominated and was reflected by that of the other Romance countries. Spain, after an attempt at neoclassicism, went over to the romantic approach with Saavedra, Bécquer, and Larra, then turned increasingly to realism and the depiction of the doings, habits, and language of the people with Galdós, Alarcón, Pardo Bazán, Blasco Ibáñez, Azorín, Pío Baroja, Rubén Darío, Gabriela Mistral, and García Lorca. Italy's romantic contribution, partly under

French, occasionally under German influence, began with Alfieri and Foscolo, assuming a more native aspect with Manzoni, de Amicis, Leopardi, Carducci, and Pascoli. More realistic are the works of Giacosa, Rovetta, Verga, Fogazzaro, Matilde Serao, Grazia Deledda, with D'Annunzio in a class by himself. Romanticism penetrated Portugal with such writers as Herculano and Castelo Branco, but romanticism's realistic outgrowth comes to the fore with Eça de Queiroz, Oliveira, and Pessoa. There is even a neorealism, represented perhaps more by Brazilian than by Portuguese writers (Gonçalves Dias, de Assis, da Cunha, Veríssimo). Alecsandri, Eminescu, and Caragiale are the main representatives of nineteenth-century Romanticism in Rumania.

Literary activity in the nineteenth century had a far greater impact on the languages than in earlier periods. There was more of a secular attitude after the French Revolution and the Declaration of the Rights of Man. The battle against illiteracy had finally begun. Education was becoming more widespread, reaching down into the lowest social strata and out to the more remote country districts, as schools proliferated and became free, public, and compulsory. These same schools had perforce to concentrate on the national language rather than on Latin. Military service on a nationwide scale, inaugurated by Napoleon and replacing the old professional armies, aided in the cause of education, literacy, and standardization, if only so that raw recruits would understand and follow commands issued in speech or in writing. But this elevating process of education had to shun the rarefied language of literature, poetry, and philosophy, and concentrate increasingly on the language of the masses, which in turn exerted its influence on the literary output, turning it away from the medievalistic excesses of the early Romantic movement and into realistic channels, which meant the appearance in writing not merely of the lower-class language, but even of slang and dialects. The ultimate result was that a literary production which at the outset of the nineteenth century had still been predominantly aristocratic, becoming more and more democratized as it went, passed through a rather long middle-class stage, and by the end of the First World War had become predominantly popular, journalistic, the language of newspapers and magazines directed at a mass market rather than a pundit oligarchy or even a fairly numerous bourgeoisie.

In this sense, it might be said that the romantic movement eventually led to the triumph of the spoken over the written language. There was a gradual, yet perceptible loosening of literary straight jackets, a search for elasticity, briefness, conciseness, that still characterizes modern schools of journalism, a parallel search for the picturesque, colorful, and new in vocabulary. To present the reverse of the medal, there also began to appear a tendency toward the vulgar, the sloppy, the incoherent, the inarticulate. Literature began to strain syntax, particularly in the new forms of poetry. It was perhaps part of the age-old struggle between language viewed as a means of precise communication and language viewed as a free vehicle for self-expression. Whether the peak of "democratization" in language has yet been reached is something we cannot answer.

But the movement was two-way. Monteverdi stresses the use of historical and literary characters passing into the journalistic and everyday language, so that in Italian *Perpetua* is used for "housekeeper," *Figaro* for "barber," *Cicerone* for "tourist guide," *Maramaldo* for "traitor" (he might have added *Pagliaccio* and *Pulcinella*, with their popular derivatives *pagliacciata* and *pulcinellata*, "clownish behavior," and even such foreign adoptions as *Polichinelle* and *Punch*). Spanish, with *Don Juan* for "enterprising lover," *matamoros* (literally "Moor-killer") for "braggart," and the numerous characters supplied by Cervantes that have become international (*Dulcinea, Sancho Panza, Rocinante*, the *Quijote* that gives us *quixotic*) follows suit, while French is even more productive of such international forms (*Roland, Bayard*, the *Chauvin* of *chauvinism* and *chauvinist, chassepot, gilet, guillotine, mesmerisme, saxophone*). Hall stresses the feature of regionalism in literature, as illustrated by Argentina's *lengua gauchesca* and in the writings of Fogazzaro, Verga, Gadda, and others; sometimes with overtones of separatism, as in the *Jocs Florals* of Catalonia and the *Félibrige* movement of Mistral's Provence. But he also brings out the centralizing, antidialectal force exerted by modern governments and their school systems, which insist on the national standard.

Linguistically, the latter part of the nineteenth century is marked by relative stability in sounds and grammatical structure, coupled with a vast extension in vocabulary, due in part to accretions from slang and the more popular reaches of the language; in part to the advances of science and technology, which are attended by the formation of hosts of new words, international in nature, based on Latin and Greek roots, pre-

fixes, and suffixes; in part to the admission of loanwords from abroad.[1]
The factor of snobbism and linguistic prestige of one language over an-
other is indicated by the penetration of English words into French, of
French words into Italian, Spanish, even Rumanian.[2]

Italy's cultural subjection to France during this period may in part
be attributed to such historical and political factors as the intervention
of the two Napoleons in Italian affairs before final unification was
achieved in 1870; in part to the purely cultural factor of the stability of
French usage as contrasted with the fluctuation of Italian. Both factors
began to wane after Italian troops occupied Rome. There was also the
stabilizing and nationalistic influence of such writers as Manzoni and
de Amicis. But Manzoni's attempt to re-Florentinize the language was
thwarted by the greater importance of Rome once it became the capital
of a united Italy. It is significant in this connection that most of the
words admitted to standard colloquial usage after 1870 came from
the Roman dialect (*pifferaro,* "piper"; *pignolo,* literally "pine nut,"
colloquially used in the sense of "small-minded"; *abbacchio,* "lamb";
saltimbocca, "rolled thin slices of veal with prosciutto," a Roman
specialty; *sbafare,* "to freeload"; *fifa,* "fear," especially in military action;
scalcinato, literally "having lost its plaster," idiomatically "down at the
heels"; *svignarsela,* literally "to get out of the vineyard," "to get away
unnoticed"; *spaghettata,* "spaghetti feast"; *fattacci,* "unpleasant happenings," with criminal overtones; *pupazzetti,* "little puppets," often cut
out of paper, but more recently, "comic strips").

Yet the persistence of French influence is attested, among other
things, by what Migliorini styles "Franco-Latinisms" (*ascensore, paci-
fista, pedicure*), as well as by a sample of what might be termed "modern Franco-Italian."[3]

---

1. French *vasistas,* "transom," from German *Was ist das?* "what is that?" (German soldiers in Paris, seeing a transom for the first time, inquired about it in their
language; the French seemingly thought they were giving their name for it); *chou-
croute,* "sauerkraut," with its first part "cabbage" in French, its second part "cabbage" in German; *contredanse* (from English *country dance*); *boulingrin,* "bowling
green"; *paquebot,* "packet boat"; *bifteck,* "beefsteak"; *club, tunnel, snob, bluff, wagon,*
taken over from English without change in spelling; even *jeu de l'âne salé,* "Aunt
Sally's game" (but *âne salé,* though it sounds like "Aunt Sally," means "salted donkey" in French). *Cravate,* from Serbo-Croatian *Hrvat,* "Croatian," Russian *samovar,*
knout, pogrom, are all early or late nineteenth-century borrowings.

2. Spanish *edecán, taller,* from French *aide-de-camp, atelier;* Italian popular and
semivulgar *comò, paltò,* from French *commode,* "chest of drawers," *paletot,* "overcoat."

3. See Appendix L.

The advent of a new linguistic century was heralded in Italy, even before the outbreak of the First World War, by Marinetti's Futurism, which purported to break all the restraints of conventional syntax and give words full freedom (*parole in libertà,* or, to use one of his own telescoped forms, *parolibere*). This movement, which was not too successful in Italy, at least in the linguistic field, was to have vast international repercussions in art, architecture, music. Linguistically, some of its "dynamic" features appear in the contemporary works of Marshall McLuhan, as well as in some of the modern schools of poetry, particularly in the United States. Another precursor of the twentieth century was Gabriele D'Annunzio, whose spectacular political and military activities before, during, and immediately after the Great War were attended by a spirit of linguistic creativity exemplified by his use of *velivolo* for "airplane," *capolavorare,* "to work at masterpieces," and the *eja, alalà* first used by his *Arditi* and legionnaires, later taken over by the Fascists.

Each of the three major Romance countries ran into a period of crisis during the first half of the twentieth century. In Spain, it was the great Civil War of 1935–1938, with its attendant cruelties, destruction, and bloodshed. In France, already weakened by the supreme effort exerted in the First World War, it was the military collapse of 1940, followed by the German occupation and ultimate liberation; but this was followed by the gradual disintegration of France's second colonial empire. Italy's crisis came first, with Mussolini's seizure of power in 1922, and lasted longest, till the end of the Second World War in 1945, and beyond. All three, in different measure, had linguistic repercussions.

Spain, a country still partly isolated from the rest of Europe and undergoing a torment which, though painful, lasted for a comparatively short time, underwent little in the way of basic linguistic change beyond what would have reached it under more peaceful circumstances. There were some vocabulary innovations, and the repristination of old terms in new meanings.[4]

---

4. *Caudillo,* "chief," once used for El Cid, later applied to Franco; *falange,* "phalanx," applied to a Fascist-type organization; *carlista,* once a supporter of Don Carlos, applied to the ultraconservatives; *miliciano,* "militiaman," applied to irregular Loyalist troops; *requeté,* onomatopoeic for the blare of a bugle, applied to Navarrese Franco supporters; *Alcázar,* "citadel," specifically applied to the Alcázar of Toledo, which held out under Republican siege; later *Valle de los Caídos,* "Valley of the Fallen," the huge mortuary erected to those who died on both sides.

In very recent times, there was a movement for the purification of the Spanish language from foreign intrusions (mainly of United States origin) which was a very pale reflection of the similar movement carried on in France, and described below. To this purification Ramón Menéndez Pidal, greatest of Spanish philologists and at that time still Minister of Education, lent some theoretical and half-hearted support before his recent death.

The French situation was more complex. France had been subjected to invasion from abroad in two great wars and to prolonged foreign occupation in the course of the second one. But France had also suffered a loss of linguistic prestige which began at the time of the first war and was accelerated by the second, caused in part by the relentless encroachments of English. This led to an attitude of defensive linguistic nationalism that in some ways equaled that of the sixteenth century. French, its defenders proclaimed, was not merely still a great international language; it was *the* international language, and should be kept pure of English infiltrations, from across the Channel or the Atlantic. Why use some French adaptation of *air conditioning* and *air conditioned* when terms like *climatisation* and *climatisé* could ingeniously be formed on native words? Why should French teen-agers use "Hi, pals!" as a greeting when the bountiful French language was in a position to supply *Salut les copains!?* At the most, one could accept terms like *parking* and *camping*, but why *baby-sitter* and *teen-ager?* Actually, for some of the younger generation's activities, it was French that could supply English with a slang *à gogo*, "aplenty," "in abundance," that was misinterpreted as "Go! Go!" and a *discothèque* that was borrowed untranslated by English speakers.

The great apostle of the new French linguistic nationalism was René Etiemble, whose *Le Franglais* (also labeled *Sabir Atlantique*) gave rise to such imitations as *Espanglés* or *Spanglish*. In this devastating book, which unfortunately did not receive in America the attention it deserved, possibly because the author mingled political condemnation of U.S. policies with his linguistic material, the French professor took issue not with hundreds, but with thousands of Anglo-American innovations in contemporary colloquial, newspaper, and even literary French. They run all the way from the frivolous (*high society, party, deb, joke, playboy, pin-up, petting, glamorous, cover girl, call girl*) to the deadly serious (*blackout, holster, gunman, muscle man, trigger man, kidnapper, under-*

world); from the utilitarian (*pipeline, scooter, roadster, hardtop, jet, nonstop, businessman, part time*) to the pleasurable (*hamburger, hot dog, lunch, crackers, grapefruit*); from drugstore items (*cold cream, Kleenex, Airwick*) to *motel, bird watcher, girl scout*. There are bilingual combinations like *quick lait*, "milk bar," *shopping-libre*, "supermarket," *self-beauté*, "home permanent"; loan translations like *argent dur*, "hard cash"; newspaper phrases featuring English syntax like *Il est beaucoup parlé du fait que la France rajeunit* ("The fact that France is growing younger is much talked about"), *La solution est loin d'être sous contrôle* ("The situation is far from being under control").

Lest it be thought that Etiemble's is a one-man crusade, here are a few suggestions issued as recently as 1973 by a French government bureau for the replacement of such Anglo-American words as *flashback, one-man show, hit parade, features, zoning, jumbo jet, show business, scoop, spacecraft, kitchenette, know-how: rétrospectif, spectacle solo, palmarès* (literally "honors list"), *variés, zonage, gros-porteur* (literally "big carrier"), *industrie de spectacle, exclusivité, aéronef* (this literally is "airship"; might we suggest *astronef*, or the *vaisseau cosmique* favored by *Le Monde?*), *cuisinette, savoir-faire* (the last seems particularly ill chosen; *savoir-faire* has to do with personality, likability, diplomacy, getting along with people; *know-how* has strong mechanical-industrial connotations).

All this is in addition to what one would expect in the line of normal vocabulary accretion stemming from mechanical and scientific progress, coupled with the language of the media (newspapers, magazines, and particularly radio and television).

The two wars and the German occupation contributed to vocabulary growth such terms as *poilu*, "hairy," and *pioupiou*, "chirp-chirp," used to describe the French infantryman in the First War; *ils ne passeront pas*, "they shall not pass," the battle cry of Verdun; *maquis* and *résistance* (the first, literally "thickets," borrowed from old-style Corsican bandits, to describe the members of the second, which fought the German occupation from underground); *Vichy* and *Ligne Maginot* (the first a collective title of opprobrium for collaborators, particularly in the Pétain government; the latter to describe an impregnable defense that somehow fails). *Pieds noirs* (literally "black feet") refers to Algerian-born settlers of European origin and came into vogue at the time of the Algerian breakup.

Slang terms, mainly of Parisian lower-class origin, have given rise to entire dictionaries, and have had varying degrees of penetration into the standard language. Widespread colloquialisms are *type* or *zig*, "guy"; *culot* or *toupet*, "nerve," "chutzpah"; *salaud*, "scoundrel," "louse"; *cornichon* or *veau*, "sucker," "easy mark"; *boule-de-suif*, "fatty," "greaseball"; *boîte*, "dump"; *faire la bombe*, "to have a high old time," "to get plastered"; *bagnole*, "railroad cattle car," or *vieux clou*, "old nail," for "car," "jalopy"; *machin*, "gadget"; *le pèse*, "the it weighs," for "money," "dough"; *la Sainte Touche*, "St. Collect's Day," "payday"; *potin* or *tapage*, "racket," "noise"; *bain de pied*, "foot bath," for "bad coffee"; *rigolo*, "funny"; *épatant* or *formidable*, "wonderful," "great," "swell"; *fiche-moi la paix*, "leave me alone"; *fiche le camp*, "scram."

A series of very recent slang terms, culled by Anne Slack for *French Review* from *Petit Larousse 1975*, includes *pifomètre*, "flair," "intuition"; *zinzin*, "weirdo"; *magouille*, "power struggle"; *renvoyer l'ascenseur* (literally, "to send the lift back," for "to return a favor"); *c'est le pied* (literally, "it's the foot") for "perfect"; *en catastrophe*, "in a hurry," "under difficult conditions"; *dingue*, "absurd"; *banquer*, "to pay," "to bankroll"; *glander*, "to waste one's time"; *polar*, "whodunit" (seemingly a telescoping of *roman policier* in reverse); *ringard*, "actor staging a comeback"; *gonzesse*, "man without energy"; *chienlit* (literally "dogbed," for "muddled political situation").

In addition, there are recent loanwords and loan translations from English, Etiemble to the contrary notwithstanding: *planning*, *sex-shop*, *pilule*, "the Pill," *concerné*, "concerned." There are even contributions that have come to the French of France from the French of Canada: *avionnerie*, "plane factory," *bouscueil*, "pile of loose ice," *frasil*, "ice film in formation," *tire*, "pastry."

On the phonological side, two notable changes are in progress: the typically Parisian merger of two of the current four French nasal sounds, so that *un vin* is pronounced *in vin* (but this is resisted in the provinces); and a similar, but far more widespread merger of the two *a* sounds (as in *là* and *âge*), in the direction of the sound of *a* in *là*.

Italian, subjected to Fascist domination for over twenty years, underwent a certain amount of vocabulary change which did not endure. There were terms like *dopolavoro* (the after-work organization); *balilla* (the Fascist boy scouts, named after a boy hero of the wars for Italian independence); *gerarca*, "hierarch" (an important member of the Fascist high command); *podestà* (the ancient term for "mayor," but under

Fascism an official appointed by the central government); *autarchia,* "autarchy" (Mussolini's plan for Italian economic self-sufficiency); Mussolini's own *retroguardismo,* "rearguardism," "the quality of lagging behind"; *prima ora* (some Fascists were "first-hour" members, from the very inception of the party); *vivere pericolosamente,* "to live dangerously." There were some nonpolitical terms, like *portabagagli* (literally "baggage carrier," perhaps a loan translation of German *Gepäckträger,* now used for "trunk compartment" in a car); and *panino gravido,* "pregnant roll," that had replaced the older *facchino,* "porter," and *panino imbottito,* "stuffed roll," "sandwich," now restored.

One major Fascist innovation had been the replacement, at least in official usage and documents, of the polite form of address (*Lei* or *Ella* with third singular verb) by *voi* with the second plural, which had always been used in some parts of the country, notably Naples. *Lei* came back as soon as the Fascists were out.

There were also numerous words that had been banned because of their real or supposed foreign origin (*garage, chauffeur, hotel, bar, consommé, menu, club, chèque,* replaced during the Fascist era by *autorimessa, autista, albergo, mescita, brodo ristretto, lista delle vivande, circolo, assegno,* most of which antedated the era, and consequently are still around).

The downfall of the Fascist regime brought in a flood of American loanwords, many of G.I. origin and purely temporary, like *sciuscià* (from *shoeshine*) for *lustrascarpe, ciuinga* (from *chewing gum*), *segnorina* (a girl of loose morals; seemingly a crossing of Italian *signorina* and Spanish *señorita*), along with the delightful custom of using all verbs in the infinitive (*Voi dove andare?,* "You where to go?" for "Where are you going?"). But a very permanent American English influence remained, with the Marshall Plan and NATO. A few forms antedated both the war and the invasion, like *depressione, proibizionismo, secco,* "dry," *guerra dei nervi,* "war of nerves," *jazz* (often spelled *ges*), *nemico pubblico numero uno,* "public enemy number one." Others are definitely of postwar vintage: *gretagarbeggiare* and, a little later, *marlonbrandeggiare* (to act like Greta Garbo or Marlon Brando); *monroismo* (the quality of being like Marilyn Monroe); English *sigh* (in comic strips, balloons, but regularly pronounced *sig*); *giubox* or *giubosse* (from *juke box*); *blue jeans; topless; drive-in* (but *cineparco* is also used); *sexy; maccartismo* (from *McCarthyism*). On the other hand, *futbol* was rejected in favor of *calcio,* and *basketball* in favor of *pallacanestro.*

What distinguishes the Italian attitude toward transatlantic loanwords from the French is a spirit of tolerant acceptance. A *Corriere della Sera* writer, Alfredo Tudisco, after exemplifying the infiltration with an eloquent passage,[5] goes on to say: "We can swallow our anglicisms with our minds at ease. The first favorable results are already apparent in the replacement of complicated sentences full of subordinate clauses by simpler, clearer sentences based on coordinated structures."

The question, however, arises whether the new telegraphic brevity of newspaper Italian exemplified by *correntacqua* (for *acqua corrente,* "running water"), *cinema* (for the older *cinematografo*), *burosauri,* "bureausaurians" (for fossilized bureaucrats), *fantascienza,* "science fiction" (a telescoping of *fantasia* and *scienza*), is not due as much to the media as to American influence. There is in Italian, far more than in French or Spanish, a tendency to change, due in part to a late but accelerated educational process that has cut down illiteracy from the 80 percent of 1800 to the 8 percent of 1960; in part to the internal migration that accompanied postwar industrialization, shifting and mingling populations once kept apart by geography; but above all to the all-pervading press, radio, and television that have replaced literary authors as the setters of national standards.

The present-day vocabulary, strongly influenced by scientific and technological usage, makes abundant use of new compounds of which the first element is *super-, inter-, para-, radio-, tele-, auto-*. Italian linguistic creativity is illustrated by such imagery as *pescecane,* literally "shark," for "profiteer" (but this goes back to the First World War); *pappagallo* "parrot," for "masher"; *vitellone,* "big calf," for "scion of the idle rich"; *paparazzi,* origin unknown, for "inquisitive news photographers"; *sfasato,* "out of phase," for "insane"; *pollo,* "chicken," for "easy mark," "sucker"; *ragazza squillo,* "call girl" (*squillo* can be "telephone ring" or "blare of a bugle"); *spogliarella,* "strip-teaser" (from *spogliarsi,* "to undress"; here French was for a time more elegant with its *effeuilleuse,* which brings in the imagery of stripping off leaves from a tree, but it has lately gone over to *striptiseuse,* directly borrowed from English).

There is little in the way of phonological change going on in present-day Italian, outside of a tendency to neutralize the open and closed

---

5. "*È un vero playboy, molto sexy, il beniamino dell'international set; industrial design è il suo hobby, e di più è un health fiend; figurati, va dal dottore per un check-up ogni due mesi.*" ("He is a real -, very -, the pet of the - -; - - is his -, and furthermore he's a - -; imagine, he goes to the doctor for a - every two months.")

sounds of *e* (occasionally even of *o*), so that *pesca,* "peach," and *pesca,* "fishing," once distinguished by pronunciation, can be confused. The political predominance of Rome clashes with the cultural tradition of Florence where the two pronunciations differ (as in *lettera, posto, gloria*), but the tendency is toward compromise. Grammatically, there are few innovations in progress: irregular euphonic formations like *begli* and *quegli* tend to level out with the regular *belli* and *quelli; gli* before the verb tends to replace *loro* after the verb in the sense of "to them" (*gli ho dato il libro* instead of *ho dato loro il libro,* "I gave them the book").

The picture that emerges for today's Romance languages is one that does not differ too radically from that of the other great languages of the modern world: democratization, to the point of vulgarization, as the language becomes the common property of all social classes, and no longer obeys the dictates of a cultural aristocracy; a definite slackening of phonological and morphological change, typical of historical periods of national unity and centralization, but now powerfully aided by the ubiquitous media; vast changes in the fields of vocabulary and semantics, as new objects, processes, and activities call for new words that will describe them.

With the proper allowances made for historical conditions and technological factors, the situation is not too different from the one that seems to have prevailed in the ancient Roman realm at the end of the Classical period (say the third century A.D.).

Will the processes of democratization and vulgarization go on to the end that seems inevitable? Perhaps and perhaps not. There are too many factors at work today that were not operative in the days of ancient Rome.[6]

---

6. It is yet too early to estimate the effect on the languages of postwar literary writers, such as Ayala, Sender, Casalduero, Buero Vallejo in Spain; Sartre, Saint-Exupéry, Aragon, Camus, Simone de Beauvoir, Françoise Sagan in France; Malaparte, Moravia, Quasimodo, Levi, Ungaretti, Montale, Gadda, Lampedusa in Italy. In any event, it is far smaller than it was in the past, partly because present-day languages look more to the media than to books for their inspiration, partly because present-day writers are influenced by the spoken language to a greater degree than in the past.

17. The Influence of Latin-Romance on Western European Languages

The impact of one civilization upon another is measured (not too precisely) by a multiplicity of yardsticks—archaeological discoveries, artifacts, contributions to life styles, food, housing, attire, religion, literature, science, and invention. Many of these impacts are recorded in linguistic form. Loanwords and loan translations are perhaps the most reliable indication of the extent and quality of the mingling of peoples and cultures.

Measured by this yardstick, the influence exerted by Latin and Latin's descendants upon the world at large easily outstrips that of any other group.

Along with Greek, but to a larger degree, Latin is the world's main purveyor of the higher ranges of vocabulary, the terms that describe objects and activities in the areas of religion, philosophy, literature, and, above all, science and technology in all their branches. This influence is fully international in scope, especially in more recent times. It is not only the European languages that have achieved a fair measure of linguistic internationality in the upper ranges; the scientific and technological impact of Greek and Latin is perceptible in such Far Eastern languages as Japanese and Indonesian, in the tongues of India, in Semitic languages such as Arabic and Hebrew, while the religious Graeco-Latin content has been spread far and wide by Christian missionaries to the indigenous languages of Africa, America, New Guinea, Australia, the islands of the Pacific.

In addition to the Latin element, there are the big contributions that have been made both to Indo-European languages that are not Romance and to non–Indo-European tongues by French, Spanish, Italian, Portuguese, through medieval, Renaissance, and modern contacts. In recent times, the Romance languages have had to meet the competition of a formidable rival, English, which in many instances has far outstripped its closest Romance rival, French.

But English itself, while basically (that is to say, for what concerns its sound and grammatical structure) a Germanic language, is so infiltrated by both Latin and Romance elements that when it comes to vocabulary it may well be described as a mixture of Germanic and Latin-Romance, with the Germanic element having the edge in the matter of frequency of use, the Latin-Romance ahead by actual dictionary word count. In fact, this characteristic leads many nonspecialists to suppose that English is half Romance—an erroneous view, but one that can be easily accounted for.

On a straight word count, the combination of English words derived from Latin, French, Spanish, Italian, and Portuguese accounts for about 50 percent of all dictionary entries. The Germanic, including the original Anglo-Saxon with its Scandinavian admixture brought in by the Danes, plus loanwords from German, Dutch, and modern Scandinavian, constitutes at the most 25 percent of the entries. The balance is supplied by words of Greek origin, plus the very numerous contributions from other sources (Celtic, Slavic, Hebrew, Arabic, Indo-Iranian, Dravidian, Chinese, Japanese, American Indian, African, etc.) that English has freely and easily appropriated. One needs to be reminded that this proportion does not at all hold when the running words in conversation or in writing are counted. Here it is estimated that one-fourth of all our spoken language consists of repetitions of pronouns like *I, me, you, he, him, she, her, it, we, us,* high-frequency verbs like *be, have, will;* definite and indefinite articles like *the, a, an;* conjunctions like *and, but, that;* prepositions like *of, on, to, in, for;* all of which are Anglo-Saxon.[1] The same is true even in literature; the vocabulary of the King James Bible is (counting running words) 94 percent Germanic; Shakespeare's is 90 percent; Tennyson's 88 percent; Milton's 81 percent; Samuel Johnson's 72 percent. But in present-day technical writings, despite all the

---

1. The only word of Latin-Romance origin that could even remotely vie with these in frequency of occurrence is *very*, which goes back to Old French *verai*, in turn derived from Vulgar Latin *veracus*, Classical Latin *verus*, "true." *Very* displaced Anglo-Saxon *sore*, as in "I am sore wroth," whose German cognate is *sehr*. In French, *verai* went on to become *vrai*, "true."

repetitions of extreme-frequency Germanic words, the count goes down to less than 60 percent, and the Greek and Latin-Romance element rises in proportion.

Early Anglo-Saxon borrowings from Latin include words that few save specialists recognize as of foreign origin, to such an extent have they changed their form to conform to English sound structure (*street, kiln, cheese, minster, bishop, cheap,* from Latin *strata, culina, caseus, monasterium, episcopus, caupo; monasterium* and *episcopus* are Latin borrowings from Greek). The same may be said of French words imported by the Norman conquerors, or during the centuries when the kings of England still laid claim to French possessions (*very, pay, army, peach, tax, state, sir, faith, saint, judge, fine, dress, chair, joy, pain, grief, city, rage, piece, cry, kerchief, puppy, flirt, move, push, beef, pork, veal, boil, plate, dandelion,* which is French *dent de lion,* "lion's tooth," even *tennis,* which is French *tenez,* "here you are," "take this," as you serve, and its *love,* which is French *l'oeuf,* "the egg," or "zero score").

Italian contributes many words of the same description (*lumber, cash, costume, pilot, medal, gallop, cartoon, laundry, gulf, bank,* some of which it had taken earlier from the Germanic of the Ostrogoths and Longobards). Many of the Italian contributions come in by way of French; *parrucca,* for example, is borrowed by French as *perruque,* then later by English as *periwig,* then abbreviated to *wig.* With the Renaissance came new floods of French and Italian words (*violin, sumptuous, ballet, canteen, dentist, patrol, routine, cadet, grimace, prestige, trait*). Many of the more recent Italian contributions are fully naturalized and disguised in appearance (*partisan, radish, chicory, escort, manage, group, gallery, garb, compliment, caprice, cannon, concert, attack, improvise*). Others, particularly in the arts, retain their Italian appearance (*tempo, aria, piano, torso, stanza, cello, villa, vista, gala, piazza, portico, malaria, manifesto, grotto, cameo, trombone*). Much more recent are *zucchini, broccoli, confetti,* the pasta family, including *spaghetti* and *ravioli,* and, of course, *pizza* and *pizzeria,* all accepted in full popular use, despite their foreign appearance, along with *studio, trio, presto, solo, motto, ghetto, buffalo,* even *influenza* and *flu.* Quite recent are *Mafia* and *Cosa Nostra* (the latter, perhaps, coined on American soil).

By the time Spanish and Portuguese began to stream into English, it was a little late for full naturalization, though a few words made it (*cockroach, cork, molasses, alligator, sherry, port* (wine), *hoosegow, pickaninny*). But most words from that source, however popularly used, retain a foreign form (*armada, mulatto, Negro, mosquito, rodeo, sombrero, bonanza, cargo, tornado, pimento, corral, commando*). *Colonel* has French spelling but Spanish pronunciation, with *r* for *l* (Spanish *coronel*).

Reverting to Latin, the mother tongue of Romance, Middle English and the Renaissance saw the introduction of *gesture, interrupt, lunatic, nervous, picture, polite*. In many cases the Latin word was borrowed as it stood, with only an adaptation to English pronunciation (*census, genius, inferior, minor, senior, stupor*). In other cases, there was the dropping of a Latin ending, or replacement with an English one (*quiet, reject, suppress, ulcer, legal, contempt, include, popular, individual, necessary*). Then there are words which clearly betray their Latin origin, but are nevertheless in popular use (*alibi, alias, bonus, exit, extra, item, [omni]bus, propaganda, deficit, agenda, quorum, veto*). Last come a host of words based on Latin roots, but coined in relatively modern times (*Protestant, inertia, transcendental, confiscate, conclude, ascend, probity, interrogate*), plus the scientific coinages of yesterday and today (*febrifuge, pulmonary, cerebral, capillary, supersonic, deflagration, artifact, reactor, nuclear, computer*).

When it comes to words and expressions used in English but considered not naturalized, a survey of the guide words (those at the top of the page) in a special dictionary of "foreign" words and expressions is revealing. Out of a total of 358 such words, Latin accounts for 60, French for 102, Italian for 43, Spanish for 27, Portuguese for 7, Rumanian for 1. This gives a total of 240, a clear and impressive majority. By way of comparison, Greek accounts for 15, German for 43, other Germanic languages, including Dutch and Scandinavian, for 9, Russian for 6, Irish for 1, Indo-Iranian tongues (Sanskrit, Persian, Hindi, Bengali) for 10, Semitic languages (Arabic, Hebrew, Aramaic) for 16, Turkish for 3, Hungarian for 1, American Indian languages for 6, Hawaiian for 2, Chinese for 2, Japanese for 2, African tongues for 1, Basque for 1.

The impact of Latin-Romance on Germanic languages other than English (German, Dutch, Scandinavian) is more limited, but still considerable. To begin with, all have, as tongues of Western civilization, the stock of Graeco-Latin words that have entered the language of culture, literature, art, and science. Granted that no other Germanic language enjoyed the peculiar relationship with French that bound English to the Romance world throughout the Middle Ages, it is none the less true that the medieval background of Germany and the Low Countries was approximately equal to England's, and that the force of the Renaissance and Humanism struck with the same impact the Germanic lands of Western Europe. Hence the purely Classical Latin element in German, Dutch, and Scandinavian is not inferior to that of English. What is lacking is that very large body of early Romance words derived from the Old French of the Normans and from the later contacts, often hostile, that followed their conquest of England. On the other hand, from about 1400 on, German and Dutch contacts with France equalled or perhaps even surpassed those of English.

Very early contacts between Germanic and Latin speakers are often identifiable either by the fact that the borrowed Latin word had not yet palatalized or assibilated velars before *a* (in the case of French) and front vowels (as in *cerasia*, "cherry," giving rise to German *Kirsch*, Dutch *kers*, the first part of Swedish *Körsbär*; or *cellarium* "cellar," becoming German *Keller*, whence *Kellner* and *Kellnerin*, "waiter" and "waitress"; or *caseus*, "cheese," turning into German *Käse*, Dutch *kaas*; here Swedish prefers the native *ost*); or by the fact that the High German form shows the second Germanic consonant shift, whereby an initial Latin *p* becomes *pf*, a medial *p* or *b* becomes *f*, a *t* turns into *ts*, *z*, or *ss*, depending on its position (this accounts for Latin *pondus*, "weight," "unit of weight," to German *Pfund*, as against English *pound*, Dutch *pond*, Swedish *pund*); *planta*, "plant," to German *Pflanze*, as against English, Dutch, and Swedish *plant*; *piper*, "pepper," to German *Pfeffer*, but English *pepper*, Dutch *peper*, Swedish *peppar*; *strata* to German *Strasse*, versus English *street*, Dutch *straat* (here Swedish uses the native *gata* that appears in our *Newgate*, German *Gasse*); Latin *persica* becomes German *Pfirsich* (English *peach* is taken from later Old French *pesche*); the Anglo-Saxon form taken directly from Latin was *persoc*, like Dutch *persik*, Swedish *persika*. Latin *tabula* comes out in German as *Tafel*, but this is restricted to special uses; German normally uses *Tisch*, our *dish*; here English has *table*, Dutch both *tafel* and *tabel*, the latter used more specifically in the sense of "schedule"; Swedish has *tabell*, but the native *bord* (English *board*) is the customary word. Of particular interest is *paraveredus*, a late imperial Latin word for "horse," which is adopted by German as *Pferd*, by Dutch as *paard*, and does not appear in Scandinavian (Swedish prefers the native *häst*). In English it became *palfrey*, but that was a later borrowing from Old French *palefreit*, today *palefroi*. Latin *scribere* gave German *schreiben*, Dutch *schrijven*, Swedish *skriva*; it appears in English *shrive*, but English preferred the Anglo-Saxon *write*. Latin *caupo*, "itinerant merchant," gave rise to German *kaufen* with its compounds and derivatives (*verkaufen, Kaufmann*, etc.), Dutch *kopen*, Swedish *köpa*; in English it gave rise to *cheap*, but the native *buy* was preferred as a verb. *Fenestra*, "window," became *Fenster* in German, *venster* in Dutch, *fönster* in Swedish; again English preferred a native formation (really a Scandinavian borrowing) on the root of *wind*. *Brevis*, in the sense of "letter," "missive," gave English *brief* (now used mainly at law), German *Brief*, Dutch *brief*, Swedish *brev*. Place-names in what later became West Germany show interesting changes: modern Münster is Latin *monasterium*, as is our *minster*; modern Köln, which we prefer to call by its French name, Cologne, is Latin *colonia*, "colony." Though it is probable that they go no farther back than medieval Latin, German and Dutch *prosit* (or *prost, proost*) come straight from a Latin verb form, "may it be of good omen"; Scandinavian prefers its native *skål* as a drinking toast.

Later Germanic borrowings from Romance, usually French, include such forms as *Spiegel*, Dutch *spiegel*, Swedish *spegel*, from Old French *espiegle* (now replaced by *miroir*) from Latin *speculum*, "mirror." When the potato was brought back from the New World, French *tartuffe*, now *truffe*, formed from Latin *terrae tuber*, was appropriated by German as *Kartoffel*, translated by Dutch as *aardappel* and by German as *Erdapfel*, preferred in many German areas, and taken in its original form by Swedish as *potatis*.

There is one characteristic of German which perhaps goes back to the days of nineteenth-century romanticism, a sort of linguistic nationalism that leads to the creation of loan translations to replace earlier loan-words. There was an obsolete *Aquaedukt*, for instance, which *Wasserleitung* replaced (*aquaduct* still appears in Dutch, although *waterleiding* is perhaps more common). *Kasus* for "case" was replaced by *Fall*, save in a grammatical connotation. *Körper* from Latin *corpus* is more commonly used for a living body, as is also the native *Leib* (*Leiche*, usually a dead body or corpse, has a cognate in English *litchfield*, obsolete for "graveyard").

Borrowings in the Renaissance and modern times are in abundance.

Some are formed on Latin roots, or are modifications of Latin words (the names of the months fall into this category, as do such words as *president* and *student*); others come from the individual Romance languages, with a strong predominance of French forms. All Germanic languages use Latin *catus* to indicate "cat," and some form of Graeco-Latin *papyrus* for "paper." More specifically French are *chauffeur, garage, garderobe, commode, classe, intéressant, lampe, restaurant, toilette,* though spellings may vary; but *bagage* and occasionally even *omelette* are avoided by German in favor of native formations (*Gepäck, Eierkuchen;* the latter is more often used in the sense of "pancake"). Interesting individual choices in loan words are sometimes in evidence. While "lounge" may be borrowed untranslated, German and Norwegian show a preference for *foyer,* Dutch for *conversatie-zaal,* Swedish for *salong,* Danish for *vestibule.* Swedish and Norwegian prefer French *adieu* (*adjö, adjø*) for "good-by," but Danish prefers the native *farvel* (English *fare well*). German prefers the native *Amt* for "office," but French *comptoir* is the choice of the others (Dutch *kantoor,* Scandinavian *kontor*). "To cost" is taken in Vulgar Latin form (not *constare,* but *costare*): German and Dutch *kosten,* Swedish *kosta,* Danish and Norwegian *koste.*

Many military terms in German have French form, though some were previously borrowed by French from Italian: *General, Soldat, Manöver, Post, Leutnant, Offizier, Kompagnie, Bataillon, Regiment, Brigade, Division, Infanterie, Artillerie,* (*Haupt*)*quartier, Gendarmerie, Kommandant-ur, Kapitän, Marine, motorisiert. Panzer* seems borrowed from Italian *panciera,* "breastplate."

Influenza is definitely Italian, but *Fieber* seems to favor French, as do some nouns of relationship (*Familie, Onkel, Tante*) and of the table (*Serviette, Salat, Kotlett, Zitrone*). *Billet* and *Dame* are definitely French. Noncommittal as to Latin or French derivation are *Nation, Regel,* "rule," *Pest,* "pestilence," *Minute, Preis.* Among verbs from French are *rasieren,* "shave," *amüsieren,* "to amuse," *fallieren* (*faire faillite*), *retournieren, passen.* Among adjectives, *natürlich* seems to favor French; *klar* and *doppel,* Latin. *Kassa* and *Saldo* are Italian financial terms; *Acquit* is French.

Dutch and the Scandinavian languages go along with German in most of these borrowings. Dutch prefers the Latin-Italian *lucifer,* "light-bearer," for "match," to the "strike-wood" (*Streichholz*) of German or the "kindling-stick" (*tandsticka*) of Swedish, and generally uses French *par-*

don for "excuse me." Where German has taken French *Tasse* for "cup," Dutch, like English, prefers Latin *cuppa* (*kop, kopje*). *Bestie* appears in German, but is seldom used, while Dutch *-beest* (from Latin *bestia*) appears in numerous names of African antelopes.

The overall picture of Germanic borrowings from Latin-Romance is an impressive one, with English holding first place, and Dutch outstripping both German and Scandinavian, quite in accordance with historical contacts.

The contributions of Latin to the Celtic languages, with which the Italic had a special affinity, are extensive, perhaps even more so than the stream going in the opposite direction, which is considerable. The majority of Celtic contributions to Latin-Romance came from Gaulish, which became extinct and left scanty records, so that there is no way of gauging how much Latin got into Gaulish; whereas the Latin contributions to British Celtic survive fully in modern Welsh and its continental offshoot, Breton. There is also a sizable Latin element in Irish, of the Goidelic branch, imported largely by the Christian missionaries. In addition to this, modern Breton has, as might be expected, a strong French element, while modern Welsh and Irish have acquired Romance elements through English contacts, along with the international Latin of modern science.

Some of the terms brought into Britain by the Romans were themselves loan words. *Sapo,* "soap," seems to have been Germanic in origin, but the Romans passed it on to the Britons who later became Welshmen in the form *sibon. Ecclesia,* "church," originally Greek, shows up as *eglwys.* Even *caballus,* which the Romans may have acquired from the Celtic Gauls, was brought into Welsh as *ceffyl,* into Irish as *capall.* Elcock reports (p. 298) a long list of Welsh borrowings from Latin.[2] Only a few can be given here: *arma,* "weapons," to *arf; asina,* "she-donkey," to *asen; auctoritatem,* "authority," to *awdurdod; barba,* "beard," to *barf; bestia,* "beast," to *bwyst; caulis,* "cabbage," to *cawl; civitatem,* "city," to *ciwdod* (but the nominative *civitas* gives rise to *ciwed*); *corona,* "crown,"

---

2. These originally appeared in H. Lewis, *Yr Elfen Ladin yn yr Iaith Gymraeg,* Cardiff, 1943. In Welsh *f* indicates a *v* sound, *ff* an *f* sound; *dh* represents the *th* sound of *this, dd* the sound of *d; w* and *y* can have the full vocalic value of *i, u.*

to *corun;* *corpus,* "body," to *corff; crux* to *crwys* (but accusative *crucem* to *crog*); *de subito,* "suddenly," to *disyfyd; doctus,* "learned," to *doeth; fata,* "fates," to *ffawd; firmus,* "firm," to *ffyrf; focus,* "fire," "hearth," to *ffoc; fontana,* "fountain," to *ffynon; forma,* "shape," to *ffurf; fructus,* "fruit," to *ffrwyth; gentem,* "people," to *gynt; imperator,* "commander," "emperor," to *ymherawdr; infernum,* "hell," to *uffern; lactis,* "milk," to *llaeth; liber,* "free," to *llyfr; littera,* "letter," to *llythyr; maledictio,* "curse," to *melltith; memoria,* "memory," to *myfyr; mensa,* "table," to *mwys; numerus,* "number," to *nifer; oceanus,* "ocean," to *eigion; palma,* "palm," to *palf; piscis,* "fish," to *pysg; populus,* "people," to *pobl; porta,* "door," to *porth; primus,* "first," to *prif; rete,* "net," to *rhwyd; Romanus,* "Roman," to *Rhufain; scala,* "ladder," to *ysgol; scribo,* "I write," to *ysgrif; siccus,* "dry," to *sych; spiritus,* "spirit," to *ysbryd; stella,* "star," to *ystwyll; tabula,* "table," to *tafol; tempus,* "time," to *tymp; venenum,* "poison," to *gwenwyn; vinum,* "wine," to *gwin; viridis,* "green," to *gwyrdd; virtus,* "virtue," to *gwyrth.*

These borrowings cast light upon the state of the Latin language at the time when they took place (the Roman occupation of Britain, second to fourth centuries A.D.). To judge from the Welsh forms, popular Latin had lost *n* before *s* (*mensa*), and was in the habit of using a prothetic *i-* before *s* plus consonant combinations (*spiritus, stella,* to Vulgar Latin *ispiritus, istella;* Welsh would retain the *i* of the Vulgar Latin); but Latin *v* was still pronounced as *w,* showing a Welsh development parallel to that which Romance gave to imported Germanic *w* (*vinum, viridis,* to *gwyn, gwyrdd,* like Germanic *werra, wânt,* to *guerra, guanto*).

Irish, too, borrowed extensively from Latin at the time of Ireland's conversion to Christianity. A few words taken at random are: *caulis,* "cabbage," to *cal; catus,* "cat," to *cat; capitanus,* "captain," to *captaoin; calyx,* "chalice," to *cailís; arma,* "weapon," to *arm; barcus,* "boat," to *bárc; tabula,* "table," to *tabhall; privilegium,* "privilege," to *pribhléid; patronus,* "patron," to *pátrún; sanctus,* "saint," to *san; pacem,* "peace," later "kiss of peace," to *póg,* "kiss." Outside of words that have become international in relatively modern times, neither Welsh nor Irish show extensive borrowing from Romance. The case is different with Breton, which, though it originally stemmed from Welsh, lived for many centuries on French soil in intimate contact with French. In the Breton passage (Léon dialect) transcribed in the American Bible Society's *Book of a Thousand Tongues* (Mark I, 1–4), out of a total of 57 words 15 are of Latin or French origin, with a strong edge for the latter.[3] The corresponding Welsh and Irish passages show, respectively, 9 out of 63 words, and 5 out of 51, not all of which coincide with the Breton.[4]

---

3. The forms borrowed by Breton from Latin or French are: *commansament*, "beginning"; *scrivet*, "written"; *brofeted*, "prophet"; *faç*, "face"; *brepari*, "prepare"; *mouez*, "voice," from French *voix*, with Celtic mutation; *gri*, "crying"; *dezert*, "desert," "wilderness"; *preparit*, "prepare"; *vadeze*, "gone"; *brezege*, "preach"; *badiziant*, "baptizing"; *gonversion*, "conversion," "repentance"; *remission*, "remission," "forgiveness"; *pec'hejou*, "sins."

4. Welsh: *efengyl*, "gospel," from Latin *Evangelium*, originally Greek; *ysgrifennwyd*, "written," from Latin *scribenda*; *proffwydi*, "prophets," from Latin *propheta*, originally Greek; *baratoa*, "prepare," and *paratowch*, "prepared," from Latin *paratum*; *bedyddio*, "baptize," originally Greek; *diffeitwch*, "desert," probably from Latin *defectus*; *pregethu*, "preach," from Latin *praecepta*; *pechodau*, "sins," from Latin *peccata*. Irish: *scríobhtha*, "written," from Latin *scripta*; *baisteadh*, "baptized," and *baiste*, "baptism," both originally Greek; *seanmóré*, "preach," from Latin *sermo*; *bpeacadh*, "sins," from Latin *peccata*.

18. The Influence of Latin-Romance on Eastern European and Other Language Groups

As we move eastward into the Slavic world, the picture changes. Here contacts were relatively late. The Slavs, as they expanded westward after 500 A.D., had far greater contacts with the Greek culture of the Byzantine Empire than with the Latin culture of Western Europe. The result is that outside of Latin words that became international in the last few centuries, most of the Slavic borrowings have been from individual Romance languages, notably French, which exerted a particularly strong influence on the Russian court of Catherine the Great and the czars that followed her. One early Romance loan word to appear in Russian is *korabl'*, "ship," which Portuguese developed in the form *caravela*, from Latin *carabus*, of Greek origin. Russian *apel'sin*, "orange," is borrowed from German *Apfelsine*, "Chinese apple," but Polish, Czech, and Serbo-Croatian have words based on Italian *pomarancia*, while Bulgarian prefers *portokal*, which indicates Portuguese origin, and which it shares with Italian (*portogallo*) as well as with other Balkan tongues. On the other hand, Russian eschewed the Nahuatl name for "tomato," which was so generally accepted in the West, and fixed on Italian *pomodoro*, "golden apple," which it renders as *pomidor* (*tomat* seems to be an afterthought). Words that an English speaker would find recognizable in all or most Slavic languages include *address, baggage, bank, biscuit, chauffeur, doctor, dentist, interesting, advocate, lemonade, post* (in the sense of "mail"), *minute, omelet, police, republic, restaurant, card, lamp, student, captain, public, army, arrest, passport, platform, autobus* or *omnibus, class, wine* (*vino*), *menu, lady* (*dama*), the names of the months in Russian, Serbo-Croatian, and Bulgarian, but not in

Polish or Czech, which prefer Slavic names, such as Czech *Srpen,* "sickle," for "August," or Polish *Listopad,* "leaf fall," for "November."

Russian takes from French *soldat, ofitsyer* (but this probably came in through German), *komandovat',* "to command," *magazin,* "large store," *pal'to,* "overcoat," *serzhant,* "sergeant," *bombardirovat',* "to shell," "to bomb," *komod,* "chest of drawers," *bilyet,* "ticket," *kupe* (in the sense of "railroad compartment"), *zhilet,* "vest," *hotel* (which vies with native *gostinnitsa*). Italian influence appears in *pantalony,* "pants," and *kalsony* "nether underwear" in Russian, possibly in *kvartira,* "flat," "apartment," from Italian *quartiere; traktir,* "inn," from Italian *trattoria; salfetka,* "napkin," from Italian *salvietta; koleta,* "collar," from Italian *colletto; persik,* "peach," from Latin and Italian *persica. Gazeta,* "newspaper," is Italian, but *zhurnal,* "magazine," "periodical," is French, as are also *trotuar,* "sidewalk," from French *trottoir,* and *kontora,* "office," from French *comptoir.* Latin or Romance are *militsyoner,* "policeman," replacing the older and native *gorodovoy, salat* "salad," *retsept,* "prescription," *pilyulya,* "pill," *nomer,* "number." Even more noncommittal, in view of the fact that they may have passed through German, are such military terms as *mayor,* "major," *general, diviziya,* "division."

Polish features such French importations as *salon, toaleta, fryzier,* "barber," from French *friseur, komoda,* from French *commode, konfitura,* "jam," from French *confiture, prezent,* "gift." Polish *koperta,* Serbo-Croatian *koverta* (Italian *coperta,* French *couverte*) are used in the sense of "envelope," Polish *kanapka* (French *canapé*) for "sandwich." Czech goes along with Polish in using French-derived *toaleta,* while Bulgarian prefers *klozeta,* and Russian a native *ubornaya.* Serbo-Croatian prefers French *avion* to the *samolët,* "self-flying," that most of the others use for "airplane." Polish *kapelusz* for "hat" seems taken from Italian *cappello.* Czech *marmelada* is originally Portuguese. *Garderoba* for "cloak room" is shared by Polish, Serbo-Croatian, and Bulgarian. *Berberin* is Serbo-Croatian for "barber." Two forms from Italian are Bulgarian *kamerierka* for "chambermaid" (Italian *cameriera*), and the *velosiped* (Italian *velocipede*) that is used for "bicycle" by Russian and Bulgarian. *Apartament,* Bulgarian for "apartment," also seems derived from Italian *appartamento.*

There is a tendency in Russian to prefer words built on Slavic roots, such as *mezhdunarodny,* "international," to Latin forms like *internatsional'ny.* But present indications are that this phase of linguistic nationalism is dying out.

Words of the type described above are also generally current in the two Baltic languages, Lithuanian and Latvian, which have strong points of contact, both historical and linguistic, with the Slavic group.

Two additional Indo-European branches of Eastern Europe that had both early and late contacts with Latin-Romance are Greek and Albanian. There is no question that Greek gave to Latin far more than it took from Latin. As the language of a civilization that was already highly developed when Rome was founded, it was the mission of Greek to supply Latin with both loanwords and roots from which more words could be constructed to describe Rome's expanding activities. Yet there was some movement the other way. The Greek names of the months are all Latin. Greek gave up its *ailuros* in favor of Latin *catus*, "cat," which it took as *gata*, but the use of *g* instead of *c* seems to indicate that the transfer occurred after Latin had become Italian. *Porta* for "door" is noncommittal, as are *taverna, gamba,* "leg," and *palati,* "palace."

Greek contacts with the seafaring Venetians, Genoese, and Pisans during the Middle Ages and the Crusades, and later Italian contacts in the Renaissance, led to extensive borrowing from Italian (*kantina,* "cellar," *sofito,* "attic," *vazo,* "vase," *tramontana,* "north wind," *valitsa,* "valise," *ombrella, servitoros,* "servant," *oroloi,* "watch," "clock," *sapuni,* "soap," *kaltses,* "socks," *bratso,* "arm," *biskoto,* "biscuit," *kouverta,* "blanket," *bokkali,* "bottle," *piato,* "plate," *kamariera,* "chambermaid," *resta,* "small change," *kapello,* "hat," *gazoz,* "carbonated soft drink," *limonadha,* "lemonade," *petsetta,* "napkin," *portokali,* "orange," *pantalonia,* "pants," *penna,* "pen," *pipa,* "pipe," *mpompa,* "bomb," *mparberis,* "barber,"[1] *salata,* "salad"). *Narantsa,* "orange," *tirantes,* "suspenders," seem Spanish, while French contributes *paltó* and *kommó* (though these, judging by their form, may have come in through Italian), *salon, tir-bousón,* "corkscrew," from French *tire-bouchon, asenser,* "elevator," from French *ascenseur, ganti,* "glove," *lamba,* "lamp," (possibly through Arabic), *omelet, magazí, kombeinezón,* "slip," *pourboire,* "tip."

Albanian probably inherited from Illyrian, which had extensive contacts with the Romans, such words as *ar,* "gold," from Latin *aurum; ergjënt,* "silver," from Latin *argentum; numëri,* "number," from Latin *numerus; qen,* "dog," from Latin *canis; vera,* "summer," from Latin *ver; kupe,* "cup," from Latin *cuppa; mbret,* "king," from Latin *imperator;* two days of the week (*marte* and *merkurre*); five months (*fruër, mars, prill,*

---

1. *mp* is a makeshift grapheme for the sound of *b*, which modern Greek gave up in favor of *v* for the letter beta.

maj, gusht). But Albanian's Romance loan words are overwhelmingly Italian: *librarija*, "bookstore," *roba*, "clothes," *pallto*, "overcoat," *korridori*, "corridor," *ashensori*, "elevator," *spaga*, "cord," *me spiegue*, "I explain," from Italian *mi spiego, faculeta,* "handkerchief," from *fazzoletto, pjani*, "floor" "storey," *avokati*, "lawyer," *posta*, "mail," *peceta*, "napkin," *portokali*, "orange," *pague*, "to pay," *artisti i piturave*, "painter," *pjata*, "plate," *dogana*, "customs," *kartolina postare*, "postcard," *ferovija*, "railroad," *restoranti; sherbtori*, "servant," from *servitore, sherbimi*, "service," *vapori*, "steamer," *sekretari, sapuni, salata, prendvera*, "spring," from *primavera, valixhja*, "suitcase," from *valigia, studenti, itinerari*, "timetable." *Verdhë*, from Italian *verde*, "green," is used for "yellow." French are *amuzant, chauffeur, bileta, korekt, omelet*, possibly *fort* and *drejt*, "straight," from French *droit*. It is possible that *rruga*, "street," may go back to a Vulgar Latin formation that also gave French *rue* and Portuguese *rua* (in Italian *ruga* has the Classical Latin meaning of "wrinkle").

On European soil, non–Indo-European languages include Basque, which is in a class by itself (the possibility of a link with the Caucasian languages has been advanced), and Ural-Altaic tongues of Asian origin, of which the chief are Hungarian, Finnish, and Turkish.

Basque, one of the world's language mysteries, possibly the descendant of ancient Iberian, being situated at the western end of the Pyrenees, in contact with both French and Spanish, has borrowed some vocabulary items from both. Some of the borrowed words, however, seem to indicate by their form that they were taken either from Latin or from a very early form of Iberian Romance: *lagi* or *lege*, "law," *crea*, "to create," *joku*, "game," *errege*, "king," *ezpata*, "sword." Noncommittal as between Latin and Spanish are *kantu*, "song," *arrosa*, "rose," *mundua*, "world," *josi*, "to sew." *Sei*, "six," the only borrowed Basque numeral, comes from Spanish *seis*, as do *gerezi*, "cherry," *erloju*, "watch," "clock." There are some loanwords, like *eternala*, "eternal," *malecia*, "malice," that seem learned, but they are few. Spanish has borrowed far more from Basque than Basque from Spanish, indicating a strong spirit of linguistic independence on the part of the Basques, who have haughtily rejected Latin-Spanish names for the months and the days of the week, and use their own.

Hungarian, earliest of the Ural-Altaic languages to come into contact with Latin-Romance, has such words as *kastély*, "castle," *pár*, "pair," *palota,* "palace," and religious words like *templom,* "church," *szent,* "saint," *püspök,* "bishop," *sekrestyés,* "sacristan," all of which could have come from very late or medieval Latin, along with *szappan,* "soap," possibly even *fiw,* "boy," "son," and *arany,* "gold." The months have Latin names. *Móló,* "dock," "pier," *nulla,* "zero," *cédula,* "label," have Italian forms; *narancs* and *tinta* favor Spanish, but the second is more probably the German *Tinte,* which nevertheless goes back to Latin *tincta.* Then there are the "modern" words for "bank," "chauffeur," "repair," "garage," "information," "lamp," "post," "omelet," "pipe," "salad," "visa," "radio," "pistol." But generally speaking, Hungarian has borrowed more heavily from German and the Slavic tongues than from the Latin-Romance group.

Finnish, strongly influenced by neighboring Swedish, has relatively few Latin-Romance words: *pankki,* "bank," *piispa,* "bishop," *kapteeni,* "captain," *auto; kappeli,* "chapel," *konjakki,* "cognac," *kontorristi,* "clerk," (here we see the influence of Swedish, influenced in turn by French *comptoir*), *konsertti, lamppu, juristi, minuutti, pippuri, poliisi, suola,* "salt," *sihteeri,* "secretary."

Turkish contacts with the Western world began in the thirteenth century, and expanded in the fourteenth and fifteenth, as the Turks pressed in upon the Byzantine Empire. Since they were at first under Arab and Persian cultural influence, it is not surprising that most of their loan words from Latin-Romance are relatively recent, and overwhelmingly of French origin. A few, like *lamba* for "lamp," with its telltale *b* for *p,* indicate that they came into Turkish through Arabic. Some, like *fatura,* "bill," "invoice," *peçete,* "napkin," *lokanta,* "inn," show Italian derivation. *Kaptan, banka, posta, numara, pipo,* "pipe," *pasaport, salata, baston,* "stick," could also have come from Italian. But *saloni, adres, berber,* "barber," *bisküvi,* "biscuit," *şoför* "chauffeur," *pardesü,* "overcoat," *vestiyer,* "baggage room," "cloak room," *koridor, asansör,* "elevator," *jambon,* "ham," *avukat, otel, bilete, omlet, polis,* "police," *sekreter, servis, sabun,* are clearly French. Three names of months are Latin (*mart, mayıs, ağustos*).

Passing on to the Semitic languages, Arabic, having had contacts with the Roman world since the sixth century, has a large Italian assortment: *bîbâ,* "pipe," *bosta,* "mail," *bortukân,* "orange," *bantalûn,* "pants," *bitello,* "veal," *bôlîsa,* "baggage check," from Italian *polizza.* All of these show the necessary Arabic shift from *p*, which does not appear in the Arabic sound scheme, to *b*. There are also *lokanda*, "inn," *avokâto, fatura*, "invoice," from Italian *fattura, passaporto, gonella*, "skirt," from Italian *gonnella*. More noncommittal are *bank, baskawît*, "biscuit," *kahten*, "captain," *gawanti*, "glove," *numra*, "number," *salata, sâbûn*. Definitely French are *polis*, "police," *secretaire*, and the second part of *râis el gar-sonât*, "head waiter," literally, "head of the waiter corps." Arabic makes use of the Latin names of months, in addition to its own months, which do not coincide with those of the West.

Hebrew, which has its own proud system of word formation, prefers loan translations to loan words. *Sabon, chatul*, "cat," *machsan*, "store," (but this probably represents the Arabic form that gave rise to *magaz-zino, magasin*, and *almacén*), *kartis*, "ticket," are a mere handful of Latin-Romance words, well outdistanced by those that come from English (*le-flartet*, "to flirt," *le-balef*, "to bluff," *le-talfen*, "to telephone"), and the Germanic Yiddish that has crept, slangily and surreptitiously, into the Ivrit of Israel (*kumsitz*, from *komm'sitzen*, "come sit," for "evening get-together in the open").

In Asia, Indo-Iranian Persian and Hindi, being members of the Indo-European family, have many original roots in common with Latin. But contacts were limited in ancient and medieval times, and the few loan words they took came mainly from French: Hindi *sabun*, Persian *saboon* (which may have come through Arabic), Hindi *kameej*, Persian *qamis*, "shirt" (more likely to be of Spanish or Portuguese provenance), Persian *post*, "mail," *tambr*, "stamp," *lamp, garson*.

Further east, Thai has *sa-bae* for "soap," *pang* for "bread," probably from Portuguese *pão*. Indonesian, subject to Dutch influence, was also located on the Portuguese travel lanes. It has such general words as *pos*, "mail," *pilot, sabun, kertas*, "paper," *kemedja*, "shirt," *serdadu*, "soldier." More specifically French are *bagasi* and *dokumen;* more specifically Portuguese are *mentega*, "butter," *sepatu*, "shoe," *kedju*, "cheese," *roda*, "wheel."

French influence, widespread in what was once French Indochina, appears in Vietnamese *tem*, "stamp," from French *timbre, kai valise*, "baggage," possibly *xa po*, "chief," with *x* equalling French *ch*. "Soap" is *saa bong*. There is a word *chao*, used for both "hello" and "good-by," which sounds like Italian *ciao*, used in the same fashion; but the connection is doubtful.

A Far Eastern tongue that has borrowed extensively from the Spanish colonizers is Tagalog, now the official language of the Philippines. Since there is no *f* sound in Tagalog, it is replaced by *p*, which accounts for *posporo*, "match," from Spanish *fósforo*, and *prutas*, "fruit," from Spanish *frutas*, as well as for the native adaptation of the Spanish name of the country, Pilipinas. A cross section of Spanish loan words in Tagalog includes the days of the week, *pato*, "duck," *maleta*, "suitcase," *karne*, "meat," *serbesa*, "beer," from *cerveza*, *sabon*, "soap," *mantekilya*, "butter," *papel*, "paper" (*papeles* is "documents," as in Spanish), *edad*, "age," *tinidor*, "fork," *kutsilyo*, "knife," from *cuchillo*, *kutsara*, "spoon," from *cuchara*, *berde*, "green," *Diyos*, "God," from *Dios*, *sapatos*, "shoes," *tinta*, "ink," *leon*, "lion," *harina*, "flour," *kamisa*, "shirt," *mundo*, "world," *kabayo*, "horse," *keso*, "cheese," *tren*, "train," *bote*, "bottle," from *botella*, *artistang erkake*, "actor," *sambalilo*, "hat," from *sombrero*, *kahon*, "box," from *cajón*, *bola*, "ball," *kuwenta*, "bill," from *cuenta*.

Japanese, a free and easy borrower from English, has absorbed most of its Latin-Romance loan words through the intermediation of our tongue: such words as *furai ni suru*, "to fry," *sōsu*, "sauce," *henkechi*, "handkerchief," *chīzu*, "cheese," *remon*, "lemon," *shabon*, "soap," *kara*, "collar," *sarada*, "salad," *hoteru*, "hotel" (vying with native *ryokan*), *teiburu*, "table," *rampu*, "lamp," *piano*, *tenisu*, "tennis," *botan*, "button," *suteishon*, "station," *basu*, "bus," are taken from English (with the possible exception of *shabon*, which is more likely to have come in directly from Portuguese), but had previously been taken by English from Latin or French. One interesting loan word adapted directly from French is *abbaku*, representing French *avec*, "with," used to describe a Japanese "love" hotel, specially designed for temporary assignations, but furnished with (*avec*) all the comforts of home. Older words from Portuguese are *pan* "bread," and the interesting *tempura* "fried shrimp," which goes back to Latin *Quattuor Tempora*, the four Ember days, on which the Catholic Portuguese ate only fish.

Chinese, a language of ancient culture, rivals Hebrew in its rejection of foreign loan words. In their place, Chinese prefers loan translations, which often lose their character as translations and acquire Chinese imagery. When the telephone was first introduced, the attempt was made to adapt the Western word to the Chinese sound scheme, and it came out as *deh leu fung;* this was soon replaced by *dyan hwa*, "electricity talk." Neither *gazette* nor *journal* was accepted, and the newspaper was designated as *bao jr,* "inform paper." The Chinese reluctance to adapt foreign sounds to their own appears in two classes of words that could be described as loan words, personal and national names. *America* comes out as *Mei Kuo,* where *Mei* bears some resemblance to one of the Western syllables, but the combination means "beautiful land." In like manner, England becomes *Ying Kuo,* France *Fa Kuo,* Germany *De Kuo* (*De* representing the initial sounds of *deutsch*). Italy, exceptionally, comes out in full as *Yi Da Li* (but in the form of English *Italy,* not that of Italian *Italia*).

The very numerous African languages have been heavily infiltrated by the languages of their former colonizers, and have in some cases given rise to pidgins. This means that the tongues of what used to be French West Africa, Equatorial Africa, and the Belgian Congo contain heavy French admixtures; the tongues of the former British African empire are interspersed with English; those of South Africa with Dutch-Afrikaans; those of Angola, Mozambique, and Portuguese Guinea with Portuguese; those of Somalia and Eritrea with Italian. Where this has not occurred to any extensive degree, there are nevertheless a few Romance loan words, such as the *tember,* "stamp," from French *timbre, samuna,* "soap," *ansola,* "bedsheet," from Italian *lenzuolo, shemiz,* "shirt," *adrasha,* "address," *gazeta,* of the dominant Amharic of Ethiopia, which is basically Semitic and imported from southern Arabia. In Swahili, a Bantu tongue, we find *karatasi,* "paper," and *tikiti ga posta,* "postage stamp." Most of Swahili's Romance loan words are of Portuguese origin, through contacts at Dar-es-Salaam: *bandera,* "flag," *parafujo,* "screen," *sabuni,* "soap," *meza,* "table," *kasha,* "box," *bastola,* "pistol," *padri,* "father," "priest." *Garafuu,* "clove," seems to reflect Italian *garofano,* originally from Greek. *Daktari* is Latin and English for "doctor," and vies with native *mganga* and Arabic *mtabibu.* Hausa, the predominant language of northern Nigeria, and Luganda both have the almost universal word for "soap" (*sabulu, saffuu*). Hausa also has *adireshi,* "address," *takarda,* "paper," and *kare,* "dog," while Luganda has *kiizi,* "cheese."

In America, Algonquian *nasaump* from French *la soupe* is reported by Hall, and Entwistle, reporting the contributions to Spanish of the South American Indian languages, also reports a few of their borrowings from Spanish, such as Araucanian *napus, irtipu, cahuallo, aghuas, chumpiru,* from *nabos, estribo, caballo, habas, sombrero* ("turnips," "stirrup," "horse," "broad beans," "hat"); Mapuche *charu* and *ovicha* from *jarro*, *oveja* ("jug," "sheep"); Quechua *mamay* from *mamá mía;* Nahuatl *xenola* and *xalo* from *señora, jarro* ("lady," "jug"). These are all forms which indicate intimate contact on a strictly popular level.

One last measure of the international prestige of a language or language group, though admittedly a minor one, is the extent to which it is considered in the many attempts that have been made since the seventeenth century to construct an international language for purposes of communication among all the varied linguistic groups of mankind.

Well over one thousand such languages have been offered up to the present time. They are divided into a minority of so-called a priori languages, altogether arbitrary and not based upon existing tongues, and a majority of a posteriori languages, built up out of languages already in use. In the case of the latter, which are not only more numerous, but have gained more extensive followings than the others, it is almost invariably the Latin-Romance element that predominates, though there have been a few ingenious but unsuccessful attempts to give the various language groups of the world some sort of proportional representation. Among the more recent which still have a body of followers and are not museum pieces one need only mention Ido, Interlingue (or Cosmoglotta), the American Interlingua, and Esperanto. The first three are almost pure combinations of Latin, French, Spanish, Italian, with International Greek and English (mostly where it happens to coincide with Latin-Romance). Esperanto, the only constructed language in this group that attempts to give something like equal representation to the Germanic languages along with the Latin-Romance (there are also occasional Slavic forms, and words from other languages that have become international), happens to be by far the most widespread, with a speaking population scattered all over the globe that has been estimated to run up to eight million, and a true literary output, both original and in translation. It has also achieved some measure of international recognition, to the extent that various countries, not only Western but also Asian and African, teach it in their institutions of higher learning and use it in radio broadcasts and official documents.

The Esperanto vocabulary offers numerous terms taken from the two principal Germanic languages, German and English ("boy," for instance, is *knabo;* "bird" is *birdo*), but they are easily outstripped in number by the Latin-Romance element. To exemplify: Definitely Latin are *pluvo,* "rain," *glacio,* "ice," *nokto,* "night," *aŭskulti,* "to listen," *aŭdi,* "to hear," *plumbo,* "lead," *lakto,* "milk," *pomo,* "apple," *piro,* "pear," *ovo,* "egg," *ludo,* "game," *scii,* "to know," *flava,* "yellow," *sed,* "but," *post,* "after," *trans,* "across," *apud,* "among." French are *neĝo,* "snow," *mateno,* "morning," *dimanĉo,* "Sunday," *vendredo,* "Friday," *semajno,* "week," *onklo,* "uncle," *bofrato,* "brother-in-law" (this is perhaps a combination of French *beau* and Latin *frater*), *krii,* "to cry," *kompreni,* "to understand," *ĉevalo,* "horse," *abelo,* "bee," *tranĉaĵo,* "slice," *fromaĵo,* "cheese," *viando,* "meat," *citrono,* "lemon," *valizo,* "valise," *krajono,* "pencil," *plumo,* "pen," *naĝi,* "to swim," *trotuaro,* "sidewalk." Spanish seems to have been used for *meskito,* "mosquito," *ebria,* "drunk," *veneno,* "poison," *familio,* "family," *respondi,* "to answer"; Italian for *oro,* "gold," *arĝento,* "silver," *kapro,* "goat," *se,* "if," *ĉielo,* "sky," *vento,* "wind," *minuto,* "minute," *amiko,* "friend."[2]

This preponderance of the Latin-Romance element does not seem to disturb any of the numerous Esperantists who are native speakers not only of other Indo-European languages but of such far-flung tongues as Chinese, Japanese, Arabic, and Swahili. For what it may be worth, it confirms the prestige and importance that the Latin-Romance tongues have in the eyes of the world.

---

2. In Esperanto orthography, *ŭ* = low; *c* = i*ts*; *ĉ* = *ch*urch; g = go; *ĝ* = *g*eneral; *j* = *y*et; *ĵ* = mea*s*ure; *s* = *s*o; *ŝ* = *s*ure.

19. Present-Day Geography and Demography of the Romance Languages

There are many indices of the importance and prestige of a language or group of languages. Some are altogether objective (number of speakers, territorial extent). Others are reasonably objective (literacy; books, magazines, and newspapers published; scientific output and scientific periodicals; economic, industrial, commercial, agricultural, standing; gross national product, per capita income, standard of living). Least objective are the output of literature, both prose and poetry, and the production of art in all its forms. Every group loves its own literature, written or oral, its own musical and artistic forms. Subjective judgments too often come into play. Yet all these items have to enter the composite picture of what constitutes the status of a language or language group in the world.

If we limit ourselves only to the two thoroughly objective measuring sticks, the demographic and the geographic, we may nevertheless state by way of introduction that in the fields of literacy, publications, scientific output, economic, commercial, and industrial activity, the Romance nations are among the more advanced in the world. Their literary and artistic output is second to none.

Both geographically and demographically, the Romance languages occupy one of the leading positions in the Indo-European family of languages, which is spoken by almost half of the world's nearly four billion inhabitants. Of these, roughly one-half billion, or one person out of eight, is a native speaker of a Romance language.

On the demographic side, a projection of world populations to the end of 1975, based on latest available United Nations statistics, shows approximately 1.88 billion speakers of languages classified as Indo-European, in all the existing branches (Germanic, Romance, Balto-Slavic, Indo-Iranian, Greek, Celtic, Armenian, Albanian).[1]

Of these, speakers of Romance languages number about 487 million, as against 495 million speakers of Germanic, 268 million speakers of Balto-Slavic, 610 million speakers of Indo-Iranian, 10 million speakers of Greek, 4 million speakers of Armenian, 3 million speakers of Celtic, 3 million speakers of Albanian.

The Romance subdivisions are as follows: Spanish (including Catalan), 215 million; French (including Provençal and Franco-Provençal), 80 million; Portuguese (including Galician), 110 million; Italian (including Rheto-Rumansh and Sardinian), 60 million; Rumanian, 22 million.

In addition, there are speakers residing permanently abroad; speakers of pidgins based on the individual Romance languages; and non-native, cultural speakers. The numbers of all these are much more difficult to estimate, but they run, very roughly, to about 50 million for French and 10 million each for Spanish, Portuguese, and Italian.[2]

Geographically, the Romance languages are native and official in roughly ten million square miles of the world's total land surface (exclusive of Antarctica) of fifty-two million square miles. They are widely spoken and used, often with co-official status, in another seven million square miles.

The Romance languages cover southwestern Europe (France, Belgium, Spain, Portugal, Italy, southern and western Switzerland); all of the American continent south of the Rio Grande, with the exception of Guayana and Surinam; the larger Antillean islands; the province of Québec in Canada, and the French islands of St. Pierre and Miquelon;

---

1. The 1.933 billion speakers of non-Indo-European languages are distributed as follows: Semitic-Hamitic-Cushitic, 151 million; Ural-Altaic, 100 million; Sino-Tibetan, 863 million; Japanese-Korean, 155 million; Dravidian, 163 million; Malayo-Polynesian, 182 million; Black African, 250 million; Austro-Asiatic and Mon-Khmer, 47 million; American Indian, 13 million; Caucasian, 5 million; Australian-Papuan, 3 million; Basque, 1 million.

2. By way of comparison, the Germanic languages estimated above have, in addition, roughly 130 million nonnative, cultural speakers, speakers residing abroad, and speakers of pidgins; for the Balto-Slavic languages, the estimated figure is 123 million (this includes inhabitants of the Soviet Union, such as Ukrainians, Byelorussians, Uzbeks, Georgians, etc., whose mother tongue is not Russian); for Indo-Iranian, 100 million; for Greek, 2 million; for Celtic, Armenian, and Albanian, the main figure includes such speakers.

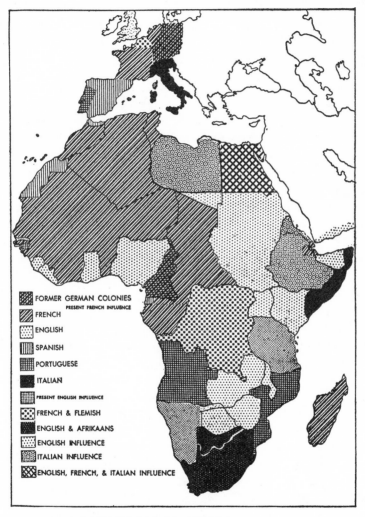

COLONIAL LANGUAGES OF AFRICA

in the Pacific, French insular possessions (Tahiti, French Samoa, etc.). In Africa, Romance languages are extensively used, both in full and pidgin form, in former French, Belgian, and Italian possessions, and in past and present Portuguese holdings. In Asia, all that remains is the vestiges of former colonization (the extensive use of Spanish, rivaling English, in the Philippines; the former Portuguese possessions of Goa, Damau, Diu, and the still Portuguese Macao and part of Timor; former French Indo-china, now North and South Vietnam, Laos, and Cambodia).

Romance pidgins or creolized forms are numerous. They began with the Lingua Franca of the Middle Ages, also known as Sabir, immortalized by Molière, which was a mixture of Italian and Provençal with Arabic and Greek elements, used widely throughout the Mediterranean area. Most numerous and widespread are the pidgin forms of Portuguese, which appear wherever the Portuguese founded colonies. There is a pidginized form of Portuguese that is spoken in Macao, another in the formerly Portuguese cities of India's west coast, a third in the Cape Verde islands, a fourth in the region of Zanzibar, a fifth in Indonesia and the Philippines, in addition to forms currently used in Portuguese Guinea, Angola, and Mozambique (these are sometimes jokingly referred to as *pretuguês*, combining *preto*, "black," with *português*). There is still some doubt whether Papiamento, the curious speech form of Surinam, is primarily based on Portuguese or on Spanish, or on a mixture of the two. Depending on the point of view, one could even classify the popular speech forms of Madeira and the Azores as dialects or pidgins. Hall, who has gone deeply into the study of pidgins, suggests that even the dialects of northeastern Brazil may be based on earlier creolized forms.

Spanish pidgins appear in the Philippines, the interior of some South American countries, and along the Mexican-U.S. border, where Pochismo (derived from *pocho*, "discolored," but applied also locally to a U.S.-born Mexican) is often used in the contacts between Mexican immigrants and U.S. border patrols. *Huachar*, "to watch," *te y ponque*, "tea and pound cake," *lleñeral*, "ginger ale," *jatqueque*, "hot cake," *fanfurria*, "frankfurter," *jamachi*, "how much?" are some of the forms of this interesting variety.

French, in addition to the mixture of French and English that often characterizes the speech of the inhabitants of Québec and surrounding regions, has given rise to a full-fledged Haitian Creole, which is current among most of the population, and is even taught in the schools (*Car Bon Dieu té r'aimé créatures-li si tant, que li baille seul Pitite-li,* "for God so loved the world that he gave His only begotten son"; French: *Car Dieu a tant aimé le monde qu'il a donné son Fils unique*). There is also a Cajun French spoken in Louisiana by the descendants of deportees from Acadia, in Canada (*papier nouvelles,* a loan translation of *newspaper,* is one of its forms). Other varieties appear in Martinique and other Caribbean islands, as well as in French Guiana, on the islands of Mauritius and Réunion, in the Indian Ocean, and in former French colonies of West Africa and Equatorial Africa, where the mixture is sometimes called *petit nègre.* French has managed to infiltrate even Pidgin English, in which a Frenchman is *man-a-wi-wi,* "the man who says *oui, oui,*" and *montou, montwar* (*bonjour, bonsoir*) are occasionally heard. Indonesian often calls a Frenchman *orang deedong* (Indonesian *orang,* "man," plus French *dis donc,* "speak up!").

Italian, which gave rise both to Franco-Venetian and the Lingua Franca of the Middle Ages, has today a number of emigrant dialects (the Italian-American described in Arthur Livingston's "L'America Sanamagogna"[3] and the Cocoliche of Argentina are typical); but these can hardly be described as stable pidgins, being doomed to disappearance within a couple of generations from the date of original migration. One could perhaps describe Maltese, which is based on Arabic, as a pidginized form of Italian, by reason of its very large vocabulary superstructure taken from Italian.

Large groups of Romance speakers permanently living abroad (as distinguished from seasonal migrant workers) are constituted by the large Hispanic groups on U.S. soil (Chicanos in New Mexico, California, Arizona; Cubans in Florida; Puerto Ricans in New York, New Jersey, etc.; a total of at least 10 million), by Portuguese speakers on U.S. soil (perhaps half a million, mainly in Massachusetts and California), by Italian speakers in both North and South America (about 10 million), by French speakers in Louisiana and New England (perhaps half a million), by Rumanian speakers on Greek and Yugoslav soil (less than half a million).

---

3. *Sanamagogna* is borrowed from *son of a gun;* other samples are *lotto* from *lot, grosseria,* from *grocery, ghenga di loffari,* from *gang of loafers,* even *Broccolino,* from *Brooklyn.*

Most difficult to determine is the number of cultural speakers of individual languages, people to whom the language is not native, but who have studied or practiced it to the point of being able to communicate in it. The extent to which they are able to communicate is another source of difficulty, since it may range from the ability to speak and understand a number of essential phrases to near native-speaker fluency and accent. Foreign-language registration in the various school systems of the world ought to give us some indication, but experience shows us that mere classroom attendance is by no means a sure yardstick of interest in or assimilation of the language studied.

In the United States, out of approximately fifteen million high school students, perhaps five million undertake the study of a foreign language, with, roughly, two million taking Spanish, fewer than two million French, one million Latin, fewer than half a million German, while Italian and Russian string along with about twenty-five thousand each. In the colleges and universities, these proportions are repeated, with Spanish at present holding a slight advantage over French; in elementary school courses, Spanish also outstrips French. At any rate, the preponderance of the Latin-Romance group in American linguistic interest is overwhelming.

Abroad, things are different, mainly because English gets into the picture of foreign-language choice. There are still a good many countries where French is more widespread than English, but they are themselves Romance lands, like Italy, Spain, Portugal, Latin America. Elsewhere, English far outstrips French at the present time. In the U.S.S.R., where French used to be the overwhelming choice of the old czarist aristocracy and bourgeoisie, the percentages for foreign language study are now roughly 45 percent for English, 35 percent for German, 20 percent for French.

Nowhere outside of the United States does Spanish attract a considerable following. In many European countries, it even runs behind Italian. There is a large number of cultural speakers of French in Near Eastern countries, such as Iran, Turkey, Egypt, Israel, and, of course, in the Arab and Black African countries that used to be French colonies, possessions, or mandates. Even though shorn of a good deal of its former universal prestige, French nevertheless remains a great cultural language, second in number of followers only to English.

As a nonnative cultural language, Italian is fairly widespread on both shores of the Mediterranean, but especially in the countries on the eastern shores of the Adriatic (Yugoslavia, Albania, Greece), where the tradition implanted by the Venetian Republic in the Middle Ages is still strong. Far more modest is the position of Italian in northern Europe and the other continents. In North and South America it is sustained mainly by second- and third-generation Italian-Americans.

Portuguese, save for its pidgin forms, has little currency outside its national territories, which are, however, extensive. Rumanian, too, has little currency outside its borders, save for what was once Bessarabia and is now the Moldavian S.S.R., and the Macedo-Rumanian enclaves in Yugoslavia and Greece.

The picture that emerges for the Romance languages as a whole is a strong one. Its speakers are numerous and widely distributed over the globe. They are active, intelligent, resourceful. They have been leaders in exploration and discovery, in commerce, in science, in all forms of art and literature. Constituting roughly one-eighth of the world's population, covering one-fifth of the earth's land surface, they can point proudly not only to their Roman heritage, but to the roster of their own individual achievements.

Distribution of ROMANCE

NATIVE AND/OR OFFICIAL

French   Spanish   Portuguese   Italian

LANGUAGES throughout the World

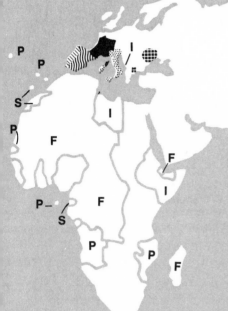

WIDELY SPOKEN BY REASON OF

(a) IMMIGRATION   (b) FORMER COLONIZATION

F   S   P   I

Rumanian

20. The Future of the Romance Languages

As the final quarter of the twentieth century dawns, the question comes up: Within the framework of coming world history, what does the future hold in store, not merely for the speakers of the various Romance languages, but for the languages themselves, taken individually and collectively?

As in the previous chapter, there are a few things connected with languages and their growth that can be objectively measured. These are primarily demography and geographical extent. For the rest, history has a way of coming up with sudden and dramatic developments. An atomic World War III cannot be altogether ruled out of the roster of possibilities, despite détentes and agreements among the major powers, when one considers that the "Atomic Club" shows definite signs of expanding its membership. But even short of drastic developments, history often manages to present a series of ups and downs, of declines and comebacks.

Consider, for example, the rise of Japan to first-class citizenship among the nations of the world, in the course of little more than one brief century; the startling changes that have occurred in the status of countries like India, only recently a jewel in the British imperial crown, today a major, independent power with a policy and a will of its own; or Iran, heir to one of the great empires of the past, the mighty Persian realm of Darius and Artaxerxes, relegated to inferior status and changed almost beyond recognition by the Arab conquest and the Mongol invasions, now jetted forth into modern-day prominence by its fortunate possession of immense oil reserves that the world desperately needs; or of the Arab countries, once almost the masters of a Mediterranean and Near

216

Eastern empire that stretched from Arabia and Mesopotamia to Spain and Portugal, then subdued and colonized by the nations of the Christian West, now emerging again into a powerful, even though loosely knit, bloc that also wields a huge oil weapon whereby to impose its point of view and will.

Linguistically, who is to prophesy what will be, a hundred years hence, the status of such widespread but hitherto scantily considered languages as Hindi, Iranian, Arabic, Japanese, Chinese, Malay-Indonesian? Nations like India, Persia, the Arab complex, Japan, China, have given proof in the past of vast capacities for civilization, invention, science, industry, commerce, political organization, not to mention literature, philosophy, and the arts. It was only what might be termed the fortunes of war that placed them temporarily among the so-called backward, or underdeveloped, or developing, nations. Now that those fortunes have turned the other way, what is there to prevent them from vying, on a plane of complete equality, with the great Western nations, or their languages from competing with our Indo-European English, German, French, Spanish, Portuguese, Italian, and Russian?

Going back to our fully objective yardsticks, geography and demography, there are lessons to be drawn from their statistics, particularly over the last ten years.

Geographically, the Western languages, including Germanic English and German, Romance French, Spanish, Portuguese, Italian, and Slavic Russian, held control until the end of the Second World War over tremendous areas of the earth, constituting over three quarters of the globe's land surface. Today, with the relinquishment of the British, French, Dutch, Belgian, Italian, and Portuguese colonial empires, a good deal of that advantage has vanished.

It is altogether true that the languages of colonization continue to be used and studied in most of the areas where they once exercised sway. In many cases, they are still official or co-official in independent lands that were formerly colonial possessions.

As late as 1966, for instance, French was still the sole official language of such countries as Chad, Dahomey, Gabon, Guinea, Ivory Coast, Mali, Senegal, Togo, Upper Volta, Zaire. It was co-official with one or more indigenous tongues in South Vietnam, Laos, Algeria, Central African Republic, Congo Republic, Malagasy Republic; semiofficial and widely used in North Vietnam, Cambodia, Morocco, Tunisia, Egypt, Niger, Mauretania. English was the sole official language of Gambia, Kenya, Liberia,

Uganda, Zambia; co-official in Tanzania, Niger, Nigeria, Sierra Leone, Ghana, Malawi, Somalia, India, Pakistan, Burma; semiofficial and widely used in Egypt, Sudan, Sri Lanka (formerly Ceylon), the Philippines. More modestly, Italian was co-official in Somalia and semiofficial and widely used in Libya and Ethiopia; Dutch was widely used in Indonesia; Spanish was co-official in New Mexico and semiofficial and widely used in the Philippines. That picture is slowly changing as the new nations gain greater confidence in themselves, their own cultures and potentialities. Kenya, for example, has shifted from English to Swahili as its official language. The Philippines have dropped both English and Spanish from their official list, and gone over to Tagalog.

The process of making indigenous tongues official is greatly retarded where a multiplicity of such tongues is spoken on the soil of any one nation, and the colonial language has to be used as a common linguistic medium, as is the case of Nigeria and Zaire. The Philippines seem to have succeeded in gaining acceptance for one of their native languages, Tagalog, which is actually the language of a minority of the population. India has not been so fortunate. After decades of trying to impose Hindi as the official national language, it has been compelled by widespread and bloody language riots to retain English for purposes of intercommunication among its sixteen major and countless minor language varieties.

Does this mean that the Romance languages will eventually have to relinquish the seven million square miles of the earth's surface to which they are not indigenous? In the long run, probably; but it is likely to be a fairly long run. At any rate, barring cataclysms, they will continue to hold the ten million square miles (one-fifth of the earth's land surface) where they are fully native and popular.

There is a good deal to be learned from statistics on population growth for various lands, since these figures are easily translated into terms of speaking populations.

It is a well-known fact, highly deplored in a good many responsible circles, that the world's population has been expanding in recent times at too fast a rate for its own good. A world population that was short of two billion at the outset of the twentieth century crossed the three billion mark shortly after the end of World War II, and is now rapidly nearing four billion. The consensus of expert opinion is that the four billion figure will be rather easily reached by 1980, considering that the end of 1975 will almost certainly see a world population of over 3.8 billion. The general implications of this situation, and the remedies, if any, that may be used to correct it, are best left to experts in other fields.

What interests us on the linguistic side is that this expansion is not taking place at anything like the same rate in all parts of the world, or, more specifically, among speakers of all languages.

Taking first the great language families and the way they have grown in speaking populations over the last ten years, this is what we find (figures under 1963 and 1974 indicate millions of speakers):

Language Family	1963	1974	Percentage Increase
Indo-European	1,600	1,880	17
Semitic-Hamitic-Kushitic	120	150	25
Ural-Altaic	85	100	17
Sino-Tibetan	750	865	13
Japanese-Korean	130	155	19
Dravidian	130	165	27
Malayo-Polynesian	135	180	33
African	175	250	40
Southeast Asian	45	50	11
American Indian	12	13	8

The language groups that show the highest percentage increases are the African (40 percent), Malayo-Polynesian (33 percent), Dravidian (27 percent), Semitic-Hamitic (25 percent). The others, including the Indo-European, show a more moderate growth (under 20 percent). The heavy increase in Semitic-Hamitic speakers is mostly due to Arabic; that of Malayo-Polynesian speakers to both the languages of Indonesia and those of the Philippines.

Shifting now to individual major languages (two, Hindi-Urdu and Malay-Indonesian, have been omitted from our table, for reasons indicated below), this is what we find:

Language	1963	1974	Percentage Increase
English	400	450	12(8)[1]
German	115	120	5
French	80	100	25(12)
Spanish	160	220	38
Portuguese	90	110	22
Italian	60	65	8
Russian	205	240	17(10)
Chinese	700	770	10
Japanese	95	105	10
Arabic	90	120	33
Bengali	85	110	30

1. Here percentage figures in parentheses indicate real native-speaker growth, shorn of the addition of nonnative, cultural speakers, who are particularly numerous in the case of English, French, and Russian.

For India, the present figure for Hindi is 140 million; to these must be added 60 million speakers of Urdu, which is in substance the same language as Hindi (the two together are sometimes labeled Hindustani). To these must be added another 100 million nonnative speakers of Hindi and Urdu, in both India and Pakistan.

The total for Indo-Iranian languages is 610 million, but this includes some 55 million speakers of Persian, Pashto, Kurdish, Baluchi, Tadjik, etc., all languages spoken outside of India and Pakistan. On the other hand, the 163 million speakers of Dravidian languages are all located on Indian soil (save for about 3 million in Sri Lanka, or Ceylon). The sum total of Indo-Iranian and Dravidian speakers in India, Pakistan, and Sri Lanka gives us 718 million, as against the 581 million of 1963. The percentage growth for these languages taken together is 24 percent.

Malay-Indonesian includes Bahasa Indonesian, the recently created official language of the Indonesian Republic, plus the older Malay that was used as a general trade language in the former Dutch East Indies. Officially, Bahasa serves a population of 115 million, all of whom are native speakers of other languages of the Malayo-Polynesian family (Javanese, Madurese, Balinese, Dayak, etc.). Actual speakers of either Bahasa or the Malay on which it is based probably do not exceed 50 million at the present time, though their numbers are steadily increasing.

The areas that reflect the largest population and speaker growth are (1) Africa south of the Sahara; (2) Latin America, where both Spanish and Portuguese have taken startling leaps; (3) Indonesia and the Philippines; (4) the Arab countries; (5) India, Pakistan, Bangladesh, Sri Lanka. The rest of the world shows what might be described as a "normal" increase, generally ranging between 10 and 20 percent, and in some instances dropping below 10 percent.

Among the world's largest languages, highest percentage growth in the last ten years has been achieved by Spanish (38 percent), Arabic (33 percent), Portuguese (22 percent), and the India-Pakistan-Bangladesh-Sri Lanka complex (24 percent).

Demographically, the lead among the Romance languages is resolutely taken by the Iberian languages, Spanish and Portuguese, while French, Italian, Rumanian, are relatively stable. This reverses the historical picture of the Middle Ages, when French and Italian were ahead of Spanish and Portuguese in numbers of speakers.

Demography and speaking populations are, of course, far from being the sole factors that determine the importance and prestige of languages. At the same time, they must be considered, especially when they apply to languages of attested and enduring civilizations. They are particularly important in connection with the more material aspects of present-day life: industry, commerce, the ability to produce and consume. It is possible that North American interest in the nations and tongues of Latin America, which has not been shared to any considerable degree by the countries of Europe, may have a sounder foundation for the future than had been envisaged since the end of World War II. This need not in any way detract from our interest in the other swiftly growing areas of the earth: Africa, the Near East, southern Asia, the island world off the southeastern coast of Asia; nor from our interest in the older, established lands of Europe, the U.S.S.R., China, and Japan.

One word of advice that might be offered to those who look to Latin America for future opportunities and development would be not to forget that Latin America includes not one, but two, large and rapidly expanding Romance languages: Portuguese as well as Spanish.

For the rest, there is no reason to suppose, short of cataclysmic occurrences, that the Romance languages will not continue to be the voice-bearers of their respective civilizations, and to contribute validly to the picture of a "brave new world" as they have contributed to the world of the past—in art, literature and philosophy, science and technology, discovery and invention, the expansion of trade, industry, agriculture, and all the activities that lead to a better material, intellectual, and spiritual life.

They may, along with the great Germanic languages (English and German) encounter stiffer competition in a world where new nations are emerging and old nations, once great, are clamoring for readmission to the world's stage. But this should not cause excessive preoccupation. If past and present history is any indication, the Romance languages can be trusted to know how to hold their own, and at the same time help the others to achieve their goals.

At the round table of the world's languages, there will always be a place of honor for French, Spanish, Portuguese, Italian, Rumanian, as well as for the Latin language from which they sprang.

A Brief History of Romance Philology and Linguistics

Linguistics is often defined as the study of language pure and simple; philology as the study of language in the framework of the cultural output of language, particularly in the field of literature. This would make linguistics an altogether factual science, recording what is and has been, while philology, in addition to being far more embracing (the literary output of any given literary tongue is, after all, a complete field of study in itself), would also contain a subjective factor of individual evaluation of so-called literary values, as well as an often hypothetical pursuit of literary influences.

Philology, more than linguistics, delves into historical causes and effects. A "pure" linguist of the more descriptive persuasion asks the question: "Why do English speakers refer to an animal of a certain kind as a 'horse'?" He answers it in this fashion: "Because that is what their ancestors called it, as far back as the English language can be traced." A philologist is not satisfied with this answer. He wants to know the whys, the wherefores, and the hows. This leads him into historical as well as purely linguistic research.

But history itself has its own thorny questions of why and wherefore and how, along with when and where. The teaching of history as a sequence of kings and dynasties, famous men, battles and dates, is somewhat out of fashion in our inquisitive age. People now want to know why a certain war took place, why its outcome was what it was, what were the causes of a given invasion or migration, what were its results. The historian knows that while some past historical events have to be reconstructed largely on the basis of hypotheses, inductions, and deductions, his research can be mightily helped by a study of whatever documentation has come down to us from the period under consideration.

The philologist, whose task it often is to interpret the documents for the historian, has the same feeling with regard to his own language specialty, which he considers as a segment of the broader historical field. He is not content with stating bald facts of linguistic change, but wants to examine the available evidence to trace, insofar as it is possible, the causes of those changes and the events, both linguistic and nonlinguistic, that brought those changes about. The documentary and historical evidence must, of course, be carefully sifted, examined, and weighed, as is evidence in a court of law. But when all is said and done, the methodology works out more satisfactorily than that of taking two points in time and arbitrarily reconstructing what "must have happened" in between.

It goes without saying that there are certain fields of language where documentary and historical evidence is totally or almost totally absent, and in these cases the reconstructive methodology is the only one available. This is true of the transition from a hypothetical Proto-Indo-European to the earliest recorded Indo-European languages, and, in lesser degree, of some existing language groups (American Indian, African, native Australian, and Papuan). It is not true of other language fields where both the historical and the documentary evidence are abundant and unbroken, and can be easily traced from the fifth century B.C. to our own times, as is the case with Latin-Romance.

This is why the term "Romance philology" antedates the term "Romance linguistics," which is today more in vogue. On the basis of etymological meaning, Romance linguistics stresses "language," that which is produced with the tongue, that which is spoken; Roman philology is the "love of the word," and the word may appear in either spoken or written form, with the written form usually supplying the historical link, and giving some indication, however imperfect, of the whys and the hows.

It might seem logical to say that Romance philology could not possibly have come into being before the rise of the Romance languages. But since those languages are the continuators of Latin in all its manifestations, Archaic, Classical, and Vulgar, it is at least as logical to say that Romance philology includes those pre-Romance manifestations.

Interest in language, its nature, origin, and links, is by no means a modern phenomenon. While the linguistic interests and views of the ancients differed from those of today, and their methodologies were necessarily less scientific than ours, their minds were as keen as our own. On the basis of their accumulated stock of information, far less extensive than what is available to us, they reached certain conclusions that hold both interest and merit for us as we view them from our modern vantage point.

To begin with, the practical aspects of language for purposes of communication between different speaking groups were as obvious to the ancients as they are to us. As far back as the confusion of tongues in the Book of Genesis, there was consciousness of what lack of linguistic understanding could do to a project that required human collaboration. The hieroglyphic representations of interpreters accompanying foreign ambassadors to the court of the pharaohs, the bilingual and trilingual inscriptions on stone for areas that had more than one language, the bilingual dictionaries of Sumerian and Akkadian inscribed on clay tablets, are indications of awareness of language diversity and its inconveniences.

But it was only with the Greek philosophers and the Sanskrit grammarians of the fourth and third centuries B.C. that we begin to find conscious interest in the problems of language. Panini's grammar of Sanskrit, composed about 300 B.C., but containing references to earlier works now lost, is a highly analytical, prescriptive and descriptive manual of the earliest Indo-European language on record.

The Greeks, more introspectively inclined, preferred to go into lengthy debates concerning the possibility of an inherent link between the object and the word that represents it in speech (the word being the Greek word; other languages were blissfully ignored, since nonspeakers of Greek were collectively styled *barbaroi*, "babblers," inferior creatures whose babbling held no true meaning). But this initial discussion eventually led to an examination of the chosen tongue, and a classification of grammatical categories and parts of speech that is still largely valid today.

The Romans, following in the footsteps of the Greeks, organized their own language into a similar grammatical scheme, something not too difficult, since both Greek and Latin share the same original Indo-European structure. But the Romans had one advantage over the Greeks, that of being able and willing to make comparisons between the two languages. Outside of Greek, which they respected as the vehicle of a culture superior to their own, they showed the same (to us) distressing unconcern for the other languages of antiquity spoken around them (Etruscan,

Gaulish, Iberian, Punic, and many more), to which they have left us only stray references on the basis of which to reconstruct those tongues.

Yet among the Romans, too, there was some measure of awareness of the problems of language, of the incipient dialectalization and vulgarization of their own tongue, of the changes that go on in language, both in time and in space.[1]

Christianity and the barbarian invasions had the effect of imparting dignity to nonclassical languages. Conversion of the newcomers called for massive propaganda efforts in the languages of the newcomers themselves, and this meant extensive translations of the Bible into Germanic, Slavic, and other tongues.[2]

At the same time, however, philosophical and speculative interest in language waned, and with the break in communications between East and West, even Greek was all but lost to speakers of Late Latin. Grammatical interest continued, but more and more on a prescriptive rather than a descriptive basis, reflecting a state of affairs no longer current among the speakers. As the Romance languages made their first timid appearance, little attempt was made to codify them into set grammatical forms. On the other hand, the Semitic-speaking Arabs, who now occupied the southern shores of the Mediterranean and made menacing inroads into the European lands of Spain, France, and Sicily, accepted for their language the grammatical categories and classifications of the Greek school of Alexandria, to which they had fallen heirs (again, this was not too difficult, for there are strong similarities of structure between Semitic and Indo-European).

The main contribution of the Middle Ages to linguistics in general (and it is a somewhat questionable one) was Roger Bacon's *Universal Grammar,* to the effect that "grammar is one and the same in all languages, so far as substance is concerned; but it may vary in individual details." This was substantially what the Greeks and Romans had implied without actually affirming it, and what the Jansenist *Port Royal Grammar* continued to imply as late as 1660. The idea of a universal grammar into which all human tongues must fit was not finally rejected until the beginning of the nineteenth century, to be revived, curiously, in the

---

1. See Part II, Chapter 4.
2. The first Germanic version of the Bible is Wulfilas' translation into Gothic, about A.D. 400; the first Slavic version is Cyril and Methodius' translation into Old Church Slavic, about A.D. 900.

twentieth by believers in the monogenesis, or single origin, of language, such as Alfredo Trombetti.[3]

Dante Alighieri's *De Vulgari Eloquentia* of 1305 marked, on the one hand, the beginning of Romance philology in the narrower sense (specific study and comparison of the Romance languages). It also marked the beginning of modern linguistic thought.

As has been seen (Part II, Chapter 10), this minor Latin work of the author of the *Divine Comedy* made the first true attempt at language derivation and language comparison, correctly describing Italian, French, and Provençal as stemming from Latin; and offering, in addition, a basically correct enumeration and classification of the Italian dialects, thus getting linguistic geography off to an early start. Dante was also the first to claim dignity for the new vernaculars, as against the crystallized Latin of universal medieval scholarship.

Dante's pronouncement was followed at some distance in time by the fall of Constantinople to the Turks, with the consequent rediscovery by the West of the treasure stores of Greek. This was both accompanied and followed by the voyages of exploration of Africa and Asia, then by the discovery of the New World, with its myriad strange tongues. It was the new and unfamiliar languages of lands other than Europe and the Mediterranean basin that led to a rethinking of the medieval position that all languages are basically similar in structure.

The Renaissance mind was an inquiring one, and it is not surprising that research and investigation, however imperfect the methods on which they were based, advanced contemporaneously along many fronts. While books and essays were being written about the new strange tongues that navigation and discovery had brought to light, Dante's pronouncements about the vernacular of Italy set off a chain reaction of discussion and

---

3. *Dell'unità d'origine del linguaggio*, Bologna, 1905; *Elementi di glottologia*, Bologna, 1922–1923. See also Oddone Assirelli, *La dottrina monogenistica di A. Trombetti*, Bologna, 1961; and, shorn of the monogenistic feature, Benjamin Lee Whorf, "Grammatical Categories" and "Language: Plan and Conception of Arrangement," in *Language, Thought, and Reality* (ed. J. B. Carroll), Cambridge, Mass., 1956; and Joseph Greenberg (ed.), *Universals in Language,* Cambridge, Mass., 1963, and *Language Universals* (Janua Linguarum, Series Minor, 59), The Hague, 1966. Also, some theorists of the school of transformational-generative analysis, founded by Noam Chomsky (see end of this chapter), have again brought the idea of a universal grammar into focus, placing traditional grammar into proper perspective again by reverting to the concerns and even specific doctrines of traditional theory, such as the question of universal properties of language, somewhat along the lines of Bacon's *Universal Grammar*.

speculation about both Italian and other literary vernaculars, now grown to adult estate.

Castilian had already been fixed and made official by Alfonso el Sabio in 1253. Now, in the sixteenth century, came Juan de Valdés and Arias Montano to duplicate for the languages of the Iberian Peninsula what Dante had done for Italian, while in France Henri Etienne, in his *Thesaurus Linguae Graecae* of 1572, propounded the thesis of dialectal division and the objective reality of documented language forms. The search for objectivity and truth rather than fancy was furthered in the following century by Mabillon and Du Cange, who established the rules for determining the authenticity and approximate dating of ancient texts, like the Oaths of Strasbourg, now rediscovered. The fanciful etymologies of Pléïade writers such as Lemaire, Ronsard, and Picard were at least partly repressed by later writers: Ménage, Bernardo Aldrete, and Nunes de Leão. At the same time, the ideological conflict of the Reformation lent new interest to both the ancient tongues of the Bible and the medieval documents that contained the real or supposed justification for the Church's immense holdings.

Major contributions to linguistic studies throughout the seventeenth and eighteenth centuries continued to lie mainly in the field of the Romance languages and their Latin ancestor, with Lacurne de Ste.-Palaye's insistence on comparison of the Romance tongues, Bonamy's stress on the *lingua rustica* of Gregory of Tours and the legal Formulas of Angers as the true direct ancestor of the Romance vernaculars, the monumental collections of medieval texts of Flórez and Muratori, and Martín Sarmiento's suggestion (1757) that a linguistic atlas of Galicia be undertaken.

The fact can hardly be overstressed that from the time of Dante, at the outset of the fourteenth century, to the close of the eighteenth, linguistic research lay overwhelmingly (1) in the Latin-Romance field, and (2) in the philological division of linguistics. The second part of this proposition holds true even throughout the crucial nineteenth century, when the current of studies initiated by Sir William Jones with his 1786 essay on the intimate relationship of Sanskrit and Old Persian with Greek, Latin, Celtic, and Germanic turned the stream of linguistic research into the Indo-European channel. But by the very nature of things, Indo-European studies had to be based on documentation. As for the comparative aspect of the new studies (laying side by side forms taken from the oldest Indo-European languages on record, and from their comparison deriving the "laws" of their separate development, along with the reconstruction of the hypothetical Indo-European parent language from which they had sprung), that methodology had been repeatedly suggested, though not directly applied, by the earlier Romanists, notably de Ste.-Palaye, Bonamy, and Sarmiento.

The story of the notable achievements of the early Indo-Europeanists (Schlegel, Rask, Bopp, Grimm, Verner, Pott), as well as such later ones as Brugmann and Delbrück, Schleicher and Paul, pertains to the story of linguistics in general. But the precise, rigorous comparative methodology they had set in motion was quickly applied to the Latin-Romance field by Friedrich Diez, who outlined it in full in his *Grammatik der romanischen Sprachen* of 1836–1844.

An entire new generation of Romance philologists came into being, which included such names as De Jubenal, discoverer of the *Chanson de Roland*, Gaston Paris, who in 1870 founded the first periodical (*Romania*) devoted exclusively to Romance philology, Paul Meyer, Hugo Schuchardt, Graziadio Ascoli, and Francesco d'Ovidio.[4]

The twentieth century is marked by a transition in the stress placed upon the various aspects of language. The previous century had been dominated by the historical, comparative, philological approach, applied equally both to the general field of Indo-European studies and to its various branches, including the Latin-Romance. Now Ferdinand de Saussure's *Cours de linguistique générale* (1916), offering a precise formulation of descriptive linguistics, presented with absolute clarity a thesis, earlier hinted at by von Humboldt, of language as a sociological phenomenon, to be viewed in relation to its living speakers and their psychological processes. Some features of the Saussurian concept are (1) the distinction between language (a system in which many individuals participate) and speech (the basic production of sounds peculiar to the individual speaker); (2) the presentation of the linguistic sign as both arbitrary (i.e., not based upon any inherent link between word and object) and constant (i.e., having universal acceptance among all members of the speaking group); (3) a static, synchronic, descriptive element that is essential to the speaker, while language change is largely a matter of convenience of articulation.

---

4. For fuller references than appear in the Bibliography, see the more extensive chapter bibliographies in M. Pei, *Voices of Man*, Harper & Row, New York, 1962 (reprinted by AMS Reprint Corp., New York, 1972), and particularly pp. 14–18, 49, 54.

While this view of language at any specific point in time is basically correct, it puts into the background the historical, dynamic factors that had prevailed in the thinking of an earlier period. It also places far less reliance on the importance of historical documentation, stressing in its place a spoken-language approach that is necessarily static. Since the living speaker of a thousand years ago is no longer present, and has left no audible record of his speech, the descriptive linguist often prefers to reconstruct what that speech must have been on the basis of such present-day indications as the divergence of modern dialects from one another, and to trace the course of the spoken language during the intervening period from his hypothetical reconstruction of the past to the ascertainable reality of the present. He is often forced to bring in written-language evidence, but is reluctant to do so, and trusts the authenticity of such evidence far less than did the comparativists of the earlier period.

Since this new methodology works well (in fact, is the only one possible) in the case of languages that have little or no known history, written form, or documentation, it was perhaps natural that it should appeal to linguists of a new generation, impatient with tradition and eager to explore new fields previously untrodden. (Something similar has occurred within the last fifty years in the fields of art, literature, music, economics, politics, even moral and ethical standards.)

Until the late 1950's, the predominant slant of linguistic studies was therefore in the direction of the descriptive rather than the historical; of phonology and, to a lesser degree, morphology and syntax as against etymology and semantics; of the spoken vernaculars, including dialect and slang, as against the written literary languages; of the mechanical, unconscious aspects as against the spiritual, deliberate manifestations of language.[5]

Nevertheless, historical linguistics goes on. Among its still most flourishing branches is the Latin-Romance. The names of important modern workers in this field are numerous (some, with their major works, are listed in the Bibliography).

The development of the Romance languages in general, following the nineteenth and early twentieth-century tradition set by Friedrich Diez, Gustav Gröber, Wilhelm Meyer-Lübke, Adolf Zauner, Edouard Bourciez,

---

5. For the development of the most recent trend in linguistics, typified by Noam Chomsky and his transformational-generative school, which perhaps indicates a return to earlier points of view, see Paul A. Gaeng's brief discussion at the end of this chapter.

all of whom wrote comprehensive comparative grammars of the Romance tongues, has been similarly treated in recent times by Angelo Monteverdi and Carlo Tagliavini in Italy, Heinrich Lausberg and Ernst Auerbach in Germany, William Elcock and Rebecca Posner in England, Walter von Wartburg in Switzerland, Robert A. Hall, Jr., in the United States. Other notable contributions have been made by Hugo Schuchardt and his pupil Leo Spitzer, Ernst Gamillscheg, Giuliano Bonfante, and Yakov Malkiel.

Historico-linguistic studies that go back to the ancient languages of the Italian peninsula include such American works as that compiled by R. S. Conway, Joshua Whatmough, and Sarah Johnson on the pre-Italic dialects of Italy, and Carl Buck's work on Oscan and Umbrian. There are in the twentieth century numerous excellent historical grammars and descriptions, as well as etymological dictionaries, of Latin, including those of A. Ernout and A. Meillet in France, W. M. Lindsay and L. R. Palmer in the United States and England, Ernst Kieckers and Ferdinand Sommer in Germany, Vittore Pisani and Giacomo Devoto in Italy. Vulgar Latin, with all the conflicting views on its nature, chronology, and development, was covered in the nineteenth century by Hugo Schuchardt in Germany and F. G. Mohl in France, then, in the twentieth, by Charles Grandgent, H. F. Muller, and Ernst Pulgram in America, Carlo Battisti in Italy, Karl Vossler and Helmuth Schmeck in Germany, Veikko Väänänen in Finland, S. da Silva Neto and Theodoro Maurer in Brazil.

Collections of medieval documents, such as Jules Tardif's *Monuments historiques* of 1866 and G. Bonelli's *Codice paleografico longobardo* of 1908, began to be flanked by new, updated versions, fortified by photostats of the actual documents, designed to permit the researcher to solve for himself questions of doubtful spelling and interpretation. Outstanding among these are Ph. Lauer and Ph. Samaran's *Les diplômes originaux des Mérovingiens* (1908) and L. Schiaparelli's *Codice diplomatico longobardo* (1929-1933). The photostatic method is also being increasingly used for manuscripts and collections of medieval Romance texts that formerly appeared in critical editions (with the extant manuscript reconstructed and transcribed in accordance with the compiler's idea of what the lost original must have been) or diplomatic versions (where the text appears as an exact transliteration of the extant manuscript, but is likewise subjected to the reading of the compiler).

Detailed studies of the documentary evidence concerning Vulgar Latin, which had begun to accumulate in the days of Flórez and Muratori, continue in our century with such works as E. Bechtel's and E. Löfstedt's separate studies of the *Peregrinatio Sylviae;* H. F. Muller and Pauline Taylor's *Chrestomathy of Vulgar Latin;* studies on the language of the Merovingian and Carolingian documents of France by Jeanne Vielliard, George Trager, Louis F. Sas, and Mario Pei; of the Longobardic documents of Italy by Robert and Frieda Politzer; of the *Forum Judicum* of Spain by Paul Cooper; of Christian Latin by Christine Mohrmann.

The evidence of the Latin inscriptions, barely skimmed by K. Sittl and a few other nineteenth-century scholars (though it had been available since the 1860's in the monumental *Corpus Inscriptionum Latinarum*), began to be examined in detail at the outset of our century by J. Pirson and A. Carnoy, who studied, respectively, the inscriptions of Gaul and Spain; then by Ernst Diehl, whose specialty was the Christian inscriptions. Later Veikko Väänänen of Finland made a careful examination of the inscriptions of Pompeii. Very recently Paul A. Gaeng has made a comparative study of the Christian inscriptions of Gaul, Spain, and Italy, from which some of the very earliest phenomena of later Romance dialectalization can be deduced. Other similar studies are in preparation to cover the Latin inscriptions of Africa, Britain, and the Balkans.

Curiously, America, which took an early start in the modern descriptive approach to linguistics, also holds a lead of sorts in these philological activities, which are firmly grounded in the work of earlier centuries. A promising new development, though yet unpublished, is the work of Thaddeus Ferguson, who combines reconstructive and philological methods, using the second to check the first.

Dealing especially with French linguistic development and history are numerous twentieth-century works, including the monumental *Histoire de la langue française,* composed by Ferdinand Brunot and Charles Bruneau in thirteen volumes over a period that extended from 1905 to 1969. More specifically devoted to Old French is the grammar and collection of medieval dialect texts prepared by Eduard Schwan and D. Behrens, originally published in German in 1888, but updated and translated into French by Oscar Bloch in 1913. Good historical grammars of the language are the works of K. Nyrop, E. Lerch, A. Dauzat, M. Cohen, Mildred Pope, Alfred Ewert, Urban T. Holmes and Alexander Schutz. W. von Wartburg, whose production ranges over the entire Romance field, has one of the most readable works on the subject, *Evolution et structure de la langue française.* Joseph Bédier, primarily a literary scholar in the earlier reaches of Old French literature, has contributed a good deal to our information about the language in its primitive stages. The tradition of historical and etymological French dictionaries, initiated for Old French and its dialects by F. Godefroy, A. Hatzfeld, and A. Darmesteter in the 1880's, continued with Oscar Bloch and W. von Wartburg, has now been revived by a team of philologists from Heidelberg and Laval universities, under the general editorship of K. Baldinger.

The Spanish field is dominated by the extraordinary output of Ramón Menéndez Pidal, who from the beginning of this century until his very recent death covered practically every angle of Spanish linguistics and medieval literature, with side excursions into the Old French epic. Excellent historical grammars of Spanish are the work of Amado Alonso, Rafael Lapesa, and William Entwistle. In addition to the *Diccionario de la Real Academia,* there is a historical and etymological dictionary of the language by Juan Corominas. The question of the Spanish substratum has been explored in depth by Frederic Jungemann.

The Portuguese field has been amply covered by the work of José Leite de Vasconcellos, Antenor Nascentes, author of an etymological dictionary of the language, Edwin Williams (*From Latin to Portuguese*), and Manuel de Paiva Boléo, the distinguished director of Coimbra's *Revista Portuguesa de Filologia.*

Italian studies offer historical grammars of the language that range from the earlier ones of F. d'Ovidio and W. Meyer-Lübke and Charles Grandgent to the more recent works of Bruno Migliorini and Mario Pei, and to the painstaking volumes of G. Rohlf's *Historische Grammatik der italienischen Sprache und ihrer Mundarten* and P. Tekavčić's *Grammatica storica dell'italiano.* An excellent etymological-historical dictionary is the work of G. Alessio and C. Battisti. Other notable contributions are those of G. Bertoni, M. Bartoli, C. Merlo, G. Pellegrini, O. Parlangèli, A. Schiaffini, and A. Menarini, while the *Bibliography of Italian Linguistics* of Robert A. Hall, Jr., is a model of its kind.

The earlier workers in the field of Rumanian, O. Densusianu, M. Gaster, and I. Iordan, have been followed in more recent times by G. Weigand, S. Pop, E. Petrovici, with their linguistic atlas of Rumania; their collaborator, S. Puşcariu (author also of an etymological dictionary of Rumanian); Maria M. Manea; A. Graur; and A. Rosetti, author of a history of Rumanian more up-to-date than that of Densusianu.

The field of both Old and modern Provençal, explored in the nineteenth century by F. Raynouard and F. Mistral, has had more recent attention from V. Crescini and C. Appel, both compilers of extensive Old Provençal chrestomathies, as well as from J. Anglade, with his historical grammar, and A. Jeanroy, with his profound studies in the older literature.

Greatest exponent of Catalan studies is A. Griera i Caja, with his historical grammars of the older language and his linguistic atlas of Catalonia today. J. Corominas has in preparation an etymological-historical dictionary of Catalan.

The foremost specialist in Sardinian is M. L. Wagner, with his *La lingua sarda* and an extensive dictionary. U. Pellis and P. E. Guarnerio have also contributed to our knowledge of the Sardinian varieties.

The Swiss varieties of Rheto-Rumansh have been covered by R. von Planta, C. Decurtins, and T. Gartner, while the Italian variants have formed the topic of extensive studies by Carlo Battisti.

For our knowledge of Vegliote, the last modern descendant of Dalmatian, we are indebted to Matteo Bartoli. Dalmatian, in its relation to the Balkan languages, has also been the subject of extensive studies by P. Skok, R. Hadlich, and Žarko Muljačić, while an excellent study of the Vegliote vocabulary in comparison with other Romance languages is the work of John Fisher.

Judaeo-Romance in its medieval French versions has been gone into in depth by D. S. Blondheim, Raphael Levy, and Menahem Banitt, who under the name of Max Berenblut also contributed an important study of the Italian versions. Modern Judaeo-Spanish (Ladino) has formed the subject of several interesting studies by A. Agard, M. L. Wagner, and Max Luria, among others.

Among important twentieth-century periodicals devoted exclusively to Romance philology and linguistics one may mention *Romania* and *Revue des Langues Romanes* of France, *Zeitschrift für romanische Philologie* and *Romanische Forschungen* of Germany, *Archivio Glottologico Italiano* and *Lingua Nostra* of Italy, *Archivum Romanicum* and *Vox Romanica* of Switzerland, *Revista de Filología Española* of Spain and Spanish America, *Revista Portuguesa de Filologia* of Portugal, *Revista Brasileira de Filologia* of Brazil, *Studii și Cercetări Lingvistici* of Rumania, *Romance Philology* of the U.S.; but this cursory list not only omits many other important periodicals but also fails to mention the numerous ones which combine Romance philology and linguistics with Romance literatures (like *Romanic Review, Modern Language Notes, Modern Language*

Review, Symposium), or with linguistic studies in general (like the American *Language* and *Word,* England's *Medium Aevum,* and Rumania's *Revista de filologia romanică și germanică.*

Two developments that pertain almost exclusively to the twentieth century call for special mention. One, definitely linked to historical and philological studies, is the historical-etymological dictionary, either of the Latin-Romance field as a whole, or of a specific Romance language. While it is true that attempts at this sort of work were made as far back as the days of Ménage, and, on a more fanciful basis, of Isidore of Seville and Varro, it was the nineteenth-century work of Diez and the later ones of Körting and Meyer-Lübke that really set the pace for modern times. The updated fourth edition of Meyer-Lübke's *Romanisches etymologisches Wörterbuch* gives fairly ample coverage of the entire field (with some reservations, especially for Rumanian), while some of the dictionaries recently compiled for individual Romance languages follow the practice of the *Oxford English Dictionary* of tracing the entire history of each word from its earliest recorded appearance. The value of such a tool for historical-philological studies is obvious.

The second innovation, although more descriptive and synchronic than philological and historical, nevertheless had its inception in the nineteenth-century controversies concerning the importance of dialects vis-à-vis literary languages as trustworthy indicators of past historical developments in language. Once it became evident that official, literary tongues, however firmly established and of practical importance, were only sublimations of one dialect or conglomerations of many dialects, the dialectal composition of individual languages began to be examined in depth. The examination revealed that the number of dialectal variants in any given language is almost infinite, with divergences appearing even within two parts of a village separated by a brook or rise of ground. The study of these dialectal differences peculiarly lent itself to the descriptive, synchronic, speech-oriented methodology that was coming into vogue, with field studies by linguistically trained observers who would go into each chosen area and ferret out, by dint of ingenious questioning, from the least literate part of the population, what the localism was by which certain objects or actions were designated. Often the investigators would not even use the official designation of the object, but show a picture (of a horse, for instance) and ask their informant: "What do you call this?" The replies, duly recorded in phonetic transcription (this was in the days before tape recordings and cassettes), were inscribed on large maps of the total area (say France), with a single map being used for each word or phrase, so that the word that appears in standard French as *cheval* now appeared in hundreds of local variations charted out on a single map of the entire French area. The hundreds or thousands of individual maps, gathered together in a collection of several volumes, would then constitute a linguistic atlas of France.

First among the comprehensive works of this nature was the *Atlas linguistique de la France* of J. Gilliéron and E. Edmont (1902), followed at a distance by the *Sprach- und Sachatlas Italiens und der Südschweiz* of K. Jaberg and J. Jud (1928); both atlases have had numerous revisions and updatings, which have revealed how the dialects change in approximately the same measure as the official tongues.

We now have similar atlases for the Iberian peninsula (T. Navarro Tomás), the Rumanian area (Weigand and associates), the Catalan area (A. Griera), Corsica (G. Bottiglioni), and numerous limited regions, including various countries of Latin America.

The linguistic atlas vogue easily spread from the Romance to other language fields, and it was relatively easy for Hans Kurath and his associates to apply the methodology first to New England, then to the United States as a whole, particularly since a similar methodology was already being used by scholars in the field of American Indian languages, such as Franz Boas and Leonard Bloomfield. The methodology itself and the rules for its application are summarized in Sever Pop's two-volume *La dialectologie* of 1950, which also goes into a detailed description of dialectal studies and linguistic atlases throughout the world.

The linguistic atlas proves that collaboration between descriptive and historical linguists is possible, and that the fruits of their joint research and methodologies can be of benefit to all who view language as something more than a medium of elementary communication.

Yet no useful purpose can be served by any attempt to force an absolute merger into a single field of what Saussure so clearly proved to be a divided area. Historical linguistics, of which Latin-Romance philology forms so integral a part, has its own problems, subject matter, methodology, procedure, and nomenclature, evolved over a very long period of trial and error.

Romance philology is the branch of historical linguistics that casts the greatest amount of light upon the rise and development of our Western civilization, of which the decline and fall have been repeatedly prophesied, but which, through tremendous changes, has displayed a singular power of adaptability and the will to survive. Like true art, music, literature, it is no mere fad or hobby, but something that gives a clear understanding of the past and present, and an insight of the ways into which to direct our future course.

Noam Chomsky and the Transformational-Generative School

BY PAUL A. GAENG

The essentially empirical approach of previous decades, marked by Saussurian structuralism and prejudices against the mentalist constructs of traditional grammar, caused a sharp reaction on the part of some theorists who felt that Saussure and his followers, particularly the American linguists Edward Sapir, Leonard Bloomfield, and Charles Fries, by basing their analysis of language on a finite set of actual utterances, had failed to account for the infinite set of sentences that a native speaker is able to produce. The new theoretical approach, first developed by Noam Chomsky in his *Syntactic Structures* (The Hague, 1957), has since come to be known as transformational-generative grammar. Briefly, the aim of this new theory is to construct a formal grammar that seeks to explain how an infinite number of sentences can be produced from a limited number of basic structures by applying a variety of rules so as to "generate" larger and more complex sentences. The requirements of such a theory, according to Chomsky, are to specify and predict all the sentences in a given language that a native speaker is able to understand and produce, even though they may have never been spoken or written before. Thus, while the structural linguist was satisfied with describing and identifying the structural features of the sentences that people say, the generative grammarian goes a step further in that he also seeks to explain how these sentences are produced.

The fundamental goal of transformational-generative theory, then, is to find a set of rules by which *all* the grammatical sentences and *only* the grammatical sentences of a language may be generated, and none of the ungrammatical ones. Every native speaker, so its theorists claim, is equipped with an "internal grammar" which enables him to produce and understand sentences that have never been spoken or written before. It is this linguistic "intuition" that tells the native speaker of English, for example, that *colorless green ideas sleep furiously* is a well-formed, that is, grammatical sentence, even though it is rather meaningless, whereas *furiously sleep ideas green colorless* is neither grammatical nor meaningful. In the same way, the native speaker of English is readily aware of the ambiguity in *flying planes can be dangerous,* or that the pair of sentences (1) *John is easy to please* and (2) *John is eager to please* are really quite different, despite their apparent identity of structure on the surface. The native speaker uses this intuitive knowledge of his language, this *competence,* to produce and understand novel sentences and to reject utterances not in keeping with his native language pattern, as opposed to the *performance,* that is, the actual use he makes of his language in a given situation. Thus, generative grammar comes to be a model of the speaker's and hearer's competence, this internal grammatical mechanism which underlies the concrete act of speech, the performance.

In contrast to the approach taken by structural linguists who have traditionally begun the analysis of a language by taking its sounds as a starting point (a "sound to sentence" approach), transformational-generative analysis moves from sentence to sound, so to speak, by focusing on the syntax of the language and proceeding from there down to the level of basic sound units. It begins with the assumption that certain sentences are basic and that other sentences are derived from them by a process of transformation. For example, *the dog bit the policeman* is a basic sentence type (basic in the sense that it cannot be derived from any other sentence that underlies it) which may be transformed into such nonbasic sentence types as *the policeman was bitten by the dog,* or *did the policeman bite the dog?,* or even the phrase *the dog's biting the policeman,* which, although not a sentence by itself, could occur with another sentence, such as *the dog's biting the policeman resulted in a court action for the owner.* The core of grammar, accordingly, is made up of a relatively small number of basic sentence types which are the foundation, as it were, upon which all sentence structures rest.

Changes in some of the theoretical concepts and methods of transformational-generative grammar have been swift since their first statement in Chomsky's seminal work, and today the theory differs in many respects from its original version; these changes, however, involve methods of analysis rather than basic aims and objectives.

Appendixes

Appendix A

The Indo-European Languages

The world's languages, over three thousand in number, may go back to a single ancestor, but of this there is no sure evidence. They can, however, be subdivided into families, among the members of most of which there is a provable structural and genetic link. Others, for lack of information, have to be presented on a geographical basis.

Of these families, the most important in terms of number of speakers is the Indo-European (so called because its members extend from northern India to western Europe). Speakers of Indo-European languages today include nearly two billion of the world's total population of slightly less than four billion.

It is supposed, but not proved, that there was once a Proto-Indo-European language, of which no records have come down to us, but which can to some extent be reconstructed by comparing the oldest recorded members of each branch. From this parent language the various branches are believed to have broken off, becoming highly differentiated in the course of their migrations, though still recognizable as stemming from a common source.

The living branches of the family are eight in number. Two other extinct branches, Hittite and Tokharian, have been clearly identified.

The living branches of Indo-European with their main subdivisions are as follows:[1]

Germanic (1) East Germanic: †Gothic; (2) West Germanic: Low—†Anglo-Saxon, English; Dutch-Flemish, Frisian, Afrikaans; Low German; High—German; (3) North Germanic or Scandinavian: †Old Norse; Icelandic; Norwegian, Danish, Swedish.

Italic (or Latin-Romance) (1) †Oscan-†Umbrian; (2) †Faliscan-Latin (Latin gave rise to Portuguese, Spanish, Catalan, French, Provençal, Sardinian, Italian, Rheto-Rumansh, †Dalmatian, Rumanian).

---

1. For the approximate number of present-day speakers of each branch, see Part II, Chapter 19. A cross (†) before the name of a language indicates that it is now extinct.

241

Balto-Slavic (1) Baltic: †Old Prussian, Lithuanian, Latvian; (2) Slavic: †Old Church Slavonic; Russian, Ukrainian, Byelorussian; Polish, Czech, Slovak; Serbo-Croatian, Slovenian, Macedonian, Bulgarian.

Indo-Iranian (1) Iranian: †Old Persian, †Avestan, Modern Persian, Pashto, Kurdish, Tadjik; (2) Indian: †Sanskrit, †Prakrits, Hindi-Urdu (Hindustani), Bengali, Mahrati, Punjabi, Gujarati, Bihari, Rajasthani, Sinhalese, Sindhi, Assamese, Oriya, Nepali, etc.

Greek: †Minoan, †Homeric, †Classical Greek, †Byzantine Koine, Modern Greek.

Celtic (1) †Gaulish; (2) Goidelic: Irish, Scots Gaelic, Manx; (3) Brythonic: Welsh, Breton, †Cornish.

Armenian: †Classical Armenian; Modern Armenian.

Albanian: †Illyrian; Modern Albanian (Gheg, Tosk).

Here are some other important language families; the connection of some of them with Indo-European has been claimed, but for this the evidence is doubtful.[2]

Semitic-Hamitic-Kushitic (1) Semitic: †Akkadian, †Punic, †Aramaic; Arabic, Hebrew, Syriac, Amharic, etc.; (2) Hamitic: †Ancient Egyptian, †Numidian; Coptic, Berber; (3) Kushitic: Somali, Galla, etc.

Ural-Altaic (link between Uralic and Altaic disputed) (1) Uralic: Hungarian, Finnish, Estonian, Mordvinian, etc.; (2) Altaic: Turkish, Tatar, Kazakh, Azerbaijani, Turkmen, Kirghiz, Uzbek, etc.; (3) Mongol-Tungus: Kalmuk, Khalkha, Uigur, etc.

Sino-Tibetan (1) Chinese (Mandarin, Cantonese, Wu, Min, Hakka, etc.); Thai; (2) Tibetan, Burmese, etc.

Japanese-Korean (link disputed) (1) Japanese; (2) Korean.

Dravidian: Tamil, Telugu, Malayalam, Kannada, etc.

Malayo-Polynesian: Malay-Indonesian, Javanese, Madurese, Dayak, Sundanese, Balinese, etc.; Tagalog, Ilocano, Bisayan, etc.; Malagasy; Hawaiian, Maori, Samoan, etc.

Black African (1) Sudanese-Guinean (geographical rather than genetic classification): Mossi, Fula, Yoruba, Mandingo, Hausa, Ibo, Fanti, Ewe, Efik, etc.; (2) Bantu: Zulu, Xhosa, Ruanda, Swahili, etc.; (3) Khoisan: Hottentot, Bushman.

Austro-Asiatic and Mon-Khmer: Vietnamese, Cambodian, Lao, Munda, etc.

American Indian and Eskimo-Aleut (geographic rather than genetic classification, though a tentative grouping into over thirty seemingly unrelated families has been essayed) (1) Arawak, Carib, Tupi, Quechua, Aymará, Araucanian, Maya, Zapotec, Mixtec, Uto-Aztec, Athapaskan, Algonquian, Iroquoian, Siouan, etc.; (2) Eskimo, Aleut.

Caucasian: Georgian, Lesghian, Avar, Circassian, etc. (possible link with Iberian, Etruscan, and other ancient "Mediterranean" languages).

Australian-Papuan (geographic rather than genetic classification).

Iberian-Basque (link disputed) †Iberian, Basque.

Ainu and Hyperborean (Ainu; Kamchadal, Yukagir, etc.).

---

2. For approximate number of present-day speakers, see Part II, Chapter 19.

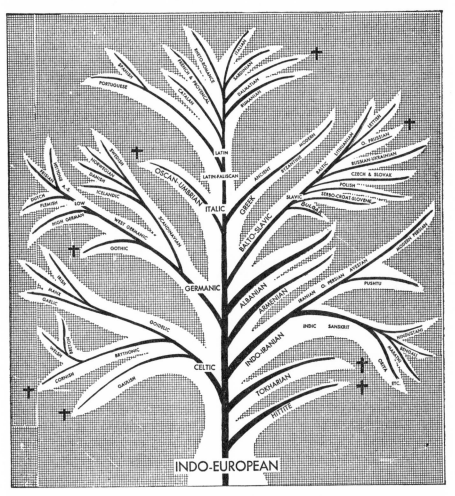

THE INDO-EUROPEAN FAMILY TREE

Crosses indicate extinct branches and languages. It is probable that numerous other languages of antiquity belonged to the Indo-European family. The eight existing branches are Indo-Iranian, Armenian, Albanian, Balto-Slavic, Greek, Italic-Romance, Germanic, Celtic.

Appendix B

The Tongues of Ancient Italy;
Archaic and Pre-Classical Latin

Etruscan

The problem of interpreting the Etruscan language and determining its linguistic affiliation is rendered difficult, if not impossible, by the lack of a long bilingual text (such as the Rosetta stone which, thanks to parallel inscriptions in Greek, in Ancient Egyptian demotic writing, and in hieroglyphic characters, provided a key to the deciphering and interpretation of Ancient Egyptian). Nevertheless, certain striking points of resemblance between Etruscan and Classical Latin or later Romance developments have been noted, such as:

(1) The use of three different symbols to represent the unvoiced velar sound *k* (as in *car*): *K* before *a*, *C* before *e, i,* and *Q* before *u*. This corresponds to the archaic state of affairs in Latin; it is possible that the Romans may have borrowed this alphabetical feature from the Etruscans.

(2) The occasional change of *C* to *ś* before *e* and *i* (e.g., *face, faśe*), suggesting *palatalization* (see Appendix E), a phenomenon that also occurs in Umbrian, in later Vulgar Latin, and in the Romance languages. Whether it is connected with the later general palatalization in Romance is, however, doubtful.

(3) The change of initial *f* to *h* appears (*fap-, hap-,* in a family name). This phenomenon occurs also in some Italic dialects, as well as some Romance languages and dialects, e.g., Spanish *hambre* from Latin *fam(i)ne;* Calabrian *hiuri* from Latin *flore*. A relationship between the Etruscan and the Romance phenomenon, however, is most unlikely.

Here are two brief passages in Etruscan with Latin equivalents suggested by the Italian linguist Trombetti:

surinaś śacni θui ceseθce = *Surinas sacellum hic fundavit*

("Surinas founded a chapel in this place").

eulat tanna larezul ame = *utinam hoc faustum sit*

("Would that this were a favorable omen").

The Etruscan enigma still awaits solution.

Oscan and Umbrian

The Oscan linguistic family, extending throughout the south of Italy, and the Umbrian in the east show several traits in common. They are both closely allied to Latinian, from which they differ, however, in some important aspects, as for instance:

(1) In both Oscan and Umbrian the voiceless velar qu (as in *quick*) is shifted to the labial p (Oscan *pís, píd;* Umbrian *pisi, piře* = Latin *quis, quid*).

(2) Fall of short unstressed vowels indicative of strong accent on the stressed syllable, similar in type to the popular Latin form *caldus* for *calidus* (Oscan *úpsannam* = Latin *operandam;* Umbrian *poplu* = Latin *populum*).

(3) In both dialects confusion appears between $\bar{e}$ and $\breve{i}$ and between $\bar{o}$ and $\breve{u}$. Since this important linguistic feature is characteristic of later Latin and general Romance developments, a connection between the Oscan-Umbrian and the later Romance phenomena may be sought, although the question is still an open one.

(4) In Oscan the z sound (as in English *rose*) is retained between vowels while it is changed to r in Latin (Latin *genus, generis* for *genesis*). Oscan has *-azum* for its genitive plural feminine ending, while Latin has *-arum*.

(5) The change of Indo-European intervocalic *-bh-* to *-f-* (= Latin *-b-*) (Umbrian *trifu* = Latin *tribus;* Oscan *prúfatted* = Latin *probavit*) and the shift of *-nd-* to *-nn-* (Oscan *úpsannam* = Latin *operandam*) show traces not only in modern central and southern Italian dialects but also in other Romance languages and dialects. Thus, French *siffler* and Spanish *chiflar* as well as Italian *zufolare* must be traced back to a popular Latin *sifilare* rather than the Classical *sibilare* form. (But note Spanish *silbar* and Italian *sibilare*, which go back to the Classical Latin form.) A reflex of the shift of *-nd-* to *-nn-* may be seen in Roman *annamo* for standard Italian *andiamo*.

Here is a sample of an Oscan inscription from Apulia with its Latin equivalent and an English translation:

suae pis pru meddixud altrei castrous auti eituas zicolom dicust, izic comono ne hipid ne pon op toutad petirupert urust

si quis pro magistratu alteri de agro aut pecunia diem dixerit, is comitia ne habuerit priusquam apud populum quater oraverit

("If anyone, in his capacity as magistrate, appoints a day for another concerning land or money, let him not have the vote of the assembly until he has spoken four times before the people")

Our most comprehensive source for Umbrian are the so-called *Iguvine Tablets* (bronze tablets discovered at *Iguvium*, an ancient city in Umbria, now *Gubbio*). Here is a section with Latin equivalent and English translation:

inumek via mersuva arvamen etuta; erak pir persklu uřetu; sakre uvem kletra fertuta, aituta; arven kletram amparitu; eruk esunu futu; kletre tuplak prumum antentu

tunc via justa in arvum eunto; ea ignem cum supplicatione adoleto; sacrum ovem lectica ferunto, agunto; in arvo lecticam collocato; eo sacrum fiat; lecticae furcam (duplex) primum intendito

("Then by the right way they shall go to the field; there let him light the fire with prayer; they shall bear and push forward the sacred sheep on a stretcher; he shall place the stretcher on the field; there let the sacrifice take place; he shall first lay out the fork on the stretcher")

Faliscan

Despite its close alliance with Latin, Faliscan presents some dialectal peculiarities, among them:

(1) Intervocalic Indo-European *-bh-* appears as *-f-*, as in Oscan and Umbrian, not as *-b-*, as in Latin.

(2) Apparent absence of final *-s*.

Here is an example of a short Faliscan inscription, with its Latin equivalent:

foied uino pipafo, cra carefo = Latin *hodie vinum bibam, cras carebo*
("to-day I'll drink some wine, to-morrow I won't have any")

Archaic and Pre-Classical Latin

The early inscriptions discussed below can be found in Part II, Chapter 1, together with Classical Latin equivalents and English translations:

(1) *manios med fhefhaked numasioi*

The following linguistic features are of interest: Archaic *-os* ending for Latin *-us* to show nominative singular masculine (subject case); Archaic final *-d* to show indirect object (also a feature of Oscan); reduplicated perfect (retained only sporadically in Classical Latin); retention of intervocalic *-s-*, which later changes to *-r-* in Latin (see [4] above under Oscan and Umbrian); the *-oi* ending in the dative (indirect object case), which later becomes *-ō*.

(2) *duenos med feced en manom einom duenoi ne med malo statod*

Here we may note the following: older *dṷ* for later *b* (*duenos* for later *bonus*); disappearance of reduplication (*feced* rather than *fhefhaked*); *-os, -om, -oi,* for later Latin *-us, -um, -ō*, endings.

(3) *sei quis scies violasit iovei bovid piaclum datod*

Let us note the following features: the diphthong *ei* has not yet contracted to *ī* (*sei* and *jovei* for later *sī* and *jovī*); the dropping of *n* before *s* in *scies* for *sciens* (a characteristic feature of later popular Latin); final *-d* is still retained in *bovid, datod;* fall of the short unstressed vowel (as in *piaclum*); an Archaic future or future perfect form in *-ss-*, actually a subjunctive-optative form (*violasit*).

(4) *honc oino ploirume cosentiont r(omai) duonoro optumo fuise viro* (or *virorum?*) *luciom scipione*

The following features are worth noting: the diphthong *oi* is not yet contracted to *ū* (*oino* for later *ūno*); the *dṷ* group has not yet been replaced by *b* (*duonoro* for *bonorum*); frequent fall of final *-m* (also very characteristic of Post-Classical Latin); interchange of *ŭ* and *ĭ* in unstressed positions (*optumo*, Classical Latin *optimo*).

For further particulars and textual examples concerning the languages of ancient Italy, consult Mario Pei, *The Italian Language,* Vanni, New York, 1941, pp. 162–63, 167–72.

THE ANCIENT LANGUAGES AND DIALECTS OF ITALY
This map is not to be taken as exact or complete, but only as a rough approximation.

Appendix C

The Structure of Classical Latin—
A Brief Description

The following is not intended to give a full picture of the Classical Latin declensional and conjugational systems. For that, the reader is referred to any good school grammar of Latin. This summary merely highlights those morphological phenomena that have bearing on subsequent developments of Latin into Romance.

The Noun

(1) The Latin noun is never accompanied by an *article*, either definite or indefinite. Thus, *amīcus* can have the meaning of "friend," "the friend," or "a friend."

(2) Nouns, pronouns, and adjectives are *inflected* (changed by means of endings) to show their relationship to other words in the sentence. The inflectional ending of such a word shows its *number, gender,* and *case.* For instance, the ending *-ōrum* of the word *amicōrum* adds to the basic idea of "friend," represented by the root *amīc-*, those of "genitive" (possessive case) and "plural," so that the complete form comes to mean "of the friends," or "of friends."

(3) Because Latin expresses grammatical relationship by means of inflectional endings it is called a *synthetic* language, in contrast to so-called *analytic* languages, which tend to express such relationship by means of articles and prepositions (in case of nouns) and auxiliaries (in case of verbs). It appears that popular, spoken Latin was characterized by analytic structures, if one is to judge by Post-Classical writings and inscriptions. Instead of saying, for instance, *lector ipsius ecclesiae,* "reader of the church (itself)," (using the genitive case of the intensive pronoun *ipse* and the noun *ecclesia*), people tended to say *lector de ipsa ecclesia,* with the possessive preposition *de* and a common "oblique" case form which represents the merger of various cases, coinciding in this instance

248

with the subject. This analytic structure is fully borne out by the Romance languages in general, cf. French *de l'église*, Italian *della chiesa*, Spanish *de la iglesia*.

(4) *Gender* in Latin is, for the most part, *grammatical* rather than being related to natural gender (such as the distinction between male and female or animate and inanimate). Thus, a word like *agricola*, "farmer," which is naturally male, appears in a predominantly feminine declension. And just as inanimate objects are often masculine or feminine in gender, the neuter sometimes also designates animate beings, e.g., *mancipium*, "slave." Certainly, the neuter in Latin no longer corresponds to a psychological reality (inanimate object); it is this fact, no doubt, that is largely responsible for its gradual absorption by the masculine and feminine genders in the Post-Classical and Pre-Romance periods, with only traces of the old neuter surviving in the Romance languages.

(5) The grammatical gender of a Latin noun may thus be identified (occasionally) by its meaning; more often by the ending of the nominative singular, in accordance with the following scheme covering the five declensional classes:

	I	II	III	IV	V
masculine	—	-ŭs	-s	-ŭs	—
feminine	-ă	—	-s	—	-ēs
neuter	—	-ŭm	-ĕ	-ū	—

Examples: port-a, "door"; *amīc-us*, "friend"; *membr-um*, "limb"; *hiem-s*, "winter"; *mar-e*, "sea," *frūctus*, "fruit"; *gen-ū*, "knee," *di-ēs*, "day."

Admittedly, this is an oversimplified representation of the Latin noun system. Thus, in the second declension some masculine nouns whose root ends in *-r* do not show a *-us* ending, e.g., *puer*, "boy," (rather than *puerus*) and *vīr*, "man." The third declension presents a number of complexities in the nominative ending, particularly for what concerns the neuter nouns, e.g., *lac*, "milk," *ŏs*, "bone," *cŏr*, "heart," *mĕl*, "honey," and others. This declension is also the most complex in terms of gender identification, while exceptions in the others are rather few.

(6) The nominative endings in the plural may be summarized as follows:

	I	II	III	IV	V
masculine and feminine	-ae	-ī	-ēs	-ūs	-ēs
neuter	—	-a	-(i)a	-ua	—

Examples: port-ae, "doors"; *amīc-ī*, "friends"; *membr-a*, "limbs"; *hiem-ēs*, "winters"; *mar-ia*, "seas"; *fruct-ūs*, "fruits"; *gen-ua*, "knees"; *di-ēs*, "days."

(7) The remaining four Latin cases are summarized in the following table. Note, however, that what is often referred to as the sixth case, the *vocative*, or case of direct address, is not shown because it generally coincides with the nominative, save in the singular of nouns of the second declension, e.g., *Marce*, "oh, Marcus," *amīce*, "oh, friend," or *fīlī*, "oh, son," rather than *Marcus, amīcus*, and *fīlius*, respectively; the only exception to this rule being the word *dĕus*, "God," which keeps its nominative form.

It should also be noted that all neuters have the identical form in the nominative and accusative cases.

Declension		Genitive	Dative	Accusative	Ablative
I	Sing.	-ae	-ae	-ăm	-ā
	Plur.	-ārum	-īs	-ās	-īs
II	Sing.	-ī	-ō	-ŭm	-ō
	Plur.	-ōrum	-īs	-ōs/-a	-īs
III	Sing.	-ĭs	-ī	-ĕm	-ĕ/-ī
	Plur.	-(i)um	-ĭbus	-ēs/-īs/-(i)a	-ĭbus
IV	Sing.	-ūs	-uī/-ū	-ŭm/-ū	-ū
	Plur.	-ŭum	-ĭbus	-ūs/-ŭa	-ĭbus
V	Sing.	-ēi	-ēi	-ēm	-ē
	Plur.	-ērum	-ēbus	-ēs	-ēbus

Some third declension nouns, called *i*-stems, sometimes have -*ī* in the ablative singular, -*ium* in the genitive plural, and -*īs* in the accusative plural. In the fourth declension singular the dative, accusative, and ablative of neuter nouns are identical in form.

These endings combine with the *base* of any noun to make up a word, the base being the unchanged part of the word that remains after cutting off the ending of the genitive singular. For instance, the base of *pŏrta* is *pŏrt-(ae)*, of *sŏcer*, "father-in-law," is *sŏcr-(i)*, and that of *hŏmō*, "man," is *hŏmin-(is)*.

(8) Vulgar Latin (see Part II, Chapter 4) has reduced the five declensions to three, the fifth having been absorbed by the first (the *pŏrta* type) and the fourth by the second (the *amīcus* type) due to the numerical weakness of these two declensional classes, as well as the identity of gender and similarity of ending of second and fourth, and first and fifth, declensions. (Some fifth declension nouns in -*ēs* had alternative forms in -*a* already in Classical Latin, e.g., *materiēs* and *materia*, used interchangeably.) The first, second, and third declensions are, therefore, normally the ones that give rise to later Romance forms.

(9) With the fall of final -*m* in the accusative singular and the obliteration of vowel quantity distinctions in the final syllable (see Part II, Chapter 5), the nominative *portă*, the ablative *portā*, and the accusative *portăm*, the dative-ablative *amīcō* and the accusative *amīcŭm*, the accusative *hominĕm* and the ablative *hominĕ*, fell together. This means that at that point, around the fifth century, only the forms *porta* and *porte* (from genitive/dative *portae*) were left in the first declension singular and the forms *amicus*, *amici*, and *amico* in the second declension singular. In the third, where other case endings presumably remained distinct somewhat longer, there was no more distinction between accusative *hominem* and ablative *homine*.

In the plural, where case distinctions were phonetically more stable, there also occurred an eventual obliteration and loss of cases, leaving an essentially one case system in the modern Romance languages (for Rumanian, see Part II, Chapter 11). The following scheme gives an idea of the development of Romance noun forms in Old French (of interest because of its two-case system), standard Italian, and Spanish.

First Declension

Singular
port-a
  -ae
  -ae
  -am
  -ā
⟶French *porte*, Italian *porta*, Spanish *puerta*

Plural
port-ae————————Italian *porte*
  -ārum
  -īs————————Old Italian *porti*
  -ās————————French *portes*, Spanish *puertas*
  -īs

Second Declension

Singular
mur-us————————Old French *murs*
  -ī
  -ō————————Old French *mur*————Spanish *muro*
  -um————————Italian *muro*
  -ō

Plural
mur-ī————————Old French *mur*
  -ōrum
  -īs————————Italian *muri*————Spanish *muros*
  -ōs————————Old French *murs*
  -īs

Note: The old nominative singular and plural in Old French disappear around
    the fourteenth century, leaving a single case in modern French: *mur* vs.
    murs.

Third Declension

Singular
pan-is————————Old French *pains*
  -is
  -ī
  -em————————Old French *pain*, Spanish *pan*, Italian *pane*
  -e

Plural
pan-ēs————————Old French *pain*, Italian *pani*
  -um
  -ibus
  -ēs————————Old French *pains*, Spanish *panes*
  -ibus

Note: The nominative plural of Old French should call for a form with -*s*. By imitation of the standard pattern established by second declension nouns (-*s* in the nominative singular, never in the plural), however, the -*s* is dropped. The Italian nominative plural form in -*i, pani,* could not have developed phonetically from Latin -*ēs* and is seemingly due to analogy with second declension nominative plurals, cf. *murī.* (For a different view see Appendix I.)

(10) The eventual breakdown of the Classical Latin noun system cannot be sought in phonetic phenomena exclusively, and it must be assumed that the disappearance of cases that could have survived is due to psychological causes, such as analogy (the imitation of a standard pattern). The fact is that in Post-Classical and Late Latin the confusion of morphologically distinct cases is quite frequent. Indeed, the most important change in Latin, with far-reaching and complex consequences for the entire grammatical system in its development into the Romance languages, is the reduction of its case system.

The Adjective

(1) According to their grammatical form, adjectives fall into two main classes: (a) those of the *bŏnus, -a, -um* type, which represents a combination of first and second declension, with the masculine forms declined like *amīcus* or *sŏcer,* the feminine like *pŏrta,* and the neuter like *membrum;* and (b) those that follow the third declension pattern, which, in turn, are classified as adjectives of three terminations, with separate endings for all three genders, like *acer, acris, acre,* "sharp," "pungent"; adjectives of two terminations, with the same endings for masculine and feminine, like *brĕvis, brĕve,* "short," "brief"; and adjectives of one termination, with the same nominative singular for all three genders, like *prudens,* "sagacious." In general, adjectives follow the declensional pattern of *i*-stems in that the ablative singular ends in -*ī,* the genitive plural in -*ium,* and the accusative plural in -*īs.*

(2) With the loss of the neuter gender in the noun system, it was also lost in the adjectives; thus, those of three terminations were reduced to two, e.g., Spanish *bueno, buena,* and those of two terminations to one, as in Spanish *feliz, útil, breve,* etc. The neuter survives only sporadically, as in Spanish *lo bueno* or *lo cómico,* where it expresses an abstract idea.

(3) There are three degrees of comparison. The *comparative* is formed by adding to the base form of the adjective the endings -*ior* for the masculine and feminine and -*ius* for the neuter; in the *superlative* the endings -*issimus, -a, -um* are added to the base, e.g., *grand-is, grand-ior, grand-issimus.* The comparative follows the pattern of third declension adjectives, while the superlative is declined like the *bŏnus, -a, -um* type adjective.

(4) While most Latin adjectives are compared in this manner (compare the English comparison in -*er* and -*est,* as in *greater* and *greatest*), some adjectives ending in -*ius* and -*eus* form their comparative form by preceding the positive form with the adverb *magis* and their superlative form by using *maximē* with the positive form, as in *idōneus,* "suitable," *magis idōneus, maximē idōneus.* This analytic comparative with *magis,* and also *plus,* became the practice in Post-

Classical and Vulgar Latin, people preferring to say *magis* (or *plus*) *grandis* rather than *grandior*. Except for the survival of some "organic" forms in high-frequency words, like French *meilleur*, Italian *migliore*, and Spanish *mejor*, from the irregular Latin comparative form *melior*, "better," (positive form *bonus*), and also in some learned words (surviving also in English *superior*, *ulterior*, *exterior*, etc.), the Romance languages generally favor the analytic construction, French and Italian having chosen Latin *plus* (*plus*, *più*), while the Iberian languages and Rumanian opted for the adverb *magis* (Spanish *más*, Portuguese *mais*, Rumanian *mai*).

(5) The Latin organic superlative in *-issimus*, *-a*, *-um*, fulfilled a double function in Latin, as relative and as absolute superlative (*grandissimus* meaning both "the greatest" and "very great"). In the former function it was gradually replaced by the new Romance comparative preceded by the definite article, as in French *le plus grand*, Italian *il più grande*, and Spanish *el más grande*. The *-issimus* form used as an absolute superlative survives in such forms as Spanish *riquísimo*, "very rich," (base form *rico*) and the frequently heard Italian *bravissimo*.

The Adverb

(1) Adverbs of manner are normally formed by adding the endings *-ē* and *-iter* to the base of the adjective; thus, from the first and second declension adjective *longus*, *-a*, *-um*, "long," one may derive the adverb *longē*, while the third declension adjective *fŏrtis*, *-e* becomes *fortiter*, "strongly." The adverbs of manner also have comparative and superlative forms. The former, as a matter of fact, happens to coincide with the neuter of the comparative form of the adjective, the whole pattern being *longē*, *longius*, *longissimē*.

(2) The adverb in *-iter* has been completely lost in the Romance languages; those in *-ē* have left a few traces, e.g., *bĕne*, giving rise to French *bien*, Italian *bene*, and Spanish *bien*. (The English noun/adjective *Romance*, incidentally, derives from a Post-Classical adverb *romanice*, "in the Roman manner," built on the adjective *romanicus*.)

(3) Occasionally, the neuter form of the adjective is also used in adverbial function, as in *forte* (neuter of *fortis*, "strong") or *multum*, "much." This process has to some extent also survived in the Romance languages, e.g., French *parler fort*, "to speak loud." (Cf. also English *drive slow*.)

(4) The Latin adverb of manner, however, has largely been replaced in the Romance languages by a Post-Classical formation involving the feminine ablative form of the noun *mēns*, "mind," (ablative, *mente*) combined with the feminine ablative form of an adjective, e.g., *clārā mente*, literally, "with a clear mind," replacing the Latin *clārē*. Originally, this construction probably applied to mental states, but it gradually lost this connotation to assume a purely adverbial function, as in French *clairement*, Italian *chiaramente*, and Spanish *claramente*, "clearly."

(5) Other Latin adverbs, such as those of location and time (e.g., *ubi*, "where," *hodiē*, "today," *herī*, "yesterday," etc.) have sporadically survived to

this day, e.g., Spanish *hoy* from *hodiē*, French *hier* from *hĕrī*, and others we cannot deal with in this brief sketch.

The Pronouns

Contrary to noun and adjective inflection, a fair number of Latin inflectional forms have survived in the Romance languages; however, it must be noted that in the course of their development from Latin to Romance the functions of these pronominal forms have often changed. (The historical development of pronouns is a rather complex one and can hardly be dealt with in a few paragraphs. In any event, we limit our discussion to developments in three of the major Romance languages, French, Italian, and Spanish.)

PERSONAL PRONOUNS

(1) The personal pronouns of the *first person* are *ego*, "I," and *nōs*, "we"; of the *second person*, *tū*, "you," and *vōs*, "you," in the singular and plural, respectively. Personal pronouns for the *third person* ("he," "she," "it," "they") are lacking in the Latin system; to make up for this deficiency the language uses a *demonstrative* pronoun in this function.

Ego, tū, nōs, and *vōs* are declined. Here is the inflectional pattern with corresponding developments in French, Italian, and Spanish.

Nominative *ego;* by way of an assumed Vulgar Latin form *eo,* it developed into French *je* (used only in conjunction with a verb form in the modern language; in Old French it could be used in stressed position also), Italian *io,* and Spanish *yo.*

Genitive *meī,* "of me": it did not survive.

Dative *mihi,* "to me": by way of an alternate *mī* form already attested in Classical Latin, it is continued in the Italian and Spanish *mi* forms, with different functions, however. While in Italian it appears only in unstressed *proclitic* (occurring immediately before the verb) or *enclitic* (occurring immediately after the verb) positions, e.g., *mi dà,* "he (she, it) gives me," or *parlami,* "speak to me," in Spanish it is used in stressed position as object of a preposition, e.g., *para mí,* "for me."

Accusative *mē,* "me," and

Ablative *mē,* "by, for, etc., me": the accusative/ablative form *mē* becomes, without change of form, a stressed pronoun in Italian, e.g., *a me,* "to me," while Spanish *me* is relegated to unstressed position, e.g., *me dice,* "he (she, it) tells me," or *dame,* "give me." In French, where the dative *mihi* (*mi*) does not survive, the Latin *me* keeps the same form in unstressed position, e.g., *il me voit,* "he sees me," while in stressed position the Latin *ē* vowel has diphthongized, giving rise to Old French *mei,* Modern French *moi,* as in *avec moi,* "with me." *Moi* is also used as an emphatic form of the first person, "I," where Italian and Spanish use *io* and *yo,* respectively.

Nominative *tū:* it survives in all three languages, French *tu,* Italian *tu,* and Spanish *tú.*

Genitive *tuī:* it did not survive.

Dative *tibi:* by analogy with Latin *mi,* the dative became *ti* in Vulgar Latin. The accusative/ablative form *tē* has also survived intact.

Accusative *tē;* Ablative *tē:* the development and functional distribution of *ti* and *te* in Italian and Spanish, and that of *te* in all three languages, closely parallel those of *mi* and *me;* thus, Italian *ti dà* but *a te;* Spanish *te dice* but *para tí;* and French *il te voit* but *avec toi. Toi,* like *moi,* is also used as emphatic "you," where the others use *tū.*

In the plural, the genitive was also lost. Nominative and accusative, and dative and ablative, are identical in form, *nōs, vōs,* and *nōbīs, vōbīs,* respectively.

Only *nōs* and *vōs* have survived in the languages under reference: French *nous* and *vous,* Italian *noi* and *voi,* and Spanish *nos* and *os* (*vos* as a subject pronoun survives only dialectally). While in French these forms may be used both in stressed and unstressed positions (e.g., *il nous voit,* "he sees us," and *avec nous*), the Spanish forms are used only in proclitic and enclitic positions (e.g., *nos ve,* "he (she, it) sees us"). In stressed position this language has added a derivation of Latin *alterōs, -ās,* "others," to *nos* and *vos,* giving rise to the modern forms *nosotros, nosotras, vosotros,* and *vosotras.* In Italian, on the other hand, *noi* and *voi* are used in stressed position only. In unstressed position, as verb objects, there developed, through a process of analogy, the forms *ce, ci,* and *ve, vi,* e.g., *ci dà,* "he (she, it) gives us," but *ce lo dà,* "he (she, it) gives it to us."

(2) Personal pronoun forms of the third person, as mentioned before, do not exist; instead, Latin borrows demonstrative pronouns for this function, particularly *is, ea, id; iste, ista, istud;* and *ille, illa, illud,* "he," "she," "it," with varying shades of meaning, *iste* often with a connotation of contempt and *ille* conveying a note of reverence and glorification.

DEMONSTRATIVE PRONOUNS

(1) The demonstratives, functioning either as adjectives or as pronouns, serve to point out a special person or thing. In Classical Latin they were six in number: *hic, haec, hōc,* "this (here)"; *is, ea, id,* "this," or "that"; *iste, ista, istud,* "that (nearby)"; *ille, illa, illud,* "that (over there)"; *idem, eadem, idem,* "same"; and the reflexive *ipse, ipsa, ipsum,* "self," used as an emphatic pronoun. All of them, of course, are fully inflected for gender, number, and case. The pronoun *idem* having completely disappeared from the Romance languages and only traces of *hic* and *is* remaining (e.g., *hōc ille* ultimately giving rise to French *oui* from Old French *oïl*), the surviving *ipse* (assuming also the functions of *idem*), *iste,* and *ille* embarked upon new careers, so to speak, by extending their functions far beyond those they had in Classical Latin.

(2) While *ipse, iste,* and *ille* all survive in some form or other as demonstratives in the Romance languages (see below), both *ipse* and *ille* have given rise to what is generally considered to be a Romance development—the *definite article.* It is of interest to observe, however, that in Post-Classical texts (beginning with about the fourth century) these two pronouns are increasingly used in conjunction with nouns where the demonstrative function does not seem appropriate. In saying *ille* (or *ipse*) *homō,* rather than *homō,* "the man," people seem to have felt the need of concretizing the object expressed by the word. That is probably why originally the definite article is used only with nouns designating con-

crete and specific objects rather than abstract ideas (cf. English *the woman is beautiful* versus *life is beautiful*).

(3) The pronoun *ipse* survived as a definite article in a few Romance areas only (e.g., in Sardinian as *so, sa, sos, sas,* for the two genders in the singular and plural, from Latin *ipsum* [accusative of *ipse*], *ipsa, ipsōs,* and *ipsās*). The modern literary languages have all chosen derivations of *ille,* which underwent a three-fold development according to its use as (a) subject pronoun (*ille amat,* "he loves"); (b) object pronoun (proclitically with a verb, as in *illum videō,* "I see him"); and (c) definite article (proclitically with a noun, as in *ille homō,* "the man"). This threefold development appears to have been conditioned by a double system of accentuation, the subject pronoun keeping its original accent (on the first syllable), while the object pronoun and article shift it to the second syllable. In addition, new forms developed in the spoken language (attested in Post-Classical texts) which partially replaced Classical Latin forms of *ille.* Some of the subsequent developments in the Romance languages can only be explained on the basis of these "popular" forms. The following summary (necessarily simplified) purports to show this threefold development of *ille.* (Note that "stressed" means subject pronoun development, while "unstressed" means object pronoun or article.)

Singular (genitive and dative are identical in all three genders)

Nominative: *ille* → Vulgar Latin *illī* → (a) *stressed:* French *il,* Italian *egli;* (b) *unstressed:* French *le,* Italian *il* (article). Spanish *él* (pronoun) and *el* (article) descend from the Classical Latin form direct.

Nominative: *illa* (see accusative/ablative).

Genitive: *illīus* → Vulgar Latin *illuius* and *illaeius,* the latter surviving only in Old Provençal *l(i)eis.*

Dative: *illī* → Vulgar Latin *illui* (masculine) and *illei* (feminine) → (a) *stressed:* French *lui* (Old French *lei*), Italian *lui, lei;* (b) *unstressed:* French *lui* (Old French *lei, li*), Italian *gli, le* (object pronoun). Spanish *le* (pronoun for both masculine and feminine) comes from the Classical form.

Accusative/Ablative: *illum, illō* → (a) *stressed:* Italian *ello,* Spanish *ello* (neuters); (b) *unstressed:* French *le* (Old French *lo*), Italian *lo* (both article and pronoun), Spanish *lo* (pronoun).

Accusative/Ablative: *illam, illā* → (a) *stressed:* French *elle,* Italian *ella,* Spanish *ella;* (b) *unstressed:* French *la,* Italian *la,* Spanish *la* (both article and pronoun).

Plural (dative and ablative are identical in all genders)

Nominative: *illī* → (a) *stressed:* French *il(s),* Italian *eglino* (archaic); (b) *unstressed:* Italian *li, gli* (pronoun), and *i, gli* (article).

Nominative: *illae* → (a) *stressed:* Italian *elleno* (archaic); (b) *unstressed:* Italian *le* (both article and pronoun).

Genitive: *illōrum* → (b) *unstressed:* French *leur(s),* Italian *loro* (pronoun).

Genitive: *illārum;* the feminine form of this case entirely disappeared in Post-Classical Latin.

Dative/Ablative: *illīs* → (b) *unstressed:* Italian *i, gli, li* (see nominative plural), Spanish *les* (pronoun).

Accusative: *illōs* → (a) *stressed:* French *eux* (Old French *els*), Spanish *ellos;* (b) *unstressed:* French *les* (Old French *los*), Spanish *los* (both article and pronoun).

Accusative: *illās* → (a) *stressed:* French *elles,* Spanish *ellas;* (b) *unstressed:* French *les,* Spanish *las* (both article and pronoun).

(4) With the general weakening of the demonstrative value of Latin demonstrative forms, the need arose for new ones. Already in Pre-Classical Latin one finds examples of *iste* and *ille* prefixed by the exclamatory particle *ecce* (also *eccum*), "behold"; thus, *eccillum* and *eccistam* in Plautus (*eccistam videō*). This process becomes increasingly frequent in Post-Classical writings, e.g., *ecce ista via quam vidētis* ("this [here] road that you see") in a fifth-century account of a trip to the Holy Land by the Spanish nun Aetheria. Hence, the demonstrative series (*i*)*cist,* (*i*)*ceste,* (*i*)*cil,* (*i*)*celui,* (*i*)*cele,* (*i*)*cels,* etc., in Old French deriving from Latin *ecce istī* (for *iste*), *ecce ista, ecce illī* (for *ille*), *ecce illui, ecce illa, ecce illos,* respectively, although there is good evidence to the effect that in these instances the reinforcing particle may have been the demonstrative *hic* rather than *ecce* (see Mario Pei, "Old French Demonstratives," *Studies in Romance Philology and Literature,* Chapel Hill, 1963, pp. 17–21). The fusion of *ecce, eccum,* and also *atque* (a copulative particle) with *iste* and *ille* is also reflected in the various forms of Italian *questo* and *quello,* Spanish *aquel,* Rumanian *acest* and *acel,* and other major and minor Romance languages.

(5) Uncombined *ipse* and *iste* have also survived, particularly in Spanish and Portuguese, where they serve to show the threefold distinction of relative distance which in Latin was expressed by *hīc,* "this (near the speaker)," *iste,* "that (near the person spoken to)," and *ille,* "that (over there)." With the loss of *hīc,* the pronoun *iste* (Spanish *este,* Portuguese *êste*) moved into this position, while *ipse* took over the function formerly assigned to *iste* (Spanish *ese,* Portuguese *esse*). The third dimension is expressed by *eccum* (or *atque*) *ille* (Spanish *aquel,* Portuguese *aquêle*), the simple form *ille* having lost much of its demonstrative force. The *iste/ille* contrast is also kept in Italian (*questo* versus *quello*), with a non-compulsory intermediate form *codesto,* "that (near you)," while it was lost in Modern French which, for the purpose of distinction of distance, uses the particles *-ci* and *-là,* as in *ce livre-ci* versus *ce livre-là.*

POSSESSIVE PRONOUN-ADJECTIVES

(1) The possessive pronoun-adjectives in Latin are: *meus, -a, -um,* "my, mine," *tuus, -a, -um,* "your," *noster, nostra, nostrum,* "our," *vester, vestra, vestrum,* "your," in the singular and plural. They follow the declensional pattern of first and second declension adjectives, and correspond to the personal pronouns *ego, tū, nōs,* and *vōs.*

(2) The reflexive possessive *suus, -a, -um,* "his (own)," "her (own)," "its (own)," "their (own)," which corresponds to the third person reflexive pronoun *sē* (which has no nominative, but is otherwise inflected like forms of *ego* and *tū,* with identical developments into the Romance languages; see above), refers to the subject of the sentence only. Whenever a person other than the subject was involved, Latin used the genitive form of demonstratives like *is* and *ille* instead,

namely the forms *eius* and *eōrum* (genitive singular and plural of *is*) and *illīus* and *illōrum* (genitive singular and plural of *ille*).

(3) Among significant developments in Post-Classical Latin we may note the following: (a) Classical *vester* becomes *voster*, probably by analogy with *noster*, although the Archaic form is, indeed, *voster* (e.g., in Plautus); (b) confusion of function between *suus* and *eius, eōrum*, etc., that is, nonobservance of the Classical Latin distinction between "his own" and "his (someone else's)"; (c) creation of short forms *mum, tum, sum, ma, ta, sa*, etc. (for *meum, tuum, suum, mea, tua, sua*), forms that have gained universal extension in French (*mon, ton, son, ma, ta, sa*) and also appear sporadically in Italian dialects, e.g., *sorata*, "your sister," (cf. French *ta soeur*). All these developments are duly attested in Post-Classical texts and inscriptions.

(4) Without going into details or attempting to explain a great number of phonetic irregularities in the development of possessives from Latin to Romance, let us sample French, Italian, and Spanish forms with respect to corresponding Latin ones: While French *mien* develops from the Latin accusative *mĕum*, Italian *mio* and Spanish *mío* descend from an oblique form *meo* (merger of Latin dative, accusative, and ablative). French *tien* and *sien* have no roots in any Latin form; they are analogically rebuilt on the first person "mine." Italian *tuo, suo*, Spanish *tuyo, suyo*, develop from Latin *tŭo* and *sŭo*. In addition, Spanish has also developed a set of unstressed forms like French *mon, ton*, etc., except that Spanish *mi, tu, su*, and the plurals *mis, tus, sus*, are merely shortened forms of the regular feminine *mía, tua, sua* developments as a result of proclitic use with a noun (Old Spanish *la tua madre*, Spanish *tu madre*) and do not continue Post-Classical forms as French does.

In the plural, French *notre, votre*, Italian *nostro, vostro*, and Spanish *nuestro, vuestro*, descend from Latin *nŏstrum* and *vŏstrum* (for Classical *vestrum*). French alone distinguishes between stressed and unstressed forms, e.g., *notre livre* versus *le nôtre*, "our book," "ours." These possessives, like those of the singular, have also developed feminine forms.

(5) The pronoun-adjective *suus*, which, as stated before, was used as a reflexive possessive in Classical Latin, lost this restriction in the Romance languages. However, of the three languages, only Spanish has kept Latin *suus* in both singular and plural, e.g., *su libro*, "his (her, their) book," while French and Italian have chosen derivations of Latin *illōrum*, e.g., French *leur livre*, Italian (*il*) *loro libro*, "their book."

The Verb

(1) The Latin verb is also inflected to express mood, voice, tense, person, and number. The inflection of the verb is called *conjugation*. There are four regular conjugational classes in Latin, each one characterized by a *thematic* or *stem* vowel, which is arrived at by removing the infinitive ending *-re*. These four classes are as follows: I *laudā-re*, II *monē-re*, III *legĕ-re*, IV *audī-re*. To these stems personal endings are added, three for the singular and three for the plural.

Singular		Plural	
"I"	-ō or -m	"we"	-mus
"you"	-s	"you"	-tis
"he," "she," "it"	-t	"they"	-nt

In addition to personal endings, mood and tense signs are also added to the stem to differentiate between, say, present and imperfect, or indicative and subjunctive. For instance, -bā- signals the imperfect indicative of all conjugations, while -bi- is a tense sign for the future indicative in conjugations I and II, but not in III and IV, which use -a- for the first person singular and -ē- in all other persons.

Examples: Present—laud-ō, "I praise," *laudā-s,* "you praise," *lauda-t,* "he (she, it) praises," *laudā-mus,* "we praise," *laudā-tis,* "you praise," *lauda-nt,* "they praise."

Imperfect—laudā-ba-m, "I was praising," *laudā-bā-s,* "you were praising," etc.

Future—laudā-b-ō, "I shall praise," *laudā-bi-s,* "you will praise," etc.

Note: In the first person present the stem vowel merges with the ending, while in the future it absorbs the vowel of the *-bi-* syllable.

(2) The person markers in Latin fulfill essentially the function of the English *I, you,* etc., pronouns. Latin *ego, tū, is,* etc., are only used for the purpose of emphasizing the meaning expressed by the verb ending. This state of affairs is still very much prevalent in most Romance tongues (Spanish *canto* means "I sing"). In modern French, where only first and second person plural are left with distinctive endings in most tenses, the use of the subject pronouns is as necessary as in English. As a matter of fact, the pronoun has become such an integral part of the verb form that one can speak of inflectional *prefixes* (*il-aime,* "he loves") equivalent to inflectional *suffixes* in Latin (*ama-t*).

(3) The morphology of the Latin verb rests essentially on the opposition of two tense stems: the *present* stem, obtained by removing the *-re* ending of the infinitive (*laudā-re*), and the *perfect* stem, which remains after removal of the *-ī* ending from the third principal part of the verb (*laudō, laudāre, laudāv-ī*). These two verbal stems represent the two verbal *aspects,* called *infectum* and *perfectum.* Largely inherited from the old Indo-European system, these two stems relate to the type of action expressed by the verb, the present stem (also called *durative*) referring to *continuous action* (an action viewed in the process of accomplishment), while the perfect stem presents the state resulting from the action. For each of these aspects Latin developed a *tense* system consisting of present, past, and future. In the *infectum* they are *laudō, laudābam,* and *laudābō* (see [1] above); in the *perfectum* they are *laudāv-ī,* "I have praised," *laudāv-era-m,* "I had praised," and *laudāv-er-ō,* "I shall have praised."

(4) Examples given so far represent *indicative active* forms. The *indicative* is the mood of assertion and interrogation. There is also a *subjunctive* mood used in commands, conditions, and dependent clauses, as well as an *imperative* mood, also used for command and exhortation. In English the Latin subjunctive is often translated by such auxiliaries as *may, might, would,* and *should;* however, it is difficult to attach a particular meaning to an isolated subjunctive form like *laudem* (present subjunctive active of *laudāre*) because of the variety of its uses.

Each subjunctive form, therefore, calls for a special translation. Contrary to the indicative, there is no future tense in the subjunctive. Personal endings are the same as those of the indicative. In the present and imperfect the forms that correspond to *laudō* and *laudābam* are *laude-m* and *laudā-re-m*.

The present imperative active is generally identical to the present stem, e.g., *laudā*, "praise"; the ending *-te* is added in the plural, e.g., *laudā-te*.

(5) The *perfectum* consists of three tenses in the indicative: perfect, pluperfect, and future perfect, but only perfect and pluperfect in the subjunctive. Personal endings are essentially those of the *infectum*, except that in the first person perfect there is an *-ī*, rather than *-ō* or *-m*, and a *-tī* ending in the second person for normal *-s*.

		Indicative	Subjunctive
Examples: Perfect—		*laudāv-ī,* "I have praised"	*laudāv-eri-m*
		laudāv-is-tī, "you have praised"	*laudāv-eri-s*
		laudāv-i-t, "he (she, it) has praised"	*laudāv-eri-t*
		laudāv-i-mus, "we have praised"	*laudāv-eri-mus*
		laudāv-is-tis, "you have praised"	*laudāv-eri-tis*
		laudāv-ēru-nt, "they have praised"	*laudāv-eri-nt*
Pluperfect—		*laudāv-era-m,* "I had praised"	*laudāv-isse-m*
		laudāv-era-s, "you had praised"	*laudāv-isse-s*
		laudāv-era-t, "he (she, it) had praised"	*laudāv-isse-t*
		etc.	etc.
Future Perfect—		*laudāv-er-ō,* "I shall have praised"	
		laudāv-eri-s, "you will have, etc."	
		laudāv-eri-t, "he, she, it, etc."	

(6) The perfect system of Latin is very complex. Generally speaking only first and fourth conjugation verbs had stems ending regularly in *-v*, as in *laudav-* and *audiv-*. Most second and all third conjugation verbs showed a number of perfect stem endings, such as those in *-u* (*monuī* from *monēre*), stem vowel lengthening (*lēgī* from *lĕgere*), stem reduplication (*canō*, "I sing," but *cecinī*, "I sang"), and others. Both the "regular" or "weak" (like those in *-āvī, -ēvī, -īvī*) and the "irregular" or "strong" perfect (like *monuī*, etc.) have survived in the Romance languages. The development of the former has been rather regular, e.g., Latin *amāvī, amāvistī, amāvit, amāvimus, amāvistis, amāvērunt* → French *aimai, aimas, aima, aimâmes, aimâtes, aimèrent;* Italian *amai, amasti, amò, amammo, amaste, amarono;* Spanish *amé, amaste, amó, amamos, amasteis, amaron.* That of "strong" perfects, however, is quite complicated, involving considerable phonetic modification, interchange of types (e.g., perfects in *-u* showing up with a different vowel, as in Italian *volli*, "I have wanted," from Latin *voluī*, but French *voulus*), and analogical rebuilding of regular patterns disrupted by phonetic developments. Among the major Romance languages, speakers of Spanish and Portuguese regularly use the Latin perfect (also called the past definite, or the preterite) as their main past-tense form; in standard Italian, however, it is rarely used, while French has completely relegated it to the written language.

(7) Latin has a special set of forms for the *passive voice*, which, generally speaking, corresponds in meaning to the passive in English. The personal endings

of the passive forms are the same in both the indicative and the subjunctive of the *infectum*, namely: *-(o)r, -ris (-re), -tur, -mur, -minī, -ntur.*

Examples: Present Indicative—laud-or, "I am praised," *laudā-ris,* "you are praised," etc.
Imperfect Indicative—laudā-ba-r, "I was praised," *laudā-bā-ris,* "you were praised," etc.
Future Indicative—laudā-bo-r, "I shall be praised," *laudā-be-ris,* "you will be praised," etc.
Present Subjunctive—laude-r, laudē-ris, laudē-tur, laudē-mur, etc.
Imperfect Subjunctive—laudā-re-r, laudā-rē-ris, laudā-rē-tur, laudā-rē-mur, etc.

In the *perfectum,* however, the passive forms are formed by means of a participial form, the so-called *perfect passive participle,* combined with the present, imperfect, and future forms of the verb *esse,* "to be," which in the first person are *sum, eram,* and *erō.* These participial forms end in *-tus, -ta, -tum* in all conjugations and are inflected like adjectives of the *bonus, -a, -um* type. The *perfectum* forms of *laudō* are *laudātus sum,* "I have been (was) praised," *laudātus eram,* "I had been praised," and *laudātus erō,* "I shall have been praised."

(8) In addition to the passive inflection, there are also a number of verbs that are passive in form but active in meaning, e.g., *ūtor,* "I use," *sequor,* "I follow," and *hortor,* "I exhort." Some verbs also had an active meaning in both active and passive forms, e.g., *mereō* and *mereor,* "I deserve," so that it is not surprising that confusions arose even in Classical times (*hortō* for *hortor* already in Plautus), a confusion that was accentuated in Post-Classical Latin and soon led to complete elimination of this verb category, even before the dawn of the Romance languages.

(9) Discussion of the verbal system would not be complete without at least a passing mention of the noun and adjective forms of the verb. These include four *participles* which are really adjectives in inflection and meaning but have the power of verbs in syntactic constructions and also, since they express tense, in marking time. They also express voice. The endings, which are identical in all conjugations, are (a) *-ns, -ntis,* for the present active participle, e.g., *laudāns, laudantis,* "praising," (formed on the present stem and declined like a third declension adjective); (b) *-tūrus, -a, -um,* for the future active participle, e.g., *laudātūrus, -a, -um,* "about to praise," (remember the famous *moritūrī tē salūtāmus,* "we who are about to die greet you"?); (c) *-tus, -a, -um,* for the perfect passive participle (see [7] above); and (d) *-ndus, -nda, -ndum,* for the future passive participle, also known as the *gerundive,* e.g., *laudandus,* "must be loved," or "ought to be loved," (cf. the name *Amanda,* "girl who ought to be loved").

(10) The nominal forms of the verb are the *gerund* and the *supine.* The former is a verbal noun, active in meaning, corresponding to the English verbal noun in *-ing,* e.g., *ars scrībendī,* "the art of writing." As a noun it is declined, but only in the so-called oblique cases, i.e., other than nominative: *laudandī, laudandō, laudandum, laudandō,* "praising."

The supine is a verbal noun of the fourth declension, but it is used only in the accusative and ablative cases. When used in the accusative, its function is to express purpose, mainly after verbs of motion, as in *vēnit laudātum,* "he came to praise." The ablative in *-ū* is not very common; it is used mainly with verbs of saying and hearing, as in *mīrābile dictū*, "wonderful to tell."

In terms of the knowledge of all forms of a Latin verb, the supine is important because it supplies the fourth principal part of the verb, which is arrived at by removing the *-um* ending. Actually, however, the perfect passive participle form serves this purpose just as well. Here then are the four principal parts of the four verbs which we have used to illustrate the Latin conjugational classes:

I *laudō, laudāre, laudāvī, laudātum*	ā stem
II *moneō, monēre, monuī, monitum*	ē stem
III *legō, legĕre, lēgī, lectum*	ĕ stem
IV *audiō, audīre, audīvī, audītum*	ī stem

These principal parts provide the *three* stems from which all the forms of the Latin verb are derived. Of course, there are exceptions, like the verb *esse*, "to be," and others, but there is no rule without exception.

Students of Latin are most likely to find gaps in this necessarily brief sketch of the Latin verb system. They may wonder why we did not mention the fact that there are three sets of infinitives, each with active and passive forms, and that there are imperatives besides those in the present active, like the present passive imperatives (*laudāre*, "be you praised," and *laudāmini*) and the future imperatives (*laudātō*, "you shall love," and *laudātōte*); but like so many other synthetic forms these were lost in Romance and in keeping with our stated purpose we wanted to highlight especially those morphological phenomena of Latin that bear upon subsequent developments in Romance. Even so, we must be quite selective in choosing the features to be briefly touched upon in the following paragraphs.

(11) Contrary to what may be observed in Post-Classical texts as regards the breakdown of the Latin noun inflection, changes in the general structure of the Latin verb are neither numerous nor revolutionary. While the study of these texts is most instructive for the evolution of the nominal inflection in Vulgar Latin, they are much less so in terms of the conjugational system. It is only by comparing the verb structure of Romance with that of Latin that we are able to grasp the general thrust of the evolution as it occasionally surfaces in the non-Classical features we come upon here and there in Late Latin texts. Thus, we can state with some measure of certainty that the Latin deponents were eliminated from the language in the Post-Classical period (although traces of them still survive, as in French *je suis né*, Italian *sono nato*, Old Spanish *soy nado*, from Latin *nātus sum*, "I was born"), but we are rather hard put to determine the time of disappearance of all inflected passive forms (*laudor, laudābar*, etc.) and those of the Classical future (*laudābō, laudābis*, etc.). And although Post-Classical and Late Latin texts do show an unmistakable preference for the use of analytic and periphrastic constructions where synthetic forms would be used in Classical Latin (as when St. Augustine says in one of his sermons: *metuō . . . vōs habēbam fatīgātōs*, "I fear . . . I must have tired you," rather than something like *metuō . . . vōs fatīgāverim*, the inflected perfect subjunctive form of *fatīgāre*), on the whole, the use of verbs conforms to the Classical Latin standard. The Romance languages, as a matter of fact, present essentially the same verb structure as Latin by continuing to express tense, mood, voice, person, and number by means of a

complex interplay of personal endings, changes in the verbal root, and the use of auxiliaries.

(12) Among the Latin verb forms that were discarded in the major Romance languages we may note the following:

(a) all deponent verb forms, except as noted in the preceding section, to which we may also add the form *mortuus*, e.g., *mortuus est* → French *il est mort*, "he died." A reflex of deponent verbs of motion (e.g., *ingredior*, "I enter," *ingressus sum*, "I have entered") is evident in the passive participle + *esse* construction of the *venutus est* type (French *il est venu*, Italian *è venuto*, "he has come"), which is built precisely on the analogy of such verbs.

(b) all inflected forms of the passive, except the perfect passive participle (*laudātus, -a, -um*), which, in combination with various forms of *esse*, "to be," serves to form the passive state of being, i.e., the result of a previous action (cf. English *the house is being built* versus *the house is built*). Of the future passive participle (the gerundive) a few traces survive, as in Spanish *hacienda*, "farm," from Latin *facienda*, "things to be done." (Cf. also English *agenda*, gerundive of *agĕre*, "to set in motion.") With the disappearance of the inflected passive forms, the passive infinitive endings in -*rī* and -*ī* (*laudārī*, "to be praised") naturally also disappeared. Those passive and deponent verbs that became active (e.g., *moriō* for *morior*, "I die") also correspondingly changed their infinitive forms to -*re*; thus, *morirī* became *morire*.

(c) the supine (*laudātum, laudātū*).

(d) the perfect active infinitive (*laudāvisse*).

(e) the gerund, except for the ablative form (*laudandō*), which became the new present participle (cf. Spanish *cantando*, "singing"), while the old Latin present participle (*laudāns*) became either an adjective or a noun, e.g., Spanish *cantante*, "singer," (Latin *cantāns, cantantem*).

(f) the inflected (synthetic) forms of the future, which are replaced by a new analytic construction (see below).

In addition, there are a few Latin verb forms that may be said to have disappeared through phonetic merger with others, e.g., *laudāverim* (perfect subjunctive active) and *laudāverō* (future perfect indicative active) → Spanish *loare*, the future subjunctive form, a form that is missing from the Latin system.

(13) One of the most notable innovations in verbal inflection is the replacement of the synthetic Latin future in -*bō*, -*bis*, -*bit*, etc. (*laudābō, monēbō*) and in -*am*, -*ēs*, -*et*, etc. (*legam, audiam*) by a periphrastic construction involving the *infinitive* of the verb and forms of *habēre*, "to have," used as an auxiliary. The disappearance of the Latin future seems to be due to both phonetic and psychological causes: the phonetic similarity of *laudābit* (future) and *laudāvit* (perfect) on the one hand, and *legĕt* (future) and *legĭt* (present) on the other hand, and the general tendency of the spoken language to use periphrastic constructions (cf. French *je vais partir*, "I am going to leave" for the more literary *je partirai*, "I shall leave").

The use of the *habēre* plus infinitive construction appears sporadically in Classical and Post-Classical authors with the original meaning of "to have to," "must" (as in *scrībere habeō*, "I must write," used by Cicero). Increasingly, however, it comes to be used with the meaning approaching that of the simple future tense and even appears in synthetic form in a seventh-century text: *daras,* "you shall give," (a contraction of *dare habēs*), which is the precursor of Spanish *darás* and Italian *darai.* (French *donnerai* is a contraction of Latin *donāre habeō,* rather than *dare habeō.*) It is of interest to observe that most Romance forms have become synthetic again, as they were in Classical Latin.

(14) Another syntactic means to render the idea expressed by the verb more concrete led Latin speakers to the creation of a new past tense known as the present perfect, the *passé composé* of French, a compound tense made up of a past participle (the Latin perfect passive participle) combined with present tense forms of *habēre,* e.g., *habeō laudātum* → French *j'ai loué,* Italian *ho lodato,* Spanish *he loado.* The origin of this innovation is found in Pre-Classical texts already; thus, Plautus uses a past participle in an adjectival function in combination with *habēre* in constructions of the *habeō cultellum comparātum* type ("I have [here] a knife which has been bought"). Not uncommon in the works of Classical authors, this type of periphrastic construction becomes increasingly frequent in Post-Classical writings, in Christian authors especially, in what appears to be a desire to stress the completion of an action. The transition from "I have a knife (which has been) bought" to "I have bought a knife" is relatively easy; hence, when Bishop Gregory of Tours writes *episcopum invītātum habēs* in one of his sixth-century writings, we are safe in rendering this sentence as "you have invited the bishop."

Once established, this construction could not be limited to the present perfect. *Laudātum habeō* gave rise to *laudātum habēbam* (or *habuī*), "I had praised," *laudātum habēbō,* "I will have praised," *laudātum habēre,* "to have praised," (replacing the Classical *laudāvisse* infinitive), etc.

(15) The inflected passive in the Latin *infectum,* as noted already, was replaced in all tenses and moods by periphrastic forms composed of the perfect passive participle (*laudātus*) plus a form of *esse.* In other words, *laudātus sum,* "I have been praised," moved up to the present tense meaning of "I am praised," the slot formerly occupied by *laudor.* The disappearance of the inflected forms and this replacement by a periphrastic construction is often attributed to analogy with such expressions as *bonus sum,* "I am good," or *cārus est,* "he is dear," which are said to have exerted influence on *laudātus sum* in such a way as to change its meaning from past to present. This explanation is somewhat of an oversimplification, however. In the first place, inflected, i.e., synthetic passive forms, occur all through the Vulgar Latin period in a variety of texts, even the most "incorrect" ones (incorrect with respect to the Classical Latin language); in the second place, it must be pointed out that the true passive of Latin (expressing immediate action) is hardly ever replaced by an analytical passive in the Romance languages. *Laudor* means "I am being praised," which in French would be expressed by *on me loue* rather than *je suis loué,* or in Spanish by *me loan,* "they praise me," rather than *soy loado,* since the Latin *laudātus sum* construction refers to a state of being rather than an action.

Whatever the causes of the disappearance of synthetic passive forms may have been, the fact is that we have no clear picture of this linguistic development. We only know the Latin and Romance state of affairs; the bridge leading from one to the other seems difficult to reconstruct.

(16) Apart from these major developments in the Latin verb system in its evolution into Romance, the changes involve mainly individual verb forms whose independent phonetic developments often lead to new irregularities in the conjugational scheme. To forestall what might have become a complete anarchy of forms had the individual phonetic developments gone unchecked, the subconscious popular analogical forces (and sometimes even conscious ones) constantly intervened by drawing back into regular schemes those irregularities which normal phonetic changes in individual verb forms had brought about. Speakers, often aided by the conscious efforts of grammarians, felt that different forms of the same verb somehow belong together. For example, when Latin *prŏbō*, "I try," "I prove," became Old French *pruef*, as a result of the phonetic "law" according to which all stressed Latin short *o*'s become a *ue* diphthong in French (cf. Latin *nŏvem* → Old French *nuef*, Modern French *neuf*, "nine"), but Latin *probámus*, "we try," "we prove," developed to Old French *prouvons* (because unstressed Latin *o*'s either remained *o* or turned into an *u* sound (spelled *ou*), the regular present tense pattern was reestablished by adopting the *ou* as a root vowel, so that instead of the *pruef/prouvons* opposition, the pattern was regularized to *prouve* in the singular as well.

For further and considerably more detailed information the reader is referred to existing manuals dealing with the development of the Romance languages, listed in the Bibliography. There exist excellent handbooks in English both on the *ensemble* of Romance languages (such as those of W. Elcock, R. Hall, Jr., and R. Posner) and on individual languages (e.g., those of W. Entwistle, A. Ewert, and M. Pei).

Appendix D

The *Appendix Probi;* Pagan and Christian Inscriptions; The Graffiti of Pompeii

Here are brief linguistic analyses of the texts referred to in Part II, Chapter 4, The Triumph of Vulgar Latin.

The Appendix Probi

(1) *columna* ("column") *non colomna*

The use of stressed *o* for *u* in *colomna* is a sample of the widespread interchange between short *u* and long *o* that led to the later Romance merging of the two sounds.

(2) *vetulus* ("old") *non veclus, calida* ("warm") *non calda, tabula* ("table") *non tabla, auris* ("ear") *non oricla*

The forms *veclus, calda, tabla,* and *oricla* all exemplify the fall (syncopation) of unstressed vowels, but *calda* was acceptable even in Classical Latin. In addition, *vetulus* and *auricula* (or *oricla*) show the widespread popular tendency to use diminutives ("little old," "little ear"), which later lose their diminutive connotation and become the regular Romance words: French *vieil, vieux, oreille;* Spanish *viejo, oreja;* Portuguese *velho, orelha;* Italian *vecchio, orecchia*—all go back to the Latin diminutives *vetulus* and *auricula,* not the standard *vetus* and *auris.* The form *oricla* also shows the change of the diphthong *au* to *o,* which occurred in most major Romance languages. Sporadically it had also appeared earlier, e.g., *Claudius* and *Clodius.*

(3) *olim* ("formerly") *non oli*

The censured form *oli* shows the dropping of the final *-m* in nouns, adjectives, adverbs, and numerals, a Pre- and Post-Classical phenomenon.

(4) *vinea* ("vineyard") *non vinia*

The spelling *vinia* reflects the popular tendency to turn the vowels *e* and *i* in hiatus (before another vowel) into a *y*-glide, thus reducing the number of syllables in the word and palatalizing the preceding consonant, as in French *vigne,* Spanish *viña,* Portuguese *vinha,* and Italian *vigna.*

(5) *coquens* ("cooking") *non cocens*
The censured *cocens* form shows the tendency to reduce *qu* (pronounced *kw*) to *k* before front vowels: Latin *coquere* → French *cuire*, Spanish *cocer*, Portuguese *cozer*, and Italian *cuocere* (cf. also *cinque* for *quinque*, attested in inscriptions, hence French *cinq*, Italian *cinque*, Spanish *cinco*).

(6) *sibilus* ("whistle") *non sifilus*
The popular Latin *sifilare* for the Classical *sibilare* shows Oscan influence (see Appendix B); it is the censured form which gives rise to French *siffler*, Spanish *chiflar*, and Italian *zufolare*.

(7) *februarius* ("February") *non febrarius*
There is a popular tendency to drop *u* in hiatus, as reflected in French *février*, Spanish *febrero*, and Italian *febbraio*.

(8) *mensa* ("table") *non mesa*
The dropping of *n* before *s* is attested in both Pre- and Post-Classical Latin (see p. 45, 69–70), cf. Spanish *mesa*. Also, from Latin *mensis*, "month," we get French *mois*, Spanish *mes*, and Italian *mese*, by way of Vulgar Latin *mesis*.

(9) *aqua* ("water") *non acqua*
This "irregularity" shows the typical Italian doubling of consonants.

(10) *pauper mulier* ("poor woman") *non paupera mulier*
The feminine adjective form *paupera* for the classical *pauper* (an adjective of one termination, see Appendix C) shows a declensional shift to bring it in line with the *bonus, -a, -um* type adjective. This new feminine form is reflected in Italian *povera*, but not in Spanish *pobre* (from Latin *paupere*, the oblique case), while French *pauvre* may come from either the Classical or the Vulgar Latin form.

Pagan Inscriptions

(1) *ispose rarissime fecit* for *sponsae rarissimae* ("made [it] for his beloved wife").
Several interesting features to be noted in *ispose*: (a) Fall of *n* before *s* (see above, *Appendix Probi*). (b) Prothesis, i.e., the prefixing of a vowel to initial *sc-, sp-, st-* consonant clusters. In Vulgar Latin, the prothetic vowel is almost universally *i*, which Italian retains but restricts to cases where the preceding word ends in a consonant (*la Spagna*, "Spain," but *in Ispagna*, "in Spain"; *la strada*, "the street," but *per istrada*, "on the street"). Spanish, Portuguese, and French change the prothetic vowel from *i* to *e*, and retain it universally, save for French learned (book) words like *spécial*. In popular words, fourteenth-century French drops the *s* but retains the *e* with an acute accent, as in French *épouse*, Old French *espose*, cf. Spanish *esposa*. Compare also Latin *schola*, Italian *la scuola* (but *in iscuola*), Spanish *escuela*, Portuguese *escola*, Old French *escole*, Modern French *école*, which developed through an attested Vulgar Latin form *iscola*. (c) Reduction of the Classical Latin diphthong *ae* to *e*, and thus pronounced. The same phenomenon also occurs in *rarissime*. Occasionally, we find examples of so-called inverse spelling, as in *aeclesiae* for *ecclesiae*. The stonecutter, realizing that his spoken *e* represents not only written *e* but also *ae*, occasionally slips

into the opposite phenomenon of writing *ae* for what he pronounces *e* (and what should be written *e* also).

(2) *hic so et non so* for *hic sum et non sum* ("I am here and I am not here").

On this inscription from Naples (no date given), the form *so* illustrates: (a) The fall of final *-m*, already current in Pre-Classical Latin, appears universally in later Romance, save for some words of one syllable, e.g., Latin *rem*, "thing," which gives rise to French *rien*, "nothing." (b) Merger of unstressed final *-u* and *-o* (see Chapter 5). A similar phenomenon may be observed in *co filio* (for *cum filio*), appearing on an inscription from Rome.

(3) *Lepusclu Leo qui vixit anum et mesis undeci et dies dece e nove perit septimu calendas agustas* for *Lepusculus Leo* (or *Lepusculo Leoni*) *qui vixit annum et menses undecim et dies decem et novem* (or *undeviginti*) *periit septimo* (*die*) *kalendas augustas* ("[to] Lepusculus Leo who lived one year and eleven months and nineteen days, died on the seventh day before the Kalends of August").

Features of interest in this 404 A.D. inscription from Tusculum (present-day Frascati, just south of Rome) are the following: (a) Syncopation, i.e., the fall of an unstressed vowel caused by the concentration of stress accent on the stressed syllable in *Lepusclu* (cf. the form *calda* in the *Appendix Probi*). Also, this proper name leaves us in doubt whether it is meant to be nominative *Lepusculus* (in which case it would illustrate the fall of final *-s*, a phenomenon that occurs universally in standard Italian) or dative *Lepusculo*, with a confusion of final unstressed *u* and *o*. (In this case *Leo* would be an incorrect dative for *Leoni*.) Syntactically, either case would fit the context. (b) *Anum* for *annum* shows the reduction of a double consonant to a single; this appears in Pre-Classical writings as well, but does not fit later Italian development. (c) In addition to the fall of *n* before *s*, the *mesis* form (for *menses*) also illustrates the confusion of unstressed *e* and *i* in a final syllable. There may be another explanation for final *-is* for *-es* also: in view of the frequency of this interchange in the plural accusative of third declension nouns in Post-Classical texts, an extension of old *i*-stem noun endings to non-*i*-stem nouns is also possible (see noun inflection, Appendix C and Appendix I). (d) The numerals *undeci, dece*, and *nove* illustrate the fall of final *-m* (cf. Italian *nove, dieci, undici*). (e) *Septimu* for the expected *septimo* again shows the confusion of unstressed *u* and *o*. (f) The fall of *-t* in the conjunction *et* is quite in accord with later Italian development. It seems that in this instance (having written *et* correctly twice previously), the stonecutter let his spoken language habits interfere with his spelling. (g) Finally, *agustas* illustrates the reduction of *au* to *a* in the initial position, as reflected in Italian-Portuguese-Spanish *agosto*. French *août*, in addition to this reduction, also gives evidence of the loss of *g* between vowels. In fact, the form *austo* for *augusto* is indeed attested in a third-century inscription from Spain.

Christian Inscriptions

Many of the linguistic features encountered in pagan inscriptions and in the *Appendix Probi* (confusion of *u* and *o*, and *e* and *i* in unstressed syllable, syncopation, prothesis, fall of final *-m* and *-t*, fall of *n* before *s*, etc.) occur with great frequency in Christian inscriptions also. Hence, only new features will be pointed out.

(1) *Deus magnu oclu abet* for *Deus magnum oculum habet* ("God has a large eye").

In this inscription from Rome, the only feature not yet encountered is the fall of initial *h-* in *abet*. This consonant sound was weak even in Classical Latin; it completely disappeared in the spoken language and has left no trace in the Romance languages. (The so-called *h aspiré*, "aspirated [h]," of French is not a reflex of the Latin sound.)

(2) *Si aliquis sepulchru istum biolare bolueri abea anathema da patre et filiu et scm spm* for *Si aliquis sepulchrum istum violare voluerit, habeat anathema a patre et filio et sancto spiritu* ("If anyone should wish to violate this sepulcher, let him have a curse from the Father and the Son and the Holy Ghost").

Features of interest in this inscription, also from Rome, are as follows:

(a) Re *sepulchru istum:* since final *-m* is often dropped in writing, indicating that it is no longer pronounced in speech, the stonecutter is not quite sure when to use it. It is most probable that by that time (undated inscriptions are thought to belong in the sixth century) both words were pronounced with final *-o*, regardless of spelling. Note also *scm spm* (*sanctum spiritum*), the accusative case for the expected ablative (*sancto spiritu*), which appears in the preceding *patre* and *filiu* (for *filio*, but keep in mind the frequent confusion of unstressed *o* and *u*, particularly in the final syllable). This confusion of accusative and ablative in Post-Classical texts, resulting in the eventual merger of these cases (see noun inflection, Appendix C), is further illustrated in a seventh-century inscription from Spain, *siquis temtaverit isto monumento* for *temptaverit istum monumentum* ("if anyone should tamper with this monument [i.e., tomb]"), where the stonecutter no doubt spells the way he pronounces. (b) The verb forms *biolare* and *bolueri* are probably indicative not of a *b* but of a *v* pronunciation. As the classical *w* sound becomes *v* in popular speech, the tendency is to reserve the written symbol V for long and short *u*, and to use the symbol B for both the *b* sound and the new *v* sound, which are close to each other. (c) The preposition *da* is a typical Italian formation from *de ab* but it also occurs sporadically in early Spanish (*da*) and in Sardinian (*daba*).

(3) *membra ad duus fratres* for *membra duorum fratrum* ("the remains of two brothers").

Of particular interest in this inscription from Gaul is the replacement of the Classical genitive case (possessive) by a circumlocution with the preposition *ad* followed by the plural accusative *duos* (here *duus* due to vowel confusion). This construction with *ad* to indicate possession is typically French, as in *ce livre à moi*, "this book of mine."

The Graffiti of Pompeii

(1) *ama, valia, peria* (for *amat, valeat, pereat*)

The full text of the inscription reads: *quisquis ama valia, peria qui nosci amare* ("let him who loves be well, may he who knows not how to love die"). In addition to the fall of *-t* in verb forms (a characteristic feature of Italian), let us also note in *valia* and *peria* the change of *e* in hiatus to a *y*-glide (represented by the vowel *i*), with reduction in number of syllables and, in the case of the former, palatalization of preceding *l* (as in *million*), cf. French *vaille,* Italian *vaglia.*

(2) *verecunnus* (for *verecundus,* "ashamed," "bashful")

The change of *-nd-* to *-nn-* is a characteristic feature of Oscan, the former language of Pompeii, and continues in modern local dialects. (See also Appendix B.)

(3) *scriserunt* (for *scripserunt,* "they wrote")

The reduction of the *-ps-* consonant group to *-s-* may indicate a double *s* pronunciation, as in Italian *scrissero.*

(4) *settembris* (for *septembris,* "of September")

This example illustrates what is known as an *assimilation,* which, in Italian, leads to a great many double consonants, as in *settembre;* also *sette* from Latin *septem, fatto* from Latin *factum, sonno* from Latin *somnum,* etc.

(5) *abiat Venere Bompeiiana iratam qui hoc laeserit* for *habeat Venerem Pompeiianam iratam qui hoc laeserit* ("let him who damages this have the anger of the Venus of Pompeii").

In addition to the fall of initial *h-* and final *-m* (note the confusion of forms in *-a* and *-am* in the same grammatical function), the change of *P-* to *B-* is of interest, illustrating the phenomenon known as sonorization of voiceless consonants (turning them into voiced consonants) between vowels.

Appendix E

Vocalic and Consonantal Developments
from Latin to Romance

The following pages are meant to give a brief outline of the historical development of Latin vowels and consonants into the Romance languages, particularly French, Italian, and Spanish.

The Vowel System

(1) The Classical Latin vowel scheme consisted of five pure vowels, *a, e, i, o,* and *u.* Each of these could be long or short. The duration (length) of each was a *phonologically* significant feature in that the essentially same vowel quality could make a difference in the meaning of the word according to whether it was long or short, e.g., *pŏpulus,* "people," versus *pōpulus,* "poplar-tree," *vĕnit,* "he (she, it) comes," (present tense) versus *vēnit,* "he (she, it) came," (perfect tense), or *rosă,* "rose," (nominative) versus *rosā,* "by (with, etc.) the rose," (ablative).

(2) While it is possible that long vowels may have had a slightly more closed and short vowels a more open quality already in Classical Latin, the fact is that in Vulgar Latin distinctions of length or *quantity* gradually disappeared and there emerged a new phonological opposition of *quality,* brought about by the amount of opening or closing of the mouth during the emission of the vowel sound. Long vowels came to be pronounced more closely than short ones, which took on a decidedly more open quality. Thus, *vĕnit* and *vēnit,* which in Classical Latin were differentiated in meaning on the basis of short versus long *e* (*ĕ* versus *ē*), came to be opposed on the basis of open versus closed vowel, conventionally transcribed as *ę* and *ẹ,* namely *vęnit* versus *vẹnit.* Except for the vowel *a,* where originally long and short merged into one phonologically significant quality, a series of mergers took place, beginning, no doubt, with vowels in unstressed syllables.

(3) The following scheme illustrates how the system of *stressed* vowels was reorganized in Vulgar Latin:

Classical Latin	ā	ă	ĕ	ē	ĭ	ī	ŏ	ō	ŭ	ū
Vulgar Latin		a		ę	ẹ		i	ǫ	ọ		u

Evidence of this rearrangement is amply furnished by Post-Classical texts, inscriptions, and statements of grammarians, particularly the *Appendix Probi* (see Appendix D). These changes are further borne out by the Romance languages, which also enable us to determine their extension; thus, only Sardinian has kept both Latin *ē* and *ĭ* and *ō* and *ŭ* apart (having merged homophonous vowels, i.e., *ĕ* with *ē*, *ĭ* with *ī*, etc.), while Balkan Romance (largely represented by Modern Rumanian) has only partially participated in these changes, since it merged *ē* and *ĭ* but *not ō* and *ŭ*. This latter change also suggests that the Vulgar Latin merger of back vowels (*ō, ŭ*) may have occurred at a later date than that of front vowels (*ĭ, ē*), at any rate after Dacia had become separated from the western portion of the Roman Empire.

(4) The main factor in the transformation of vowels in Vulgar Latin and later Romance was *stress*. It tended to lengthen the vowels on which it fell, often leading to their segmentation into two vowel qualities, i.e., the formation of a *diphthong*. At the same time, however, stress on the main syllable also weakened the unstressed vowels, which all became short and in many cases dropped out altogether. Since stress plays such an important role in the later history of Latin vowels, the distinction between stressed (*tonic*) and unstressed (*atonic*) vowels is essential.

THE STRESSED VOWELS

(1) The Romance outcome of Latin stressed vowels depends on whether they are in *free* or *checked* position. A vowel is said to be in free position when it comes at the end of a syllable (e.g., the first syllable in Latin *pā-nis, mā-trem*); when the vowel is followed by a consonant in the *same* syllable, it is in checked position (e.g., *par-tem*).

(2) The following table summarizes the development of Latin vowels in both free and checked positions. The Old French stage is also given since in a number of instances it substantially differs from that of Modern French. (A dot under a vowel means closed quality, while a hook means open quality [see above]. No diacritic mark under a vowel means that it can be open or closed according to the syllabic structure in the modern language, e.g., French *été* with *ę* versus French *mer* with *ę*, both *e*'s coming from an original free Latin *a*, namely *aestā-tem* and *márem*, respectively.)

		Free Position				Checked Position			
Classi-cal Latin	Vulgar Latin	Ital-ian	Span-ish	Old French	Modern French	Ital-ian	Span-ish	Old French	Modern French
a, ā	a	a	a	ę	e	a	a	a	a
ĕ, ae	ę	ę/ie	ie	ie	ie	ę	ie	ę	ę
ē, i, oe	ẹ	ẹ	e	ei	oi(=wa)	ẹ	e	ẹ	ę
ī	i	i	i	i	i	i	i	i	i
ŏ	ǫ	ǫ/uo	ue	uo/ue	eu(=ö)	ǫ	ue	ǫ	ǫ
ō, ŭ	ọ	ọ	o	ọ/ou	eu(=ö)	ọ	o	ọ	ou(=u)
ū	u	u	u	u(=ü)	u(=ü)	u	u	u(=ü)	u(=ü)

(3) The evolution of vowels in *checked* position is far less complex than that of vowels in free position. It seems that the consonant which closes the syllable

has prevented the vowel from either too much lengthening or displacement on the vocalic scale. Yet, it will be noticed that Spanish treats Vulgar Latin ę and ǫ identically in free and checked syllables, since they become diphthongs in both instances. Here is an example for each vowel development:

Classical Latin	Vulgar Latin	Italian	Spanish	Old French	Modern French
părtem, "part"	parte	parte	parte	part	part
tĕrram, "earth"	tęrra	tęrra	tierra	tęr(r)e	tęrre
lĭttera, "letter"	lęttera	lęttera	letra	lętre	lęttre
vīlla, "estate"	villa	villa	villa	ville	ville
pŏrtam, "door"	pǫrta	pǫrta	puerta	pǫrte	pǫrte
cohŏrtem, "cohort"	cǫrte	cǫrte	corte	cǫr/cour	cour
gūstum, "taste"	gusto	gusto	gusto	irregular development	
fūstem, "stick"	fuste	fuste	—	fust	fût

(4) Vowels in *free* position are much less stable, as will be seen from the following examples. Note that the Latin diphthongs *ae* and *oe* develop into the Romance languages like Latin ĕ and ē, respectively, e.g., Latin *caelum,* Vulgar Latin *cęlo,* Italian *cielo,* Spanish *cielo,* French *ciel;* Latin *poena,* Vulgar Latin *pęna,* Italian *pęna,* Spanish *pena,* French *peine* (pronounced, however, with open *e,* contrary to normal French development of Latin ē in free position).

Classical Latin	Vulgar Latin	Italian	Spanish	Old French	Modern French
prātum, "field"	prato	prato	prado	pręt	pré
pĕtra, "stone"	pętra	pietra	piedra	piedre	pierre
pĭra, "pear"	pęra	pęra	pera	peire	poire
vīta, "life"	vita	vita	vida	vide	vie
nŏvum, "new"	nǫvo	nuovo	nuevo	nuef	neuf
flŏrem, "flower"	flǫre	fiǫre	flor	flǫr, flour	fleur
mūrum, "wall"	muro	muro	muro	mur	mur

The only vowels which have remained intact under stress are Latin ī and ū; but even so, over a large area long *u* has assumed an *ü* pronunciation, specifically in the whole French area, including Provençal, in Rheto-Rumansh, in northern Italian dialects, and even in some Portuguese ones. In northern France, furthermore, Latin *a* in free position has become *e.* The most notable phenomenon, however, is the lengthening of the stressed vowel to the point of breaking up into two vowel sounds. Here again, Modern French seems to have carried diphthongization furthest, at least among the major Romance languages, since not only Latin short *e* and *o* but also the corresponding long vowels have undergone this kind of segmentation.

(5) Whatever the causes of this *spontaneous diphthongization* may have been, it is far from being a universal phenomenon in the Romance languages. It does not take place in Portuguese, for instance, which opposes *pedra* to Spanish *piedra.* And because it seems to have occurred under varying conditions in those areas where it did happen (in French and Italian only in free syllables, while in Spanish and Rumanian—in the latter only involving Latin *e*—in both free *and* checked positions), some scholars think that diphthongization must have devel-

oped in each region independently. Others, like W. Elcock, for example, maintain that this phenomenon had begun spontaneously already in the Vulgar Latin period. The fact is that we have no sure evidence of this phenomenon in Post-Classical documents and inscriptions. All we can state for certain is that the general area of diphthongization is not a continuous one; hence, it is quite possible that in addition to the stress accent other factors may also have contributed to creating the "varying conditions" under which this vocalic development took place.

THE UNSTRESSED VOWELS

(1) Not all unstressed vowels are equally weakened as a result of the concentration of energy on the stressed vowels. Indeed, their evolution from Latin into Romance depends on their position with reference to the accented syllable. Accordingly, we must distinguish vowels in the (a) *initial* (first syllable of the word), (b) *intertonic* (immediately preceding or following the stress accent), and (c) *final* syllables.

(2) Vowels in the *initial* syllable were pronounced with enough clarity to be fairly well preserved in Romance. In Vulgar Latin they were reduced to five: *a, ę, i, ǫ, u,* in accordance with the following scheme:

Classical Latin: ā ă ĕ ē ĭ æ œ ī ŏ ō ŭ ū
Vulgar Latin: a ę i ǫ u

The Vulgar Latin pattern survives rather intact in Spanish (a*migo, seguro, in-vierno, colgar, mu*dar). In Italian, Vulgar Latin *e* normally develops to *i*, as in *sicuro* from Latin *sēcūrum* (not without exceptions, however, as in Italian *venire* from Latin *vĕnīre*); otherwise, it closely parallels the Spanish development (a*mico, inverno, collocare, mutare*). In French, Vulgar Latin *a, i,* and *u* generally remain intact, except for the quality of *u*, which turns into an *ü* sound as in the stressed syllable (a*mi, hiver, muer*); Vulgar Latin *e* weakens to a *schwa* sound (sometimes erroneously called "*e* mute") in a free syllable but generally remains open *e* in checked position, e.g., *devoir* versus *errer* from Latin *dēbēre* and *ĕrrāre*, respectively; initial *o* generally turns into an *u* sound (spelled *ou*) in a free syllable, while in a checked one it remains open *o*, as in *mourir* (from Latin *mŏrīre*) versus *dormir* (from Latin *dŏrmīre*). Exceptions to all these phonological "rules" are numerous, however, and often brought about by neighboring sounds (see below, "conditioned" changes).

(3) In the *final* position, Latin vowels were further reduced. Italian keeps Vulgar Latin *a, e, i, o* (*canta, dice, venti, tempo*), while Spanish reduces them to three only, *a, e, o* (*canta, dice, veinte, tiempo*). Of all final vowels French retains only Latin *a*, which, however, it turns into a *schwa* [ə], written *e*, as in French *rose* from Latin *rosa*. The final Latin *e* and *o* may, nevertheless, survive also in the form of [ə] when needed to support a consonant cluster, e.g., Latin *pătrem* → Old French *pedre* → Modern French *père;* Latin *pŏpulum* → early Old French *poblo* → Modern French *peuple*.

(4) A natural consequence of the Vulgar Latin stress accent, which tended to concentrate vocal energy on the accented syllable to the detriment of other

parts of the word, particularly of the vowels of the adjoining syllables, was the loss of vowels in *intertonic* position. The phenomenon of *syncopation*, as is called the loss of an unstressed vowel in this position, is widely attested in Vulgar Latin documents and inscriptions (see Appendix D). Among the major Romance languages, this definitely popular phenomenon is much more operative in French and Spanish than it is in Italian (e.g., Italian *popolo* versus Spanish *pueblo*, French *peuple;* Italian *anima* versus Spanish *alma*, French *âme*), although syncopation is by no means unknown in this language, particularly in those cases in which the phenomenon is attested in Post-Classical texts, e.g., Latin *dŏmina* → Vulgar Latin *domna* → Italian *donna*, Spanish *dueña*, French *dame*.

(5) Syncopation has greatly affected the phonetic make-up of Latin words by reducing the number of syllables. This is particularly true of words of more than two syllables which were stressed on the *antepenult* (third from the last syllable), called *proparoxytones*, e.g., *pópulum*. Generally reduced to *paroxytones* in the Iberian languages (Spanish and Portuguese, in particular) and Old French (accent on the *penult*, or next to the last syllable), with the eventual disappearance of final vowels in pronunciation and the consequent fall of the accent on the new last syllable, Latin proparoxytones (as well as paroxytones) have been reduced to *oxytones* in Modern French. The resistance of Italian (and also Rumanian) to reducing Latin proparoxytones through syncopation of the intertonic vowel has led to the distinction that some scholars have drawn between Eastern and Western Romance languages, contrasting, for instance, Italian *uómini*, Rumanian *oámeni* with Spanish *hombres*, Portuguese *homens*, French *hommes* from Latin *hóminēs*.

Vowels in Hiatus

(1) The *Appendix Probi* urges its readers not to spell *vinia, cavia, lancia,* for the correct *vinea, cavea, lancea*. Conversely, it censures the spelling *lileum* and *aleum* for *lilium* and *alium*. Vowel combinations like *-ea-, -eo-, -ia-, -io-, -ua-, -uo-,* in which one vowel directly precedes another one without forming a diphthong with it, are pronounced as two separate syllables in Classical Latin. The first vowel in such combinations is said to be in *hiatus*. With the vocal energy concentrating on the stressed vowel, however, it seems that speakers neglected to articulate carefully two successive vowels not separated by a consonant, with the result that the hiatus vowel either dropped out altogether (as in Italian *parete*, Spanish *pared*, French *paroi*, from Latin *pariētem*, originally accented on the *i*, but with the accent subsequently shifting to the more open *e*, leaving *i* unstressed), or assumed a semivocalic quality (as in English *yes*), which then combined with the following vowel to form a diphthong, reducing at the same time the number of syllables of a given word. For instance, Latin *vīnea* (syllabicated *vi-ne-a*) was reduced to *vinya* (syllabicated *vi-nya*) and Latin *alium* (*a-li-um*) to *alyo* (*a-lyo*). Scholars have given the name of *yod* to this newly developed sound (not unknown in Classical Latin where it existed in words like *jam*, *jānuārius, jocōsus, jūdex*, etc., in syllable initial position). The yod, as will be seen in subsequent discussion, has played an eminently important part in the development of new sounds and groups of sounds that did not exist in Classical Latin. In addition, this semivowel has also interfered with spontaneous vowel

developments and has been an important factor in bringing about changes not in accord with the normal operation of phonological "laws."

DIPHTHONGS

(1) As was seen in connection with the development of Latin stressed vowels, the diphthongs *ae* and *oe* merged in Post-Classical Latin with short and long *e*, respectively. The third diphthong, *au*, generally remained intact during the Vulgar Latin period, although instances of its reduction to *o* are attested here and there, as in *oricla* for *auricula* (diminutive of *auris*, "ear"), censured by Probus (see Appendix D). As a matter of fact there are extensive areas where Latin *au* has survived to this day (Rumanian, Rheto-Rumansh, dialects of southern France and Italy); in most Romance languages, however, this diphthong was generally reduced to open or closed *o* by way of a diphthong *ou*, still attested in Portuguese orthography, though now also reduced to *o* in pronunciation, e.g., Latin *aurum* → Portuguese *ouro*, Spanish, Italian *oro*, French *or*, but remains *aur* in Rumanian and Provençal.

(2) In addition to the survival of Latin *au*, there arose a secondary diphthong *au* in Vulgar Latin, also through contact of *a* and *u*, due to the loss of an intervocalic consonant, as in Latin *parabola*, "word," (borrowed from the Greek *parabolé*, "comparison," and brought into the language with the meaning of "word" by the Christians), developing to Vulgar Latin *paraula* (unattested, but reflected in Provençal *paraula*) and giving rise to Italian *parola*, French *parole*. (In Spanish *palabra*, the unstressed *u* dropped out before *a* and *u* had a chance to form a diphthong.) Another source of this secondary diphthong was the Latin perfect ending *-āvit*, which, through contraction, became *-aut* in Vulgar Latin (the form *consumaut* for *consumavit* is attested), resulting in the Italian and Spanish *-ò* and *-ó* perfect endings, respectively, e.g., Latin *cantāvit* → Vulgar Latin *cantaut* → Italian *cantò*, Spanish *cantó*.

(3) Through loss of intervocalic *-v-* in the first person perfect ending *-āvī*, another Vulgar Latin diphthong arose: *-ai*. Accordingly, Latin *cantāvī* → Vulgar Latin *cantai* → Italian *cantai*, Rumanian *cântai*, while in Spanish and French the diphthong was reduced to *e*, Spanish *canté*, French *chantai*, even though in the latter the old diphthong is still reflected in the orthography, since in Old French the diphthong was pronounced. (Orthography is sometimes centuries behind pronunciation!) The intermediate stage between *ai* and *e* is still reflected in Portuguese *cantei*.

"SPONTANEOUS" VERSUS "CONDITIONED" DEVELOPMENTS

(1) The vowel changes in stressed and unstressed positions that we have discussed so far may be called "spontaneous" because they are supposed to have been caused by the nature of the sounds themselves, quite independently of the influence of surrounding sounds. Thus, stressed Latin *a* in free position becomes *e* in Modern French (*pátrem* → *père; aestâtem* → *été*), the quality of the vowel (open or closed) depending on the syllable structure in the modern language. A "conditioned" sound change, on the other hand, is determined by surrounding sounds, the phonetic environment, and is predictable in terms of this environment. We have seen, for instance, that stressed Latin *a* in both free and checked

positions remains *a* in Spanish. Yet, when this *a* is immediately followed by the semivocalic yod it combines with it to form a diphthong first, which then is reduced to a monophthong: e.g., Latin *laicum* (*lá-i-cum*), "layman," becomes Spanish *lego* (also reducing the original three syllables to two). This same kind of conditioning by yod is also operative when the semivowel does not immediately follow the stressed vowel but occurs in the following syllable: e.g., Latin *bāsium,* "kiss," becomes Spanish *beso* through an assumed *baiso* → *beiso* → *beso* development. (Again, the intermediate stage is attested by Portuguese *beijo*.) The same development also takes place when *a* is in an unstressed initial syllable, e.g., Latin *bāsiāre,* "to kiss," becomes Spanish *besar,* with the expected "intermediate" diphthong *ei* in Portuguese *beijar*. French closely follows this Spanish development, at least in pronunciation if not in orthography, e.g., *baiser* (pronounced [beze]). On the other hand, Italian does not participate in this development. While, as was seen, the *a* combines with an immediately following yod to form a diphthong, it is not affected by this semivowel when it occurs in the following syllable; hence, Latin *bāsium* → Italian *bacio.*

(2) The influence of the yod may also be seen with other vowels. Specifically, it tends to close open vowels of Vulgar Latin, thus interfering with their normal development. This is particularly true of Spanish, where all stressed vowels in contact with a yod close up one degree (a → ę/ẹ; ę → ẹ; ẹ → i; ǫ → o; ǫ → u), preventing open vowels from diphthongizing, e.g., Latin *fŏlia* → Spanish *hoja* (for the expected *ue*) or Latin *tĕneō* → Spanish *tengo* (for the expected *ie*), in contrast to French *feuille* and *tien(s)*, which have the expected, normal diphthongs.

(3) Hiatus vowels *e* and *i* are one of the main sources of the yod. There are others. This palatal semivowel may also proceed from the *vocalization* (i.e., the change of a consonant to a semivowel or vowel) of the palatal element in the Latin *-ct-* (pronounced [-kt-]) and *-cl-* (pronounced [-kl-]) consonant groups. In the Latin word *lacte,* "milk," for instance, the [k] sound lost its consonantal nature and turned into a semivocalic yod which, then, combined with the preceding vowel, very much in the way already illustrated. Latin *lacte* becomes French *lait* (reflecting the first diphthongal stage in orthography but now pronounced [lę]), Portuguese *leite* (intermediate stage between *ai* → *e*), Spanish *leche*. Similarly, Latin *ŏctō,* "eight," first became *oito* (the Portuguese stage) and then *ocho* in Spanish, preventing diphthongization of Latin short *o* under stress. In French, on the other hand, where vowels in checked position do not normally diphthongize, the development of a semivowel from a palatal consonant seems to have favored segmentation of the preceding vowel, which then combined with the following yod eventually to give French *huit*. We must assume a development along the following lines: Latin *ŏctō* → late Vulgar Latin *oito* → early Old French *ueit* (not attested) → Modern French *huit*. In a similar vein, from Latin *ŏculum,* through a Vulgar Latin stage *oclo,* we get Spanish *ojo,* but Old French *ueil,* Modern French *oeil,* with diphthongization. Once again, Italian does not share in this development: the palatal element in the *-ct-* consonant group (the [k]) is assimilated to the following *t,* e.g., Latin *lacte* → Italian *latte;* Latin *ŏctō* → Italian *otto,* while the Latin *-cl-* consonant group retains the [k] element but turns *l* into a semivowel, e.g., Latin *ŏculum* (Vulgar Latin *oclo*) → Italian *occhio*

(pronounced [okkyo]), leaving the stressed vowel intact. Note, however, that Italian is not quite immune to the closing influence of yod, e.g., Latin *cĭlium,* "eyelid," → Italian *ciglio* (not *ceglio*), with the closing of Latin *ĭ* to *i*. (Cf. also French *cil,* but Spanish *cejo* is "irregular.")

(4) Changes of the kinds illustrated in the foregoing paragraphs, in which the quality of a preceding vowel is altered under the influence of a following semivowel, are generally subsumed under the heading of *metaphony*. Also known as *vowel mutation* or *umlaut,* this phenomenon is due to some sort of assimilative influence and always depends on phonetic environment. It is widely attested in Germanic languages, as in English *foot* versus *feet*. Here, the change of the root vowel in the plural is ultimately caused by a front vowel in a once existing ending which was lost even before the historical appearance of English. In Primitive Germanic an unattested *fōtiz* was the plural form of *fōt,* "foot"; the *ō* vowel of the root was fronted to *ē* by anticipation of the *i* in the ending, so that by the time Old English appears the form *fēt* as the plural of *fōt* was already established. (Later *ē* shifted to *i* and *ō* to *u* in pronunciation.)

(5) Latin final *-ī* and *-ŭ* have in many cases also modified the stressed vowel. The perfect form *fēcī,* "I have done," survives in Spanish and French as *hice* and *fis,* respectively, as against Italian *feci*. The final *-ī* changed the root vowel to *i* before it dropped out in French and turned into *e* in Spanish, in accordance with the normal development of final vowels in this language. Actually, the end result of this phenomenon is quite similar to that brought about by vowel contact with yod. This kind of metaphony occurs in many Romance dialects, particularly Italian varieties, where it often brings about diphthongization of a stressed vowel which normally would not be diphthongized, serving to distinguish masculine from feminine forms, e.g., southern Italian masculine *buonǝ* from Latin *bŏnŭ(m),* *bŏnī,* versus feminine *bonǝ* from Latin *bŏna, bŏnae*. In Portuguese, Latin final *-ŭ* effects the closing of open *e* and *o,* hence the qualitative distinction between singular *mǫrto* and plural *mǫrtos* from Latin *mŏrtŭ(m)* and *mŏrtōs,* respectively. In Rumanian, both *-ī* and *-ŭ* have exerted a similar influence, but only on stressed open *o*. Of special interest is the fact that in this language final *-a* and *-e* have also affected this same vowel, breaking it up into an *oa* diphthong, e.g., Latin *formōsu(m)* → Rumanian *frumǫs,* but *formōsa* → *frumoásă*.

(6) Another "conditioned" vowel development is brought about by the vocalization of *l,* which, in contact with another consonant, tends to become a semivowel yod or *wau* (the semivowel *u,* as in *water*). In Spanish, Portuguese, and French (rarely in Italian) this *l* before a consonant turns into the semivowel *u* and combines with the preceding vowel, usually *a,* to form a diphthong: Latin *alterum* → French *autre* (now pronounced with *ǫ,* however), Portuguese *outro,* Spanish *otro*. This phenomenon occurs with greatest regularity in French, e.g., Latin *alba* → French *aube,* but Italian, Spanish *alba;* Latin *saltum* → French *saut,* but Italian, Spanish *salto* (however, Portuguese *souto*).

Italian, as we said, only rarely makes use of this kind of vocalization; but it quite regularly vocalizes *l* to the semivowel *i* after a consonant and before a vowel, particularly in the *pl-, fl-,* and *cl-* consonant groups, as in *piano, fiamma, chiamare,* from Latin *plānum, flamma, clāmāre,* respectively. This feature sets Italian squarely apart from its sister languages.

(7) *Nasalization* is another important vocalic development conditioned by contact with a neighboring sound. We may define this phenomenon as the throwing of a vowel resonance into the nasal passage in anticipation of a following nasal consonant. It is peculiar to French, Portuguese, and some northern Italian dialects. Unknown in Classical Latin, it is not reflected in Vulgar Latin documents, but evidence of it in the earliest documents of Old French is unmistakable (cf. *meon* from Latin *meum* in the Strasbourg Oaths; see Appendix G). Indeed, nasalization is one of the fundamental characteristics of the French vowel system. If Latin *bŏnum* has become French *bon*, it is because the *n* has transferred its nasal resonance to *o* before dropping out in pronunciation. (The French word is phonetically represented as [bɔ̃].) In the feminine form *bonne* (phonetically [bɔn]), however, from Latin *bŏna*, the *n* reappears in speech, thus "denasalizing" the preceding vowel. This process of denasalization is represented in writing by doubling the consonant. (In former days, as a matter of fact, even the feminine form was nasalized, the first *n* marking the nasalization of the preceding vowel and the second one the consonant to be pronounced; people said [bɔ̃nə].) Nasalization has not affected all Latin vowels simultaneously. It must have begun with the most open vowel, the *a*; but when it reached *i* and *u*, the high tongue position was immediately lowered to a more open vowel quality. Thus, open *ö* and *e* are actually nasalized in Latin *ūnum* → French *un* and Latin *vīnum* → French *vin*, instead of *i* and *u*, respectively. The nasal equivalent of *a*, generally spelled *en* or *an*, appears in a word like *enfant* [ãfã] from Latin *infantem*.

Nasalization has also played an important part in the evolution of Portuguese. In checked position, in words like *fonte* and *tempo*, the vowel is nasalized but the consonant is also articulated (very much as in Old French). There are also many words in which *n* between two vowels has dropped out altogether after nasalizing the preceding vowel. Thus, a number of nasal diphthongs have arisen, as in *mão* (Latin *manum*), *lições* "lessons," (Latin *lectiōnēs*, "readings"), *cães*, "dogs," (Latin *canēs*), etc. If the posttonic vowel happened to be identical with or similar to the quality of the stressed vowel, it was absorbed by the latter, as in *lã*, "wool," (Latin *lāna*), or *bom*, pronounced [bõ], (Latin *bonum*).

Instances of nasalization in some northern Italian dialects closely follow the French model.

The foregoing sketch, which necessarily excludes many details concerning the spontaneous and conditioned developments of Latin vowels in the Romance languages, may give some idea of the manifold and complex changes that confront the student who wishes to probe further the mystery of linguistic change. One fact that emerges from the comparison of the Latin and Romance vowel structures is that not all the languages have undergone the same changes and that some have kept closer to the Latin prototype than others. For instance, the stressed vowels of Italian *prato, tẹrra, avẹre, amico, pọrta, gọla, muro*, and the corresponding Portuguese forms *prado, tẹrra, havẹr, amigo, pọrta, gọla, muro*, rather faithfully preserve the seven vowel qualities of Vulgar Latin. To this extent, these languages are more of an echo of Latin than is, say, French, which, among the major Romance languages, has diverged most from its ancestor through the development of two new vowel series, the nasal and the so-called middle vowels (*ö, ü*), that give this language its very individual and distinctive character. And even though some languages and dialects share in the French developments, none of the Romance languages, we believe, have exploited the phenomena of nasalization and front vowel rounding (the *ö* sound being actually an *e* pronounced with rounded lips), the *e* being open or closed according to the syllable structure in the modern language, thus giving open *ö* in a syllable ending in a consonant sound and closed *ö* in a syllable ending in a vowel sound (*peur* versus *peu*), while *ü* is really an *i* sound also produced with rounding of lips) as fully as French has. What this language may lack in the kind of sonority and "musicality" displayed by, say, Italian and Spanish, with their many *a*'s and *o*'s in both stressed and unstressed syllables, it certainly makes up in originality.

The Consonant System

(1) The Classical Latin consonant scheme is rather poor when compared with the consonantal structures of the Romance languages. It consists of the following series: (a) *labials: p, b;* (b) *dentals: t, d;* (c) *velars: k* (generally spelled *c*), *g*, and the combinations *qu, gu* [kw, gw]; (d) *spirant: f;* (e) *sibilant: s;* (f) *lateral: l;* (g) *nasals: m, n;* (h) *vibrant: r* ("rolled"); (i) *aspirate: h;* (j) *semivowels: y, w* (written *i, u*). Most striking is the absence of the *palatal* series (the English sounds represented by *ch* in *church, j* and *dg* in *judge, sh* in *show, s* in *measure, lli* in *million, ny* in *canyon, ts* in *tsetse*). Also, some consonants have no voiced counterparts, such as *f* and *s* (the latter always pronounced as in *see*); there are no equivalents of the sounds represented in English by *th,* as in *thing* and *this.* The Romance languages have all made up for these deficiencies in one way or another.

(2) Changes that Latin consonants have undergone in the historical evolution from Latin to Romance depend largely on the position they occupied in the word, i.e., whether they were *initial, interior* (*intervocalic* or part of a consonant group), or *final.* Also, the fate of *simple* consonants was different from that of *double* consonants or clusters. For example, the single, intervocalic *t* in *amata* was treated differently from the double *tt* in *mĭttit,* or the *pt* group in *captat.*

(3) Consonants in the *initial* position tend to be stable and, generally speaking, they have remained intact. The most notable exception, and one that sets Spanish apart from its sister Romance languages and most dialects, is the loss of initial Latin *f.* Turning first into an aspirated *h* sound, this aspiration subsequently disappeared from pronunciation (probably around the sixteenth or seventeenth century), although it can still occasionally be heard in some southern Spanish and Spanish-American dialects of the lower classes. The *h* is reflected in orthography, however, e.g., Spanish *hacer,* "to do," *hijo,* "son," *humo,* "smoke," from Latin *facere, fīlium, fūmum,* respectively. Compare this outcome with Portuguese *fazer, filho, fumo;* Italian *fare, figlio, fumo;* French *faire, fils, fumée,* and Rumanian *fi, fiu, fum.* The change of initial Latin *f* to Spanish *h,* which is so characteristic of literary Spanish, is by no means a universal phenomenon. There are many words—and not necessarily book (learned) words, where a certain amount of conservatism in evolution would be expected—which keep initial Latin *f* intact, particularly where it is followed by the diphthong *ue* or an *r,* as in Spanish *fuerte* and *frente* from Latin *fŏrtem* and *frŏntem,* respectively.

A great deal of ink has flowed to account for this sound change. Since the *h* pronunciation for Latin *f* is said to have begun in a northwestern corner of the Spanish peninsula immediately adjacent to Basque country, whence it spread southward, some scholars have attributed this phenomenon to the influence of Basque speech habits, since initial *f* is absent in this language. At any rate, words of Latin origin that have found their way into Basque either omit this consonant sound (e.g., Latin *fīlum*, "thread," → Basque *iru*) or replace it by *b* or *p* (e.g., Latin *festa*, "feast," → Basque *pesta*). Others claim that the change from initial Latin *f* to *h* in Castilian (literary) Spanish is quite independent of such influence and can be accounted for by the fact that initial *f* was pronounced by the Romanized inhabitants of the peninsula as a *bilabial* sound (much the way we blow out a match) which, in time, was relaxed into an aspiration. (A similar phenomenon may be observed in modern Japanese where bilabial *f* interchanges with aspirated *h*, in accordance with the nature of the following vowel sound.)

(4) The changes that the Classical vowel system underwent in Vulgar Latin are not paralleled in the area of consonants. It may be said that, on the whole, the Classical system is fairly well preserved in Post-Classical texts and inscriptions. Some changes were taking place, of course, as will be seen from a glance at the texts given in Appendix D. When the grammarian Probus censures the form *cocus*, "cook," used instead of the correct *coquus*, we must assume that in the spoken language the semivowel *u* [w] had merged with the following *u* vowel, a fact which is confirmed by other censured forms, e.g., *rivus non rius* (where the *v* symbol stands for [w]). It is the censured form *rius* that survives in Italian *rio* and Spanish *río*, respectively.

(5) Among other consonantal developments attested (sometimes only suggested) in Vulgar Latin documents, we may list the following: (a) The change of *u* semivowel (as in *wine*) to the voiced spirant *v* (voiced counterpart of *f*), sometimes the voiced bilabial *b* also (as in Rumanian *bătrân*, "old," from Latin *veterānus*), probably passing through a bilabial spirant stage (as in Spanish *lavar*, with the two lips barely touching), e.g., Latin *lavāre* (v = w) → Italian *lavare*, French *laver;* this phenomenon is suggested by the frequent interchange of *v* and *b* in texts and, particularly, inscriptions, e.g., *bir* for *vīr*, "man," *alva* for *alba*, "dawn," *lebanto* for *levanto*, "I raise," and countless others. (b) The fall of initial *h* (*abere* for *habere* in many inscriptions), which is only preserved in orthography, e.g., Spanish *haber*, Portuguese *haver*, Italian *ho*, "I have." (c) The fall of final *-m*, attested even in Pre-Classical Latin, with far-reaching consequences on morphological developments (see Appendix C). The Romance languages have kept no traces of final *-m* except in a few monosyllabic words, in which this consonant turned into *n*, e.g., Latin *rem*, "thing," → French *rien;* Latin *cum* → Italian, Spanish *con*. (d) The occasional fall of final *-t*, particularly in conjugational endings, as evidenced in inscriptions and Pompeiian graffiti, as well as later Vulgar Latin documents. This consonant is largely lost in Italian and Spanish documents from the time these languages are first attested, but survives in French, even if it is no longer pronounced in the modern language except in liaison, as in *il est à la maison*, e.g., Latin *cantant*, "they sing," → Italian *cantano*, Spanish *cantan*, French *chantent*. (e) The fall of *n* before *s*, also attested in Pre-Classical inscriptions, as in *cosul* for *consul* (see Appendix B). It is said that

the well-known first century B.C. grammarian Varro pronounced *mesa* for *mensa,* a form that survives in Spanish, Portuguese *mesa,* French *moise,* "tie beam." (f) The reduction of certain consonant groups by assimilation of the first to the second consonant, as in Latin *septembris,* which appears in a third-century inscription from Italy as *settembris* (Italian *settembre*), or in *issa* for Latin *ipsa* on a Pompeiian graffito (Italian *essa,* "she"); in a similar vein, the Latin intervocalic *ct* [kt] and *x* [ks] groups are also reduced. We read *ottobres* for Latin *octobris* and *visit* for Latin *vixit* on inscriptions; cf. Italian *ottobre* and *visse,* "he (she, it) lived." For the vocalization of the palatal element in the Latin *ct* consonant group in French, Portuguese, and Spanish, see (3) above under "Spontaneous" and "Conditioned" Developments. It may be of interest to mention here a peculiar development of this intervocalic consonant group in Rumanian where *c* [k] turns into *p,* as in *lapte* from Latin *lacte* (Italian *latte*).

(6) The history of final *-s* is more complex. In Archaic Latin inscriptions this consonant is often omitted in the old masculine *-ŏs* (later *-ŭs*) ending; this is also reflected in metrics where *-s* is dropped after a short vowel before a word beginning with a consonant. The fact that final *-s* was an indispensable morphological marker no doubt contributed to its reestablishment in the Classical Latin period. Contrary to final *-m,* for instance, final *-s* appears to be quite stable in Post-Classical documents, even in such spontaneous outbursts of love, enthusiasm, hatred, and vengeance as the graffiti of Pompeii, which, like graffiti scribbled on the walls of restrooms and subway stations, would be more likely to reveal speech habits of the semi-literate. If this final consonant had disappeared in popular speech, it would surely be reflected in these texts. Documentary evidence, it would seem, is not of great help in ascertaining Romance trends in connection with this particular phenomenon. All we can say is that the whole Romance area is divided up into two halves with respect to final *-s:* the Iberian languages (Spanish, Portuguese, Catalan, and their dialects), the French and Provençal languages and their dialects, the northern Italian dialect area (which follows the French system in so many respects anyway), Rheto-Rumansh, and Sardinian all retain it, while central and southern Italian dialects (standard Italian being, in essence, based on central dialects) and Rumanian have discarded it. Italian and Rumanian, however, keep a reflex of final *-s* in monosyllabic words in the form of an *i,* as in Italian, Rumanian, *noi, voi,* from Latin *nōs* and *vōs.*

(7) The loss or retention of final *-s* is one of the important features in the development of the Romance languages. Two others that must especially be singled out are: (a) the weakening of intervocalic voiceless stops (*p, t, k*), also called *sonorization,* and (b) the phenomena subsumed under the general term of *palatalization.*

SONORIZATION OF INTERVOCALIC VOICELESS STOPS

(1) This phenomenon, which is essentially an assimilation of the intervocalic consonant to the sonority of surrounding vowels, is not pan-Romance; but it is very important because, like the treatment of final *-s,* it squarely divides the Romance language area into two parts, often referred to as the *Western* and the *Eastern.* The phenomenon of sonorization is only sporadically attested in

early Vulgar Latin documents and inscriptions, e.g., *imudavit* for *immūtāvit,* "he (she, it) has changed," *lebra* for *lepra,* "leprosy," *pagatus* for *pācātus,* "appeased," and a few others. Examples begin to multiply after the fall of the Empire (end of the fifth century) and appear with increasing frequency in Merovingian documents (northern France) of the seventh and eighth centuries.

(2) In the intervocalic position, the voiceless stops *p, t, k* tend to become the voiced counterparts *b, d, g.* In some cases they also lose their occlusion (the phenomenon called *spirantization,* i.e., articulation of the sound without interrupting the flow of breath, as in Spanish *saber,* pronounced with both lips closely brought together without complete closure) and even drop out altogether. Here are some typical examples illustrating this phenomenon:

Latin	Italian	Portuguese	Spanish	Old French	Modern French
sapĕre, "taste"	sapere	saber	saβer	saveir	savoir
mātūrum, "ripe"	maturo	maduro	maðuro	meür	mûr
sēcūrum, "sure"	sicuro	seguro	seɣuro	seür	sûr

Note: The symbols β, ð, ɣ in Spanish indicate spirantization.

(3) Similarly, when *p, t, k,* were followed by *r* or *l* (except the *cl* [kl] consonant group), they were also subject to sonorization:

Latin	Italian	Portuguese	Spanish	Old French	Modern French
capra, "goat"	capra	cabra	caβra	chievre	chèvre
pĕtra, "stone"	pietra	pedra	pieðra	pieðre (pierre)	pierre
lacrima, "tear"	lacrima	lagrima	laɣrima	lairme	larme

(4) It may be seen from these examples that literary Italian sets itself apart from its Western Romance sister languages in the treatment of intervocalic stops in that it closely reflects the Latin state of affairs. Since Rumanian goes pretty much hand in hand with Italian in this respect (e.g., Latin *sāpōnem,* "soap," → Italian *sapone,* Rumanian *săpun;* Latin *fŏcum* → Italian *fuoco,* Rumanian *foc,* as against Portuguese *sabão, fogo,* Spanish *jaβon, fueɣo,* French *savon, feu*), it has been customary to divide the Romance area into an Eastern and a Western part on the basis of this phenomenon also, the Western languages being those that customarily sonorize, spirantize, or drop voiceless stops (the same that also retain final *-s*), while the Eastern languages generally retain these consonants in their Latin state (and also drop final *-s*). Exceptions to this general trend are numerous, however, e.g., Italian *padre, madre, pagato, strada,* from Latin *patrem, mātrem, pācātum, strāta;* in many instances words displaying such "irregularities" are borrowed from dialects in which sonorization of intervocalic voiceless stops has occurred, specifically the northern Italian dialects. In French, intervocalic *k* sometimes turns into a *y* sound, rather than dropping out, e.g., *payer* from Latin *pācāre,* but this is due to the nature of the vowel that follows.

(5) Paralleling the sonorization of intervocalic voiceless stops, the original Latin *b, d, g* in this position also tend to weaken to the point of disappearance in many cases. Except for Spanish, where *b* becomes a spirant [*β*], in the other lan-

guages this consonant turns into a *v*, e.g., Latin *habēre* → Italian *avere*, Rumanian *aveá*, Portuguese *haver*, French *avoir*, but Spanish *haber*. As to original Latin *d* and *g*, they generally remain intact in Italian and Rumanian; *d* sometimes drops out in Spanish and Portuguese, as in Spanish *ver* and *fe*, Portuguese *vêr* and *fé*, from Latin *vidēre* and *fidem*, respectively, but it is only spirantized in Spanish *sudar*, "sweat," and (*des*)*nudo*, "naked," while the corresponding Portuguese forms, *suar* and *nú*, suggest greater propensity to drop this consonant, following the French example: *voir*, *foi*, *suer*, *nu*. An interesting phenomenon occurs in Provençal, which turns this intervocalic *d* into a *z* (*vezer* from Latin *vidēre*), probably by way of a spirantized *d*.

Original Latin *g* in this position is generally preserved in Rumanian, but in Italian it is sometimes dropped, as in *reale* from Latin *rēgālem* (cf. Spanish, Portuguese *real*), or *maestro* from Latin *magistrum* (Spanish *maestro*, French *maître*, Old French *maistre*); however, cf. Italian *legare* from Latin *ligāre*. Generally preserved as a spirant in Spanish [ɣ] and in Portuguese in its Latin form (*ligar, agosto*, in both languages), this consonant either drops out in French altogether (*lier*) or turns into a yod, as in *royal* from Latin *rēgālem* (Old French *reiel*).

(6) Latin intervocalic *s* was voiceless. It has remained thus in the so-called Eastern Romance languages, but it was sonorized in the Western ones to a *z* sound, except that around the sixteenth or seventeenth century it fell victim to a general devoicing trend in Castilian Spanish, so that *rosa* is now pronounced with a voiceless *s*, much like the Latin prototype. Speakers of standard Italian, particularly those from the North, are wont to give intervocalic *s* a *z* pronunciation also.

(7) Somewhat related to the weakening of intervocalic stops is the general simplification of double (geminated) consonants. Among the major Romance languages only Italian has kept them, as in *bella, fiamma, gatto, grosso, bocca*, from Latin *bella, flamma, cattum, grossum, bucca*. The others have reduced them to a single consonant, e.g., Rumanian *flamă, gros*, Spanish *boca, gato*, Old French *bele, flame*. (Note that in Modern French forms like *belle, flamme, année, terre*, etc., are merely imitations of Latin spelling; the double consonant is always pronounced as a single one.) The apparent predilection for geminates in Italian has also brought about the doubling of originally single Latin consonants, a trend that is occasionally attested in Post-Classical texts already, as in *acqua*, censured in the *Appendix Probi*, instead of Latin *aqua*; cf. Italian *acqua*, but Spanish *agua*, Portuguese *água*, French *eau*.

Palatalization

(1) Palatalization, in essence, may be defined as the shifting of the point of articulation of a sound into the palatal zone. While that of *l* and *n* (*ly* and *ny*), caused by a yod, as in Vulgar Latin *vinia* (pronounced *vinya*) or *filio* (pronounced *filyo*), is relatively easy to grasp, other phenomena of palatalization are much more complex and difficult to follow in detail. The most important and universal is unquestionably the palatalization of *k* and *g* before the front vowels

i and *e*. Except for a restricted area in central Sardinia, it has affected all Romance languages and dialects.

(2) In Classical Latin, both *k* (mostly written *c*) and *g* were pronounced like the initial sounds in English *kill* and *gill*. This is called a velar pronunciation and, hence, *k* and *g* are generally identified as *velar* consonants, although this is not quite accurate phonetically because before front vowels their point of articulation is on the *hard* rather than the *soft* palate, as would be the case before *o* and *u*. The fact is that in the course of sound evolution from Latin to Romance these consonants became quite unstable when followed by front vowels and fell an easy prey to assimilative influences exerted by the phonetic surrounding. It is very difficult, if not impossible, to determine at what point these "palatal" consonants began to shift toward the vowel which followed. Some scholars believe that by the third century the *k* in words like *cēna, caelum, cinque*, etc., had come to be pronounced with initial *ky* (*kyena*), subsequently moving forward to a *ty* stage (*tyena*), and eventually either to *tsh* or *ts*, depending on the particular region. The *ts* sound (as in *tsetse fly*) is only attested in the early stages of the major Western Romance languages, having been reduced to an *s* sound in French and Portuguese, in particular, while it shifted to a *th* (as in *thing*) in Castilian Spanish. Southern Spanish dialects, however, have followed the French/Portuguese example (*ts* → *s*), which is also characteristic of the Spanish spoken throughout Spanish America. Thus, Italian *cinque*, Rumanian *cinci* (with *tsh*), are opposed in treatment of *k* followed by *e* and *i* to French *cinq*, Portuguese *cinco* (with *s*) and Spanish *cinco* (with either *th* or *s*).

(3) Paralleling the development of *k* before *i* and *e* was the corresponding voiced "palatal" *g*. The first stage of development was presumably *gy*, moving subsequently to *dy* and eventually to either *dzh* (as in *judge*) or *dz*, the voiced equivalents of *tsh* and *ts*. Italian and Rumanian, as might be expected, have chosen *dzh*, as in Italian *genero*, Rumanian *ginere*, from Latin *gĕnerum;* but so did Old French and Old Portuguese, although in the modern languages this sound was reduced to *zh* (as in *measure*), e.g., French *gendre*, Portuguese *genro*. In Spanish, on the other hand, the *g* before stressed *i* and *e* became *y*, as in *yerno* (Latin *gĕnerum*) but otherwise disappeared, e.g., *hermano*, "brother," from Latin *germānum* (cf. French *germain*). The *dz* sound survives only in some northern Italian dialects.

(4) The development of initial *g* followed by front vowels happens to coincide with the results of the palatalization of initial *y*, as in Latin *jam*, "now," and *jānuārius*, "January," (Italian *già, gennaio*, Portuguese *já, janeiro*, French (*dé*)*jà, janvier*, but Spanish *ya, enero*), and initial *dy* (spelled *di*), as in Latin *diurnum*, "daily," (Italian *giorno*, Portuguese *jornada* [Vulgar Latin *diurnata*], French *jour*).

(5) In the northern part of Gaul and some Alpine regions, initial *k* and *g* also palatalized before *a* in a fashion similar to that of these consonants before front vowels. It would seem that in these regions *a* had a decidedly palatal quality which favored this process. By way of the same presumed intermediate stages of *ky* and *ty* the evolution reached the *tsh* and *ts* stages, except that French stopped at the former (Old French *chief*, pronounced *tshyef*), which was later reduced

to *sh* in Modern French *chef* from Latin *caput*. The nature of the following vowel (*a* or *e*) depends on whether the original Latin *a* is in free or checked position; thus, *chef* is opposed to *char* from Latin *carrum*.

Paralleling this development, *g* before *a* becomes *dzh* or *dz* in these same areas, e.g., French *jambe* from Latin *gamba*, "hoof," (notice the semantic shift from "hoof" to "leg").

The *ts* and *dz* developments are attested in Franco-Provençal and modern Provençal dialects only.

(6) Among the consonantal groups that underwent palatalization, the development of initial *pl*, *kl* (written *cl*), and *fl* is of interest, because it sets French apart from its Italian, Spanish, Portuguese, and Rumanian relatives, not on account of its innovation but rather its conservatism, since it has retained these groups intact with respect to Latin. For instance, in Latin *plēnum*, *clāmāre*, and *flamma*, Italian turns the *l* consonant of the group into *y* (*pieno*, *chiamare*, *fiamma*); Spanish palatalizes the *l* and drops the initial consonant (*lleno*, *llamar*, *llama*); Portuguese turns the group into a *sh* sound (*cheio*, *chamar*, *chama*); Rumanian palatalizes the *l* only in the *kl* group (*chemá*, pronounced *kyemá*), keeping *pl* and *fl* otherwise intact (*plin*, *flamă*); the corresponding French forms are *plein*, *clamer*, and *flamme*. (Within a word, as was seen earlier, French also palatalizes the *kl* group, as do the others, as in *oeil* from Vulgar Latin *oclo*.)

(7) There are many palatalizations of consonant groups in word interior position. Typical are *k* and *t* followed by a semivowel, as in Vulgar Latin *facia*, "face," (Classical Latin *faciēs*), which becomes French *face*, Italian *faccia*, Spanish *haz* (pronounced *fas*, *fatsha*, *ath*), through a process that is identical to the palatalization of *k* before front vowels, and Latin *fortia*, "strong," (plural of *forte*), which gives rise to French *force*, Spanish *fuerza*, Italian *forza* (with *ts* rather than *tsh*). Between vowels, the *ti* [ty] group becomes a voiced *z* sound in French, as in *oraison* from Latin *orātiōnem*.

Details concerning the phenomena of palatalization alluded to in the preceding paragraphs are many and can hardly be dealt with in a few pages. It is, after all, one of the most significant developments in the evolution of the Latin sound structure into Romance. For further information on this particular subject and the vowel and consonant developments in general, the reader is referred to the manuals mentioned at the end of Appendix C.

Note on the Simplification and Voicing
of Intervocalic Consonants

BY MARIO PEI

The most widespread and noticeable feature in Romance consonantal development is without doubt the progressive weakening of consonants in the intervocalic position, coupled with the almost universal tendency to simplify Latin double consonants in the same position; so that an original Latin group *-atta-* tends to become *-ata-*, while original *-ata-* tends to go in successive stages to *-ada-*, then to *-aða-*, and ultimately, with complete fall of the consonant, to *-aa-*.

For these twin phenomena, various explanations have been offered, of which the most common is that the speakers tend to follow a line of least resistance, or what might be styled "economy of articulatory effort." What leads the speakers to seek this economy of articulatory effort? Is it laziness or carelessness pure and simple, or is there another underlying cause?

Most linguists are agreed in attributing the widespread changes in the vowel system to the stress accent tendency, which, by concentrating vocal effort on the stressed vowel in the word, causes it to lengthen and break into a diphthong, or otherwise alter its nature, while it reduces the vocal energy available for other vowels in the word, which accordingly are weakened, blurred, shortened, and ultimately dropped.

It is my belief that the stress accent also supplies the phonetic explanation for the reduction of double consonants to singles, and for the weakening of single consonants from unvoiced to voiced plosives, then to voiced fricatives, ultimately to their complete fall, in a progression that runs parallel with the weakening of unstressed vowels; while at the same time the stressed vowel in the word, receiving an increased concentration of vocal effort, lengthens to the point of breaking into a diphthong, like a thin strip of metal subjected to constant hammering that finally breaks in two. This makes the entire process a case of conservation of energy, operative in phonetics as in physics.

If the original unvoiced or voiced plosive is double, it weakens by simplifying, which requires less vocal effort (-*ata*- is easier to handle than -*atta*-, which calls for a break in the breath stream followed by a brief holding period before the consonant is released).

In the case of original -*ata*-, the -*t*- is (a) unvoiced, (b) plosive. The vowels on either side are both voiced sounds and continuants. The consonant tries to assimilate itself to the all-important stressed vowel, and the first step in this assimilation is to make the vibration of the vocal cords continuous, instead of interrupting and then resuming it; therefore, -*t*- changes to -*d*-, which is, like the vowels surrounding it, voiced. But -*d*- is still a plosive, albeit voiced; this means that another interruption remains, this time in the breath stream rather than in the vocal cords, between the continuant -*a*- and the voiced plosive -*d*-, and between the latter and the second continuant -*a*-. This can be eliminated by shifting from -*d*- to -ð-, which is a fricative, and therefore a continuant, like the vowels. Now we have three contiguous phonemes which are all both voiced sounds and continuants, calling for no break, either in the vibration of the vocal cords or in the breath stream, but only for modifications in the point of articulation. If we want to concentrate still more of our limited vocal energy on the stressed vowel, the only other thing we can do is to eliminate the consonant altogether, and remain with nothing but contiguous vowels. So in the case of a language with maximum stress accent, like French, we have the following sequences: -*atta*- to -*ata*-; -*ata*- to -*ada*- to -*aða*- to -*aa*- (*amāta* to *amada* to *ameðe* to *aimeé;* or popular Spanish *amatum* to *amado* to *amaðo* to *amao*).

In the case of labials, we have -*appa*- to -*apa*-; -*apa*- to -*aba*- to -*ava*- or -*aβa*-; but seldom to -*aa*- (*rīpa* to *riba* to French *rive,* Italian *riva,* Spanish *riβa*). In the case of velars, the progression is -*akka*- to -*aka*-; -*aka*- to -*aga*- to -*aɣa*- to -*aįa*-

(*pācāre* to Italian *pagare*, Spanish *payar*, French *payer; advocātum* to Spanish *aβoyaδo*, French *avoué*).

If we start with a voiced plosive in Latin, we have a better chance of reaching the zero stage (°*dormībat* to Italian *dormiva*, archaic *dormia*, Spanish *dormía*, Old French *dormeiet*, Modern French *dormait; scrībō, caballum*, to Rumanian *scriu, cal*); and still more if we start with a voiced fricative (*rivum* to Spanish *río*).

This theory offers a cause for the "economy of effort" on the part of the speakers. They are trying to make things easier for themselves, but not out of sheer sloth or carelessness; rather, because of a redistribution of vocal energy, of which they have only a limited supply. If they use too much of it on the stressed vowel, not only will all unstressed vowels suffer (some more than others, depending on their position) but also the more exposed (i.e., intervocalic) consonants. It is no accident that a language that shows the greatest degree of diphthongization of stressed vowels, like French, likewise shows the greatest degree of weakening and fall of unstressed vowels, and of weakening and occasional fall of exposed consonants.

The situation naturally varies from one language to another, at different historical periods, and in accordance with the nature of the surrounding vowels involved (front or back). It is of interest, however, that the two languages, French and Spanish, that have the highest degree of spontaneous diphthongization also show the highest degree of simplification and voicing of intervocalic consonants, while the Romance variety that has no diphthongization, Sardinian, has the lowest rate of simplification and voicing. Of special interest is the case of Rumanian, which has a low percentage of spontaneous diphthongization. It does not voice intervocalic consonants, save for the fall of -*b*- and -*v*-, but it does show universal reduction of Latin double consonants to singles. Italian, also with a low rate of spontaneous diphthongization, shows simplification and doubling of intervocalic consonants in approximately the same degree, as likewise voicing and resistance to voicing. Here the mixture of dialectal influences that go into the standard language is probably the cause of the confusion. Provençal and Portuguese, both lacking spontaneous diphthongization, display simplification and sonorization to a degree that is intermediate between that of Sardinian, Italian, and Rumanian and that of French and Spanish.

Further study of dialectal varieties and of subsidiary factors in phonological development is in order before this theory can be offered in final form.[1]

---

1. For the development, and particularly the diphthongization, of stressed vowels in the major Romance groups, see Mario Pei, "A New Methodology for Romance Classification," in *Studies in Romance Philology and Literature*, Chapel Hill, N.C., 1963.

Appendix F

Vulgar Latin Texts from Spain and Italy

Two Texts from Northern Spain (A.D. 905)

. . . testes qui in ista carta rovoraturi estis, cognosite quia fecimus ea . . . ("[you] witnesses who are about to sign this document, know that we made it out")

Rovoraturi for *roboraturi* shows progression of *b* between vowels to *v; cognosite* for *cognoscite* may indicate palatalization; *ea* shows fall of final *-m;* the construction *quia fecimus* after a verb of knowing, replacing Latin accusative with infinitive, is typical of Romance.

Dum essere pausati in domo istius Gundefredo presentes fuimus . . . ("While we were guests at the house of this [man] Gundefredus, we were present [i.e., witnessed a signature].")

The verb form *essere* has replaced *esse*, which is normal for French or Italian (while Spanish *ser* is derived from Latin *sedere*); *pausati* is reminiscent of Spanish *posada*, "inn," "resting-place"; *dum* followed by the infinitive (rather than the present indicative to denote continued action in the past time) is indicative of syntactical confusion; *in* is not used with *domo* in Classical Latin (but cf. Spanish *en casa de*, "at the house of"); *Gundefredo* is a form in *-o* used in the genitive function, for the expected form in *-i* (*Gundefredi*), while *istius* is a correct Latin genitive.

Short Text from Northern Spain (A.D. 916)

Sit tivi concessum ("Let it be granted to you")

Tivi for *tibi* shows *b* between vowels progressing to *v*, probably indicating spirantization (see Appendix E, The Consonant System), cf. *rovoraturi*, above; *sit concessum* (literally "let it have been granted to you," where the Classical tongue would use *concedatur*) shows the new Romance formation of the present passive.

Five Short Texts from Italy

(1) From a Lucca document (A.D. 746)

de uno latum decorre via publica nomero quindeci ("on one side runs public highway number 15")

Here there is obvious confusion between ablative *latere* and nominative-accusative *latus*, compounded by the substitution of *-um* for *-us,* indicating possible fall of final *-m* and *-s* (Italian *lato*, Spanish *lado*, Old French *lez*, all deriving from *latus*); *decorre* is good Italian for Latin *decurrit,* with fall of final *-t, e* replacing unstressed *i, o* replacing stressed short *u,* as happens also in *nomero* for Latin *numero* (Italian *numero* is learned; the popular development is shown by *novero*, "number"). Compare an acceptable Latin *de uno latere decurrit via publica numero quindecim* with Italian *da un lato decorre (la) via pubblica numero quindici,* and it will be evident why there is sometimes difficulty in determining whether the language is very late Vulgar Latin or very early Italian.

(2) From a Lucca document (A.D. 765)

. . . duo congia de pulmentario faba et panico mixto, bene spisso, et condito de uncto aut oleo ("two measures of relish of broad beans and millet, mixed, quite thick, and dressed with fat or oil")

Here we have new syntactical conditions with the old genitive case replaced either by the noun in single-case form (*faba, panico*), or by *de* with the single-case form (*de pulmentario*). The construction with *de* is also used where the Classical language would have used the ablative, either alone or with *in* (*condito de uncto*). The use of a neuter plural form (*congia*) for a masculine noun develops into a fairly frequent process in early Italian (*le mura, le focora*).

(3) From an Abruzzian document (A.D. 819)

ego Paulo homo liver filio quondam Lupi et abitatur locus qui bocatur Quintianu . . . intus sagrosanctu altaro me hoffero . . . sicut et alis monachi me hobligo . . . ut hubicunque me inbenire potuerit monacho Sancti Benedicti potestate me habeas de prendere in lligamen ("I, Paul, a free man, son of the deceased Lupus and inhabiting a place which is called Quintianus . . . offer myself within the holy altar . . . like the other monks I bind myself . . . that wherever a monk of Saint Benedict may find me (you) may have power to take me into bonds" [this presumably in case he leaves the monastery and is sought and found.])

Here we have *-o* forms in the nominative singular masculine, alternating with *-u* in the accusative; *alis monachi* showing alternation of *-i* and *-is* in the plural; survival of Latin genitive forms in proper names (these continue into early Italian); survival of Latin passive forms (*abitatur, bocatur*).

(4) From a Nocera document (A.D. 850)

. . . per longu passi sidici et gubita trea et pede unu ("in length sixteen paces, three ells, and one foot")

Noteworthy in this brief passage is the use of a second declension nominative for the Classical accusative plural (*passi* for *passus*), evidencing the shift of fourth declension nouns to those of the second declension (see Appendix C, Nouns).

(5) The Verona riddle of the eighth or ninth century:

separeba boves alba pratalia araba & albo versorio teneba & negro semen semi-naba ("it separated the oxen, plowed white fields, and held a white steering rope, and sowed black seed")

The reference is to a writing hand, whose fingers (oxen) are parted, guiding the white quill (steering rope) to plow white parchment (fields) and writing with black ink (sowing black seed). While this passage favors Vulgar Latin rather than Italian, it shows fall of final -*t* in verb forms; also -*o* endings for masculine singular nouns in the accusative function; *boves*, however, is a Latin plural.

This undecided state of affairs (Vulgar Latin versus Italian) continues into the ninth and early tenth centuries, while in France documents appear which are unmistakably French, not Latin.

Appendix G

Analyses of the Language of Selected Passages from Early French, Spanish, and Italian Texts

FRENCH

Oaths of Strasbourg

Pro Deo amur et pro cristian poblo et nostro commun salvament, d'ist di in avant, in quant Deus savir et podir me dunet, si salvarai eo cist meon fradre Karlo, et in aiudha et in cadhuna cosa, si cum om per dreit son fradra salvar dift, in o quid il mi altresi fazet; et ab Ludher nul plaid nunquam prindrai qui, meon vol, cist meon fradre Karle in damno sit.

("For the love of God and for the safety of the Christian people and our own common safety, insofar as God grants me the knowledge and the power [to know and to be able], so will I assist this my brother Charles, both in help and in all things, as one by justice should assist his brother, provided he does the same with me; and with Lothair I shall never make any pact which, of my will, may be to the detriment of this my brother Charles.")

(a) Vowels of the final syllable, already quite weak in the Late Vulgar Latin of this region, have fallen, save where they survive in French (feminine nouns ending in *-a*, which in French turns to *-e*; or those needed to support a previous troublesome consonant cluster; but final *-a* has not yet become *-e*, at least in writing [*aiudha, cadhuna cosa*], save in *fazet* from *faciat*, while the supporting vowel indicates an orthographic uncertainty that probably reflects an indefinite schwa sound [*poblo, nostro, damno, fradre* and *fradra, Karlo* and *Karle*], as in the first vowel of English *about*). (b) Stressed vowels are still in their Vulgar Latin state (*amur* for *amore, cristian, poblo, savir* and *podir* for *sapere* and *potere*, respectively, *dunat* for *donat, cosa* for *causa*); stressed *a* in free position does not yet show the later change to *e* (*cristian, fradre*); there is no indication of the later diphthongization of Latin free short *e* to *ie* (*Deo*), or of free short *o* to *uo, ue,* ultimately *eu* (= *ö*), or of long *o* to *ou* (*amur*), or of long *e* to *ei* (*savir, podir*); the diphthongs that appear (*dreit, plaid*) owe their *i* to the palatalization of an original velar in *directum, placitum.* (c) Intervocalic consonants have progressed from unvoiced to voiced plosives; voiced plosives to voiced fricatives or to complete fall (*populo* to *poblo; ab ante* to *avant; sapere, potere,* to *savir, podir; fratrem* to *fradre; ego* to *eo*); the *dh* spelling in *aiudha* from *adjuta, cadhuna* from *kata una, Ludher* from *Lotharium,* is probably indicative of further progression from *t* to *d* to ð, the sound of *th* in English *this.* (d) Assibilation of Latin *ci* plus vowel to *ts* is indicated in *fazet* from *faciat.* (e) Probable nasalization in *meon* from *meum.* (f) *Cosa* indicates typical French palatalization of *c* before *a,* which had to take place before the *au* of *causa* became *o.*

Structurally, we find the Old French two-case system for masculine nouns in operation, with nominative (*Deus*) opposed to a general oblique case used in the function of a genitive (*Deo*), ablative (*amur, cristian poblo, nostro commun salvament, ist di, Ludher, damno*), accusative (*fradre Karlo, dreit, plaid*), dative (*fradre Karle*). The new French future appears in *salvarai* (from *salvare habeo*), *prindrai* (from *prehendere habeo*). The new French demonstrative appears in *cist* (from *ecce* or *hic istum* or *isto*).

In vocabulary, Old French *ab* replaces Latin *cum; savir* (from *sapere*), *podir* (from *potere*), replace *scire, posse;* Greek *kata* plus *una* replaces *quisque. Avant* from *ab ante, altresi* from *alterum sic,* are new Romance formations. *Om* (from *homo,* "man") is used in the sense of French *on.*

Sequence of St. Eulalia

Buona pulcella fut Eulalia, / Bel avret corps, bellezour anima.
Voldrent la veintre li Deo inimi, / Voldrent la faire diavle servir.
Elle non eskoltet les mals conseilliers, / Qu'elle Deo raneiet chi maent sus en ciel.
Ne por or ned argent ne paramenz, / Por manatce regiel ne preiement;
Niule cose non la pouret omque pleier / La polle sempre non amast lo Deo
    menestier.

> ("Eulalia was a good girl, / She had a beautiful body, a more beautiful soul. / The enemies of God wanted to overcome her, / Wanted to make her serve the devil. She does not listen to the evil counselors / That she should renounce God Who dwells up in heaven. Neither for gold nor silver nor attire, / For royal threat or entreaty; Nothing could ever bend her / So that she would not continue to love God's service.")

In this poem, nearly half a century after the Oaths of Strasbourg, we find the following: (a) Latin free stressed *a* has turned into French *e* (*presentede* from *presentata*). (b) Diphthongization of free Latin short *e* to *ie* (*ciel* from *caelum*), and free short *o* to *uo*, later progressing to *ue* → *eu* [= ö], (*buona* from *bona*); Latin long free *e* has gone on to *ei*, later *oi*, (*concreidre* from *concredere*), and long *o* to *ou*, later *eu*, (*bellezour* from *bellatiorem*). (c) All final vowels have fallen save for *-a*, which still appears as *-a* (*buona, pulcella, anima*), but now more often as *-e* (*auret* from *habuerat, elle* from *illa, eskoltet* from *auscultat*). (d) Progression of intervocalic unvoiced plosives to voiced is in evidence (*presentede, spede,* from *presentata, spata*), as are assibilation (*czo* from *ecce hoc,* later spelled *ço,* still later *ce*), and typically French palatalization of *c* before *a* (*chielt* from *calet, chief* from *caput*); but graphic uncertainty appears where *chose* is spelled *kose* and *qui* is spelled *chi.*

The Old French two-case system for masculine nouns is in evidence throughout, with the oblique case used in genitive function (*li Deo inimi* for *illi Dei inimici*) but also in the accusative (*lo Deo menestier*). We also have here the full appearance of the Old French definite article (*li, les, la, lo*). Old French is definitely on its way by the end of the ninth century.

Valenciennes or Jonah Fragment (Latin forms in roman type; French forms in italics)

Dunc, co dicit, Ionas profeta habebat *mult laboret e mult penet a cel populum; e* faciebat *grant iholt, et eret mult las* et preparavit Dominus *un edre sore sen cheve, quet umbre li fesist e repauser s'i podist* . . . *e cum cilg eedre fu seche, si vint grancesmes iholt* super caput Ione . . .

> ("Then it says this, Jonah the prophet had greatly labored and greatly suffered with those people, and it was very warm, and he was very tired, and God prepared an ivy over his head, that it might make shade for him and he could rest there . . . and when that ivy was dry, there came a very great heat over Jonah's head.")

(a) *Dunc,* from *deumquam,* goes on later to *donc.* (b) *Co* represents the same word and presumably the same pronunciation as *czo* in the *Eulalia;* it will eventually become *ce.* (c) *Mult,* from *multum,* is the regular Old French word for "much," "very," replaced later by *beaucoup, très.* (d) *Cilg* and *cel* show the typical French demonstrative adjective; the first represents the masculine nominative, more commonly spelled *cil,* the latter the oblique case. (e) Other features of interest are: *grant* from *grandem; iholt,* a curious spelling for *chalt,* later *chaud,* "hot," from *calidum; eret* from Latin *erat,* later replaced by *esteiet, était,* from *stabat,* "stood"; *edre, eedre,* come from *hederum* (instead of *hedera,* which is a feminine noun in Latin); *eedre* may indicate an attempt to show the initial stage in the diphthongization of Latin free short *e* (*hederum* → *edre, eedre, iedre;* ultimately, with fusion with the preceding article, *illum hederum* → *lierre*); *grancesmes* showing continued survival of the Latin superlative *grandissimus.*

ITALIAN

Montecassino Testimonial Formulas

Capua, 960: *Sao ko kelle terre per kelle fini que ki contene trenta anni le possette parte Sancti Benedicti*

Sessa, 963: *Sao cco kelle terre per kelle fini que tebe monstrai Pergoaldi foro que ki contene et trenta anni le possette*

Teano, 963: *Kella terra per kelle fini qi bobe mostrai Sancte Marie e et trenta anni la posset parte Sancte Marie*

Teano, 963: *Sao cco kelle terre per kelle fini que tebe mostrai trenta anni le possette parte Sancte Marie*

Capua, 960:   ("I know that those lands within those boundaries which here contains [which are described herein] the Party [Monastery] of Saint Benedict owned them for thirty years.")

Sessa, 963:   ("I know that those lands within those boundaries which I showed you were of [belonged to] Pergoaldus, which here contains [which are described herein], and he owned them for thirty years.")

Teano, 963:   ("That land within those boundaries which I showed you is of Saint Mary, and the Party [Monastery] of Saint Mary owned it for thirty years.")

Teano, 963:   ("I know that those lands within those boundaries which I showed you the Party [Monastery] of Saint Mary owned them for thirty years.")

The following features are of interest in these texts: (a) The typical Italian system of plural endings, -i for masculines, -e for feminines, -i for third declension nouns (*anni, kelle terre, fini*). (b) The Italian fall of final -t (*contene, possette*). (c) The Italian feminine plural object pronoun *le*. (d) The absence of diphthongization in *contene* and the fall of *u* in *ko* (from Latin *quod*, "that") and *kelle* (for Italian *quelle*) may be attributed to the local dialect (southern); conversely, *sao* (from Latin *sapio*, "I know," later developing to Italian *so*) shows a more northern development: Latin *sapio* becomes *saccio* in the Neapolitan region, but *saio, sao, so*, in more northern dialects. (e) The expression *parte sancti Benedicti* may be a Latinism, like *parte sancte Marie* in two of the other documents, a survival of the Classical genitive in stereotyped formulas; but the Sessa document has a Latin genitive even for an unadorned personal name (*Pergoaldi*, "of Pergoaldus"). Such Latin genitive forms for proper names appear sporadically later in Old Italian and may be the source of Italian family names in -i (e.g., *Petri, Tondi, Vivaldi*). (f) The verb form *foro* (from Latin *fŭĕrunt* for *fuĕrunt*) is a more exact phonetic development than the later Italian *furon(o)*. (g) The forms *tebe* and *bobe* come from Latin *tibi* and *vobis*, respectively, while *mostrai* is the normal Italian development of the Latin perfect *monstravi*, "I have shown."

Umbrian Confession Formula

Me accuso de lu genitore meu et de la genitrice mia, et de li proximi mei, ke ce non abbi quella dilectione ke me senior Dominideu commandao . . . de la decema et de la primitia et de offertione, ke nno la dei siccomo far dibbi . . . Et qual bene tu hai factu ui farai en quannanti, ui altri farai pro te, si sia computatu em pretiu de questa penitentia. Se ttou judiciu ene ke tu ad altra penitentia no poze accorrere . . . si sie tu rappresentatu ante conspectu Dei, ke lu diabolu no te nde poza accusare . . .

("I accuse myself of my father and my mother, and of my relatives, that I did not have for them that love that my lord God commanded . . . of the tithe and the first fruits and the offering, that I did not give it as I should have done . . ." "And whatever good you have done or will do henceforth, or another will do for you, may it be counted as the price of this penance

. . . so that you may be represented before the presence of God, so that the devil may not accuse you of it.")

Of interest are the following: (a) The -*u* ending in noun forms as against the -*o* ending in verbs; the -*u* ending is scantily used today in Umbria. (b) The verb forms *abbi, dibbi,* indicating older developments from Latin *habui, debui* (modern Italian *ebbi, dovei*). (c) Strictly phonetic development from the Latin originals in *meu, mei, ttou;* note also *mia* from Latin *mēa* and the shortened *me* in *me senior.* (d) *Inde,* often combined with the verb (*pregonde la sua sancta misericordia,* "I ask for His divine mercy," elsewhere in the Formula), appears as *nde,* ultimately becoming *ne* in Modern Italian, e.g., *ve ne prego,* "I ask you (of it)"; cf. French *je vous en prie.* (e) A curious shift from -*t* to -*i* in *ui* from Latin *aut,* "or." (f) The verb form *commandao* showing the intermediate stage between Latin *commandavit,* "he has ordered," and Modern Italian *comandò.* (g) Finally, the singular form *altri* which shows a formation analogical to that of *egli,* and the singular demonstrative pronouns *questi* and *quegli,* from a Vulgar Latin masculine singular *illī,* replacing Classical *ille.*

SPANISH

From the *Glossary of San Millán*

. . . *Et ecce repente* [*lueco*] *unus de* . . . *et suscitabi* [*lebantai*] . . . *et suscitabi* [*lebantavi*] *conmotiones* [*moveturas*] . . . *et submersi* [*trastorné*] *nabes* . . . *Et tertius veniens* [*elo terzero diabolo venot*]. . . . *Indica* [*amuestra*] *mici.* . . . *Et inveniebit* [*aflarat*] *illum* . . . *non nobis sufficit* [*non convienet anobis*] *quod.* . . . *siquis* [*qualbis uemne*]. . . . *Ayt enim apostolus* [*zerte dicet don Paulo apostolo*] *quia* . . . *vide quid agas* [*ke faras*]. . . .

"And behold, suddenly [then] one of the . . . and I aroused movements (commotions) . . . I submerged ships. . . . And the third (one) coming [the third devil came]. . . . He shows me. . . . And he will find him . . . it does not suffice us [does not suit us] that . . . if anyone [whatever man]. . . . For the apostle says [indeed Saint Paul the apostle says] . . . take heed of what you will do."

. . . *adjubante domino nostro Iesu Christu cui est honor et imperium cum patre et spiritu sancto in secula seculorum* ("with the help of our Lord Jesus Christ, to Whom is honor and dominion with the Father and the Holy Ghost in the centuries of centuries")

The glossary reads as follows: *cono aiutorio de nuestro dueno, dueno Cristo, dueno salbatore, qual dueno get ena honore, e qual duenno tienet ela mandatione cono Patre, cono Spiritu Sancto, enos sieculos de lo sieculos* ("with the help of our Lord, Lord Christ, Lord Savior, which Lord is in the honor, and which Lord holds the command with the Father, with the Holy Ghost, in the centuries of the centuries")

In these samples we find the following: (a) Full Castilian diphthongization of Latin stressed short *e* and short *o* in both open and closed syllables (*lueco, amuestra, convienet, uemne, nuestro, dueno, tienet, sieculos*). (b) Final vowels that have resisted fall, as is normal in Spanish. (c) No passage of unvoiced plosives to voiced (*moveturas, aiutorio, sieculos,* though Latin *adjutorium,* "help," loses intervocalic *d*), which may be due to a dialectal influence from the neighboring Rioja region, where intervocalic -*p*-, -*t*-, -*k*- plosives have remained unchanged to this day. (d) Initial Latin *f* has not yet turned to *h* (*faras*), nor *fl* to *ll* (*aflarat*). (e) Final -*s* is kept. (f) Final -*t*, which later falls, here disappears only occasionally (*amuestra* versus *tienet, aflarat*). (g) Assibilation of *c* before *e* is indicated by *zerte*. (h) Palatalization of Latin *mn* consonant group seems indicated by *duenno* from *dom'num* (syncopated form of Latin *dominum*); cf. Spanish *dueño.*

In the area of morphology: (a) The Spanish single case for both singular and plural nouns appears throughout (-*o*, -*a*, -*e*; -*os*, -*as*, -*es*). (b) There is fluctuation in the ending of the first singular perfect (*levantavi, lebantai, trastorné,* the latter representing the modern Spanish outcome). (c) Future forms are Spanish (*aflarat, faras,* from *adflare habet* and *facere habes,* respectively). (d) The definite article, derived from *ille,* still keeps the initial vowel (*elo, ela*), but contracts with prepositions in a fashion later retained by Portuguese (*cono, eno, enos,* where modern Spanish would have *con lo, en lo,* and *en los*). (e) Finally, the form *get* (to be pronounced *yet*) from Latin *est* is probably an attempt to represent the initial diphthong *ie* (from stressed Latin short *e*) in this verb form. It is an old form current in the dialect of Rioja and other Spanish dialects but not in Castilian proper, in which it was and still is *es,* "he (she, it) is."

Appendix H

Samples from Medieval Romance Poetry

These works are identified in Part II, Chapter 7, Medieval Romance Languages and the Rise of Romance Literatures.

Chanson de Roland

As the story opens, Charlemagne has conquered all of Spain except the city of Zaragoza, where the Moslem king Marsile still holds out:

> Charles li reis, nostre emperedre magnes,
> Set ans toz pleins at estet en Espaigne;
> Tres qu'en la mer conquist la tere altaigne.
> Chastel ni at ki devant lui remaignet,
> Murs ne citet n'i est remes a fraindre
> Fors Sarragoce qu'est en une montaigne;
> Li reis Marsilies la tient, ki Deu nen aimet,
> Mahomet sert ed Apollin reclaimet:
>   Nes poet guarder que mals ne l'i ataignet!
> ("Our ancient lord and leader Charlemagne
> In seven years had conquered all of Spain.
> From sea to sea he won that haughty land.
> His catapults no castle could withstand.
> Before his onset yielded every town
> Save Zaragoza, whence Marsile looked down
> Upon a land, ravaged and torn by war,
> That hated Christ, and Allah did adore.
> Mohammed's aid he sought, to vent his hate,
>   But no wise could escape impending fate.")

Marsile is sorely troubled, and calls a council of his emirs. His counsellor Blancandrin advises that a peace embassy be sent to Charlemagne, with an offer of submission. If Charlemagne departs from Spain, Marsile will follow him to his capital city of Aix, in France, take the oath of fealty, and be converted to Christianity. Once the Frankish host is out of Spain, says Blancandrin, it will never return. True, the hostages they must give to Charlemagne as pledges of their good faith will die. But better that than utter defeat and ruin. The embassy starts on its journey, with cunning Blancandrin at its head.

Charlemagne, having listened to the peace offer, calls a meeting of his barons. Roland, the firebrand, at once urges rejection of the peace overtures, but Ganelon rises to voice his opposition. He points out that the army is weary, and the offer undoubtedly sincere. His counsel prevails. Now a Frankish ambassador must be sent back with Blancandrin to Marsile's court. Who shall be appointed? The mission is a dangerous one. On a previous occasion, Marsile has slain Frankish envoys sent to him in good faith by Charlemagne. Roland, Oliver, Turpin, the emperor's chief counsellor, Duke Naimon, offer themselves in turn. Charlemagne shakes his head. He cannot spare them. Then Roland suggests the name of Ganelon, the man who has urged appeasement. Ganelon is incensed. Why should Roland, of all men, pick him out for the thankless task, thereby marking him as expendable? But the council approves the choice. Ganelon accepts, but in the presence of the emperor and all the barons he swears vengeance against Roland and his supporters.

As they ride toward Zaragoza, Blancandrin persuades Ganelon, who does not require much persuasion, to betray the Christian cause.

Riding back to Charlemagne, Ganelon informs his liege lord that all conditions have been accepted. The Franks joyfully prepare to leave Spain. But as they approach the mountain passes of the Pyrenees, the choice of a commander for the rearguard becomes imperative. If the Moslems are inclined to treachery, the rearguard will bear the brunt of their attack. Now Ganelon triumphantly suggests Roland for the post. Roland feels honored, and proudly accepts. Charlemagne is worried, and offers him additional forces; these Roland haughtily rejects.

The bulk of the army begins its long march across the pass. Meanwhile, Marsile, in accordance with the plan conceived by Ganelon, gathers all his forces to fall upon the Frankish rearguard. The battle is joined at the pass, but not until Oliver has repeatedly voiced his plea to Roland to sound his horn so that Charlemagne, hearing it, may be warned of the danger and lead back the main body of the host to rescue his rearguard. Foolhardy Roland contemptuously dismisses this plea. "We alone suffice to take care of all the Moslems!" he boasts. "Never, by God, or His Saints, or His Angels, shall my clan be disgraced because I called for help!"

In the series of bloody encounters that follow, Roland's twenty thousand Franks perform prodigies of valor, but they are finally overwhelmed by the vastly superior Moslem forces. Roland sounds the horn at last; the emperor turns back and rides at full speed to the aid of his nephew. But it is too late for Charlemagne to save the men of his rearguard. He can only avenge them.

On the battlefield, Roland dies, after vainly trying to destroy his sword so it shall not fall into enemy hands:

> "E! Durendal, bone si mare fustes!
> Quant jo mei pert, de vos nen ai mais cure!"

(" 'Good Durendal, of what avail to me?
Since I must die, it's time to set you free!' ")

Charlemagne arrives on the scene, pursues the fleeing Moslems, destroys them, takes Zaragoza, then returns to the field of slaughter to mourn his dead:

"Amis Rodlanz, jo m'en irai en France:
Com jo serai a Lodon en ma chambre,
De plusor regnes vendront li home estrange.
Demanderont: 'O est li quens chataignes?'
Jo lor dirai qu'il est morz en Espaigne.
A grant dolor tendrai puis mon reialme.
    Jamais n'iert jorz que ne plor ne nem plaigne!"
(" 'My nephew fair, when I return to France
Reproachful eyes will meet my every glance.
Strange men will come to me from far-off lands
And ask upon what foreign, doleful strands
I left my best and doughtiest capitain.
I shall reply that you lie dead in Spain!
My kingdom I shall hold with bitter grief.
    May life for me be mercifully brief!' ")

The conquest of Spain is completed, and Charlemagne at last returns to his capital. There Aude, sister of Oliver and Roland's betrothed, meets him and inquires what fate has befallen her dear ones. Charlemagne replies that they are dead. He offers her the hand of his own son as compensation for the man she has lost; but Aude proudly rejects the offer. She falls dead at the emperor's feet.

Now Charlemagne brings up Ganelon for trial. But though the count's guilt is apparent, he has found a champion in the person of one of his kinsmen, Pinabel. But the emperor has also found a champion in Thierry of Anjou. In single combat, Thierry slays Pinabel, and Ganelon is condemned to die, drawn apart by four swift steeds, like the traitor he is:

Hom ki traist altre, n'en est dreiz qu'il s'en vant!
("He who betrays another may not boast!")

Cantar de myo Cid

The following passage tells of the Cid's original unjust exile:

De los sos oios tan fuerte mientre lorando
Tornaua la cabeça & estaua los catando.
Vio puertas abiertas & vços sin cañados,
Alcandaras uazias sin pielles & sin mantos,
E sin falcones & sin adtores mudados.
Sospiro myo Çid, ca mucho auie grandes cuydados.
Fablo myo Çid bien & tan mesurado:
"Grado ati, señor padre, que estas en alto!
Esto me an buelto myos enemigos malos."
("His sad eyes peered about him, and his cheeks were wet with tears;

His head he kept on turning, in his heart were bitter fears.
The doors he saw were open, and the shutters had no locks.
The houses bare and empty, and the fields without their flocks.
No hunting-hawks or falcons graced the stands that once were filled.
The Chieftain sighed with sorrow, for his fondest hopes were killed.
He spoke in measured accents low and sadly raised his eyes:
'I thank You, Father, Lord of all, Who art up in the skies!
My evil foes have conquered me, and this Thou has allowed!' ")

Another brief passage describes the Cid's departure for the campaign against the Moors, and his leave-taking from his beloved wife:

La oraçion fecha, la missa acabada la an.
Salieron de la eglesia, ya quieren cabalgar.
El Çid a dona Ximena yva la abraçar.
Dona Ximena al Çid la manol va besar,
Lorando de los oios, que non sabe que se far.
("The prayer is completed, and the final Mass is said.
They're ready for the battle, and are willing to be led.
The Chieftain takes Ximena in his strong and proud embrace.
She lays her lips upon his hand, while tears run down her face.
The tears of bitter parting, for who knows what lies ahead?
Will God restore her lord to her victorious or dead?")

Altabiskarco Cantua

Oyhu batditua izan da
Escualdunen mendien artetic.
Eta etcheco-jaunac, bere athearen aiteinean chutic
Ideki tu bearriac, eta erran du: Nor da hor? Cer nahi dautet
Eta chacurra, bere nausiaren oinetan lo zaguena,
Alchatu da, eta karrasiz Altabiscarren inguruac: bethe ditu.
("From far away, amid the mountain vales,
A cry is heard, that echoes to the plains;
Echeco-jauna stands before his gate,
Hearkens, and says: 'What seek these people strange?'
The dog, that at the feet of Jauna lay,
Summons to arms the neighbors with his bay.")

Arnaut Daniel

Lo ferm voler qu'el cor m'intra
No'm pot jes becs escoissendre ni ongla
De lausengier, qui pert per mal dir s'arma;
E car non l'aus batr'ab ram ni ab verga,
Sivals a frau, lai ou non aurai oncle,
Jauzirai joi, en vergier o dinz cambra.
("Firm and steadfast is my longing

> For bridal room with heavy silken hanging
> Where soft and low a nightingale is singing.
> Nor beak nor claw to slanderer belonging
> Can to that chamber keep my heart from winging,
> Or love's sweet tribute to my lady bringing.")

Rambaut de Vaqueiras

Here is the *envoi* in which the first two lines are in Provençal, the next two in Italian, the next two in French, the next two in Gascon, and the last two in a mixture of Spanish and Portuguese. In the latter, however, note that *mon* is French and *avetz* is Provençal.

> Belhs cavaliers, tant es car
> Lo vostr'onratz senhoratges
> Que cada jorno m'esglaio.
> Oi me lasso! Que farò
> Si cele que j'ai plus chiere
> Me tue, ne sai por quoi?
> Ma dauna, he que dey bos
> Ni peu cap Santa Quitera,
> Mon corasso m'avetz treito
> E, mot gen favlan, furtado.
> ("Oh, if I again could hear you
> Speak those words that fired my heart:
> 'I want only to be near you!
> Noble knight, we'll never part!'
> But instead you choose to slay me
> And you do not tell me why!
> You have chosen to betray me;
> So my five tongues say: 'Good-bye!' "

Here are the last two stanzas of the bilingual *tenzó*, the first one in Provençal and the last in the Genoese dialect:

> Domna, en estraign cossire
> M'avez mes, et en esmai.
> Mas enqera'us preierai
> Qe voillaz q'eu vos essai
> Si cum provenzals o fai
> Qant es poiaz.
> ("Lady, you do not alarm me
> With your threats of sword and mace.
> You but fascinate and charm me.
> Let me show you how we race
> One we hold in love's embrace
> When we mount!")
> Jujar, no serò con tego,

Poss'così te cal de mi.
Meill vara' per sant Marti'
S'andai a ser Opeti',
Que dar v'a fors'un ronci',
Car sei jujar!
("I will never be your filly
Or submit to your embrace!
You will always find me chilly.
If a horse you want to race,
Buy one in the market-place,
Troubadour!")

Cielo d'Alcamo

Rosa fresca aulentissima—c'apar inver la state,
Le donne ti disiano—pulzell'e maritate.
Traimi d'este focora—se t'este a bolontate.
Per te non aio abento notte e dia,
Penzando pur di voi, madonna mia!
("Rose that is most delectable—when summertime's impending,
To maiden fair and married spouse—your charm and beauty lending,
To draw me from the fires of love—upon you I'm depending.
Because of you I rest not, night or day;
You've haunted me through April and through May."

After initial rejection of the lover's plea, the lady finally relents and willingly yields to his desires:

Meo sire, poi iurastimi—eo tuta quanta jncienno.
Sono a la tua presenza—da voi non mi difenno.
S'eo minespreso aoti—merze', a voi m'arenno.
A lo letto ne gimo a la bon'ora,
Che chissa cosa n'e data jn ventura!
("My lord, now you have promised me—my heart is all aflame.
I stand before you, free from all—false modesty and shame.
If I was proud and haughty once—I'm humble now, and tame.
So take me in your arms and off to bed.
May happiness and rapture lie ahead!")

St. Francis of Assisi's *Cantico delle Creature*

Altissimu, onnipotente, bon Signore,
Tue so' le laude, la gloria e l'honore et onne benedictione.
Ad te solo, Altissimo, se konfano,
Et nullu homo ene dignu te mentovare.
("Highest, all-powerful, good Lord,
Thine are the praises, the glory, the honor and all the blessings.

They befit only Thee, Most High,
And no man is worthy to mention Thy Name.")

Laudato sie, mi Signore, cum tucte le tue creature:
Spetialmente messor lo frate Sole,
Lo quale è jorno, et allumini noi per lui;
Et ellu è bellu e radiante, cum grande splendore;
De te, Altissimo, porta significatione.
("Praised be Thou, my Lord, with all Thy creatures:
Especially lord brother Sun,
Who is the day, and Thou givest us light through him;
And he is beautiful and radiant, with great splendor.
Of Thee, Most High, he bears the symbol.")

Laudato si', mi Signore, per sora Luna e le Stelle,
In celu l'ai formate clarite et pretiose et belle.
("Praised be Thou, my Lord, for sister Moon and the Stars.
In heaven Thou hast formed them, clear, precious and beautiful.")

Martin Codax' *Cantiga de Amigo*

Ondas do mar de Vigo
Se uistes meu amigo!
E, ay Deus, se uerrá cedo?

. . . .

Se uistes meu amado
Por que ei gran coidado!
E, ay Deus, se uerrá cedo?
("Waves of the stormy sea,
Bring my lover back to me!
When will he come back, my Lord?
The one that I love most
On the whole Galician coast!
When will he come back, my Lord!")

Song of Love Attributed to King Sancho

Se Deus me leixe de vos bem aver,
Senhor' fremosa, nunca vi prazer,
Des quando m'eu de vos parti

. . . .

Ouve tal coita no meu coração
Que nunca vi prazer, se ora não,
Des quando m'eu de vos parti.
("So grant me God your favor to enjoy,
My lovely lady, never saw I joy
Since from your side I did depart.

My heart was filled with such unending pain
That only now do I know joy again
Since from your side I did depart.")

Lyric Poem by Camões

Alma minha gentil, que te partiste
Tão cedo desta vida descontente,
Repousa lá no céu eternamente,
E viva eu cá na terra, sempre triste.
Se là no assento etéreo onde subiste
Memória desta vida se consente,
Não te esqueças daquele amor ardente
Que já nos olhos meus tão puro viste.
("My gentle Darling, who so soon departed
From troubles that are life's too heavy price,
Repose forevermore in Paradise,
While I live on, alone and broken-hearted.
If God permits some measure of recalling
Of past events in Heaven's realms above,
Do not forget that ardent, burning love
That makes my present solitude so galling.")

Original English verse translations by Mario Pei. For fuller versions and translations, see recording and script FL9578, *Medieval Romance Poetry*, Folkways Records, New York, 1961.

Appendix I

Other Theories about Italian Plurals

First Declension Feminine Plural in -*a*

The generally accepted theory that standard Italian first declension plural *rose* is a historical continuation of the Latin nominative plural *rosae* has been challenged by a number of scholars, who have, indeed, been able to show that this feminine plural form in -*e* could also derive from the Classical Latin accusative in -*as*, by way of an intermediate attested -*es* form, which subsequently lost final -*s* when this final consonant was generally lost in all standard Italian verb forms. The historical development would seem to have been as follows: -*as* → -*es* → -*e*. In view of the fact that forms in -*as* are frequently found on inscriptions and other documents in the plural nominative function in the Italian area, these scholars feel that standard Italian -*e* feminine plural is the direct descendant of a popular -*as* plural nominative form, which some regard as a reflex of the Indo-European plural nominative in -*ās* preserved in some Italian dialects (e.g., Oscan *scriftas* versus Latin *scriptae*), rather than an extension of the Latin accusative case.

References: Robert L. Politzer, "On the Origin of Italian Plurals," *The Romanic Review*, 43 (1952), 272–281; Berengario Gerola, "Il nominativo plurale in -AS nel latino e il plurale romanzo," *Symbolae philologicae gotoburgenses,* in *Acta Universitatis Gotoburgensis.* Göteborgs Högskolas Årsskrift, LVI, No. 3 (1950), 328–354; Paul Aebischer, "La finale -*e* du féminin pluriel italien. Etude de stratigraphie linguistique," *Studi linguistici italiani,* I (1960), 5–49; Paul A. Gaeng, "A Postscript to the Problem of the -*ās* Nominative Plural Ending in Latin and the Origin of the Feminine -*e* Plurals in Standard Italian," *Rivista di Studi Classici,* XIX, No. 2 (1971), 228–234.

Third Declension Plurals in -*i*

The problem of the origin of third declension plurals of the *i cani* type (from Classical Latin *canēs*) has been somewhat controversial, in that several possibilities have been advanced to account for it. The prevailing theory still is that the Latin masculine nouns of the third declension patterned themselves on the second, the most extensive masculine declension, which means that the normal outcome of Latin *canēs*, Italian *cane*, eventually changed to *cani* as the result of the analogical pull exerted by plurals of the *o*-declension nouns (e.g., singular *gallo* versus plural *galli*). This analogy seems to have been further aided by the need to keep singular *cane* and plural *cani* apart by means of a distinctive plural ending.

Another theory to account for the *cani* form from Latin *canēs* is known as "Meyer-Lübke's phonological law," which states that Latin *-ās* and *-ēs* become *-i* in Italian, e.g., *florēs* → *fiori*.

A third explanation of the Italian *cani* form is based on the fact that Latin *ē, ĕ, ĭ*, and the diphthong *ae* in an unstressed final syllable frequently show an *-i* rather than *-e* outcome, e.g., *dieci* from Latin *decĕm*, while *avanti* derives from Latin *ab antē*.

A fourth theory suggests that the *-i* outcome of third declension plurals in standard Italian represents a reflex of the Latin *i*-stem accusative plural endings in *-īs*. Accordingly, Italian *cani* would be a direct historical continuation of Latin *canīs* rather than *canēs*. This theory is built on the premise that this *-īs* ending was subsequently also extended to nominative plural forms in Latin, which normally ended in *-ēs*, even for *i*-stem nouns. Indeed, instances in which *-īs* is used for *-ēs* in this grammatical function are recorded in Classical Latin already, and they steadily increase over the centuries, to the extent that by about the sixth century nominative and accusative forms in *-is* (e.g., *mensis* for *menses, parentis* for *parentes, fratris* for *fratres*) prevail over those in *-es*, regardless of whether they were originally *i*-stem or consonant stem. There would seem to be good reason to believe that the old *-īs* ending of old *i*-stem nouns persisted in the spoken language and that after the fall of final *-s*, the *-i* ending remained as a plural marker of all third declension masculine and feminine nouns.

References: Gerhardt Rohlfs, *Historische Grammatik der italienischen Sprache und ihrer Mundarten.* Bern, 1949, II, p. 49; Mario Pei, "Latin and Italian Final Front Vowels," *Modern Language Notes*, 58, No. 2 (1943), 116–120; F. D'Ovidio and W. Meyer-Lübke, *Grammatica storica della lingua e dei dialetti italiani.* Milano, 1932, p. 90; Paul Gaeng, "The Plural *i*-Ending of Third Declension Masculine Nouns in Italian," in *Studies in Honor of Mario A. Pei.* Chapel Hill, N.C., 1972, pp. 105–114.

Appendix J

Language Samples of Sardinian, Rheto-Rumansh, and Vegliote

Sardinian

(1) Excerpt from an eleventh-century charter from Cagliari, in the Cam pidanese area:

. . . *ca lli damus ass'archiepiscobatu nostru de Caralis, et pro remissione dessos peccados nostros et dessos maiorales dessa terra nostra, totus sus liberus de paniliu cantu sunt per totu Caralis, ki serviant ass'archiepiscobatu nostru de Caralis de tres setmanas una in serbiciu cali abet boler s'archiepiscobu ki aet esser in s'archiepiscobadu, in co asserbiant usque modo assu rennu; et serbiant illi in terra et in mari per tota sa Sardinia in serbiciu cale aet boler s'archiepis-cobu ki aet esser in s'archiepiscobadu. . . .*

("that we give to our archbishopric of Cagliari, for the remission of our sins and [the sins of] the chief men of our land, all the freemen [serfs] of the same kind, as many as there are in all Cagliari, that they may serve our archbishopric of Cagliari one week out of three, in such service as may be desired by the archbishop who will be in the archbishopric, that they may serve the realm properly; and let them serve him on land and on sea in all Sardinia, in such service as may be desired by the archbishop who will be in the archbishopric.")

(a) Conservation of final *-s* and *-t*, and of the original quality of Latin stressed vowels (*damus, serviant, maiorales, peccados, totus, sunt, archiepiscobu*). (b) Some sonorization of intervocalic consonants (*peccados, archiepiscobadu*). (c) The use of *ipse* as an article (*su, sa, sos* [*sus* in the text], *sas*) and in contraction with a preposition: *assu* (from *ad ipsu*); cf. the same phenomenon, which appears also in Italian, with Latin *ille*, e.g., *alla, della, nella*, etc. But note the use of *lli* (Latin *illī*) as a pronoun. (d) Plural forms derived from the Latin accusative (*peccados, liberus*), still undecided phonetically as to the final vowel. (Eventually, Campidanese universally opts for final *-i* and *-u* for *-e* and *-o*). (e) Uncontracted future in *abet boler* (Latin *habet volere* [for *velle*] and *aet esser*

(Latin *habet essere* [for *esse*]), surviving to this day. (f) Change of *gn* to *nn* in *rennu* for Latin *regnum*.

(2) Excerpts from the twelfth-century *Condaghe di San Pietro di Silki* ("Contracts of *San Pietro di Silki*"), from the Logudorese area:

Ego Maximilla abbatissa de Sanctu Petru de Silki ki lu renovo custu condake, ad unore Deus innanti, e de Sanctu Petru, e de Sancta Iulia, e ccun boluntate dessu donnu meu iudike Gunnari, e dessu fiiu iudike Barusone, e dessos frates, e dessos maiorales de Locudore, dandem'isse paragula de renobarelu su condake. . . . Et Ithoccor de Laccon Pinna kertaitili ka "non bi la posit, ka kene limba morivit." . . . Et ego battusi sos destimonios atteru die. . . .

("I, Maximilla, abbess of Saint Peter of Silki, who am renewing this contract, in the honor of God henceforth, and of Saint Peter and Saint Julia, and in accordance with the will of my lord Judge Gunnari, and his son Judge Barusone, and the brothers, and the elders of Logudoro, they giving me their word that they are renewing the contract. . . . And Ithoccor de Laccon Pinna testified that 'he did not put it there, that he died without speaking.' . . . And I brought in the witnesses on another day.")

(a) Preservation of the distinction between final *-o* and *-u* (*renovo, ego*, versus *donnu* (Latin *dominum*), *fiiu* (Latin *filium*)). (b) Preservation of Classical Latin velars and absence of palatalization (*iudike; kertaitili* from Latin *certavit illi*). (c) Phenomena of syntactic phonology in *battusi* (Latin *adduxi*) and *sos destimonios* (Latin *ipsos testimonios*, where the sonorization of initial *t* probably comes from intervocalic singular use). (d) Use of *ipse* as a definite article (*sos, dessu, dessos*) and *ille* in pronominal function (*lu renovo, renobarelu, la posit*). (e) Note the forms *paragula* (Latin *parabola*), *atteru* (Latin *alterum*), *custu* (Latin *eccum istum*), and *limba* (for Latin *lingua*, with the reduction of labialized velars to labials, *gu* → *b*, which is also characteristic of Rumanian).

(3) Modern Logudorese:
Here is The Lord's Prayer, together with a translation into the reconstructed Vulgar Latin of Sardinia and the original Latin text:

Babbu nostru, qui stas in sos chelos; sanctificadu siat su nomen tou; benzat a nois su regnu tou; fiacta siat sa voluntade tua, comente in su chelu asi in sa terra; su pane nostru de ogni die donanostu haë, et perdònanus sos peccados nostros, comente nos ateros perdonamus sos inimigos nostros. Et ne nos lasses ruere in sa tentatione; sinò liberanos de male.

Babbu (cf. Italian *babbo*, "daddy") nostru qui stas in ipsos celos; sanctificatu siat (for *sit*) ipsu nomen tuu; veniat a nobis ipsu regnu tuu; facta siat ipsa voluntate tua qua mente in ipsu chelu at sic in ipsa terra; ipsu pane nostru de omni die tu nos dona(re) habes et nos perdona ipsos peccatos nostros, qua mente nos alteros perdonamus ipsos inimicos nostros. Et ne nos laxes ruere in ipsa tentatione; si non libera nos de male.

Pater noster, qui es in caelis; sanctificetur nomen tuum. Adveniat regnum tuum; Fiat voluntas tua, sicut in caelo, et in terra. Panem nostrum cotidianum da nobis hodie. Et dimitte nobis debita nostra, sicut et nos dimittimus debitoribus nostris. Et ne nos inducas in tentationem. Sed libera nos a malo.

Rheto-Rumansh

For the sake of comparison with a major Romance language, an Italian translation of the original text is given, as well as an English version.

(1) *Friulian:* Song from the Carnic Alps

O ciampanis de sàbide sere	O campane del sabato sera
che pe fieste sunàis di ligrie,	che suonate liete per la festa,
vês te vôs simpri gnove poesie	avete nella voce una poesia sempre nuova
di confuârt, di speranze e prejere.	di conforto, di speranza e preghiera.
Par i prâz, pes culinis vie vie	Lungo i prati, lungo i colli via via
come a vòngulis rive a nô il son,	come ad onde ci arriva il suono
e ogni cûr al devente plui bon	e ogni cuore diventa più buono
tal scoltâ cheste musiche pie.	nell'ascoltare questa musica pia.
O ciampanis de sàbide sere	O campane del sabato sera
che pe fieste sunàis di ligrie	che suonate liete per la festa
tignît cont de plui biele armonie	serbate l'armonia più bella
par sunâle a la fin de la uere!	per suonarla alla fine della guerra!

"Oh, Saturday night bells / That ring happily because of the holiday / You have in your voice an ever new poetry / Of comfort, hope and prayer. / Along the meadows, away among the hills / Their sound comes to us as in waves, / And each heart becomes better / As it listens to this pious music. / Oh, Saturday night bells / That ring happily because of the holiday / Keep your loveliest harmony / To play it at the end of the war."

Note the palatalization of *c* before *a* (*ciampanis*); the survival of final -*s* (*ciampanis, sunàis, culinis*); the conservation of *pl* (*plui*) and of Germanic *w* (*uere;* the form *werra* for Latin *guerra* is already attested in very late Vulgar Latin); change of final *a* to *e* (*sere, fieste*); and the diphthongization of *ĕ* in checked position (*fieste*).

(2) *Swiss Rumansh* (Engadine Variety)

Ils teis bels ölgs nairs	I tuoi begl'occhi neri
Quels m'han fat inamurar	Che m'han fatto innamorare
. . . .	. . . .
Eu veng per tuot il muond intuorn	Io vengo per tutto il mondo intorno
E tü restast aquâ	E tu restasti qua

("Your beautiful black eyes / That made me fall in love / . . . I travel all around the world / And you stayed here.")

Note especially the use of front rounded vowels *ö* and *ü,* which generally occur only in the Swiss varieties of Rumansh.

Here are a few proverbs in this particular dialect with their Italian and English equivalents:

(a) *Oz a mi, dameun a ti.* Oggi a me, domani a te ("Today is my turn, tomorrow yours.")

(b) *Megler cun in egl en parvis che cun dus egl uffiern.* Meglio con un occhio in paradiso che con due nell'inferno ("Better with one eye in paradise than with two in hell.")

(c) *Tgi va pleun, va lunsch, va seun.* Chi va piano va sano e va lontano ("Who goes gently goes safely and far.")

(d) *Di mi cun tgi ti vas, ed jeu vi dir tgi che ti fas.* Dimmi con chi vai, e io ti dirò quel che tu fai ("Tell me whom you go with and I'll tell you what you do.")

Vegliote

The following excerpt is a fragment of a religious poem (with Italian and English translations):

Al lank de la suónta kráųk i v-inkiodúa,	Al legno della santa croce essi v'inchiodavano
La vestra santa búka da bár la dimandúa,	La vostra santa bocca da ber la domandava,
E kol fiél e kol akáįt i ve la intoskúa.	E col fiele e coll'aceto essi ve l'avvelenavano.

("They nailed you to the wood of the holy cross / Your holy mouth asked for a drink / And with gall and vinegar they poisoned it for you.")

Note the preservation of Latin velars (*kráųk, akáįt*); extreme diphthongization and transformation of stressed vowels (*suónta* from Latin *sancta*, *kráųk* from Latin *cruce*(*m*), *akáįt* from Latin *acetum*); use of third singular as a plural form (*inkiodúa*).

Appendix K

Samples of Old and Modern Rumanian and Its Varieties

Excerpts from a Letter Written in 1521

The following was written by a Wallachian gentleman to one of the judicial officials of the Transylvanian city of Brașov to inform him of the movement of Turkish ships along the Danube.

. . . dau știre domnietale za lucrulŭ Turcilorŭ, cumŭ amŭ auzitŭ eu că împăratulŭ au ieșitŭ den Sofia, și aimintrea nu e, și se-au dusŭ în susŭ pre Dunăre. . . . să știi domniiata că au venitŭ un omŭ dela Nicopoe de mie me-au spusŭ că au văzutŭ cu ochii loi că au trecutŭ ceale corabii ce știi și domniiata pre Dunăre în susŭ. . . . spui domnietale de lucrulŭ lu Mahamet-begŭ, cumŭ amŭ auzitŭ de boiari ce săntu megiiași și de genere miu Negre, cumŭ i-au datŭ împăratulŭ slobozie lu Mahamet-begŭ, pre io-i va fi voia pren Țeara rumănească iară el să treacă. Ipacŭ să știi domniiata că are frică mare și Băsărabŭ de acelŭ lotru de Mahamet-begŭ. . . . spui domnietale că mai marele miu, de ce amŭ întelesŭ și eu. . . . I Bogŭ te veselit. Amin.

("I inform Your Lordship of Turkish doings, since I heard that the emperor left for Sofia, and not otherwise; and he went up the Danube valley. . . . And also know Your Lordship that a man has come from Nicopolis and he told me that he saw with his own eyes a string of ships (know your Lordship that also) sailing up the Danube. . . . Also let me tell Your Lordship about the doings of Mahamet-bey, for I heard from men close to my son-in-law Negro that the emperor has given Mahamet-bey permission to cross Rumanian territory wherever he pleases. Also, know Your Lordship that Besarab greatly fears that thief Mahamet-bey. . . . I am reporting to Your Lordship, as my superior, all I have heard. . . . May God grant You joy. Amen.")

Note the following characteristic features of Rumanian phonology: (a) Merger of Latin long and short *u* (*lucrulŭ* from Latin *lūcrum illum*, *susŭ* from Latin *sūrsum*); recall that Latin long and short *o* remain *o* in Rumanian. (b) No diphthongization of Latin stressed short *o* (*omŭ*, cf. Italian *uomo*). There is no

312

clear-cut example of the diphthongization of Latin stressed short *e* in our text; the form *țeară* (Latin *terra*) does not show this phenomenon on the surface, because in addition to the spontaneous diphthongization (°*tiera*), there has also occurred a metaphony (see Appendix E) brought about by final *-a*, turning the *ie* diphthong into an *iea* triphthong (°*tieara*). Then, the first element of the triphthong acted upon the preceding dental (*t*) by converting it into an assibilated *ț* (as in *tsetse*) sound; in modern Rumanian the assibilated dental has also absorbed the following *e: țară*. (c) Umlaut influence of final *-a* upon stressed *e* and *o*, turning these vowels into the diphthongs *ea* and *oa* respectively (*rumănească*). (d) Weakening of final *-a* to a shwa sound [ə] (*iară, țeară*), and of final *-u* from Latin *-o* (*auzitŭ* from Latin *audito, omŭ* from Latin *homo*), the latter having completely disappeared in the modern language. (e) The central vowel represented by the letter *î* (also *â* in the modern language), pronounced like Russian *yeri* (like *y* in *rhythm*). (f) Fall of final *-s* (*mai* from Latin *magis*). (g) Preservation of intervocalic voiceless consonants (*auzitŭ, venitŭ, văzutŭ*; cf. Italian *udito, venuto, veduto*). (h) Evolution of *-di-* to *-z-* in *auzitŭ* (Latin *auditum*) and by analogy of *vezi*, "you see," (Latin *vides* by way of an assumed *vedi* form) in *văzutŭ*. (i) Palatalization of *c, g,* and *qu* before *e, i* (*treace* from Latin *traicere, genere* from Latin *generum, ce* from Latin *quid*). (j) Palatalization of *s* and *t* before *e, i* (*și* from Latin *sic, țeară* from Latin *terra*), while the *sc* consonant group before the same front vowels becomes *șt* (*știre* from Latin *scire*).

In morphology, the feature that sets Rumanian radically apart from the other Romance languages is the postposition of the definite article, which is well reflected in this text: e.g., *lucrulŭ* (Latin *lucrum illum*), *țeara* (Latin *terra illa*), *ochii* (Latin *oculi illi*), etc. We furthermore find the following: (a) Survival of the genitive-dative case, as reflected in *Turcilorŭ* (Latin *Turci illorum*), and that of the synthetic dative feminine in *domnietale*, "to Your Lordship" (Latin *dominae tuae illae*). (b) The comparative form of the adjective expressed by means of *mai* (Latin *magis*), as in *mai mare*, "bigger." (c) Merger of Latin *esse* and *fieri* to give the conjugational pattern of *a fi*, "to be," (in our text the form *e* from Latin *est* is replaced by *va fi*, "he (she, it) will be" from Vulgar Latin *volet fieri*). Note that Rumanian uses *volere* rather than *habere* as an auxiliary to form the Romance future, e.g., *voi cînta* (Vulgar Latin *voleo cantare*) versus Italian *canterò* (Latin *cantare habeo*). (d) The auxiliary *habere* → *avea* with both transitive and intransitive verbs (*au ieșitŭ* from Latin *habet exitum*; cf. Italian *è uscito; au văzutŭ* from Vulgar Latin *habet vidutum*; cf. Italian *ha visto*). (e) Subjunctives introduced by the conjunction *să* (Latin *si*), e.g., *să știi domniiata*, "know Your Lordship."

In the matter of vocabulary, the Slavic element is in evidence: *boiar*, "man," *corabie*, "ship," (but Slavic seems to have borrowed this from Italian *caravella*), *slobozie*, "permission," *veselit*, "rejoice," and *Bog*, "God." Among the Latin elements, of interest are those words that did not survive in the West, e.g., *ști* (Latin *scire*), *întelege* (Latin *intellegere*), *treace* (Latin *traicere*), *lucru* (Latin *lucrum*) in the sense of "matter," "business," and the adjective *mare* (Latin *magnus + talis*) in the meaning of "big," "large." The characteristic formula of courtesy, *domniiata*, polite "you" (here "Your Lordship") occurs several times. Still in wide use today in the form *dumneata*, used with the second singular form of the verb. The plural *domnie vostre, dumneavoastră* in the modern language, used with the second plural of the verb, refers to more than one person, but it is also used to address one person as an expression of the highest respect.

Tombstone Inscription (Early Seventeenth Century)

> *Această piatră pre groapă Radului Buzescul*
> *Rugate lui Dumnezeu în zi și în noapte*
> ("This stone (lies) on the body of Radu Buzescu
> Pray God by day and by night")

Note the following: (a) The umlaut effect in *această* from Latin *atque ista* and *piatră* from Latin *petra* (*e* → *ea* [*ia*]), as well as *groapă* from German *cruppa* "back," and *noapte* from Latin *nocte* (*o* → *oa*). (b) The possessive forms *Radului* and *lui Dumnezeu*, showing how the third person possessive may be expressed by *lui* (Vulgar Latin *illui*, for Classical Latin *illī*). (c) Initial *di-* changing to *z-* (*zi* from Latin *die*). (d) The change of Latin *ct* [kt] group to *pt* in *noapte*.

Early Macedo-Rumanian

The following is from the Lord's Prayer:

Ćaće nostru karle ješti en ćer, neka se posveta lumele tev; neka vire tae kraljestvo; fia tae volja ka ši en ćer aša ši pre pemint.
("Father our which art in heaven (may) hallowed be Thy name; (may) come Thy Kingdom; be done Thy will as in Heaven so also on earth.")

The same text in early Daco-Rumanian, taken from a Protestant catechism of 1559, runs as follows:

Tatăl nostru ce ești în ceri sfînțească-se numele tău, sa vie împărăție ta, fie voia ta cum în ceri așă și pre pămînt.

For the sake of comparison, here is this opening sentence in modern literary (Daco) Rumanian:

Tatăl Nostru care ești în ceruri, sînțească-se numele tău; vie împărăția Ta; facă-se voia Ta precum în ceruri și pe pămînt.

Note the relatively few changes that have occurred from Old to Modern Daco-Rumanian. The hybrid subjunctive form *sfînțească-se*, "hallowed be," deriving from a Romance *sînt* and a Slavic *sfînt* has been Latinized to *sînțească-se*. The word *tată*, which appears in both versions, comes from the special vocabulary of children ("daddy") and has displaced the traditional *pater*.

Modern Daco-Rumanian

The following lines are from a poem by George Sion (1821–1892) in praise of the Rumanian language (with a reconstructed text in Vulgar Latin and an English rendition).

Limba Românească	Lingua Illa Romanesca
Mult e dulce și frumoasă	Multum est dulcis sic formosa
Limba ce vorbim!	Lingua illa quid verbamus
Altă limbă armonioasă	Alteram linguam harmoniosam
Ca ea nu găsim!	qua illa non (of uncertain origin)
Saltă inima 'n plăcere	Salta(t) anima in placere
Când o ascultăm	Quando illam auscultamus
Și pe buze aduce miere	Sic per (of uncertain origin) adducit mel
Când o cuvântăm	Quando illam conventamus
Românașul o iubește	Romanus ille illam iubescit (Slavic)
Ca sufletul său	Qua sufflatum illum suum
O! Vorbiți, scriți românește	O! Verbate, scribite romanice
Pentru Dumnezeu!	Per inter Dominum Deum!

("Very sweet and beautiful is the language that we speak!
None other do we find that is so harmonious!
Our heart is jumping with joy when we hear it
And honey flows from the lips when we speak it.
The Rumanian loves it like his own soul,
Oh, speak and write Rumanian, in the name of God!")

Modern Istro-Rumanian

Here are some proverbs with Italian and English equivalents for comparison:

Apetitu vire munkându. L'appetito viene mangiando ("One's appetite grows as one eats.")

Breku ke latra, nu mucka. Cane che latra non morde ("The dog that barks does not bite.")

Draku ne aude predikele. Il diavolo non ascolta le prediche ("The devil does not listen to sermons.")

Galjira ke kanta, fakut-a ovu. Gallina che canta, fatto ha l'uovo ("Hen that cackles has laid an egg.")

Nu-j rosa far de spire. Non c'è rosa senza spine ("There is no rose without a thorn.")

Appendix L

Modern Franco-Italian Jargon

From the parody *Giobbe,* in which the heavily Frenchified verses of Francesco Fontana are satirized:

Voilato di nebbie	Veiled in fog
Parigi ho *apperçuto*	I caught a glimpse of Paris
e la *siloetta*	and of the silhouette
che il domo del Pantheon	that the dome of the Pantheon
nel cielo *progetta.*	projects into the sky.
Promenasi il popolo	The French populace
francese la notte;	strolls about at night;
nel fango *pietinano*	through the mud wade
gommosi e *cocotte,*	streetwalkers and girls of easy virtue,
guardati dai mille	watched by
col *sabre* nel fodero	the thousand constables
sergenti di *ville.* . . .	with sheathed sabres.

The words in italic are either French or Frenchified. (a) Used without change of form are: *cocotte, sabre, ville. Siloetta* (French *silhouette*) is slightly adapted to the Italian sound system and, like *sergenti* (French *sergents*), also to the Italian noun system (*la siloetta*). (b) French verb stems to which Italian endings are added: *voil-ato* (French *voil-é*), *progett-a* (French *projett-e*), *promen-a si* (French *se promèn-e*), *pietin-ano* (French *piétin-ent*), *apperç-uto* (French *aperç-u*). Note also in the last example the characteristic doubling of Italian consonants.

Glossary of Linguistic Terms
Appearing in This Work[1]

ABLATIVE *See* CASE.

ABLAUT The changes occurring in a vowel sound according to the position of
the pitch accent in the parent language, or of the stress accent at a later
period. English *sing, sang, sung,* represent ablaut variations reflecting conditions in the parent Indo-European language, where the accent was on
the root, or on preceding or following syllables later lost. A modern example is Spanish *dormir,* where the *o* is retained where unstressed, but replaced by *ue* when stressed, as in *duermo.* The ablaut alternation regularly
denotes a distinction in meaning, such as different tense forms of a verb.
Synonym: APOPHONY.

ACCENT An increase of stress (greater amplitude, or loudness), or a change
of pitch (higher or lower frequency), giving prominence to one syllable
of a sequence over the adjacent syllables. In writing, a diacritic mark
indicating syllabic stress (Spanish *habló*), vowel quality (French *élève*),
or vowel quantity (length: Czech *dobrý*). The term is also used to describe a person's speech habits with respect to his own or an acquired
language ("a Southern accent," "a foreign accent").

ACCUSATIVE *See* CASE.

ACTIVE *See* VOICE.

AFFIX A collective term used for PREFIXES, INFIXES, and SUFFIXES (q.v.). It
is generally used to produce derivatives (*un-* in *undo, -ide* in *bromide*) or
inflectional forms (*-s* in *dogs* and *speaks*).

AFFRICATE A sound articulated as a stop (*t*), then passing into a fricative
(*sh*) without shifting the point of articulation (*church,* where *ch* represents *t* immediately followed by *sh*).

AGREEMENT Correspondence of one word with another as to gender, number, case, person, etc. (Spanish *las buenas muchachas,* where *las* and
buenas are both feminine and plural to agree with *muchachas*).

---

1. For fuller discussions of these terms, see Mario Pei, *Glossary of Linguistic
Terminology* (New York: Columbia University Press, 1966).

ALLITERATION   The recurrence of the same sound or sound group, usually initial, in successive words (the *w*'s in *wild and wooly*).

ALVEOLAR   A consonant produced by placing the tip or blade of the tongue in contact with the alveoli, or ridge of the upper gums (English *t, d*).

AMELIORATION   Betterment in the meaning of a word (Germanic *marah skalk*, "horse groom," developing into *marshal*). *Synonym:* ENHANCEMENT.

ANALOGY   The occasional, largely unpredictable tendency of a word or form to be pulled out of its natural orbit of development by the attraction of another word or form with which it has a real or fancied resemblance or connection; the process of modifying words on the model of existing patterns (a child's use of *sheeps* as the plural of *sheep* because most English nouns form their plural by adding -*s*).

ANALYTICAL LANGUAGE   A language in which AUXILIARY (q.v.) words are the chief means of indicating grammatical relationships to the total or partial exclusion of inflections, and where the separate meanings are expressed by words that can be used in isolation (English *I shall wait*, where *I* indicates first person singular, *shall* indicates futurity, and *wait* conveys the basic meaning of the action, as contrasted with Latin *amābō*, where *ama-* conveys the basic meaning, -*b*- indicates futurity, -*ō* first person singular). *Synonym:* ISOLATING LANGUAGE; *Opposite:* SYNTHETIC LANGUAGE.

ANTEPENULT   The syllable or pronounced vowel which is third from the end of a word (the first syllable in English *eagerly* and Latin *oculus*).

APHERESIS   The disappearance of an initial vowel, often because of absorption by the final vowel of the preceding word (English *cute* from *acute;* Vulgar Latin *illa ecclesia* to Italian *la chiesa*). *Opposite:* PROTHESIS.

APICAL   A sound produced with the tip or apex of the tongue as the articulator (Castilian apical *s*).

APOCOPE (or APOCOPATION)   Loss of a final vowel (Middle English *helpe* to *help;* Italian *amor* for *amore*). *Opposite:* PARAGOGE.

APOPHONY   *See* ABLAUT.

A POSTERIORI (LANGUAGE)   An artificial language constructed with reference to, and on the basis of, existing languages, and blending different living language elements (Volapük, Esperanto, Ido, Interlingua). *Opposite:* A PRIORI LANGUAGE.

A PRIORI (LANGUAGE)   An artificial language constructed without reference to or similarity with existing languages (Solresol, Suma, Ro). *Opposite:* A POSTERIORI LANGUAGE.

ARTICULATION   The formation of a speech sound by the vocal organs. *See also* POINT OF ARTICULATION.

ASPECT   A verbal category indicating whether an action or state is viewed as completed (PERFECTIVE) or in progress (IMPERFECTIVE), instantaneous or enduring, occasional or habitual.

ASPIRATE   The sound [h] and its variations. A stop consonant characterized by the addition of a puff of breath, or ASPIRATION (q.v.); a sound whose pronunciation involves intensity in the expulsion of air from the oral cavity (English word-initial *p, t, k;* the Greek sounds indicated by the letters *theta, phi, chi,* in the earlier stages of the language [*th* in *outhouse, ph* in *uphill, ckh* in *backhouse*]; Sanskrit and Hindi sounds indicated in transcription by such combinations as *bh, dh, jh*).

ASPIRATION   The addition to a stop consonant of a perceptible puff of breath (in English, *p, t, k,* are usually aspirated in word-initial position, but unaspirated after *s-*). Or an *h*-sound unmarked in English writing.

ASSIBILANT   An AFFRICATE (q.v.) consisting of a dental or alveolar stop plus a sibilant release (*ts* in *its, dz* in *adze*).

ASSIBILATION   A process of ASSIMILATION (q.v.) whereby a nonsibilant dental or alveolar stop adds a sibilant release, articulated at the dental or alveolar point of articulation (Latin *vitium* to Italian *vezzo*).

ASSIMILATION   A phonetic process whereby two phonemes acquire common characteristics or become identical. The assimilation may be PARTIAL (Latin *in-possibilis* to *impossibilis,* where the *n* acquires the labial feature of the following *p,* but not its unvoiced stop feature), or TOTAL (Latin *ad-facio* to *afficio,* where the voiced dental stop *d* turns to the labio-dental unvoiced spirant *f.*) When both phonemes affect each other, the assimilation is RECIPROCAL (Latin *rapidum* to *rap'du* to Italian *ratto,* with unvoicing of *d* to conform to the preceding *p,* and dentalizing of *p* to conform to the following *d*). The assimilation is CONTIGUOUS if the two phonemes are adjacent, as in the examples above; NON-CONTIGUOUS if they are separated (Latin *denarium* to Italian *danaro,* where the *e* of the initial syllable is assimilated to the *a* of the stressed syllable). The assimilation may be PROGRESSIVE (Latin *hominem* to *hom'ne* to French *homme; London* to Cockney *Lunnon*); or REGRESSIVE, or RETROGRESSIVE. (Latin *domina* to *dom'na* to Italian *donna; give me* to vulgar *gimme*). *Opposite:* DISSIMILATION.

ASSONANCE   Repetition in verse of stressed vowel sounds, but not of accompanying consonants (Old French *magnes, Espaigne, fraindre, aimet, ataignet,* all occurring at the end of verses in a single *laisse* of the *Chanson de Roland,* having in common the stressed vowel *a,* followed or not by a *y*-glide).

ATONIC   Without stress or pitch accent (in *furthering, -er, -ing* are atonic syllables; *-e-* and *-i-* atonic vowels). *Synonyms:* UNACCENTED, UNSTRESSED. *Opposites:* TONIC, ACCENTED, STRESSED.

AUXILIARY   A word having no complete meaning in itself, but used in combination with another word which has a complete meaning (prepositions, conjunctions, auxiliary verbs such as *may, will, should*).

BACK FORMATION   Derivation of one word from another assumed to be a derivative (*sculpt* from *sculptor, buttle* from *butler,* on the analogy of *act* from *actor*); forming one word from another by cutting off a real or supposed suffix (French *cri* from *crier,* English *peddle* from *peddler*). *Synonyms:* RE(TRO)GRESSIVE FORMATION, RÜCKBILDUNG.

BACK VOWEL   A vowel whose point of articulation is in the rear of the oral
cavity, and which is pronounced with the back part of the tongue arched
toward the soft palate ([o], [u]). *Synonyms:* BROAD, DARK, DEEP, VELAR
(VOWEL).

BASE   The simple form of a word, to which inflectional endings are appended;
it may be the primary root of the word, or the root with a THEMATIC
SUFFIX (q.v.) (in Latin *agimus, ag-* is the bare root, *agi-* the stem, with
the addition of the thematic morpheme *-i-*).

BILABIAL   A sound produced with both lips (*p, b, m*).

BLOCKED   *See* CHECKED.

BREAKING   *See* DIPHTHONGIZATION.

BREVE   A diacritic mark placed over a vowel to indicate either a special sound
(Rumanian *casă*), or short quantity (Latin *portă*).

CASE   Broadly, the grammatical function of a noun or pronoun in the sentence
(in *the boy is here, boy* is in the nominative, or subjective, case; in *I see
the boy*, it is in the accusative, or objective, case). But often the distinction involves form as well as function. A CASE FORM is a specific variant
of a noun, adjective, or pronoun that indicates by its appearance (usually,
but not invariably, its ending) the function it has in the sentence. English has no separate case forms for adjectives; for nouns only two forms
that differ from the general singular or plural (the possessive, or genitive,
as in *the boy's book, the boys' books*); some pronouns add a distinction
between subject and object forms (*I, my, me; who, whose, whom*). Sanskrit, one of the oldest Indo-European languages on record, indicates
eight case forms for nouns, adjectives (including participles), and pronouns, which tend to fall together to varying degrees in the various
branches. They are as follows: NOMINATIVE (or SUBJECTIVE): usually
indicates the subject or a predicate nominative (Latin *puer est bonus;
Romulus est puer*). GENITIVE (or POSSESSIVE): usually indicates ownership or possession, but may be used in a variety of other functions, depending on the language (English *the boy's house;* Latin *domus pueri*).
DATIVE: usually indicates the indirect object, but may be used in other
functions, depending on the language. Modern English indicates this
function either by position (*I give the boy the book*), or by using the
preposition *to* (*I give the book to the boy;* Latin *puero librum do*). AC-
CUSATIVE (or OBJECTIVE): usually indicates the direct object, but may be
used in other functions according to the language. In Modern English,
position indicates that the noun is the object (*I see the boy*); but a special case form appears for some pronouns (*I see him;* Latin *puerum video*).
VOCATIVE: the form used in direct address (Latin *quid agis, Petre?*). For
the most part, the vocative tends to fall in with the nominative, though
some languages retain separate vocative forms to this day (Russian vocative *Bozhe* versus nominative *Bog;* Serbo-Croatian *djevojko* versus *dje-
vojka*). ABLATIVE, INSTRUMENTAL and LOCATIVE indicate a variety of
functions which Modern English generally expresses by the use of prepositions. The ablative, originally, indicated removal (*I took it from the boy*),

or direction away from (*from the city*); the instrumental, means by which (*I write with a pen*); the locative, place where (*in the city*). The use of case endings originally permitted Indo-European speakers to dispense with prepositions, but in many languages, both classical and modern, both case endings and prepositions are used. The PREPOSITIONAL case of the Slavic languages is another name for the locative, used because, while prepositions may appear in connection with other cases, this is the only one which cannot be used without a preposition. The OBLIQUE case of Vulgar Latin and Old French represents a merger, or falling together, of the former Latin cases, outside of the nominative which remained distinct in form. When these terms are applied to languages outside of the Indo-European group, they are generally loosely used to indicate something analogous or similar, but seldom quite identical (other terms have been developed for some, like the illative, elative, abessive, etc., of Finnish).

CHECKED POSITION   Descriptive of a vowel followed by a consonant in the same syllable (Latin *par-tem*). *Opposite:* FREE POSITION.

CHECKED SYLLABLE   A syllable ending in a consonant phoneme (in Latin *partem,* the stressed syllable *par-* is checked). *Synonyms:* BLOCKED or CLOSED SYLLABLE.

CHECKED VOWEL   A vowel followed by a consonant in the same syllable (*see above*). *Synonym:* BLOCKED VOWEL. *Opposite:* FREE VOWEL.

CLASSICAL   A stage of a language, often archaic, appearing in literary texts of high standing, and used as the basis for teaching that language (Classical Latin, Classical Arabic).

CLOSED SYLLABLE   A syllable ending in a consonant sound. *Synonyms:* BLOCKED or CHECKED SYLLABLE. *Opposites:* FREE or OPEN SYLLABLE.

CLOSED VOWEL   (1) A vowel pronounced with the mouth less open and the tongue raised toward the palate (*i* is more closed than *a*). *Synonym:* HIGH VOWEL. (2) Sometimes used for BLOCKED or CHECKED VOWEL (q.v.).

CLUSTER   Two or more consecutive consonants (or vowels) in a speech segment (*spr* in *spree, sts* in *lists*).

COGNATES   Words in two or more languages from the same original source (English *man,* German *Mann*). Deceptive cognates result from a shift of meaning in one of the languages (English *rent,* French *rente,* "income"; English *knave,* German *Knabe,* "boy"). False cognates may result from accidental resemblance of form (English *estate,* Italian *estate,* "summer").

COINAGE   The creation, deliberate or accidental, of a new, artificial word which had no previous membership in the language (Burgess's *blurb,* Lewis Carroll's *chortle*).

COMPARATIVE METHOD   A method consisting in laying side by side forms from various languages to determine their similarities and differences, their phonological and morphological correspondences, their common and divergent lexical features, ultimately the relationships among the languages in question and the probable structure of the common parent tongue, if unknown.

CONDITIONED SOUND CHANGE   A change predictable in terms of other sounds in the environment (the normal palatalization of *c* before *e* and *i* in Italian).

CONJUGATION   The system of changes in the verb, by means of prefixes, suffixes, internal flexion, auxiliaries, etc., in accordance with factors of person, number, tense, mood, voice, etc.

CONSONANT   A class of speech sounds characterized by constriction accompanied by some measure of friction, or closure followed by release, at one or more points in the breath channel; a generic term for PLOSIVES, FRICATIVES, NASALS, LATERALS, TRILLS or FLAPS, GLOTTAL CATCHES or STOPS, as well as the first (GLIDE) element of a rising diphthong ([p], [g], [n], [s], [l], [r], [w]). *Opposite:* VOWEL.

CONTAMINATION   The combination into a single word or expression of elements from different words or expressions, or from different languages (*irregardless,* from the blending of *irrespective* and *regardless;* Old French *brusler,* Modern French *brûler,* from the blending of Germanic *brennen* and Latin *ustulare*).

CONTINUANT   A speech sound in which there is no stoppage of the air stream, and the flow of breath is channeled but not interrupted; this includes fricatives, resonants, and vowels. *Opposite:* PLOSIVE.

CREOLE   A contact vernacular of PIDGIN (q.v.) that has become the sole or primary language of communication of a speech community; usually characterized by a morphological simplification of the language of colonization from which it is normally derived (the Creole French of Haiti).

DATIVE   *See* CASE.

DECLENSION   The system that appears in connection with nouns, pronouns, and adjectives in Indo-European and other languages, whereby the form of the word changes in accordance with its function in the sentence, as well as with other factors, such as number and grammatical gender.

DEFECTIVE   A word lacking one or more of the forms normal for its class (*ought,* which has no past tense).

DEDIPHTHONGIZATION   The change of a diphthong into a single vocalic sound (Latin *auricula* to Vulgar Latin *oricla*). *Synonym:* MONOPHTHONGIZATION.

DELABIALIZATION   The dropping of an element of speech involving a labial element (Latin *quinque* to Vulgar Latin *cinque*).

DEMOTIKE   The vernacular or colloquial form of Modern Greek, characterized by a simplification of some grammatical forms and by the use of Turkish and other loanwords. *Opposite:* KATHAREVOUSA.

DENASALIZATION   The elimination of nasalization or of a nasal element (Latin *mensem* to Italian *mese*).

DENTAL   A sound made by placing the tip of the tongue against the upper teeth (Spanish *d* and *t* in *dotar*). Sometimes loosely used for ALVEOLAR (q.v.).

DENTOLABIAL   *See* LABIODENTAL.

DEPONENT   In Latin, a verb having only passive form, but with active meanings (*morior,* "to die").

DERIVATION   The formation of a word from an earlier word or from a base by the addition of a prefix or suffix (*rebuild, boyish*), by functional change (*to picnic*), or by back formation (*to peddle* from *peddler*).

DESCRIPTIVE   Concerned with the description of the structure of a language at a specific point in time, with the exclusion of historical and comparative considerations.

DEVOICING   *See* UNVOICING.

DIACHRONIC   As applied to linguistic phenomena, occurring over a period of time. *Synonym:* HISTORICAL. *Opposite:* SYNCHRONIC.

DIACRITIC   A mark added to a letter (over, under, after, or through the letter) to modify its value (*č, ç, l', ł*).

DIAERESIS   A diacritic mark placed over one of two adjacent vowels to indicate that it does not form a diphthong with the other vowel, but is to be given full, independent phonetic value in pronunciation (French *Noël,* Spanish *averigüe*).

DIALECT   A specific branch or form of a language spoken in a given geographical area, differing sufficiently from the official standard or literary form of the language to be viewed as a distinct entity, yet not sufficiently different from the other dialects of the language to be regarded as a separate language.

DIALECTALIZATION   The breaking up of an originally unified language into various dialects, or local forms. *Opposite:* STANDARDIZATION.

DIGRAPH   A two-letter symbol used to represent a single speech sound (*th* in *this, ng* in *thing, ea* in *each*).

DIMINUTIVE   A word or affix indicating smallness, lovability, pity, sympathy, etc. (*Jeanie, Peg, lambkin, -ette, -ling*). Some languages distinguish carefully between the pet name, indicating fondness, and the true diminutive, indicating smallness (Italian *vezzeggiativo, diminutivo*). *Opposite:* AUGMENTATIVE.

DIPHTHONG   The combination of a syllabic and a nonsyllabic vowel; a sound made by gliding continuously from the position for one vowel to that for another (*ice,* French *toi,* German *heute,* Spanish *cueva*). In a FALLING DIPHTHONG, the syllabic or stressed element precedes the nonsyllabic glide, and there is less stress on the second than on the first element (*noise*); in a RISING DIPHTHONG, the opposite holds true (French *huit*). *Synonyms:* GLIDE; OFF-GLIDE (for FALLING DIPHTHONG); ON-GLIDE (for RISING DIPHTHONG).

DIPHTHONGIZATION   The process whereby a monophthong (single vowel sound) turns into a diphthong (the *e* of Latin *ferrum* becomes *ie* in Spanish *hierro*).

DISSIMILATION   Sporadic sound change whereby a dissimilarity develops between two identical or closely related phonemes (Latin *peregrinum* to French *pèlerin,* where the first of two *r*'s is dissimilated to *l*). If the two phonemes are adjacent, the dissimilation is CONTIGUOUS (Latin *anima* to *an'ma* to Spanish *alma*); if they are not adjacent the dissimilation is NONCONTIGUOUS, or DISTANT (Latin *januarium* to Italian *gennaio,* where one of 2 *a*'s has changed to an *e*). If the phoneme that produces dissimilation precedes the one that is dissimilated, the dissimilation is PROGRESSIVE (Latin *rarum* to Italian *rado*). If the dissimilated phoneme precedes the other, the dissimilation is REGRESSIVE, or RETROGRESSIVE (Latin *quaerere* to Italian *chiedere*). *Opposite:* ASSIMILATION.

DORSAL   *See* VELAR.

DOUBLE CONSONANT   Orthographically, a letter occurring twice (*tunnel*). Phonetically, an acoustic impression apprehended or functioning as two consonants, produced by prolonging the articulation (*bus seat,* Italian *asso*), repeating the articulation (Spanish *perro*), or prolonging the interval between occlusion and release (*coat tail,* Italian *fatto*). *See also* GEMINATION.

DOUBLING   *See* GEMINATION.

DOUBLETS   Two or more words stemming from the same original word, but currently used with different meanings, and often displaying different stages of popular or learned development (*frail, fragile; dish, disc, desk, discus, daïs*).

DUAL   *See* NUMBER.

ELISION   The use of a speech form lacking a final or initial sound that a variant speech form has (*it's* for *it is;* French *l'été* for *le été*).

ENCLITIC   A word pronounced as part of the preceding word (the abbreviated form of *am* in *I'm going home;* Latin *-que* in *senatus populusque*). *Opposite:* PROCLITIC.

ENHANCEMENT   *See* AMELIORATION.

EPENTHESIS   The interpolation in a word or sound group of a sound or letter which has no etymological justification, but whose usual purpose it is to ease the transition between two other sounds (Anglo-Saxon *brēmel* to English *bramble;* Latin *hominem* to *om'ne* to *om're* [by dissimilation] to Spanish *hombre;* Norse *knīf* to French *canif*). Vowel epenthesis is sometimes called ANAPTYXIS. The vowel or consonant so used is called EPENTHETIC.

ETYMON   The original form which supplies the etymology of a given word (Latin *caballum* is the etymon of French *cheval,* Spanish *caballo,* Italian *cavallo.*) The forms stemming from an etymon are called its REFLEXES.

EUPHEMISM   The substitution of a word of more pleasant connotations for one of unpleasant or disagreeable connotations (*pass away* for *die*).

EUPHONY   A pleasing sound or combination of sounds, and the acoustic effect it produces (Italian inserts vowels into the *Landsknecht* it borrows from German, and turns it into *lanzichenecco*). *Opposite:* CACOPHONY.

FINAL POSITION   The position of the last sound, morpheme, or syllable of a word; it is customary, however, to describe a vowel as in final position if it is the last vowel in the word, even if followed by one or more consonants (*e* in Latin *vident*).

FIT   The relationship between a writing system and the language it represents (examples of a good FIT: *sit, set, rub;* of a bad FIT: *though, women, nation*).

FIXED   As applied to stress: stress which always falls on a specified syllable, regardless of flectional or other changes, or of syntactic function (Polish stress always falls on the next to the last syllable; Czech stress always on the initial syllable). As applied to word order: a word order which cannot be changed without destroying the meaning of the utterance (*John sees George*, where a reversal of *John* and *George* would alter the meaning, and any other arrangement would be contrary to usage). *Opposite:* FREE.

FLAP   A sound produced by the very rapid vibration of an articulator, such as the energetic single tap of the tip of the tongue against the hard palate in British-pronounced *very*.

FLECTIONAL ENDINGS   Elements in the word which have no independent existence or use, but are added to the root to yield declensional and conjugational forms, and add accessory meanings (*-s, -ed, -ing,* of *walks, walked, walking*).

FOLK ETYMOLOGY   Change in spelling or pronunciation of words to make them look or sound more similar to familiar words, with little regard for meaning or derivation (*sparrowgrass* for *asparagus; crayfish* from French *écrevisse*). *Synonym:* POPULAR ETYMOLOGY.

FREE POSITION   Descriptive of a vowel that comes at the end of a syllable (the first vowel in Latin *ca-nis, pa-trem*). *Opposite:* CHECKED POSITION.

FREE STRESS   Stress which may fall on any syllable of a word, according to the flectional form or the syntactic function in which it is used (Russian *vodá*, plural *vódy;* Latin *íter*, genitive *itíneris*). *Opposite:* FIXED STRESS.

FREE WORD ORDER   Words in an utterance which may occur in any position, at the discretion of the speaker, without changing the basic meaning of the utterance (Latin *Paulus amat Petrum, Petrum amat Paulus, Amat Paulus Petrum*, etc., all meaning "Paul loves Peter"). *Opposite:* FIXED WORD ORDER.

FRICATIVE   A consonant produced by friction caused by the air moving through a sustained narrow passage; this may be VOICELESS (the initial sound in *fit, thing, see, shore*) or VOICED (*v* in *liver*, the initial sound in *this* and *zest, s* in *measure*). *Synonyms:* CONSTRICTIVE, SPIRANT. *Partial synonym:* CONTINUANT.

FRONTAL   A sound made with the front part of the tongue, in the area of the hard palate.

FRONTED   Used to describe a sound produced with the tongue advanced from a given position.

FRONTING   Bringing a sound from the back to the front part of the mouth (*u* in Latin *luna* has undergone fronting in French *lune*).

FRONT VOWEL   A vowel whose point of articulation is in the front part of the mouth (*i* in *machine, e* in *met*). *Opposite:* BACK VOWEL.

FUNCTIONAL CHANGE   The use of a word, without change in form, in syntactic functions assigned to different parts of speech (*to contact someone*).

GEMINATION   Doubling or prolonging, especially of consonant sounds; in writing, it is usually indicated by a double letter (Italian *detto;* Finnish *kuusi*). In speech, there is a lengthening of the sound, or of the HOLDING PERIOD (the period of complete closure) preceding the release of a PLOSIVE. *Synonym:* DOUBLING. *See also* DOUBLE CONSONANT.

GENDER   A grammatical category which may or may not be inflectional. In the Indo-European and Semitic languages, the classifications are animate versus inanimate, with a further distinction of masculine, feminine, and sometimes neuter. NATURAL GENDER, which largely prevails in English, classifies inanimate objects as neuter, then subdivides animate objects according to sex. GRAMMATICAL GENDER, which prevailed in most ancient Indo-European languages and prevails in some modern ones, usually follows sex distinctions for animate objects, but subdivides inanimate objects arbitrarily into masculine, feminine, and neuter. The Semitic languages, as well as the Indo-European Romance tongues, discard the neuter, and classify inanimate objects into masculine and feminine. Other language groups classify nouns into categories which are sometimes styled "genders" in accordance with different concepts, which may include such things as caste, roundness, flatness, etc.

GENITIVE   *See* CASE.

GEOLINGUISTICS   The study of languages in their present-day state, with particular reference to number of speakers, geographical distribution, economic, scientific, and cultural importance, as well as identification in spoken or written form. The term should be distinguished from LINGUISTIC GEOGRAPHY (q.v.).

GERUND   A form of the verb used as a noun (English *I like walking;* Latin *ars amandi,* "the art of loving"; French *en marchant,* "while walking").

GERUNDIVE   A form of the verb similar to the gerund, but inflected and used as an adjective (Latin *amanda est,* "she is loveworthy").

GLIDE   A transitional sound produced by the passing of the vocal organs to or from the articulating position for a speech sound. *See also* DIPHTHONG.

GLOSS   An interlinear or marginal notation in an ancient or medieval manuscript giving a translation or explanation of a word or passage.

GLOTTAL   A sound produced in the larynx by narrowing or constricting the vocal cords (the catch between the two *o*'s of *coordinate*).

GRAPHEME   The smallest unit of writing that distinguishes one meaning from another (English *b, c, d, f*).

GUTTURAL   *See* VELAR.

HAPLOLOGY   Sporadic sound change whereby there is an omission in speech of one of two identical or similar consecutive sounds or syllables (*prob'ly* for *probably*).

HIATUS A pause or break in sound between two successive vowels (Latin *vinea;* French *la image,* where the hiatus is broken by elision, *l'image*); the position wherein a vowel stands before another vowel without an intervening consonant, and does not form a diphthong with the following vowel (*naïve*).

HIGH VOWEL A vowel produced with the tongue raised toward the roof of the mouth (*i* in *machine*). *Opposite:* Low VOWEL.

HOLDING PERIOD The period of complete closure between the formation of the articulation for a plosive and the release of the breath stream (as before the double *tt* in Italian *fatto*).

HOMOPHONE A word identical in sound with another, but different in written form, origin, and meaning (*to, too, two*).

HYBRID A word composed of elements originating from more than one language (*automobile,* with *auto-* from Greek, *-mobile* from Latin).

IDIOLECT The individual's use of language, with his own speech habits and use of words.

IDIOM A word or group of words having a special meaning which is not inherent to or determinable from its component parts (*look out* in the sense of *be careful*).

IMPARISYLLABIC Not having the same number of syllables in all singular declensional cases (Latin *iter,* genitive *itineris*). *Opposite:* PARISYLLABIC.

IMPERATIVE *See* MOOD.

IMPERFECT *See* TENSE.

INDECLINABLE Having only one form, and incapable of showing distinctions of gender, number, case, etc. (English *the;* Russian *kino*).

INDICATIVE *See* MOOD.

INFECTUM *See* ASPECT (IMPERFECTIVE).

INFINITIVE *See* MOOD.

INFIX A type of AFFIX inserted within the word (Latin *-n-* in *linquo,* whose stem is *lic-;* British colloquial *inde-damn-pendent*).

INFLECTION The addition of certain endings to the stem of a word to express grammatical relationships, functions, and aspects. *See also* CONJUGATION, DECLENSION.

INITIAL POSITION Position at the beginning of a word; in the case of a vowel, it may be said to have initial position if it is the vowel of the initial syllable, even if it is preceded by a consonant or consonant cluster (*o* in Latin *monui*).

INTERTONIC Between the main and the secondary stress in a word of several syllables (*-ter-* in *interésting*).

INTERVOCALIC Between vowels; said of consonants and consonant groups (both *m* and *t* in Latin *amatus*).

INVERSE SPELLING An erroneous spelling due to overcorrection on the part of the writer (Latin *diaebus* for *diebus* because the stone-cutters were conscious of the fact that they were prone to use *e* for *ae*).

ISOGLOSS   A line separating areas where the language differs with respect to a given feature, and marking the boundaries within which a given language phenomenon appears.

JOBELYN   The underworld cant used by the Paris lower classes in medieval times, illustrated in the writings of François Villon.

KATHAREVOUSA   Modern literary Greek, as opposed to colloquial DEMOTIKE; it generally conforms to Classical usage and rejects non-Greek vocabulary.

KOINE   The form of Greek used during the Hellenistic and Roman periods, the result of a merger of the ancient Greek dialects.

LABIAL   A consonant produced with one or both lips, or a vowel for which the lips are rounded (*p, b, m, f, v, w, u*); a sound in which the lower lip touches the upper lip (BILABIAL), or the upper teeth (DENTOLABIAL or LABIODENTAL).

LABIALIZATION   Lip rounding, protrusion of the lips. Historical process whereby an unrounded sound becomes a labial. *Synonym:* ROUNDING. *Opposite:* DELABIALIZATION, UNROUNDING.

LABIALIZED VELAR   A VELAR sound produced with accompanying lip rounding (*kw-* in *quality*).

LABIODENTAL   A consonant sound produced with the lower lip touching the upper front teeth (*f, v*). *Synonym:* DENTOLABIAL.

LAMBDACISM   Substitution of the phoneme *l* for another, usually *r* (Chinese immigrant dialect *chelly* for *cherry*). *Opposite:* RHOTACISM.

LANGUAGE OF COLONIZATION   The language of a politically, economically, or culturally superior or stronger nation imposed upon a conquered or dependent nation, or adopted by the latter, as the language of officialdom, business, and cultural interchange, parallel with or replacing the native language (English in India). *Synonym:* SUPERIMPOSED LANGUAGE.

LANGUAGE OF IMMIGRATION   The language of another country, spoken in communities composed of immigrants from that country, usually with the admixture of words and constructions borrowed from the language of the host country; sometimes applied to the language of the host country as distorted by the immigrants' native speech habits. *Synonym:* IMMIGRANT LANGUAGE.

LANGUAGES IN CONTACT   Two or more languages coexisting in contiguous areas, and influencing one another in their development, despite the fact that they may not be genetically or typologically related (Rumanian, Bulgarian, and Albanian, all Balkan area tongues, but of different Indo-European branches, seem to have developed in common the feature of a postposed definite article).

LATERAL   A consonant sound produced with complete closure in the front of the mouth, but incomplete closure at one or both sides of the tongue, to permit the escape of air (*l*).

LEARNED WORD   A word or form which did not develop popularly, in accordance with the phonetic laws of language change, but was introduced by clerical or scholarly use from the Classical lexicons (*episcopacy*, as opposed to the popular *bishopric*). *Synonym:* BOOK WORD. *Opposite:* POPULAR WORD. *See also* SEMILEARNED WORD.

LEVELING   *See* ANALOGY.

LEXICON   The total stock of words, morphemes, or both in a given language. The list of all the words in a language.

LIAISON   *See* LINKING.

LINGUA FRANCA   A contact vernacular used during the Middle Ages and Renaissance throughout the Mediterranean basin, and based primarily on Italian, but with admixtures from Arabic, French, Spanish, Greek, etc. *Synonym:* SABIR. Also used to describe any tongue of common intercourse among people of different language backgrounds (English among people from different parts of India).

LINGUISTIC GEOGRAPHY   The study and classification of the geographical extent and boundaries of linguistic phenomena; the study of language differences in a given speech area, and the mapping or charting of their distribution. *Synonyms:* AREA LINGUISTICS, DIALECT GEOGRAPHY, GEOGRAPHICAL LINGUISTICS. To be distinguished from GEOLINGUISTICS (q.v.).

LINGUISTICS   The study of man's speech habits; the descriptive analysis of the structures, or systems, in language (PHONEMICS, MORPHEMICS, MORPHOPHONEMICS, SYNTAX). DESCRIPTIVE LINGUISTICS describes languages and dialects. STRUCTURAL LINGUISTICS analyzes the structure of a language. HISTORICAL or DIACHRONIC LINGUISTICS deals with chronological changes in languages, SYNCHRONIC LINGUISTICS with one or more languages at one point in time. COMPARATIVE LINGUISTICS may be SYNCHRONIC, dealing with relationships at one point in time between different languages, or DIACHRONIC, comparing different forms of one language at different points in time. *Synonyms:* GLOTTOLOGY, LINGUISTIC SCIENCE, SCIENCE OF LANGUAGE.

LINKING   A phenomenon occurring when the final consonant sound of one word is pronounced without a pause before the vowel-initial word that follows, but not before a following consonant-initial word. (French *les autres* versus *les livres*). *Synonym:* LIAISON.

LIQUID   A sound type articulated with only partial closure; it is frictionless and capable of being prolonged like a vowel; it can, on occasion, be syllabic, and function as a vowel, as in Czech *vrh*, *mlh* (*l*, usually *r*, occasionally *n*, *m*).

LITURGICAL LANGUAGE   The language used in religious services and, occasionally, as a means of communication among its religious users (Latin for Roman Catholics, Classical Arabic for Moslems).

LOAN TRANSLATION   An expression brought into one language through translation of the constituent parts of the term in another language (*reason of state* for the French *raison d'état*).

LOAN WORD   A borrowed or adopted word from another language (English *very* from Old French *verai*). *Synonyms:* BORROWING; ALIEN, DOMESTICATED, or NATURALIZED WORD.

LOW VOWEL   A vowel produced with the tongue in the lower half of the mouth, which is relatively wide open (*aw* in *awful, e* in *met*). *Synonym:* OPEN VOWEL. *Opposites:* CLOSED OR HIGH VOWEL.

MEDIAL POSITION   Noninitial or nonfinal position of a sound within a word (the first *d* in *unaided*).

METAPHONY   *See* UMLAUT.

METATHESIS   Transposition of the order of sounds within the word (Anglo-Saxon *bren* to Modern English *burn;* Latin *miraculum* to Spanish *milagro*).

MIDDLE VOICE   *See* VOICE.

MIDDLE VOWEL   A vowel pronounced with the tongue at a middle position in the mouth, between the highest and the lowest elevation (*u* in *but*). *Synonym:* HALF OPEN VOWEL.

MONOGENESIS   The theory that all languages in the world had one ancestor. *Opposite:* POLYGENESIS.

MONOGLOT   Speaking, understanding, and using only one language. *Synonyms:* MONOLINGUAL, UNILINGUAL. *Opposites:* POLYGLOT, BI- or TRI- LINGUAL.

MONOPHTHONG   A phoneme produced as a single sound. A vowel sound that throughout its duration has a single, constant articulatory position (*a* in *father*).

MONOSYLLABIC   Consisting of a single syllable (English *gun;* Latin *sed*).

MOOD (OR MODE)   Distinction of form and meaning in a verb to express the manner in which the action described is thought of. The INDICATIVE MOOD represents the action as a definite fact (*he loves*). The SUBJUNCTIVE MOOD represents the action as hypothetical or subordinated to another action (*whether he be; if I were*). The IMPERATIVE MOOD expresses a command or exhortation (*write to him!; let us go!*). The INFINITIVE, often described as a mood, usually presents the action without reference to a subject (*to go*). Some languages, like Greek, have an OPTATIVE MOOD, used primarily to express a wish (*would that he were here!*).

MORPHEME   A minimal unit of speech that is recurrent and meaningful; it may be a word or part of a word (*un-friend-ly; speak-s.*) The morpheme is FREE if it can be used in isolation (*friend* of *unfriendly*); BOUND if it cannot be so used (*un-, -ly*).

MORPHOLOGY   The study of MORPHEMES and their formation into words, including INFLECTION, DERIVATION, COMPOSITION, and distinct from SYNTAX and WORD ORDER.

MUTE   See PLOSIVE. As an adjective, it is applied to a vowel which contributes to the pronunciation of a word, but does not form a separate syllable (the final *e* in English *mate* and French *porte*).

NASAL   A sound uttered with nose passage open and mouth passage occluded at some point (lips for *m*, tongue tip for *n*); or with mouth open, and nose passage producing resonance (French *en, un;* Portuguese *em, um*).

NASALIZATION   The lowering of the velum so as to leave the nasal cavity accessible to the air stream. Historically, the addition of full or partial opening of the mouth to the original nasal consonant sound (Latin *annum* to French *an*).

NATURALIZED WORD   A LOAN WORD (q.v.) which has been in the borrowing language long enough to assume the borrowing language's phonemic pattern, stress, and orthographic form (*very* from Old French *verai; bishop* from Latin *episcopus*).

NOMINATIVE   *See* CASE.

NUMBER   Grammatically, the distinction in form or meaning of a noun, adjective, pronoun, or verb to denote one or more than one of the objects mentioned. The SINGULAR number denotes one. The PLURAL number denotes more than one. The more ancient Indo-European languages (Sanskrit, Greek) and the Semitic tongues also have a DUAL number, usually for objects that go in pairs (eyes, hands); traces of the dual appear in such languages as Latin and Russian. Some languages have forms indicating three or four objects, while others seldom bother to make number distinctions, unless it is strictly necessary (Chinese, Japanese).

OBLIQUE CASE   In Classical languages, a collective term for all declensional cases other than NOMINATIVE and VOCATIVE. In Old French and Provençal, the term is used to denote the single declensional form which represents a merger of the Latin oblique cases, and is opposed to the NOMINATIVE, which is extended to cover the VOCATIVE.

OBSOLESCENT   Falling into disuse, usually because the object it represents is becoming extinct (*trolley car*).

OBSOLETE   No longer in current use (*sparking light, yclept*). A distinction is sometimes made between OBSOLETE (*sparking light*) and ARCHAIC (*yclept*).

OCCLUSIVE   *See* PLOSIVE.

OFF-GLIDE   *See* GLIDE.

ON-GLIDE   *See* GLIDE.

OPEN SYLLABLE   A syllable ending in a vowel sound (both syllables in Spanish *to-ro*). *Synonym:* FREE SYLLABLE. *Opposites:* BLOCKED, CHECKED, or CLOSED SYLLABLE.

OXYTONE   A word where the final syllable bears the main stress (*police*). *See also* PAROXYTONE, PROPAROXYTONE.

PALATAL   A consonant formed by placing the front, or blade, of the tongue against the hard palate (English, *sh* in *shore*, *s* in *pleasure*, *ch* in *church*, *j* in *jet;* German, *ch* in *ich;* French, *gn* in *agneau;* Italian, *gli* in *figlio*).

PALATALIZATION   Historically, the change from a nonpalatal to a palatal sound (Latin *centum*, with $c = k$, to Italian *cento*, with $c = ch$).

PALEOGRAPHY   The study of ancient and medieval ways of writing, including the decipherment and interpretation of texts painted or traced with ink or colors on paper, parchment, and other soft materials. Distinguished from EPIGRAPHY, the study of inscriptions carved or engraved into stone, clay, and other solid materials.

PARADIGM   A complete set of all the conjugational or declensional forms of a word (the complete declension of Latin *mūrus*, through its six cases in the singular, and its six cases in the plural).

PARISYLLABIC   Having the same number of syllables in all or almost all inflectional forms (all the singular case forms of Latin *mūrus*). *Opposite:* IMPARISYLLABIC.

PAROXYTONE   A word with its main stress on the penult syllable (*occurring*). *See also* OXYTONE, PROPAROXYTONE.

PARTICLE   A word not denoting an idea in itself (articles, prepositions, conjunctions, interjections). *Partial synonyms:* EMPTY, FUNCTION, RELATIONAL, or STRUCTURE WORD, MARKER, POINTER.

PASSIVE   *See* VOICE.

PATOIS   The popular, unwritten speech in a given locality; the local dialect of the lower social strata, normally unwritten. *See also* DIALECT.

PATRONYMIC   A name describing the paternity or ancestry of the bearer, and usually derived from the name of a father or ancestor (*The Atreides*, "sons or descendants of Atreus"; *Johnson, Williams, Ivanovich, McHugh, Fitzgerald, O'Brian*). MATRONYMIC describes feminine ancestry (Helgason, di Luisa).

PEJORATION   A semantic lowering in meaning (Spanish *alguacil*, "constable," Italian *aguzzino*, "hangman's helper," from Arabic *al-wazir*, "vizier"). A PEJORATIVE may also be a word marked by the addition of a pejorative suffix (*poet-aster*, Italian *libr-accio*, "bad book"). *Opposites:* AMELIORATION, ENHANCEMENT. *Synonym:* DEGENERATION OF MEANING.

PENULT (OR PENULTIMATE)   The next to the last syllable in a word (*-la-* in *capillary*).

PERFECTIVE   A verbal ASPECT expressing a nonhabitual or one-time action, or an action considered from the standpoint of its completion, conclusion, or result (Russian *dat'*, as opposed to *davat'*). *Synonym:* MOMENTARY. *Opposites:* DURATIVE, IMPERFECTIVE.

PERIPHRASTIC   Grammatically, a conjugation formed by using one or more auxiliary verbs (Latin *amaturus sum*, "I am about to love," for *amabor*, "I shall love"; French *je vais écrire*, "I am going to write," for *j'écrirai*, "I shall write").

PHILOLOGY   The scientific study of language, with the inclusion of literary texts; the study of a language and its entire literary output. *Partial synonym:* HISTORICAL LINGUISTICS.

PHONEME   The smallest unit of speech distinguishing one utterance from another; a class of sounds accepted by the speakers as a single sound, though phonetically different (the different *p* sounds of *spit*, *pit*, *lap*).

PHONETICS   The study, analysis, and classification of speech sounds, including their production, transmission, and reception.

PHONOLOGY   A study of the changes, modifications, and transformations of speech sounds during the history and development of a language (HISTORICAL PHONOLOGY). The sounds of the language and their permissible combinations at any given historical stage (DESCRIPTIVE PHONOLOGY).

PIDGIN   A creolized or hybrid version of a language, usually characterized by simplified grammar and a limited and often mixed vocabulary; sometimes used chiefly for intergroup communication (Melanesian Pidgin English); occasionally becoming the first language of the community (Haitian French Creole).

PITCH   Highness or lowness of tone; difference in the relative vibration frequency of the voice; sometimes contributing to the total meaning by being an integral part of the word and essential to its meaning, as in Chinese; more often associated with secondary overtones of the same meaning, as in English (*John is here; John? Are you there?; John! How could you!*) *See also* ACCENT.

PLOSIVE   A consonant that momentarily halts the flow of breath; it is produced by completely closing the nasal and oral air passages (IMPLOSION), resulting in a retention of air (HOLDING PERIOD), and then suddenly opening the closure and releasing the breath (EXPLOSION); this final phase may not inevitably occur, as in American English *on your lap*. The principal plosives are represented by *b, d, g* (VOICED), *p, t, k* (VOICELESS). *Synonyms:* EXPLOSIVE, MUTE, OCCLUSIVE, STOP.

POINT OF ARTICULATION   The point where the movable speech organs (tongue, lips, uvula) meet the immovable speech organs (teeth, alveoli, palate, velum or soft palate, pharyngeal walls). It helps to determine the nature of the speech sound that is produced.

POPULAR ETYMOLOGY   *See* FOLK ETYMOLOGY.

POPULAR WORD   A word developed in full accord with the phonological laws of its language (French *frêle*, as against *fragile*) *Opposite:* LEARNED WORD.

PORTMANTEAU WORD   A word coined by combining the first part of one word with the last part of another (*smog*, from *smoke* plus *fog; motel*, from *motor* plus *hotel*).

POSITIONAL VARIANT   A variant of a sound due to distribution, environment, or context (the PHONEME *k* has a front articulation in *key*, a back articulation in *cool*). *Synonym:* ALLOPHONE. Positional variants are said to be in COMPLEMENTARY DISTRIBUTION.

POSTTONIC   After the main accent (in *manner, e* is in posttonic position).

PREFIX   An AFFIX placed before a word, with which it forms a single unit, but whose meaning it changes (*un-* in *unlikely*).

PRESCRIPTIVE   Indicating what should be said, rather than what is actually said, as applied to grammar. *Synonym:* NORMATIVE. *Opposite:* DESCRIPTIVE.

PRETONIC   Before the main accent (in *policeman, o* is in pretonic position).

PROCLITIC   A word pronounced as one phonetic unit with the word that follows, losing its own accent (the abbreviated form of *it* in *'tis*). *Opposite:* ENCLITIC.

PROPAROXYTONE   A word bearing its main stress on the third syllable from the end (*nitrogen*). *See also* OXYTONE, PAROXYTONE.

PROTHESIS   The prefixing of an inorganic vowel to a word, for easier pronunciation or other reasons (Latin *spiritum* to Vulgar Latin *ispiritum*). *Synonym:* PROSTHESIS. The vowel so prefixed is called PROTHETIC or PROSTHETIC.

QUALITY   The identifying characteristic of a vowel sound, determined by the resonance of the vocal chambers, in turn determined by the position of the movable speech organs (tongue, lips).

QUANTITY   Duration or length; relative amount of time during which the vocal organs remain in the position required for the production of a sound.

RECESSIVE ACCENT   Historically, the accent on the initial syllable of words of Germanic origin; or, as in Greek and Latin, as far back as the accentual laws of the language permit (no farther back than the antepenult).

REDUCTION   The process whereby a full form is cut down to a shorter form (*flu* from *influenza*).

REDUPLICATION   A process whereby there is a repetition of a letter or syllable, usually at the beginning of a word (Greek *pempō*, perfect tense *pepompha*, with reduplicative prefix; Latin *dō*, perfect tense *dedī*).

REFLEXIVE   *See* VOICE.

RHOTACISM   The use of *r* instead of another sound (usually *l*) in certain positions (Roman dialect *er cortello* for *il coltello;* Portuguese *branco* from *blank*).

ROOT   *See* BASE.

ROUNDED VOWEL   A vowel produced with rounded lips (*u* of *rule*).

ROUNDING   Pronouncing a sound with lips rounded. *Synonym:* LABIALIZATION.

SCHWA (also SHWA, SHVA)   The colorless, indistinct, neutral vowel sound represented by the symbol [ə] (both *a*'s in *America*, *e* in *under*, *o* in *neighbor; e* in French *je*, first *e* in *lever*).

SEGMENTATION   *See* DIPHTHONGIZATION.

SEMANTICS   The study of meaning in language, including the relation between language, thought, and behavior, as well as historical changes in the meanings of words and expressions.

SEMICONSONANT   *See* GLIDE, DIPHTHONG.

SEMILEARNED   A form whose popular development in accordance with the phonetic laws of the language has become arrested, usually because the word at one point of history becomes the exclusive property of the more learned classes (French *esprit* from Latin *spiritum* if fully popular should have gone on to *éprit* or *épri;* if fully learned it should have been *spirite;* its form indicates that it had fully popular development until about the fourteenth century, then became arrested). *See also* LEARNED WORD, POPULAR WORD.

SEMIVOWEL   *See* GLIDE, DIPHTHONG. Some phoneticians reserve SEMIVOWEL for the OFF-GLIDE *y* or *w* of *boy, bow,* and use SEMICONSONANT for the ON-GLIDE of *yes, was.*

SIBILANT   A fricative consonant in the production of which the tongue comes into contact with the hard palate (*s* in *soft, z* in *zone, sh* in *shore, z* in *azure, ch* in *church, j* in *jet*); the term is sometimes restricted to *s* and *z* alone, with the other sounds described as composite (palatal stop plus palatal fricative), palatal fricatives, or affricates.

SIMPLIFICATION   The reduction of a double, or GEMINATED, to a single consonant sound (Latin *abbatem* to Spanish *abad;* Latin *communem* to Italian *comune*). *Opposite:* GEMINATION, DOUBLING.

SLANG   A type of language in common use, produced by the popular adaptation and extension of the meaning of existing words and the coinage of new words without regard for standard usage; it is peculiar to certain social groups or age groups; it is sometimes local, sometimes nationwide.

SOCIAL STRATIFICATION   Those differences in the language of a single locality which are due to the social or educational level of the speakers.

SONANT   *See* VOICED.

SONORIZATION   *See* VOICING.

SPIRANT   *See* FRICATIVE.

SPONTANEOUS SOUND CHANGE   A change assumed to have been caused by the character of the sound itself, independently of any influence from its phonetic environment. *Synonyms:* AUTONOMOUS OR UNCONDITIONED SOUND CHANGE. *Opposites:* COMBINATORY, CONDITIONED, DEPENDENT, or FUNCTIONAL SOUND CHANGE.

STARRED FORM   A word or form to which an asterisk has been prefixed to show that it is hypothetical and unattested, and reconstructed on the basis of known data and linguistic laws (Indo-European *swesor,* the hypothetical ancestor of *sister* and kindred forms). *Opposite:* ATTESTED FORM.

STEM   *See* BASE.

STOP   *See* PLOSIVE.

STRESS   *See* ACCENT.

STRONG   As applied to verbs, nouns, or adjectives, undergoing internal modification (*sing, sang, sung; goose, geese*). *Opposite:* WEAK.

STRUCTURE   The regularities and patterns of a language considered as a system in which the elements are defined in terms of relationship to other elements.

SUBJUNCTIVE   *See* MOOD.

SUBSTRATUM   A language displaced as the dominant tongue in its area by another language of conquerors, colonizers, etc., but possibly responsible for certain changes in the language that suppresses or replaces it (SUBSTRATUM THEORY). *See also* SUPERSTRATUM.

SUFFIX   A phoneme, syllable, or syllables added to the end of a word to modify its meaning or to form new derivatives (*dog-s, work-ing, friendli-er*). *See also* AFFIX, PREFIX, INFIX.

SUPERSTRATUM   The language of a culturally, economically, or politically superior group introduced into an area and affecting the language of the more numerous subject population, but itself eventually disappearing from the area (Germanic in the Western Roman Empire; Norman French in England). The belief that this influence takes place constitutes the SUPERSTRATUM THEORY. The ADSTRATUM THEORY includes both SUBSTRATUM and SUPERSTRATUM, plus any reciprocal influences produced by contiguity across borders.

SUPINE   A verbal noun which does not appear in English. In Latin, it appears in only two case forms, the accusative, to denote purpose after some verbs of motion, and the ablative, which functions as an ablative of specification (*mirabile dictu*, "wonderful with respect to the saying," "wonderful to relate").

SUPPORT VOWEL   A parasitic vowel developing at the end of a word to facilitate the pronunciation of a preceding troublesome consonant cluster (the final *e*-mute of French *peuple*). *Synonym:* VOYELLE D'APPUI.

SUPRASEGMENTAL PHONEME   Such elements as pitch, stress, juncture, occasionally nasalization, voice, or voicelessness, that are not normally distinguished in writing, as the SEGMENTAL PHONEMES are by letters, but are apparent in speech and add to the meaning of the expression (*What are we having for dinner, mother?* versus *What are we having for dinner, steak?*).

SURD   *See* UNVOICED, VOICELESS.

SYLLABLE   A group of phonemes consisting of a vowel or continuant, alone or combined with one or more consonants, constituting a unit of word formation. *See also* OPEN SYLLABLE, CLOSED SYLLABLE.

SYNCHRONIC   *See* LINGUISTICS.

SYNCOPE (OR SYNCOPATION)   The loss of a medial vowel, due generally to stress accent elsewhere in the word (Latin *domina* to Vulgar Latin *dom'na*).

SYNTAX   The study and rules of the relation of words to one another as the expression of ideas and the formation of phrases and sentences; the study of WORD ORDER.

SYNTHETIC LANGUAGE   A language where grammatical relationships are expressed chiefly through INFLECTIONS, and several concepts are united into one word. *Opposite:* ANALYTICAL LANGUAGE (q.v.).

TABOO   The avoidance of certain words, and their replacement by euphemistic expressions, for superstitious, moral, or social reasons (English four-letter words).

TAP   A short, single FLAP of the tongue (Spanish pe*r*o; British ve*r*y).

TELESCOPED WORD   A word obtained by combining parts of two or more words (*smog*, from *smoke* plus *fog*; *motel*, from *motor* plus *hotel*). *Synonyms:* BLEND, CROSSING, PORTMANTEAU WORD.

TENSE   The modification of verb forms to express time. The PRESENT tense indicates what happens habitually, or is happening now (*I go, I am*

going). The PAST tense indicates what happened (*I went*). The IMPER-
FECT tense indicates what was happening, or used to happen (*I was going, I used to go*). The FUTURE tense indicates what will happen (*I shall
go*). COMPOUND TENSES are formed by an auxiliary verb combined with
the past participle: PRESENT PERFECT (*I have gone*), PAST PERFECT (*I
had gone*), FUTURE PERFECT (*I shall have gone*). This scheme differs
from language to language. In Latin, there are no compound tenses in the
active voice (Present *amō;* Imperfect *amābam;* Future *amābō;* Perfect
[serving as both Past and Present Perfect] *amāvī;* Pluperfect, or Past Perfect, *amāveram;* Future Perfect *amāverō*). In Greek, the functions of the
Latin Perfect are subdivided between an AORIST (or Past) tense, *epempsa*,
and a PERFECT (or PRESENT PERFECT), *pepompha*. In the Romance languages, the functions of the Latin Pluperfect are subdivided between a
PLUPERFECT, compounded of the Imperfect of the auxiliary plus the past
participle, and a PAST ANTERIOR, compounded of the Past (called Past
Definite in French) plus the participle. PRESENT and PAST CONDITIONAL
paradigms, which did not exist in Latin, have been created in Romance.
Similar tense schemes appear in the SUBJUNCTIVE MOOD.

THEME   *See* BASE.

TILDE   A diacritic used over letters in writing to indicate a modified pronunciation (Spanish ñ; Portuguese ã, õ).

TONE   The musical pitch of the voice; a rising, falling, level, or falling-rising
inflection of the voice in pronouncing certain words which are otherwise
identical (as in Chinese). If the tone alone distinguishes meanings attached to these words, the language is said to be a TONE LANGUAGE.

TONIC   Pertaining to the ACCENT. The TONIC ACCENT is the relative phonetic
prominence, as from greater STRESS or higher PITCH, of a spoken syllable
or word (some authorities prefer to use the term as a synonym for PITCH
alone). *See also* PRETONIC, POST-TONIC.

TOPONYMIC   A place-name (New York). A word denoting a geographical
feature (*bayou, butte*).

TRADE LANGUAGE   *See* CREOLE, LINGUA FRANCA, PIDGIN.

TRANSCRIPTION   The rendering of a speech unit into written symbols, which
may be alphabetic (*I wanna go*), International Phonetic ([kæt] for *cat*),
or phonemic (/bo/ for *bow*). *See also* TRANSLITERATION.

TRANSLITERATION   The representation of an utterance from one language into
the conventional symbols of another language or writing system (*Khru-
shchev* for Russian Хрущев).

TRANSPOSITION   *See* METATHESIS.

TRIAL   *See* NUMBER.

TRIPHTHONG   A combination of three vowel sounds functioning as a single
unit (*sway, wow;* Italian *miei, buoi*).

TRIPLETS   Three words of the same language any one of which represents a
DOUBLET (q.v.) with either of the other two (Italian *fiaba, fola, favola*,
all from Latin *fabula*).

UMLAUT   An internal vowel change caused by the partial retrogressive assimilatory influence of a vowel, semivowel, or even consonant in the following syllable; the fronting or raising of a back or low vowel (*a, o, u*) caused by an *i* or *y* in the following syllable, now usually lost or altered (English *feet* from Germanic *°fōtīz*; French *fis* from Latin *fēcī;* Spanish *hice* from Latin *fēcī*). *Synonym:* METAPHONY. As applied to German orthography, the term is popularly used to denote the DIACRITIC symbol which indicates the phonetic process (*Brüder, Sätze*).

UNCONDITIONED SOUND CHANGE   *Synonym:* SPONTANEOUS SOUND CHANGE. *See also* CONDITIONED SOUND CHANGE.

UNVOICED   A sound produced without vibration of the vocal cords (*p, t, k, f*). *Synonyms:* VOICELESS (for consonants), HARD CONSONANT, SURD. *Opposites:* VOICED (for consonants), SOFT CONSONANT, SONANT.

UNVOICING   Historically, the change from a voiced to an unvoiced consonant (Indo-European *d* of *°dent-* to Germanic *t* of *tooth*). *Synonym:* DEVOICING. *Opposites:* VOICING, SONORIZATION.

UVULAR   A consonant sound produced by contact between the back of the tongue and the uvula (Parisian French *r-grasseyé*). *Partial synonym:* POSTVELAR.

VELAR   A consonant formed by the back of the dorsum of the tongue against the soft palate or velum (*c* in *cool,* *g* in *go,* *ng* in *song,* *ch* in German *Nacht*). *Synonyms:* DORSAL, GUTTURAL. As applied to a vowel, *see* BACK VOWEL.

VELARIZED   Produced with the tongue drawn back from a given position (Spanish *x* of *Quixote,* once pronounced like English *sh,* later velarized to *kh,* with attendant change of spelling to *j*). *Synonym:* RETRACTED.

VERNACULAR   The current everyday speech of a people or area, as distinguished from the literary language. *Synonyms:* COLLOQUIAL, UMGANGSSPRACHE.

VIBRANT   A sound produced with a variable number of contacts between an articulator (normally the tongue) and one of the immovable speech organs (*r* in British *very,* *rr* in Spanish *perro*).

VOCALIC   Pertaining to or functioning as a vowel. A VOCALIC CONSONANT is a consonant that may be used as a vowel in given languages (Czech: *l* in *pln,* *r* in *smrt*).

VOCALIZATION   Historically, the change of a consonant to a semivowel or vowel (Latin *planum* to Italian *piano;* Latin *palma* to French *paume*).

VOICE   The distinction of form or inflection of a verb to indicate the relationship of the subject to the action denoted by the verb. The ACTIVE VOICE indicates that the subject performs the action (*I strike*). The PASSIVE VOICE indicates that the subject receives the action (*I am struck*). The MIDDLE VOICE, appearing in Greek, represents the subject acting upon himself or for himself, a function which has generally been taken over by the REFLEXIVE (Spanish *se afeita,* "he is shaving [himself]"), which in some languages tends also to replace the passive (*aquí se habla español,*

"Spanish speaks itself [is spoken] here"). An active verb with impersonal subject (French *on parle français,* German *man spricht deutsch*) is also used in some languages to avoid the passive.

VOICED AND VOICELESS SOUNDS   Sounds produced with (or without) simultaneous vibration of the vocal cords. The former include all vowels, semivowels, and voiced consonants, such as *b, d, g, v, z.* The latter are all consonants (*p, t, k, f, s*). *Partial synonyms:* (for VOICED SOUNDS) SONANT, RESONANT; (for *voiceless sounds*) HARD, SURD, UNVOICED.

VOWEL   A sound produced by an unobstructed passage of air through the mouth that is not constricted enough to cause audible friction; it is accompanied by vibration of the vocal cords. If the mouth is closed, a NASAL vowel sound results.

VOYELLE D'APPUI   *See* SUPPORT VOWEL.

WEAK   As applied to Germanic verbs, those which form the past and past participle by the addition of the regular inflectional ending, without internal vowel change (*work, worked, worked*). *Opposite:* STRONG.

WORD ORDER   The arrangement of words in the sentence or phrase that is normal in the language; of great importance in languages which have discarded inflections in whole (Chinese) or in part (English); of lesser moment in languages that have retained full inflections (Latin, Russian). *See also* SYNTAX.

YOD   The glide or transition sound heard initially in *yes;* the name comes from a letter of the Semitic alphabet that invariably has that value. *See also* SEMIVOWEL.

YODIZATION   A palatalization which acoustically equals the sound of *y* added to a consonant. Historically, the changing of a pure vowel, usually *e* or *i* in HIATUS, into a semivowel (Latin *vi-ne-a* to Vulgar Latin *vi-nya* to Italian *vigna,* French *vigne,* Spanish *viña*). *See also* SEMIVOWEL.

Selected Bibliography

This bibliography includes only some of the major and relevant works of scholars referred to in the preceding Brief History of Romance Philology and Linguistics. It is in no way intended to be exhaustive.

Agard, Frederick B., "Present-day Judaeo-Spanish in the United States," *Hispania*, 33 (1950), 203–210.

Anglade, Joseph, *Grammaire de l'ancien provençal ou ancienne langue d'oc.* Paris, 1921.

Alonso, Amado, *De la pronunciación medieval a la moderna en español.* 2 vols. Madrid, 1955–1969.

Appel, Carl, *Provenzalische Lautlehre.* Leipzig, 1918.

———, *Provenzalische Chrestomathie.* Leipzig, 1895.

Auerbach, Ernst, *Introduction aux études de philologie romane.* Frankfurt am Main, 1949. (English trans.: *Introduction to Romance Languages and Literatures.* New York, 1961.)

Baldinger, Kurt, Georges Straka, and J.-D. Gendron, *Dictionnaire étymologique de l'ancien français.* Paris, 1972–   .

Banitt, Menahem, *A Comparative Study of Judaeo-Italian Translations of Isaiah.* New York, 1945 (published under the name Max Berenblut).

———, *Le Glossaire de Bâle.* 2 vols. Jerusalem, 1972.

Bartoli, Matteo G., *Das Dalmatische.* 2 vols. Vienna, 1910.

———, *L'Italia linguistica.* Turin, 1927.

Bertoni, Giulio, *Profilo linguistico d'Italia.* Modena, 1940.

———, *Italia dialettale.* Milan, 1925.

Battisti, Carlo, *Avviamento allo studio del latino volgare.* Bari, 1949.

———, and Giovanni Alessio, *Dizionario etimologico italiano.* Florence, 1948–56.

Bloch, Oscar, and Walther von Wartburg, *Dictionnaire étymologique de la langue française.* 5th ed. Paris, 1968.

Blondheim, David S. *Les parlers judéo-romans et la Vetus Latina.* Paris, 1925.

Bonfante, Giuliano, "L'origine des langues romanes," *Renaissance*, I, No. 4 (1943), 537–558.

Bourciez, Edouard, *Eléments de linguistique romane.* 4th ed., rev. Paris, 1946.

Buck, Carl D., *A Grammar of Oscan and Umbrian.* Boston, 1928.

Carnoy, Albert, *Le latin d'Espagne d'après les inscriptions.* 2nd ed. Louvain, 1906.

Cohen, Marcel, *Histoire d'une langue: le français.* 3rd ed., rev. Paris, 1967.

Conway, R. S., S.-E. Johnson, and J. Whatmough, *The Prae-Italic Dialects of Italy.* Cambridge, Mass., 1933.

Cooper, Paul J., "The Language of the Forum Judicum." Unpublished Ph.D. dissertation. Columbia University, 1952.

Corominas, Juan, *Diccionario crítico etimológico de la lengua castellana.* 4 vols. Madrid, 1954–57.

Crescini, Vincenzo, *Manuale per l'avviamento agli studi provenzali.* Milan, 1926.

Dauzat, Albert, *Histoire de la langue française.* Paris, 1930.

———, *Phonétique et grammaire historique de la langue française.* Paris, 1950.

Decurtins, C., *Rätoromanische Chrestomathie.* Erlangen, 1896–1919.

Densusianu, Ovidiu, *Histoire de la langue roumaine.* 2 vols. Paris, 1901–38.

Devoto, Giacomo, *Profilo di storia linguistica italiana.* Florence, 1953.

———, *Storia della lingua di Roma.* 2nd ed. Bologna, 1944. (German trans.: *Geschichte der Sprache Roms.* Heidelberg, 1968.)

Diehl, Ernst (ed.), *Inscriptiones Latinae Christianae Veteres.* 3 vols. 2nd ed. Berlin, 1961. *Supplementum.* vol. 4. Edited by J. Moreau and H.-I. Marrou. Berlin, 1967.

———, *Lateinische altchristliche Inschriften.* 2nd ed. Bonn, 1913.

———, *Vulgärlateinische Inschriften.* Bonn, 1910.

Diez, Friedrich, *Grammatik der romanischen Sprachen.* 5th ed. Bonn, 1882.

Elcock, William D., *The Romance Languages.* London, 1960.

Entwistle, William, *The Spanish Language, together with Portuguese, Catalan, and Basque.* 2nd ed. London, 1962.

Ernout, A., and A. Meillet, *Dictionnaire étymologique de la langue latine.* 3rd ed. Paris, 1951.

Ewert, Alfred, *The French Language.* London, 1938.

Fisher, John, *The Lexical Affiliations of Vegliote.* New York, forthcoming.

Gaeng, Paul, *An Inquiry into Local Variations in Vulgar Latin as Reflected in the Vocalism of Christian Inscriptions.* Chapel Hill, N.C., 1968.

———, *A Study of Nominal Inflection in Latin Inscriptions,* Chapel Hill, N.C., forthcoming.

Gamillscheg, Ernst, *Romania Germanica.* 3 vols. Berlin-Leipzig, 1934–36.

Gartner, Theodor, *Handbuch der rätoromanischen Sprache und Literatur.* Halle, 1910.

Gaster, Moses, *Chrestomathie roumaine.* 2 vols. Leipzig-Bucharest, 1891.

Godefroy, F., *Dictionnaire de l'ancienne langue française et de tous ses dialectes.* 10 vols. Paris, 1881–1902.

Grandgent, Charles H., *An Outline of the Phonology and Morphology of Old Provençal.* Boston, 1905.

———, *Introduction to Vulgar Latin.* Boston, 1907. (Reprint: New York, 1962.)

————, *From Latin to Italian*. Cambridge, Mass., 1927.

Graur, Alexandru, *A Bird's-Eye View of the Evolution of the Rumanian Language*. Bucharest, 1963.

————, *La romanité du roumain*. Bucharest, 1965.

Griera i Gaja, Antoni, *Gramática historica del català antic*. Barcelona, 1931.

————, *Atlas lingüistic de Catalunya*. Barcelona, 1923–68.

Gröber, Gustav, *Grundriss der romanischen Philologie*. 2nd ed. Strasbourg, 1904–06.

Guarnerio, Pier E., "I dialetti odierni di Sassari, della Gallura e della Corsica," *Archivio Glottologico*, 13 (1890), 125–140; 14 (1891), 131–200 and 385–422.

Hadlich, Roger L., *The Phonological History of Vegliote*. Chapel Hill, N.C., 1965.

Hall, Robert A., Jr., *Bibliografia della linguistica italiana*. 3 vols. Florence, 1958.

————, *Bibliografia della linguistica italiana: primo supplemento decennale (1956–66)*. Florence, 1969.

————, *External History of the Romance Languages*. New York, 1974.

Hatzfeld, Adolphe, Arsène Darmesteter, and Antoine Thomas, *Dictionnaire général de la langue française depuis le commencement du XVIIe siècle jusqu'à nos jours*. Paris, 1888.

Holmes, Urban T., and Alexander Schütz, *A History of the French Language*. Rev. ed. Chapel Hill, N.C., 1948.

Iordan, Iorgu, *An Introduction to Romance Linguistics: Its Schools and Scholars*. Revised, translated, and in parts recast by John Orr. London, 1937. (2nd ed. with supplement by R. Posner, "Thirty Years On." Berkeley, 1970.)

Jeanroy, Alfred, *La poésie lyrique des troubadours*. 2 vols. Toulouse-Paris, 1934.

Jungemann, Frederick, *La teoría del sustrato y los dialectos hispano-romances y gascones*. Madrid, 1955.

Lapesa, Rafael, *Historia de la lengua española*. 5th ed., rev. Madrid, 1959.

Lausberg, Heinrich, *Romanische Sprachwissenschaft*. Sammlung "Göschen." 4 vols. Berlin, 1956–62. (Spanish trans.: *Lingüística románica*. 2 vols. Madrid, 1965.)

Lerch, Eugen, *Historische Syntax der französischen Sprache*. 3 vols. Leipzig, 1925–34.

Lévy, Raphaël, *Recherches lexicographiques sur d'anciens textes français d'origine juive*. Baltimore, 1932.

Lindsay, W.-M., *The Latin Language*. Oxford, 1894.

Löfstedt, Einar, *Philologischer Kommentar zur Peregrinatio Aetheriae*. Uppsala, 1911.

————, *Late Latin*. Oslo, 1959.

Luria, Max A., *A Study of the Monastir Dialect of Judeo-Spanish*. New York, 1930.

Kieckers, Ernst, *Historische lateinische Grammatik*. 2 vols. Munich, 1931.

Malkiel, Yakov, "The hypothetical base in Romance etymology," *Word*, 6 (1950), 42–69.

———, "Hispanic Philology," in *Current Trends in Linguistics 4*, The Hague, 1968, pp. 158–228.

Manea, Maria M., *Gramatica comparată limbilor romanice*. Bucharest, 1971.

Mazzolani, Lidia S., *L'impero senza fine*. 2nd ed. Milan, 1972.

Maurer, Theodoro H., Jr., *Gramática do latim vulgar*. Rio de Janeiro, 1959.

———, *O problema do latim vulgar*. Rio de Janeiro, 1962.

Menarini, Alberto, *I gerghi bolognesi*. Modena, 1942.

Menéndez Pidal, Ramón, *Orígenes del español*. 4th ed. Madrid, 1956.

———, *Manual de gramática histórica española*. 10th ed. Madrid, 1958.

———, *La Chanson de Roland y el neotradicionalismo*. Madrid, 1959.

Merlo, Clemente, "Il sostrato etnico e i dialetti italiani," *Revue de Linguistique romane*, 9 (1945), 176–194.

Meyer-Lübke, Wilhelm, *Grammatik der romanischen Sprachen*. 4 vols. Leipzig, 1890–1902. (French trans.: *Grammaire des langues romanes*. Paris, 1890–1906.)

———, *Einführung in das Studium der romanischen Sprachwissenschaft*. 3rd ed. Heidelberg, 1920.

———, *Historische Grammatik der französischen Sprache*. 2 vols. Heidelberg, 1913–21.

Migliorini, Bruno, and T. Gwynfor Griffith, *The Italian Language*. London, 1966. (Translation and adaptation of *Storia della lingua italiana*. Florence, 1960.)

Mohl, F.-G., *Introduction à la chronologie du latin vulgaire*. Paris, 1899.

Monaci, E., *Crestomazia italiana dei primi secoli*. Città di Castello, 1955.

Monteverdi, Angelo, *Manuale di avviamento agli studi romanzi*. Milan, 1952.

Muljačić, Žarko, "Die Klassifikation der romanischen Sprachen," *Romanistiches Jahrbuch*, 18 (1967), 23–37.

———, "La posizione del dalmatico nella Romania," *Atti del Congresso Internazionale di Linguistica Romanza*, 2 (1965), 1103–1109.

Muller, Henri François, *A Chronology of Vulgar Latin*. Halle, 1929.

———, and Pauline Taylor, *A Chrestomathy of Vulgar Latin*. New York, 1932.

———, *L'Époque mérovingienne*. New York, 1945.

Nascentes, Antenor, *Dicionário etimológico da lingua portuguesa*. Rio de Janeiro, 1932.

Nyrop, Kristoffer, *Grammaire historique de la language française*. 6 vols. Copenhagen, 1899–1930.

Omeltchenko, Stephen W., *A Quantitative and Comparative Study of the Vocalism of the Latin Inscriptions of North Africa, Britain, Dalmatia, and the Balkans*. Chapel Hill, N.C., forthcoming.

d'Ovidio F., and W. Meyer-Lübke, *Grammatica storica della lingua e dei dialetti italiani*. Milan, 1931.

de Paiva Boléo, Manuel, *Introdução ao estudo da filologia portuguesa*. Lisbon, 1946.

————, *O estudo dos dialectos e falares portugueses.* Coimbra, 1942.

Palmer, L.-R., *The Latin Language.* London, 1954.

Parlangèli, Oronzo, "Il sostrato linguistico in Sicilia," *Kōkalōs,* 10/11 (1964), 211–244.

————, *Storia linguistica e storia politica nell'Italia meridionale,* Firenze, 1960.

————, "Testi siciliani in caratteri greci," *Bollettino del Centro di Studi Filologici e Linguistici Siciliani* 7 (1962), 464–468.

Pei, Mario, *The Language of Eighth-Century Texts in Northern France.* New York, 1932.

————, *The Italian Language.* New York, 1941.

————, *Studies in Romance Philology and Literature.* Chapel Hill, N.C., 1963.

Pellegrini, Giambattista, *Le iscrizioni venetiche.* Pisa, 1965.

Pellis, Ugo, *Il Sonziaco.* Trieste, 1910–11.

Petrovici, Emil, *Kann ein Phonemsystem einer Sprache durch fremden Einfluss umgestaltet werden? Zum slavischen Einfluss auf das rumänische Lautsystem.* The Hague, 1956.

Pisani, Ettore, *Grammatica latina storica e comparata.* 3rd ed., rev. Turin, 1962.

Pirson, Jules, *La langue des inscriptions latines de Gaule.* Brussels, 1901.

von Planta, Robert, and Andrea Schorta, *Rätisches Namenbuch.* Zurich, 1939.

Politzer, Robert L., *A Study of Eighth-Century Lombardic Documents.* New York, 1949.

————, and Frieda N. Politzer, *Romance Trends in 7th and 8th Century Latin Documents.* Chapel Hill, N.C., 1953.

Pop, Sever, *Grammaire roumaine.* Bern, 1948.

————, *La dialectologie.* 2 vols. Louvain, 1950.

Pope, Mildred K., *From Latin to Modern French, with especial consideration of Anglo-Norman Phonology and Morphology.* Manchester, 1934.

Posner, Rebecca, *The Romance Languages.* Garden City, N.Y., 1966.

Pulgram, Ernst, "Spoken and Written Latin," *Language,* 26 (1950), 458–466.

————, *The Tongues of Italy.* Cambridge, Mass., 1958.

Puşcariu, Sextil, *Limba română.* 2 vols. Bucharest, 1940–65. (German translation and adaptation of vol. 1 by H. Kuen, *Die rumänische Sprache.* Leipzig, 1943.)

————, *Etymologisches Wörterbuch der rumänischen Sprache.* Heidelberg, 1905.

Rohlfs, Gerhardt, *Historische Grammatik der italienischen Sprache und ihrer Mundarten.* 3 vols. Bern, 1949–54. (Italian trans.: *Grammatica storica della lingua italiana e dei suoi dialetti.* Turin, 1966–69.)

Rosetti, Alexandru, *Istoria limbii române.* 6 vols. Rev. ed. Bucharest, 1964–66.

————, *Geschichte der rumänischen Sprache, Allgemeine Begriffe.* Bucharest, 1943.

Sas, Louis Furman, *The Noun Declension System in Merovingian Latin.* Paris, 1937.

Schiaffini, Alfredo, *Momenti di storia della lingua italiana.* Bari, 1950.

Schuchardt, Hugo, *Der Vokalismus des Vulgärlateins*. 3 vols. Leipzig, 1866–68.

Schwan, Eduard, and Dietrich Behrens, *Grammatik des Altfranzösischen*. 12th ed. Leipzig, 1925. (French translation by Oscar Bloch, *Grammaire de l'ancien français*. 4th ed. Leipzig, 1932.)

da Silva Neto, Serafim, *História do latim vulgar*. Rio de Janeiro, 1957.

Sittl, Karl, *Die lokalen Verschiedenheiten der lateinischen Sprache mit besonderer Berücksichtigung des afrikanischen Lateins*. Erlangen, 1882.

Skok, Petar, "Zum Balkanlatein," *Zeitschrift für romanische Philologie*, 46 (1926), 385–410; 48 (1928), 398–413; 50 (1930), 484–532; 54 (1934), 175–215, 424–499.

Sommer, Ferdinand, *Handbuch der lateinischen Laut- und Formenlehre*. 3rd ed. Heidelberg, 1948.

Spitzer, Leo (with Ernst Gamillscheg), *Beiträge zur romanischen Wortbildungslehre*, Geneva, 1921.

————, *Aufsätze zur romanischen Syntax und Stilistik*. Munich, 1918.

Tagliavini, Carlo, *Le origini delle lingue neolatine*. 5th ed. Bologna, 1969.

Tekavčić, Pavao, *Grammatica storica dell'italiano*. 3 vols. Bologna, 1972.

Trager, George L., *The Use of the Latin Demonstrative (especially ille and ipse) up to 600 A.D. as the Source of the Romance Article*. New York, 1932.

Väänänen, Veikko, *Le latin vulgaire des inscriptions pompéiennes*. 3rd ed. Berlin, 1958.

————, *Introduction au latin vulgaire*. 2nd ed. Paris, 1967.

Vasconcellos (Leite de), José, *Lições de filologia portuguesa*. 2nd ed., rev. Lisbon, 1926.

Vielliard, Jeanne, *La langue des diplômes royaux et chartes privées de l'époque mérovingienne*. Paris, 1927.

Vossler, Karl, and Helmuth Schmeck, *Einführung ins Vulgärlatein*. Munich, 1953.

Wagner, Max Leopold, *Caracteres generales del judeo-español de Oriente*. Madrid, 1930.

————, *La lingua sarda*. Bern, 1951.

————, *Dizionario etimologico sardo*. Heidelberg, 1960–64.

von Wartburg, Walther, *Französisches etymologisches Wörterbuch*. Bonn-Berlin-Basel, 1928–1971.

————, *Die Ausgliederung der romanischen Sprachräume*. 2nd ed. Bern, 1950. (Spanish trans.: *La fragmentación lingüística de la Romania*. Madrid, 1952. French trans.: *La fragmentation linguistique de la Romania*. Strasbourg, 1967.)

————, *Die Entstehung der romanischen Völker*. 2nd ed. Tübingen, 1951. (French trans.: *Les origines des peuples romans*. Paris, 1941.)

————, *Evolution et structure de la langue française*. 5th ed., rev. Bern, 1958.

Weigand, Gustav, *Linguistischer Atlas des daco-rumänischen Sprachgebietes*. 3 vols. Leipzig, 1898–1909.

Williams, Edwin, *From Latin to Portuguese*. Philadelphia, 1938.

Zauner, Adolf, *Romanische Sprachwissenschaft*. 2 vols. 4th ed. Berlin, 1921–26.

Index